DISCARDED

CARPE CORPUS

CARPE CORPUS

Time and Gender in Early Modern France

Cathy Yandell

Newark: University of Delaware Press
London: Associated University Presses

© 2000 by Associated University Presses, Inc.

All rights reserved. Authorization to photocopy items for internal or personal use, or the internal or personal use of specific clients, is granted by the copyright owner, provided that a base fee of $10.00, plus eight cents per page, per copy is paid directly to the Copyright Clearance Center, 222 Rosewood Dr., Danvers, Massachusetts 01923. [0-87413-704-7/00 $10.00 + 8¢ pp, pc.] Other than as indicated in the foregoing, this book may not be reproduced, in whole or in part, in any form (except as permitted by Sections 107 and 108 of the U.S. Copyright Law, and except for brief quotes appearing in reviews in the public press.

Associated University Presses
440 Forsgate Drive
Cranbury, NJ 08512

Associated University Presses
16 Barter Street
London WC1A 2AH, England

Associated University Presses
P.O. Box 338, Port Credit
Mississauga, Ontario
Canada L5G 4L8

The paper used in this publication meets the requirements
of the American National Standard for Permanence of Paper
for Printed Library Materials Z39.48-1984.

Library of Congress Cataloging-in-Publication Data

Yandell, Cathy M.
    Carpe Corpus : time and gender in early modern France / Cathy Yandell.
    p.   cm.
    Includes bibliographical references and index.
    ISBN 0-87413-704-7 (alk. paper)
       1. French poetry—16th century—History and criticism. 2. Space and time in literature. 3. Gender identity in literature.
I. Title.
PQ418.Y36   2000
841'.309—dc21   99-24088
                                                                                            CIP

PRINTED IN THE UNITED STATES OF AMERICA

For Mark, Lise, and Laura

Contents

Acknowledgments	9
Prologue: Gender and Early Modern Temporal Ideology	11
1. Forging Temporal Codes	21
2. Time in a Body: Ronsard's Corporeal Clock	48
3. By Virtue of their *Vertu:* Amplified Time in Pernette du Guillet and Louise Labé	85
4. Temporal Enclosure in Anne de Marquets and Nicole Estienne	128
5. *Le temps retrouvé:* Exemplarity and the Temporal Body in Catherine des Roches	175
Epilogue: The Bridges of Chronos	212
Notes	217
Bibliography of Works Cited	251
Index	268

Acknowledgments

Without the assistance and succor of a great number of friends and colleagues, this book would have been unthinkable, unwritable, and unwritten. I am indebted to the following readers, all of whom contributed in important ways to this project: Deborah Lesko Baker, Scott Carpenter, Leonard W. Johnson, Humberto Huergo, Alison Kettering, Dora Polachek, Anne R. Larsen, Kirk Read, Dana Strand, Susie Sutch, Carl Weiner, and Colette H. Winn. Heather Dubrow, extraordinary critic and friend, graciously read the entire manuscript and offered immeasurable wisdom. Robert D. Cottrell's personal and intellectual generosity has been vital to this project since the beginning. Gary Ferguson, who to my great fortune served as an outside reader for the manuscript, clarified my thinking in several instances through his thoughtful and astute questions. To Jackson Bryce, Anne Groton, and Chico Zimmerman, I owe a special debt for their counsel on both Latin and Greek texts. Christine Lac, Marie-Christine Massé, and Anne Ulmer have offered considerable linguistic expertise. Members of the Carleton–Saint Olaf Renaissance Colloquium have provided crucial critical insights during several stages of the project. Francine Benaben, Sue Clarke, Eve Frédérix, Mary Lewis Grow, Chérif Keïta, Brigitte Lambourion, Sylvia McNeil, Éva Pósfay, Maïmouna Touré, Gwenda and Imad Wehbé, Joel Weisberg, and Mark Williams have contributed more to this book than they realize. I have also been inspired by Marian Adams Bryn-Jones's ninety-nine years of graciousness and generosity. It is difficult to imagine conducting research in Paris without the friendship and assistance of Josette Rolinat, to whom I am continually grateful. I extend special thanks to all my students *(sine quibus non)*, whose questions and challenges have informed the project from its inception, particularly Toby Wikström and David Zucco, who in addition provided research assistance. Shira Weidenbaum's intelligent and careful editing has been exceptional. Carroll Hightower, Andrea Nixon, and Mary Tatge have kindly offered their Promethean cybernetic expertise. Susan Jaret McKinstry's contributions, much like her spirit, have been boundless.

My earliest intellectual debt is of course to my parents, whose *curiosité* (in the Tyardian sense of the term) continues to be contagious. Chronologically speaking, my next great debt is to Alan Wilson of Gallup, New Mexico, whose brilliance and love of languages and cultures have provided a model for numerous acolytes from Zuni to Zimbabwe. Lise Hoshour taught by example that beauty and rigor are not incompatible. Leonard W. Johnson, esteemed mentor and razor-sharp reader, has been a continuing intellectual inspiration. This book owes much to the pioneering studies of colleagues too numerous to mention here whose work I cite throughout the text. I trust that they will accept these citations as an expression of my esteem.

I am also grateful to the National Endowment for the Humanities and to Carleton College for grants that allowed me to pursue this work. I especially thank Dean Elizabeth McKinsey and President Stephen R. Lewis Jr. for their commitment to scholarship and their generous assistance. To the staff of the libraries of Carleton College and the University of Minnesota, as well as of the Bibliothèque de l'Arsenal and the Bibliothèque Nationale de France, particularly in the Réserve, I extend my warmest thanks.

For permission to reprint material that appeared in earlier essays, I wish to thank the *Sixteenth Century Studies Journal* ("Carpe Diem Revisited: Ronsard's Temporal Ploys"), Wayne State University Press ("Carpe Diem, Poetic Immortality, and the Gendered Ideology of Time," in *Renaissance Women Writers: French Texts/American Contexts*, ed. Anne R. Larsen and Colette H. Winn [Detroit, 1994]), and *Mediaevalia*, ed. Dora Polachek ("L'habit ne fait pas la nonne: Controversy and Authority in Anne de Marquets"). For permission to reproduce artwork, I gratefully acknowledge the Réunion des Musées Nationaux ("La jeunesse perpétuelle perdue par les hommes" by Rossi), the Bibliothèque Nationale de France (engravings of Ronsard and Cassandre), and the Photothèque des Musées de la Ville de Paris ("Le miroir de la vie et de la mort").

Finally, I record here my gratitude to Lloyd and Maurine Dunn Yandell and Carol Yandell Williams, whose support has been timeless, and to Lise Yandell McNeil and Laura Yandell McNeil, who remind me at every moment why time is worth thinking about. I owe perhaps the greatest debt of all to Mark Sanford McNeil, accomplice, wordsmith, and humorist par excellence, whose time in many ways made this book possible.

Prologue:
Gender and Early Modern
Temporal Ideology

If readers of this book begin to leaf through the pages while glancing occasionally at their watches, if they did not sleep enough last night, and if their calendars show that they are fully booked for the next month, I would submit that Petrarch is largely to blame. Among the first early modern thinkers to articulate a systematic program for making the best possible use of every passing hour, Petrarch in 1350 reveals attitudes toward time that are startlingly recognizable to today's readers. Of course Petrarch was a rather solitary scholar, and his relative freedom from day-to-day responsibilities is unfathomable to most of us in contemporary society. Still, his insistence on the preciousness of time in each individual life and his exhortation to live each moment to the fullest, even though the contexts are radically different, resonate with a number of current cultural preoccupations, both philosophical and popular.

    Like most academic projects, this study grew out of a personal passion—in this case, an obsession with time, its particular power at the dawn of the twenty-first century, its promises and its threats. The most traditional and canonized early modern French poets, many of whom were inspired by Petrarch, provide a rich stock of temporal problems, from Scève to Ronsard to Du Bartas. Through these writers one could attempt to reconstruct a compendium of attitudes toward time that govern both texts and lives in sixteenth-century France. But when I began to examine the women poets included in this study, from Pernette du Guillet to Nicole Estienne to Catherine des Roches, it became clear that underlying their adaptations of such temporal motifs as *carpe diem* (pluck the day) and *exegi monumentum* (I have raised a monument) were notions of time often radically different from those of their male counterparts. This realization led me to broaden the scope of my reading to include a number of such paraliterary texts as conduct manuals, letters and polemical writing. Through these poetic and cultural texts, I attempt in this book to discover what time means and how it functions for writing men and women in early modern France.

Despite the current flourishing of critical attention to women poets' works, our understanding of time in the sixteenth century remains almost exclusively shaped by male writers. The central connection between time and gender in both male and female poets, moreover, has been heretofore neglected. The principal drawback of a reading uninformed by female poets is not so much that it is misogynistic as that it has deprived us of a more multifaceted vision of the temporal *concordia discors* (literally, "discordant concourse") at work in all these poets. Because readings of time and temporal motifs in the early modern period have traditionally centered on only one gender, we have accepted generalizations that, upon broader examination, prove to be false. Sins of omission, in other words, have in effect produced errors of commission.

For each manifestation of temporality in sixteenth-century poetry—the *carpe diem* and *exegi monumentum* motifs, the philosophy of poetic immortality, metaphorical representations of time, and ethical considerations about the use of one's time—women poets proffer distinct visions. My study attempts to show that the works of women poets often challenge our definitions of commonplace sixteenth-century temporal topoi we thought we had fully understood, compelling us to formulate more nuanced readings of such poetic devices as *carpe diem* and indeed to rethink the meaning of time in sixteenth-century France.

This book seeks to examine notions of time in early modern poetry at two crossroads. First, the intersection of two meanings of culture comes into play—the traditional one that privileges high artistic and literary production (hence, my insistence on poetry as the vehicle of transmission) and the anthropological or social one which treats societal values, symbols, and beliefs (thus, the crucial role of conduct manuals, religious tracts, philosophical treatises, and other paraliterary texts in my analysis).[1] The intersection—and bifurcation—of male and female attitudes toward time constitutes the second nexus of my study. Of course in every study much depends on the question of what Myra Jehlen terms "the politics of vision,"[2] or the angle from which one looks at a problem. In the process of uncovering early modern women poets' perspectives on time, one must also recognize, among many other societal givens, the patriarchal structures subtending the works we will examine. Yet patriarchy, which Stanley Chojnacki calls the "conceptual nucleus around whose positive charge all matters of . . . the interaction of the sexes fly about like electrons,"[3] while omnipresent, serves not always as a barrier but often as a hurdle to be surmounted in these women poets' lives. Louise Labé urges women to "rise above" the menial tasks assigned to them, and Catherine des Roches and Anne de Marquets both carve out for themselves a living and publishing environment in which women's ideas and creativity flourish.

The two elements mentioned in the subtitle of this book, time and gender, necessitate at least a preliminary explanation. I propose to examine problems of time especially as they constitute what might be called "temporal ideology," by which I mean the conjunction of philosophical, psychological, and moral attitudes toward time and its effects. It is not only a question of temporal philosophy, but also of the human values and political implications associated with specific views of time in the texts. I will focus upon elements of temporal ideology discernible in the work of a number of sixteenth-century poets both as a topos and as a rhetorical or textual manifestation. Although lyric poetry is often considered the most atemporal of genres, the use or avoidance of certain poetic devices, shifts in subject or tense, and the insistence upon temporal themes often reveal surprisingly distinct notions of temporality. Moreover, since poetry is inevitably written within a larger social context, contemporaneous humanist recommendations and injunctions concerning time, age, and schedules will also figure prominently in my analysis.

As for the term "gender," I intend to denote what is now widely accepted as a cultural construction of the sexes, that is, the social creation of subjective identities and appropriate roles for women and men. This does not mean that the body disappears from my analysis (quite the contrary), but rather that I include gender, as Joan Scott has aptly phrased it, as "a social category imposed on a sexed body."[4] A number of sixteenth-century discourses about women show, however, that the female body serves as the nucleus of male-authored moral prescriptions. The humanist treatises on civility I examine in this book do not necessarily support the homological model of sexual difference described by Thomas Laqueur, who argues that the female body was considered to be an inversion of the male body until about 1800, and that "sex . . . was still a sociological and not an ontological category."[5] In most of the conduct manuals I have consulted, although the recommended behavior certainly implies important sociological consequences, the female body by its *nature* is considered inferior to the male body, particularly in its sexual vulnerability, but in no explicit way the male's opposite. As Jacques Ferrand notes in his 1610 *Traité de l'essence et guérison de l'amour, ou De la mélancholie érotique*, while Galen believed in the theory of sexual inversion, it had been discounted by late-sixteenth-century thinkers:

> La femme est un homme imparfait, ne differant du masle, que des parties genitales; lesquelles, dit Galien, sont en la femme retenuës et encloses au dedans, à faute de chaleur suffisante pour les pousser au dehors, ce que nature n'a voulu faire pour la conservation de l'espece. Il peut donques arriver, qu'une femme eschaufée d'une furieuse amour, pousse au dehors ses parties genitales, qui sont celles de l'homme renversées selon Galien, ausquelles nos modernes anatomistes contredisent.[6]

> [Woman is an imperfect man, only differing from the male by her genitals, which, Galen says, are retained and enclosed inside, for lack of sufficient heat to push them outside, which, for the conservation of the species, Nature did not want to do. It can happen that a woman heated by a passionate love, pushes her genitals out, which are those of a man reversed, according to Galen, but our modern anatomic specialists disagree.]

While the authors included in this study appear to discount Galen's theory of sexual inversion, many examples from sixteenth-century texts do support the Aristotelian, essentialist position regarding women's bodies and their inferior status.[7] This argument is perhaps best summarized in *Le Fort inexpugnable de l'honneur du sexe feminin* (1555) by François de Billon, who takes literally Erasmus's *Praise of Folly* and challenges the following dictum: *comme un singe est toujours singe, une femme est toujours femme*[8] (Just as a monkey is always a monkey, [so] a woman is always a woman). The Spanish moralist Juan Luis Vives, in his influential *De institutio foeminae christianae (Institution de la femme chrétienne),* also employs physical arguments to justify female subjugation:

> Si la femme estoit aussi robuste en corps & en esperit, comme se rendroit elle en la subjection d'ung pareil, ou moindre de soy? Qui la tiendroit à l'hostel? Qui conserveroit le faict domestique, consistant en tant de menues, et petites choses necessaires?[9]

> [If woman were as strong {as man} in body and in spirit, how would she become subservient to an equal or lesser being? Who would keep her at home? Who would take care of household duties, consisting of so many little and necessary things?]

A 1545 French translation of Pietro Bembo's "Les Azolains" provides another clear example of physical essentialism employed to regulate female activity, this time broadening the debate to furnish reasons for the exclusion of women from the political domain:

Comment seroit-il possible que nous peussions tout en un temps donner les loix aux peuples, & les tetins aux petis enfans?[10]

[How could we give laws to the people and breasts to the babies at the same time?]

From these physical arguments important social conclusions can be drawn. Since women by physical nature are deemed to be more suited to work in the household, it follows that men will be freer to pursue outside activities while women hold down the domestic fort.[11] These examples illustrating social expectations for men and women's use of time demonstrate only the tip of the iceberg for examining questions of gender as they intersect with time in early modern culture. Essentialist arguments concerning women's natural proclivity for idleness (which breeds moral degeneracy) underlie many of the temporal prescriptions for women that we will examine, particularly in the chapter on the Lyonnais poets. Similarly, underpinning the desire to "enclose" women in the institutions of the convent or marriage is the widely discussed notion that because of natural deficiencies in females, women's time must be regulated or shepherded by men, as we will find in the poetry of Nicole Estienne. These and other instances suggest that time should indeed be examined as a gendered phenomenon.

My book begins by establishing the temporal context of the writers included in this study, considering time as it was theorized, imagined, and lived in early modern France. I then examine Ronsard's influential notions of time, including the function of temporal topoi in his poetry. For Ronsard, time is measured through the human body, be it his own (from the early *Odes* to the *Derniers vers*) or that of a female addressee (from the early *Amours* to the *Sonnets pour Hélène*). Of all the poets I investigate in this study, Ronsard's use of the *carpe diem* motif is at first glance the most straightforward (e.g., "Mignonne, allons voir" and "Quand vous serez bien vieille") and upon closer scrutiny the most varied and complex (e.g., "Je vous envoye un bouquet que ma main" and "Versons ces roses en ce vin"). In this chapter, I examine the temporal implications of the prototypical *carpe diem* poem, including the privileging of the addressee's body as the locus of time and the projection of the poet's own fear of aging onto the female addressee. Juxtaposing specific poems of Ronsard and those of his classical models Horace and Rufinus, I demonstrate the ways in which Ronsard's poet rhetorically manifests a more pronounced desire to control both time and the lady's aging than do his classical models. In Ronsard's *carpe diem* poems, the ultimate threat to the addressee is aging (time's passage made visible), depicted as a fate worse than death. For Ronsard, time controls not only physical but also psychological human destiny: aging divides the self in two (as in the image of the subject gazing at his aged reflection in the mirror). But in Ronsard's poetic system, the poet seeks to triumph over the vicissitudes of time by literary immortality, or by projections into the future, ultimately revealing confidence in a linear temporal progression.

The works of the Lyonnais poets Pernette du Guillet and Louise Labé, addressed in chapter 3, evince very different temporal underpinnings from those discernible in Ronsard's poetry. After illustrating time's crucial role in the definition of women's virtue for the contemporaries of Pernette du Guillet and Louise Labé, this chapter examines the poets' own attitudes toward time, particularly the relationship between virtue and the way women apportion their time. An analysis of several of Pernette's key motifs (virtue, contentment, and the metaphor of the Day), particularly when set against similar terms employed by her fellow poet Scève, demonstrates Pernette's creation of what might be called a "perennial present" in her work. In so doing, she implicitly challenges the concept of poetic immortality advanced by Scève and others. Louise Labé more explicitly advances her own temporal philosophy by establishing the primordial connection between writing and memory, positing writing not as a vehicle for poetic longevity, but as a link between the past and the present, as a means of introspection, and as a transgressive activity for learned women. Insisting upon what might be called the "presentness" of the past, Louise Labé creates in her poetry a sense of magnified, recurring time. Unlike the notions of eternal return from Empedocles to Nietzsche, however, Labé's concept of recurring time takes place on a small scale, excluding the rigorous determinism of those models and including, rather, the sense of continuing production.

Time as seen from within the two hierarchical institutions in which women were "enclosed" in early modern France—marriage and the convent—provides the focus for the fourth chapter of my study. Anne de Marquets, a Dominican nun who wrote religious and polemical poetry during the second half of the sixteenth century, enacts in her writings a number of shifts or displacements in the established hierarchy, both religious and literary. These displacements result in the creation of what might be called an "alternative temporality" by the embodiment of female religious experience and concrete time in her texts. Nicole Estienne, in *Les Misères de la femme mariée*, describes the plight of the married woman from her own perspective, chronicling the inequities of the institution and reenacting in the poems the sense of time experienced by the subjugated wife.

Both Anne de Marquets and Nicole Estienne—in quite different ways—rise above the temporal framework proposed by the two institutions in question. Both poets propose, sometimes more implicitly than explicitly, a temporal schema in which women, through their spirituality or through their relationships, can thrive.

In the fifth chapter, I examine concepts of temporality in the work of Catherine des Roches, who, like her predecessors from Lyons, charts her own literary terrain to some degree in response to the male poets of her intellectual circle. In a series of forty-five poems entitled "Responces" in her *Secondes œuvres*, Catherine formulates both philosophical and psychological objections to the temporal ideology inherent in the *carpe diem* motif, often within the context of her rejection of the rhetorical aim of that motif (the woman's seduction). For Catherine, as for her poetic suitor Estienne Pasquier, one of time's primary characteristics is its physical destruction, and specifically the toll it takes on the human body. Rather than attempting to "conquer" time, however, she continually subverts the power both of bodily deterioration itself and of the poets who use it as a threat. She does so by minimizing the importance of physical beauty in comparison with the noble qualities of the soul and of *vertu*, exemplified, as her character Pasithée explains, by the practices of reading and writing. Catherine forms her own vision of the future, which holds neither the assurance of *exegi monumentum* nor the menacing terror of aging inherent in the *carpe diem* motif.

The central question I pose, then, is what the inclusion of gender brings to our understanding of temporality in early modern France. The "new subjectivism" that many scholars have identified in the early modern period takes on very different forms depending on whether the subject is masculine or feminine.[12]

In analyzing sixteenth-century male and female attitudes toward temporality, it becomes clear that on the whole men tend to view disposable time as a space within which they can move, or, to put it another way, as offering the "freedom to" pursue their chosen feats. Women, on the other hand, often conceive of available time as the "freedom from" restraints of various kinds—from the spindle and the distaff in Louise Labé, for example, and from the rule of the husband in Nicole Estienne. Yet despite this rather bleak point of departure, I argue that these women poets create original and important temporal constructs in their works. I conclude with brief reflections on the striking parallels between these early modern gendered notions of temporality and theories of time at the turn of the twenty-first century.

Many of the sixteenth-century passages in this book have been taken from sources for which there exists no modern edition. I have retained the original spelling of the books and manuscripts cited except in certain cases, which to facilitate reading I have altered as follows: distinction between *u* and *v* and between *i* and *j;* resolution of abbreviations; occasional changes in punctuation, such as the substitution of a question mark for a period in an obviously interrogative phrase; and addition of apostrophes, as in "d'estre" and "l'ame." All translations, unless otherwise indicated, are my own.

CARPE CORPUS

1
Forging Temporal Codes

> Il n'y a rien au monde plus prétieux que le Temps, plus désirable que celluy pour advenir, plus regrettable que le passé, et plus pernitieux et détestable que celluy inutilement perdu.
>
> [There is nothing in the world more precious than time, more desirable than time for the future, more regrettable than the past, and more pernicious and detestable than time uselessly lost.]
> —Jehan L'Hermite, *Le Passetemps* (ca. 1602)

Three fresco paintings entitled *La jeunesse perpétuelle perdue par les hommes* [Perpetual youth lost by mankind] in François I's gallery at Fontainebleau reveal a number of intriguing clues for the student of early modern temporality. Painted by Rosso Fiorentino circa 1536, the central panel features an altar with a number of robed pilgrims requesting eternal youth from the gods. Above them, Mercury descends from the clouds to grant their wish. In the foreground to the left, an idyllic scene includes a woman sleeping in the grass, apparently basking in the sun, and near her, accompanied by a cherub, a couple dancing. In the center of the fresco, a young woman on a donkey bends down toward a snake-dragon, and, to the right of them, a few withered elders lean on canes, facing the woman on the donkey.

This remarkable painting about the passage of time, based on an ancient fable, unfolds chronologically from back to front and from left to right. The roundels *(tondi)* flanking the central panel accentuate the temporal progression and guide the viewer's "reading" of the fable, from the young crowd approaching the temple on the left to the landscape of ruins and personifications of Old Age on the right. According to one version of the fable, after Mercury grants eternal youth to humanity, careless young people entrust Youth (personified as a young woman) to a donkey, who

La jeunesse perpétuelle perdue par les hommes, by **Rosso Fiorentino**, Fontainebleau: Musée du Château.

stops to drink at a pool. In exchange for water, the guardian snake-dragon asks the donkey for Youth, who is kissing or being kissed by the dragon in the fresco. Humanity thus definitively loses Youth, as the scene of stooping old people on the right underscores.[1]

In this fresco painting, Youth's personification as a female points to the woman's body as locus of both youth and old age. As the central figure in the fresco, she becomes the currency exchanged (the woman for water) in the transaction that leads from humanity's youth to its old age. The feminine gender of the words "iuventa," "jeunesse," and "giovinezza" of course suggests a feminine iconographic representation, but etymology alone cannot account for a parallel phenomenon in French letters throughout the sixteenth century: the woman's body serves consistently as a literary site for measuring the passage of time, from *carpe diem* poems authored by male poets to moral dialogues authored by women writers.[2]

Much like the fresco of *La jeunesse perdue*, a number of early modern French texts exhibit important intersections between gender and time, through the image of the female body or through the perspective of the women poets themselves. The female body figures prominently in sixteenth-century discourses on time, from its incarnation as a flower to be plucked *(carpe corpus)* in the Pléiade poets to its highly codified connection with female morality in contemporaneous civility manuals to its metaphoric representation of female strength in Catherine des Roches's poetry.

Much of Renaissance lyric poetry reveals an obsession with temporality, both physical time with its menacing, ravaging powers and subjective time with its grounding in human imagination and experience. Poets continually seek ways to beguile, deceive, tame or conquer time, be it by magnifying the present moment or by securing their place in the future through writing. In his study *Time in French Life and Thought*, Richard Glasser concludes that French Renaissance poets, with their insistence on the ideal rather than fulfillment, are "at odds with time."[3] Ricardo Quinones, too, characterizes time in the early modern period as "the antagonist against which [men] plan and plot and war, and over which they hope to triumph."[4] This now canonical reading of time as the enemy is indisputably borne out in the principal temporal topoi of the sixteenth century, *carpe diem* and *exegi monumentum*, which figure not only in Ronsard and the Pléiade poets, but also in Marot, Scève, Saint Gelais, Des Périers, Magny, Grévin, and Pasquier. What interpretations of temporality in the sixteenth century by earlier critics such as Glasser and Quinones fail to incorporate, however, is the critical category of gender. Beginning in the middle of the sixteenth century, a number of women poets formulate their versions of these temporal topoi, initiating a poetic dialogue with male colleagues as they reveal decidedly different attitudes toward time. Time as imagined by both women and men in early modern France can be best understood within the context of a range of contemporaneous attitudes and their presumed origins.

TIME IN THEORY

A number of discrete factors—philosophical, psychological, and practical—converge to provide a backdrop for the growing importance accorded to time in sixteenth-century culture. As the social historian Lucien Febvre points out, people in the early modern period spent countless amounts of time constructing palaces, castles, and churches, all of which were decorated with sculptures that took years to complete. But set against this notion of apparently innumerable hours is a growing fascination with the power of measuring time, be it by the privileging of regulating schedules (in 1564 Viret praises roosters that serve as reliable clocks for men who go off to war) or by the much-awaited spring-loaded mechanical clock.[5] In Strasbourg, for example, the largest and most prestigious clock of its kind ever built was begun in 1547 when the Senate contracted with Conrad Dasypodius, a professor of mathematics at Strasbourg Academy, to build a "magnificent, splendid, and artistic work . . . that would bring honor to the Senate and the people of Strasbourg."[6] Ironically, the construction of this superbly precise time-measuring device took twenty-seven years to complete. The iconographic intricacies of the clock, including a compendium of the temporal knowledge of the epoch, forcefully demonstrate the privileged position accorded to physical time:

> The automated astronomical devices included a large calendar dial with the holy days, a clock giving local time, an astrolabe with delicately wrought signs of the zodiac and planets, a mechanism that showed the phases of the moon, and a celestial sphere supported by a pelican mounted on the floor in front of the clock. The principal trains of automatons were: the tutelary gods of the days of the week being borne around in elaborate chariots; figures of the four ages of man that struck the quarter hours in their circuit; and the figures of Christ and Death dueled at the stroke of the hour with Death winning all hours except the last. Also the old restored cock was mounted on the crest of the weight tower and at midday flapped its wings, raised its head, opened its beak, shook its tail and crowed, to the accompaniment of a carillon playing bits of music.[7]

This public passion for clocks and the newly refined possibility for measuring time is accompanied by a number of contradictory humanist reflections on time and its meaning. Notions of the Epicurean instant conflict with the Neoplatonic belief that the soul must rise above time, for example. Similarly, the Virgilian *fugit irreparabile tempus* (irrecoverable time flees) clashes with the restorative and cyclic value accorded to time by Heraclitus and other ancient Greeks. Finally, the Stoic *vanitas vanitatum* (vanity of vanities) motif collides with the enthusiastic humanist exhortation to use time to the fullest. Several of these differing philosophical precepts often coexist in contemporary writings and sometimes within the same text. Poets of the Pléiade appear to popularize through the *carpe diem* motif a devotion to the Epicurean instant ("the inverse of eternity"),[8] for example, yet these same poets accord an immense importance to poetic immortality, which by definition holds eternity as a central tenet. In sixteenth-century iconography, too, the image of Time as a scythe-wielding destroyer can be set against François I's emblematic salamander, who defies the ravages of time by conquering fire ("Nutrisco et extinguo" [I am nourished by it and I extinguish it]).

What, then, are the commonalities among these differing approaches toward temporality, and why did these particular philosophies appeal to sixteenth-century audiences? The most widespread philosophical underpinning of the texts I will be examining, *fugit irreparabile tempus*, warrants further elucidation within the context of the sixteenth century. Taken from Virgil's *Georgics* (3.284), this motif insists not only on time's flight but also on its irrefutable ability to destroy both power and beauty. Rabelais's Frère Jean articulates in the *Tiers Livre* the idea that time is characterized by its causing decay and decline: "Le temps matte toutes choses. Il n'est le marbre ne le porphyre qui n'ayt sa viellesse et decadence"[9] [Time conquers all things. No marble or porphyry is immune from old age and decadence]. Du Bellay's *Antiquités* as well as a number of other works by Pléiade poets illustrate the central questions of continual change, the cycles of nature, and irretrievable time represented by deteriorating ruins or withering life.[10]

The emphasis on fleeting time in contemporaneous literature bespeaks public disquietude concerning impermanence, which is a predictable development in a society riven with civil war and political strife. Not only did the religious wars claim thousands of lives, but the monarchy also became less stable with the death of Henri II following a tournament (1559), the premature death of Charles IX (1574), and the subsequent assassinations of Henri III (1589) and Henri IV (1610). Pontus de Tyard, in his *Discours du Temps, de l'an et de ses parties,* explicitly associates the rapid passage of time with uncertainty. In order to portray someone with exactitude, he argues, "il faudrait retrancher l'aile du Temps duquel l'invisible, voire l'insensible fuite, entraîne continuellement toute notre asseurance"[11] [One must cut away the wing of Time, whose invisible, intangible flight continually steals our assurance]. Seen in this optic, time becomes principally the purveyor of incertitude.

Allied with the question of uncertainty is the theme of *vanitas vanitatum,* which underscores the futility of human effort when faced with the greater forces of time and destiny. Du Bellay's well-known "Si notre vie est moins qu'une journée" from his sonnet cycle *L'Olive* (1549), for example, combines the principle of *vanitas vanitatum* with the Neoplatonic desire for beauty:

> Si nostre vie est moins qu'une journée
> En l'eternel, si l'an qui faict le tour
> Chasse noz jours sans espoir de retour,
> Si perissable est toute chose née,
> Que songes-tu, mon ame emprisonnée?
> . . . .
> Là, ô mon ame au plus hault ciel guidée!
> Tu y pouras recongnoistre l'Idée
> De la beauté, qu'en ce monde j'adore.[12]

[If our lives are less than a day / In eternity, if the turning year / Drives away our days with no hope of return, / If every born thing is perishable / What are you dreaming, my imprisoned soul? / . . . / There, my soul, guided to the highest heaven! / You will be able to recognize the Idea / Of beauty, which I adore in this world.]

Du Bellay's later "Songe" (1558) also illustrates material fragility, both human and natural, but in this work the poet's vision assumes an apocalyptic tone, beginning with the first vision, "Voy comme tout n'est rien que vanité" [See how everything is nothing but vanity].[13] In this narrative poem recounting the poet's dream, both ambition and monuments crafted by humans are systematically destroyed. As Terence Cave has shown, physical realities of the religious wars no doubt brought the *vanitas vanitatum* motif into relief in a number of contemporaneous poets.[14]

What is particularly engaging in early modern manifestations of these temporal motifs for our purposes is the question not of *tempus rerum,* however, but of *tempus corporis.* In the 1578 poem "A Charles de Pisseleu," Ronsard explicitly draws a parallel between mutability in nature and change in the human body over time:

> Si donq tout est suget à se muer souvent,
> L'homme qui n'est sinon que fumée et que vent,

Comme le filz du Temps, ne doit trouver estrange
Si quelquefois d'estat comme son pere il change.
(L.VIII, 225; P.II, 875)[15]

[If everything is thus subject to frequent movement, / Man, who is nothing but smoke and wind, / As Time's son should not find it strange / If, like his father, he sometimes changes states.]

These verses are indicative of a widespread phenomenon in sixteenth-century humanism: the parallel established between the cosmos and the creature, with a progressively insistent focus on the human subject. Whereas in medieval thought human time is imagined as a transitory period linked to eternity (where "true time" is of unlimited duration), during the early modern period "true time" becomes the time of human life.[16] When the emphasis upon temporality shifts from the macrocosm to the microcosm, from the natural world to the human body, and from the concept of a divinely determined life span to a temporal space to be shaped by individuals, the result is what might be called a secular subjectivization of time.[17] Petrarch's writings codify and disseminate this important development.

Petrarch is not, of course, the first philosopher or poet to consider time as a human phenomenon,[18] but his formulations of time and its relationship to the thinking subject undoubtedly influenced the sixteenth-century humanist philosophy of time more than any others. Aristotle had conceived of time as a succession of instants based on the physical principle of movement, where each instant is the end of the before and the beginning of the after, where events follow each other without reference to past or future. He further noted that time is not simply the objective measure of physical mutations, but also the construction of our minds. In *Physics*, Aristotle poses the question of whether time can exist outside of the soul, and he concludes that it cannot, because the soul itself "numbers movement" (fourth book).[19] Plotinus also claims that time cannot be conceived outside of the soul (*Enneads* 3.7). Augustine adds a psychological dimension to the cosmology of time, seeing it as a more subjective phenomenon. Shifting the emphasis of time from the Aristotelian *moment* to the *present*, Augustine identifies an enunciating subject in relationship to whom both past and future are defined.[20] But whereas for Augustine, time moves at the same inexorable speed for everyone, time in Petrarch's conception, though equally merciless, can be shaped by individuals. This preexistentialist idea that human beings are ultimately responsible for their own time led to Petrarch's disquietude about his use of every hour of the day. As a result, he limited his sleep to six hours and worldly activities to two hours, devoting the remaining hours to study, reflection, and writing.

Petrarch illustrates the human repercussions of time's flight in a letter to Philippe de Cabassoles, ca. 1360:

> I noted down not the verbal felicities but the substance of thought—the distresses of this wretched life, its brevity, swiftness, haste, tumbling course, its hidden cheats, time's irrecoverability, the flower of life soon wasted, the fugitive beauty of a rosy face, the frantic flight of unreturning youth, the trickeries of stealthy age; and at last the wrinkles, illnesses, sadness, toil, and the implacable cruelty of indomitable death. . . . all these considerations have derived from my deep consciousness of the brevity of life.[21]

Given the high premium placed on time, the fear of wasting it becomes all the more acute. In an often quoted passage, Alberti, Petrarch's humanist heir, notes that the three most precious human possessions are the soul, the body, and time.[22] Petrarch himself had already formulated an ethical dimension of temporal stewardship in a letter to Father Luigi Marsili in 1373:

> I urge you, I beseech you, not to let any day slip by out of sloth, but every evening cast up your accounts, like a diligent house-holder with an unreliable steward. Say: "Today I did this, began that, learned so much, became wiser herein and better therein." I urge you no less to virtue than to knowledge, that you may not find your day has passed vainly, that you have not lived. Said Emperor Titus: "My friend, I have lost a day." If we praise him for saying this because the day had passed with no profit to others, what must we think if we have brought no profit to ourselves? I grant that we cannot remain forever bowed over a book; we cannot always be tranquil recluses. We are weak creatures; the world is a turbulent place, and we are caught in its toils. But we can still insist that no day shall pass without our reviewing it, to the refreshment of our spirits. How shall we bring aid to others' affairs if we neglect our own? Sitting, standing or walking, we can reflect on ourselves and our concerns—even at a banquet, although Cicero disagrees. . . .[23]

The notion of time's preciousness raises the larger problem of human subjectivity in temporal matters. Early modern texts both implicitly and explicitly limn the questions: To what purpose should time best be put? Should time be spent differently by males and females? Does the same amount of time appear shorter or longer depending on the circumstances? A sixteenth-century proverb states directly that the sense of time's passing varies according to individual states:

> Aux amants et aux buvants,
> chemin est court avec le temps.[24]

[For lovers and drinkers / time's path is short.]

A verse from François I's collected poems describes the opposite phenomenon, namely, that waiting lengthens perceived time: "Plus de dix ans luy dure la sepmaine / S'il ne te voit, trop grant luy est la peine"[25] [A week lasts longer than ten years for him / If he doesn't see you, his suffering is too great]. In both cases, temporal duration lies in the perception of the individual subject.

Montaigne most explicitly underscores the subjective side of time, defining it as a substance to be shaped by human will: "J'ay un dictionaire tout à part moy; je passe le temps, quand il est mauvais et incommode; quand il est bon je ne le veux pas passer, je le retaste, je m'y tiens"[26] [I have a vocabulary all my own. I "pass the time" when it is rainy or disagreeable; when it is good, I do not want to pass it—I savor it, I cling to it].[27] Here, as elsewhere, Montaigne suggests time's primordial role in human existence and its variability according to physical and psychological circumstances.

The ubiquitous temporal motifs in various genres of literary and paraliterary texts, from *fugit irreparabile tempus* and *vanitas vanitatum*, on the one hand, to the *carpe diem* motif combined with the growing insistence on time as a subjective phenomenon, on the other, initially appear to point in conflicting directions. Whereas the underlying principle of both *fugit irreparabile tempus* and *vanitas vanitatum* is human defenselessness against the greater force of time, the *carpe diem* motif explicitly interjects an element of human defiance and desire for control. Yet all of these motifs embody the sense of terror about the passage of time, whether explicitly, as in Du Bellay's ruins, or implicitly, as in Ronsard's premature aging of his young addressee within the space of the poem. This heightened awareness of life's brevity sparks human attempts to govern time by partitioning it into months, days, and hours, all of which begin to be accounted for more carefully, either as scheduled time or as free time (to be devoted to "pastimes").

Schedules and Pastimes

Sixteenth-century culture shows an obsession not only with temporal theories but also with time as a practical consideration, particularly insofar as it affects the workings of the human body and human activity. How long, for example, does a given activity take? When is the best time to undertake a particular project? How should one organize the hours of one's day? How long is the human life cycle? At what age should one marry? These are the questions that surface repeatedly in early modern texts.[28] Playing off preconceived ideas of how long various human activities should take, Rabelais taunts readers with a description of Gargantua's eleven-month gestation period.[29] Of course the epic hero's gigantic stature and his miraculous birth add to his quasi-divine status, but the contemporary problem of assigning specific durations to various phenomena is nonetheless posed and parodied from the outset.

Scientific and moral treatises, also, manifest an increased interest in various bodily functions and the time required to accomplish them. Ambroise Paré, probably the most influential medical authority of his time, considers in his *Introduction à la chirurgie* the time necessary for the "concoction des viandes" [digestion/working of the bowels] and quantifies the process as taking seven or eight hours.[30] Symphorien Champier offers advice as to what time of year and moment of the day it is best to conceive (in the spring, and before breakfast). In any case, he argues, one should wait a sufficient amount of time after meals to allow food to digest before the process of "vacquer à generation" [engaging in generation]. Otherwise, one risks "podagres, gouttes, ydropisies, et plusieurs aultres maulx et aulcune foys mort subite dons [sic] Dieu nous deffende"[31] [podagra, gout, dropsy, and other diseases, and sometimes sudden death (God forbid)].

One of the effects of this desire to measure the time required for given activities is the concomitant birth of the schedule. Gargantua's fantastic agenda is now a classic case in point: following Petrarch's recommendations, the giant's principal time-saving device consists in doubling or tripling activities. While "excreting natural digestion," for example, Gargantua reviews his lessons with his tutor, so that not even a minute will be squandered.[32] The evening meal is accompanied by further lessons, peppered with useful and learned conversation.[33] On rainy days, woodwork, painting, sculpture, and games replace outdoor exercises, while the gigantic pupil simultaneously recites ancient authors.[34]

Although scenes of Gargantua's doubled activities unquestionably rely on the burlesque, the text works against reading the schoolboy's exaggerated schedule as exclusively parodic. The unmasked ideology behind Gargantua's day is one of seizing the moment and squeezing it dry. The humanist enthusiasm for an all-encompassing education of the body, mind, and soul reveals itself not only in these chapters of *Gargantua* but also in *Pantagruel*, whose eponymous hero receives a letter from his father urging him to employ the hours of his youth wisely "en estudes et en vertus" [in study and in productive activity].[35] Near the conclusion of *Gargantua*, Frère Jean bans clocks from the utopian Abbey de Thélème, and it seems initially clear that in so doing he rejects the hegemonic importance attributed to time in regulating monastic activity. But paradoxically, Gargantua remarks that too much regulation of time is in itself a waste of time, and in so doing he rehabilitates time's primacy:

1 / Forging Temporal Codes

La plus vraye perte du temps qu'il sceust estoit de compter les heures—quel bien en vient-il?[36]

[The truest waste of time he knew of was to count the hours—what good comes of it?]

Finally, the liberating exhortation posted on the monastery's door, "fais ce que voudras," is in fact temporally governed. The residents may "do whatever they want," *whenever all* of them decide to do the same thing: "Si quelqu'un ou quelqu'une disait, 'Beuvons,' *tous* buvaient. Si disait, 'jouons,' *tous* jouaient"[37] [If some man or woman said, "Let's drink," *everyone* drank. If someone said, "let's play," *everyone* played]. For the monks and nuns of the Abbey de Thélème, freedom is thus shaped by the principle of simultaneity, motivated by identical desires: the Thelemites' liberty extends only as far as their synchronous activities permit.

Rabelais does not stand alone in his opposition to the clock's tyranny. In an attempt to undo the imposition of rigid schedules, a ravenous abbot in *Petit Jehan de Saintré* discovers a technique to emancipate himself from time's clutches.[38] By setting the clock forward an hour and a half, he is able to have his midday meal right away.

Another ostensible rebellion against rigorous schedules in fact illustrates the prevalent notion in sixteenth-century letters that men should be responsible for regulating both their own and women's time. A number of writers of course take exception to this attitude, which I will address in various ways in chapters 3–5. However, the position articulated by the male speaker in Cholières's *Matinées* of 1587 turns out to be less singular than one might expect. In the chapter "En quel temps n'est loisible au mary de toucher conjugalement sa femme" [When it is not advisable to have conjugal relations with one's wife], a few commonplace caveats are enumerated: one should not engage in sex during the woman's "defluxions Lunaires" [lunar flow] or during pregnancy, nor during Lent, fasts, or prayer days.[39] The narrator expresses his counterdesire not to be hindered by any temporal limits whatsoever in his sexual behavior. In response to the question of when it would be appropriate to have conjugal relations with his wife, he retorts with lively metaphors, both extended and mixed:

J'insiste et forme ma plainte, que la possession du fonds, qu'elle a en garde, m'appartient, que j'en dois joüir pour mon usage, partant, puisqu'il me plaist y faire couler l'eau de mon ruisseau, pour le fertiliser, qu'elle ne doit m'y empecher l'entree. . . . Quoy, di-je alors, je seray le maistre de la monture, et je ne monteray dessus? Si feray et à bel effort commence à mettre ma piece en veue. . . . Ha malheureux! (dit elle) que voulez vous faire? voulez vous

vous perdre? si aviez affaire à moy vous seriez gasté. Cependant je languis, mon canon demeure chargé. . . . J'ay appetit, j'ay la viande, j'en voudroie bien taster, et si je n'oseroie: cela est pour faire perdre patience au plus froid homme de France.⁴⁰

[I insist and register my complaint that the land that she is protecting belongs to me, and I ought to enjoy full use of it. . . . Because I would like to run the water of my river to fertilize it, she shouldn't stop me from going into it. . . . "What's this!" I say, "I'm the master of the saddle and I can't mount it? Oh yes, I can!" and I diligently begin to take out my weapon. "Ah, miserable creature!" she says. "What are you doing? Do you want to do yourself in? If you have anything to do with me now you'll be spoiled." But I'm languishing. My cannon is loaded. . . . I'm hungry, I have the meat that I would like to taste, and yet I don't dare. It's enough to make the coldest man in France lose patience.]

Cholières's speaker demands to be the author of his own schedule and the master of his sex life, without interference from anyone, including his wife. Amidst the humorous dialogue and the absurdity of the argument by twentieth-century standards, the speaker's logic remains impeccable: as the owner of the land, river, weapon, saddle, meat, and wife, he should be able to enjoy them as his desires and schedule permit.

Just as schedules are seen as a largely masculine phenomenon, so the obverse of the schedule, the idea of "passetemps" or simply passing the time, often seems to involve women in some way. Men are seen as investors of time in Renaissance representations, as Ricardo Quinones notes, whereas women are seen as wasters of time,⁴¹ an observation that will be borne out in this study. It would be inaccurate, however, to trivialize the complex term "passetemps" by limiting it to a purely gendered phenomenon or by assigning to it a single meaning.

While the term "passetemps" or "passe-temps" was employed for the first time in the fifteenth century simply as a general expression for an amusing activity (Littré), it becomes a key word in a number of early modern French authors. The genesis of the *Heptameron*, for example, lies in Parlamente's proposal to create "passe-temps" while the travelers await the floodwater's recession (the pastime as edifying activity).⁴² In a different vein, contemporaneous moral discourses, responding to the public fear that women do not have sufficient activities to keep them occupied and chaste, prescribe certain activities and proscribe others (the pastime as protector). A number of poets explicitly justify their writing as a simple pastime (the pastime as subterfuge). And finally, Montaigne calls into question the very concept of "passing the time," inviting his contemporaries to rethink the significance of temporality in individual lives (the pastime as philosophical problem).[43]

Robert Mandrou notes the growing importance of recreation and pastimes in the sixteenth century, particularly among nobles.[44] In his analysis, Mandrou draws no distinctions between men's and women's pastimes, yet of the three principal pastimes he cites (hunting, gambling, and dance), only one is regularly practiced by women. Not coincidentally, the one pastime arguably acceptable for women, i.e., dance, is deemed pernicious by early modern moralists. In his *Introduction à la vie dévote*, François de Sales discourages dancing, remarking that while dance may appear innocuous, it often leads to evil.[45] The dialoguist Jacques Tahureau classifies dance among the preposterous pastimes, particularly since men engage in it with the desire to impress women. Similarly, according to Tahureau, making music is acceptable insofar as it brings pleasure to the [male] producer of it, but it should never be undertaken in the spirit of pleasing women, to whom men all too easily become subservient.[46]

When men engage in "pastimes" involving women, some moralists maintain, idleness and degeneracy often result. First among the "pastimes" to be avoided, according to the list in La Motte-Messemé's *Le Passe-temps*, is the "accointance des femmes, principalement incapables de conception" [any liaison with women, especially those not capable of conceiving], with an addendum noting that "accointance" with fertile women is necessary purely for reasons of continuing the species.[47] According to this formulation, women are associated not with the more critical "time," but rather over a kind of para-time or "pastime."[48]

In a very different vein, Bonaventure des Périers addresses a "pastime" to his patron Marguerite de Navarre. Given Marguerite's unimpeachable character, the poet clearly intends no implicit reproach of the princess regarding her use of time. Yet he nonetheless offers edifying material for her moments of freedom:

> Pour passe temps, donc, de votre lictiére,
> Regarderez ceste triste matière
> De corps de Christ second passion. . . .[49]

[Thus to pass the time in your coach, / Consider this sad tale / Of the second passion of the body of Christ. . . .]

Each strophe of the poem ends with "Pour passe temps," and the rondeaulike structure of the poem emphasizes the repetitive necessity of the royal lady's finding activities suitable both to her station and to her gender.

Both female and male early modern writers justify in prefatory material their publications by passing them off as simple "pastimes," but the practice seems to be much more consistent in women writers. The audaciousness of their publishing is thus excused because their explicit goal is not to accomplish great feats but rather simply to pass the time that would otherwise be spent in idleness. Hélisenne de Crenne, Pernette du Guillet's editor, Louise Labé, and Catherine des Roches all present their works as a pastime, and all their prefaces are addressed to female readers.[50]

Given this close association between women and pastimes, it is ironic that women of the sixteenth century were in many ways far less likely than men to have time that was unaccounted for in their daily lives. As Natalie Zemon Davis and Arlette Farge have shown, early modern women, while consistently present in domestic, economic, intellectual, and even public fora, were ordinarily occupied by quotidian tasks.[51]

Subtending the partitioning of daily time by schedules and pastimes are once again apparently conflicting philosophical approaches. While schedules purport to subjugate time by imposing strict control over it, the notion of "passing the time" conjures up whiling away the hours, allowing time to proceed unfettered by human attempts to intervene. In both cases, the growing consciousness of time's daily passage raises larger questions about the time of the human life cycle.

Lived Time

To decipher French sixteenth-century temporal codes as they appear in poetic works of the period, it will be useful to examine the concepts of age and aging in early modern society, including such elements as life expectancy, optimal marriage age, and life stages. While life expectancy in the sixteenth century cannot be calculated with certainty, Richard Bonney asserts that on the Continent, the average life span did not exceed thirty years.[52] But what does this figure signify? The meaning of "average" as a statistical term is fraught with complications in this case. First, up to 33 percent of newborns died before the age of twelve months, and only 50 percent reached their twentieth year. Second, the century was scourged by famine, plague, civil war, and extensive death of women in childbirth. Finally, as Fernand Braudel notes, the life span of wealthier citizens exceeded that of the poor by as much as ten years.[53]

Thus, the "average" life span of thirty years takes into account many premature deaths, and a number of people lived into their eighties, some with enviable verve. Pontus de Tyard, for example, reportedly maintained appreciable vigor in both body and spirit until his death at age eighty-four.[54] It should be noted, however, that women, at least in the public imagination, were considered old at a younger age than were their male counterparts. While in their thirties, women were deemed well on their way to senectitude, judging from Marguerite de Navarre, who calls herself "pouvre vieille" [poor old woman] at age thirty-four.[55] Similarly, in her *Heptameron*, the lady from Pampelune is described as thirty, the age at which "les dames ont accoustumé de quicter le nom de belles pour estre nommée saiges" [ladies are accustomed to giving up the title of "beautiful" to be called "wise"].[56]

Gabriel Meurier, in his 1577 *Thresor de sentences*, takes a generous life expectancy to be eighty years. He also accounts for the percentage of one's life involved in various activities:

> Du cours de la vie humaine,
> a bien venir quatre-vingts ans vivions,
> dont le dormir emporte la moitié,
> autres vingt ans soing et labeur avons.
> Sans autre dix qu'enfance nous manie,
> trois ou quatre ans emporte maladie,
> ainsi n'avons de reste, que sept ans,
> ou huyt au plus, de liesse ou bon temps.[57]

[In the course of human life, / We live eighty years, / Of which sleep takes away half, / Twenty years are taken by work and care, / Ten go to childhood, / Three or four are taken away by sickness, / Thus we only have seven remaining years, / Eight at the most, of happiness and good times.]

This brutally realistic division of a human life cycle reveals a number of fascinating details. First, if Meurier's description is accurate, people in the sixteenth century slept considerably more than their twentieth-century counterparts, so that a life span of the same number of years would seem to be configured quite differently. Second, childhood (to which only ten years are allotted) is listed as tantamount to work, care, and sickness, which implies its status as an undesirable period to be endured (a notable contrast to contemporary manifestations of the "Peter Pan syndrome"). Finally, the mathematical nature of Meurier's exposition illustrates a desire (quite familiar to readers at the dawn of the twenty-first century) to apportion not only hours, days, and years, but also an entire lifetime.

Several early modern physicians, following Pythagoras, divide a life cycle more broadly by comparing human ages to the four seasons. In his

Introduction à la chirurgie, Ambroise Paré outlines the four ages of man: childhood (spring; birth to age eighteen), adolescence (summer; eighteen to twenty-five), youth or virility (autumn; twenty-five to thirty-five) and old age (winter; in two stages, from thirty-five to forty-nine and from forty-nine till death). Following Galen, Paré divides the last stage into three parts, without specific ages: "verds vieillards" [green seniors] who are still active, those who only request food and sleep, and those who desire only the grave. The last of these stages involves a return to the helplessness of childhood *(bis pueri senes)*. One cannot assign ages to these last stages, he notes, because some people are older at forty than others at fifty years of age.[58]

According to these writers, at some point during the first two stages of human development marriage punctuates the temporal progression of an individual's life. The ideal age for marriage, particularly for women, poses an immensely popular problem in early modern texts. Why is so much attention paid to the age at which one ought to marry? The obvious response is that procreation is of foremost importance in a society where the only reliable support in old age is one's children and where a sizable percentage of children die during the first years of their lives. Since marriage in the sixteenth century involves the association of two families with the purpose of perpetuating and augmenting the common good of the two spouses (and their families), it seems logical that parents would choose a spouse of optimal child-bearing or child-fathering age for their children. So many contemporaneous commentators insist upon the question, however, that readers begin to understand the ideal marriageable age as a shorthand for the fullest moment in life, the period of one's physical peak, the *aetas perfecta*. Once again, this assigned "perfect age" is not universal, however, but rather considerably younger for women than for men. Erasmus identifies virgins of seventeen years old as "in the bloom of youth" and ripe for wedlock.[59] Estienne Pasquier warns that girls should marry before their perfect ripeness has passed, and he assigns twenty as the perfect age for women to marry.[60] Ambroise Paré writes that if girls are not married soon enough (preferably at fourteen to sixteen years of age), dreadful physical reactions will ensue:

> [E]lles sont tourmentees griefvement d'une defaillance de coeur, et suffocation de matrice, principalement quand elles deviennent amoureuses, et sentent une chaleur en leurs parties genitales, qui leur demangent, titillent, et chatoüillent, qui leur cause de jetter leur semence elles seules: laquelle demeurant aux vaisseaux spermatiques, ou en la matrice, se corrompt, et se tourne en venin . . . d'où provient qu'il s'esleve des vapeurs putredineuses

aux parties nobles . . . et faict qu'elles . . . sont pensives et chagrineuses, et fort degoustees, ayant l'appetit depravé, dict Pica, ne pouvans dormir, ayant la couleur palle et jaunastre basanee bouffie, et tout le corps sembablement, de sorte qu'elles ressemblent plustost mortes que vives, et souvent meurens hydropiques et languissantes, ou maniaques.[61]

[{The unmarried girls} are greatly tormented by faintness and suffocation of the uterus, especially when they become enamored, and feel heat in their genitals, which itch, tickle, and titillate. This causes them to send out their "semen" by themselves, which, staying in the sperm's vessels, or in the uterus, is corrupted and turns into poison, from which putrefying vapors rise to the noble parts of the body. This makes the girls pensive, sorrowful, and weary. They have a depraved appetite, and, as Pica says, cannot sleep, having a pale, yellowish, swollen appearance, so that they look more dead than alive, and they often die wasting away, suffering of dropsy or madness.]

To avoid this horrible condition, Paré explains, parents need simply marry their daughter while she is young, "et estant ainsi mariee reprendra sa couleur vive et naturelle, et le teint clair, ploy, et delicat, et son corps retournera entierement en sa bonne habitude"[62] [and thus being married she will regain her lively and natural color and her clear, supple, and delicate complexion; and her body will return completely to its healthy state].

In canon law, puberty normally determines marriageable age, although the minimum age for marriage is seven years, "the age of reason," when a child is deemed capable of consent.[63] The lawyer Estienne Pasquier notes that the *Digest* compiled by Justinian specifies fourteen years for men, twelve for women, but, he adds, if one is capable of carnal cohabitation before this age, marriage is permitted.[64] But for Pasquier these are obviously theoretical considerations. It seems that while a few noble women married as early as eleven or twelve in early modern France (e.g., Jeanne d'Albret to the duc de Clèves), it was the exception rather than the rule. However, noble and royal women generally married earlier than their less wealthy counterparts, who were often obliged to engage in agricultural or domestic service to lay up a dowry.[65]

The average age difference between husbands and wives in mid-sixteenth-century Paris was approximately ten to fifteen years.[66] The notion that men and women reach their physical peaks at very different ages can be traced to Aristotle, who held that women should marry at about eighteen and men at thirty-seven (*Politics* 7.16). Aristotle's belief that men's lives were longer and healthier than women's survives well into the sixteenth century, as evidenced by Ambroise Paré's remark (among many others) that a pregnant woman will have a rosier complexion and feel better if she is carrying a male child.[67]

Social and psychological exigencies, however, may account even more than physical considerations for the age gap between men and women in early modern marriages. Younger women are malleable and will therefore be molded more easily than older women to the husbands' wishes, as Francesco Barbaro discloses:

> [I]l est plus facile d'imprimer toutes les figures sur une cire molle, mais ce qui est imprimé sur une vieille et dure cire s'efface difficilement.[68]
>
> [{I}t is easier to print all the figures on soft wax, but what is printed on old, hard wax cannot easily be erased.]

The prevailing misogynistic sentiments of the time may in fact be in part attributable to the age difference between spouses. Since men of thirty frequently married women of less than twenty years old, as Barbara Diefendorf points out, their levels of maturity and experience diverged significantly.[69] Whereas parents encouraged sons to travel, gain experience, and seek new horizons, their primary concern for daughters was to protect their chastity and thus desirability, as we will see in chapter 4. It is not surprising that under such a patriarchal social code men should wish to regulate women's actions and time. Yet, as texts of the women writers included in this study reveal, considerable resistance to these presuppositions was fermenting in a number of circles, both intellectual and popular.

While extreme differences in age between spouses (twenty years or more) did exist in sixteenth-century France (witness Louise Labé's marriage to one of her father's ropemaker colleagues who was reportedly much older than she),[70] such a wide gap is not generally recommended in moral writings of the period. In the chapter "De l'inegalite de l'aage des mariez: Si un vieillard doit prendre une jeune fille: ou une vieille rechercher un jeune homme" (On the inequality of spouses' ages: if an old man should take a young woman, or if an old woman should seek a young man), Cholières discourages considerable age differences between spouses, but he uses stronger language to condemn marriage between an older woman and a younger man than the reverse.[71] In the same work, Seigneur Libanius questions why it should be unacceptable for an older man to marry a younger woman:

> La belle Venus ne s'accoupla elle pas avec le bon vieillard Anchises, sur le bord du fleuve Symois, quoy qu'il fut ridé, roupieux et chassieuz? et de cest accrochement Aeneas n'en fut il pas basty? Vous ne direz pas, qu'elle fut

surprise, ou qu'elle pensa à ce qui n'y estoit pas: Elle en faisoit la leçon aux autres.[72]

[Did not the beautiful Venus sleep with the good old man Anchises on the banks of the river Simois, even though he was wrinkled, snotty, and bleary-eyed? And did not this union produce Aeneas? You will not say that she was caught unawares or that she was mistaken: she was teaching a lesson to others.]

Seigneur Fulgence responds that Venus was only fulfilling the Oracle,[73] thus challenging the pedagogical merit of the myth. Other texts—both moral and satirical—denounce especially marriage between a younger man and an older woman as well. Gratien du Pont notes that "Qui vieille prend, est banny de plaisir / En regret vit, et tresgrand desplaisir" [He who takes an old woman is banished from pleasure and lives in regret and dissatisfaction]. In a long series of couplets he satirizes the plight of the man who chooses an older wife: she will cost him a fortune because of the extra clothing necessary to keep her warm, she will require a chambermaid, she will wake her spouse in the night with her complaining, and she will have worms.[74]

The most frequently cited argument for the difficulties between an older man and a younger woman is the potential cuckoldry and subsequent jealousy of the husband, whereas the principal obstacle to the union of an older woman with a younger man is that of the young husband's inability to honor his aging wife.[75] Today's readers might be inclined to note the fear of two conflicting systems of power that such a marriage would evoke: gender and age. Interestingly, both sets of reasoning proposed by Cholières originate from the husband's perspective, whether he be the younger or the older of the partners. Nicole Estienne offers a lively counterpoint on the matter, spelling out the considerable disadvantages for the younger female spouse, in *Les Misères de la femme mariée, où se peuvent voir les peines et tourmens qu'elle reçoit durant sa vie*, which will be examined in some detail in chapter 4. Her poems are all the more significant because, while we have access to a great many sixteenth-century commentaries on marriage by male writers, very few such works by women are extant (in addition to Estienne, only Hélisenne de Crenne comes to mind as a woman who wrote extensively about the institution of marriage from the woman's point of view).[76]

Time as it was imagined and lived thus forms the backdrop for the literary analyses I undertake during the course of the book. The nucleus of lived time for each individual inevitably resides in the body, male or female, through which or against which all human temporal notions emerge.

Time, Gender, and the Body

Nowhere in the material world is time's passage recorded more precisely, more relentlessly, or more unmercifully than in the human body. While this is true even today, it would have been overwhelmingly more palpable before the advent of dentistry, hormone replacement therapy, ophthalmologic treatment, ad infinitum. The poets included in this study all acknowledge—to varying degrees and in distinct ways—the primacy of the body as a measure for the moments of human existence. The woman's body in particular constitutes a site for a time-lapse view of aging for a number of poets. Véronique Nahom-Grappe notes the suspect nature of female beauty in sixteenth-century iconography because of its undeniable connection with death:

> Le corps de la belle femme est lié à la mort, dont le squelette grimaçant et asexué l'étreint.... Au XVIe siècle, l'iconographie offre les images de ce couple terrible, un corps d'autant plus "corporel" qu'il est féminin, d'autant plus périssable qu'il est beau, doré, nacré. L'étreinte du squelette est absolue, bien plus étroite que toutes les étreintes amoureuses, puisque ce squelette sans sexe, cette pourriture à venir, se situe à l'intérieur même du beau corps, sous la peau.[77]

> [The body of the beautiful woman is linked with death, whose grimacing, asexual skeleton embraces it and surrounds her.... In the sixteenth century, iconography offers images of this terrible couple, a body all the more "corporal" because it is female, all the more perishable because it is beautiful, golden, pearly.... The embrace of the skeleton is absolute, much tighter than lovers' embraces, because this asexual skeleton, this future rotting, is situated inside the beautiful body, under the skin.]

The numerous satirical representations of old women in sixteenth-century texts are no doubt allied with these iconographical depictions of the woman's body aging and dying. Old women frequently provide a basis for parody, derision, and condemnation in both medieval and early modern texts.

In Marot's *Contreblason* "Le tétin," for example, the breast's ugliness is described in terms denoting old age and impending death. Much like the teats of a decaying female goat's corpse, the poet notes, the old woman's breast produces a putrid fluid:

> Va, grand vilain tetin puant,
> Tu fournirais bien en suant

1 / Forging Temporal Codes 41

> De civettes et de parfums
> Pour faire cent mille défunts.⁷⁸

[There you go, big bad stinking breast, / You could easily furnish / Civets and perfumes / For a thousand dead bodies.]

It is significant that the depiction of aging female bodies often drifts to sexually charged body parts, as the example from Marot illustrates. Similarly, in his *Controverses* of 1534, Gratien du Pont insists on the decay of the aging woman's genitals:

> Baptiste dict que le bas instrument
> De la vieille est puant vilainement
> Et si dict plus, entendez bien ces vers,
> Que bien souvent, il engendre des vers.⁷⁹

[Baptist says that the lower instrument / Of the old woman stinks dreadfully / And moreover, listen carefully to these verses, / Often, it generates worms.]

These texts beg the question of why many male poets focus on the sexual aspects of aging women's bodies, particularly when other sources reveal that the sexual prowess of older women was considered superior to that of older men. Brantôme acknowledges in *Des dames gallantes* that sexual dysfunction is far more likely to strike older males:

Luy doncques, privé de ce plaisir, s'en abstient de bonne heure, encor que ce soit en despit de luy; mais la femme, en quelque age qu'elle soit, reçoit en soy, comme une fournaise, tout feu et toute matière.⁸⁰

[Thus the man, deprived of this pleasure, abstains early, although it is in spite of himself; but the woman, no matter what her age, like a furnace, takes every fire and every matter into herself.]

Both the satires critiquing women's atrophied genitals and the metaphor of the devouring furnace may well belie a displaced anxiety on the part of these male writers. The grotesque nature of the descriptions figures on the literary continuum between the medieval danse macabre and baroque satirical poems, yet the fact that the derided aging bodies are more frequently female than male suggests the displacement of a justifiable fear of aging on the part of such writers as Marot and Gratien du Pont. But male poets' emphasis on decomposing female bodies, particularly female genitals, remains a thorny question: do the male poets employ these images to suggest that aging affects women more than men because women are defined in societal terms more by their bodies? Or does male poets' insistence on the female aging body betray the displacement of a general anxiety about all female bodies? These are the sorts of questions that subsequent chapters of this book will address.

Beyond the emphasis on sexual prowess or lack thereof, Vives's recommendation for older women betrays his conviction that the responses most befitting old women are to withdraw from society and to die gracefully:

> La matrosne venue en aage vieil, prendra exemple des oyseaulx d'Egypte, lesquelz a la fin de leur long aage, serrent buschettes de boys aromatique, pour consommer les humeurs peccantes de leur corps pour suavement et doulcement finir leur vie.[81]

> [The matron who reaches old age will pattern herself after those Egyptian birds who, at the end of their long lives, hold twigs of aromatic wood in their beaks to absorb the bad smells of their bodies and to finish their lives more graciously and gently.]

Vives's disdain for aging women, much like that of the poets who satirize decaying female body parts, undoubtedly reflects a larger disquietude about aging in a society that glorifies youth (which, for all the reasons noted above, represents an extremely limited period) and at a time when old age began early and was often drawn out. Braudel cites examples of the emperor Charles V, who was considered an old man when he abdicated at Ghent in 1555 at the age of fifty-five, and of his son Philip II, who had been considered near death a number of times during the last twenty years of his life.[82]

Male attitudes toward aging females are perhaps the easiest to gauge, since so much is written on the subject. But how do males and females perceive their own aging in the early modern period? According to a number of contemporaneous texts, aging seems at first glance to signify very different things for men and for women. For men, the greatest fear associated with aging appears to be the loss of strength *(virtù)* and virility. In his "La Concorde des deux langages" of 1513, for example, Jean Lemaire de Belges describes in precise terms what old age will bring, and specifically the concomitant loss of "vertuz" [force, energy]:

> Viellesse griefve envoira ses espies
> Tremeur, Langueur, Infrigidation,
> Dont voz vertuz seront fort assoupies,
> Car par leur sort et congelation,

> Tout vostre corps sera froit comme marbre,
> Farsy de goutte et d'aultre infection.[83]

[Old age will send its treacherous companions, / Trembling, Feebleness, Chill, / Which will greatly sap your strength, / For by their spell and freezing / All your body will be as cold as marble, / Filled with gout and other infections.]

In lines 3–5, the words "vertuz," "sort" and "corps" all immediately precede the caesura of the decasyllabic verse, thus highlighting the fate of the aging body as inevitably involving the loss of strength. The terms "tremeur," "langueur," infrigidation," and "congelation" emphasize the loss of both control and flexibility. This apprehension of physical power's diminution in aging also surfaces in the work of the Pléiade poets, notably Ronsard, who as early as age thirty laments the relentless toll that time has taken on his body:

> Antres, je me suis veu chez vous
> Avoir jadis verds les genous,
> Le corps habile, et la main bonne:
> Mais ores j'ay le corps plus dur,
> Et les genous, que n'est le mur
> Qui froidement vous environne.
>
> (L.VII,98; P.I,806)

[Caves, I remember playing in your depths / Long ago when my legs {knees} were strong; / My body was supple, my hands skillful, / But today both my body and legs / Are more brittle and rigid / Than the wall so coldly surrounding you.]

Here Ronsard equates youth with both strength and dexterity in the terms "les genous verds," "le corps habile," and "la main bonne." Aging becomes tantamount to immobility and ineptitude in the antipodal expression "le corps dur" and in the comparison between the aging body and the cave's cold wall.[84]

Quite predictably, early modern critics (much like those of the late twentieth century) identify as the greatest threat to aging women not the loss of vigor but the loss of beauty. While physical attractiveness is applicable to both genders, as Montaigne implies in "Of Physiognomy,"[85] it is more consequential, in the essayist's view, for females than for males:

Je ne puis dire assez souvent combien j'estime la beauté qualité puissante et advantageuse. Il [Socrate] l'appelloit une courte tyrannie, et Platon le privilege de nature. Nous n'en avons point qui la surpasse en credit. Elle tient le premier rang au commerce des hommes; elle se presente au devant, seduict et preoccupe nostre jugement avec grande authorité et merveilleuse impression. Phryné perdoit sa cause entre les mains d'un excellent advocat, si, ouvrant sa robbe, elle n'eust corrompu ses juges par l'esclat de sa beauté.[86]

[I cannot say often enough how much I consider beauty a powerful and advantageous quality. Socrates called it "a short tyranny," and Plato, "the privilege of nature." We have no quality that surpasses it in credit. It holds the first place in human relations; it presents itself before the rest, seduces and prepossesses our judgment with great authority and a wondrous impression. Phryne would have lost her case even in the hands of an excellent attorney, if, opening her robe, she had not corrupted her judges by her dazzling beauty.][87]

Montaigne accords great power to beauty in human relations of both genders, yet the first example he furnishes, not coincidentally, is one of a female, in frontal view. Montaigne proceeds to give examples of Cyrus, Alexander, and Caesar, "those three masters of the world, [who] did not forget beauty in carrying out their great affairs,"[88] but the references to males are clustered and lack the specificity of the female illustration.

Certainly the greatest threat to beauty voiced in the texts we will examine is the physical ravaging of old age. In Alessandro Piccolomini's *Dialogo della bella creanza de le donne* [Dialogue on women's good manners], which appeared in France in a number of adaptations and translations during the sixteenth century,[89] the dialoguist has the character Florimonde express her fears of growing old, including the threat of losing her beauty:

Florimonde: Quand je pense à part-moy combien de maux apporte avec soy la vieillesse, je ne puis faire que je ne pleigne bien ceux qui s'en sentent affligez, et ne me sçaurois garder de devenir melancolique, en pensant que tost ou tard elle nous visitera, et qu'il faut que la saison vienne (comme l'on dit) que dedans le miroir on ne se cognoistra plus. Dieu me face la grace que le cours de ma vie soit arresté et achevé devant que me voir surprise et assaillie de ces maux. Car combien que beaucoup de femmes n'ont aucunefois raison de se plaindre de leur vieillesse, si est-ce qu'ordinairement je n'en vois point, qui n'en soyent à soy-mesme, et à autruy, ennuyeuses et fascheuses.[90]

[When I think of the ills that old age brings, I cannot help pitying those who feel afflicted by it, and I cannot avoid becoming melancholy, thinking that sooner or later it will come upon us, and that the season will come (as they say) when we will no longer recognize ourselves in the mirror. God grant that my life be stopped before I am taken and battered by these ills. For although many women need not complain about their old age, I only see those who are troublesome and difficult, both to others and to themselves.]

Youth—or a youthful appearance—constitutes a prerequisite, a sine qua non, for beautiful women in early modern texts. Marcel Françon, in his study of feminine aesthetics, shows that certain standards of beauty evolve during the course of the sixteenth century; notably, a shift in taste occurs from blond hair (à la Petrarch's Laura) to brown.[91] Yet the quality of youth remains immutable for every woman described as beautiful. All of the contemporaneous descriptions of Diane de Poitiers, for example, focus in some way on her age. Some inflated attention to age is of course predictable, given that she was twenty-nine years older than her lover Henri II, yet her youthfulness or lack thereof forms the center of virtually every depiction of her. The normally hypercritical, calumnious Brantôme raves about Diane's youthful beauty, claiming that at seventy she was "aussy belle de face, aussy fraische et aussy aymable, comme en l'aage de trente ans" [as beautiful in the face, as fresh and as comely as she was at thirty].[92] Even though Brantôme's claim cannot be wholly accurate (she died at age sixty six), his formulation reflects a unequivocal cultural prejudice in favor of youth, particularly for women.

One of the most surprising details emerging during the course of this study is that women's fear of losing their physical beauty in sixteenth-century texts seems to have been largely suggested or "planted" by men. None of the women poets included in this study expresses anxiety about her own passing beauty. If any fear of aging is discernible in these women (as in one of Louise Labé's sonnets to be examined in chapter 3), the question of lost beauty is immaterial.[93] Instead, these women poets devote themselves to such pursuits as promoting literary involvement by women, advocating a particular theological perspective, criticizing the institution of marriage as it existed in early modern France, or contemplating and recording the vicissitudes of love. Indeed, many of these women, as we will see, explicitly reject the ideological underpinnings of the insistence upon female beauty.

Why is the threat of aging projected upon women in sixteenth-century texts and yet apparently—judging from the texts we will be examining—more actively feared by men? As people age, of course, gender distinctions become obscured. Diane de Poitiers in her older years was described by a nineteenth-century literary historian as being more "virile" than "feminine."[94] Today we understand that estrogen levels in women and testosterone levels in men diminish as they age, which accounts for the fact that women become more like men in some ways (e.g., the growth of facial hair) and men like women (e.g., the reduction of muscle mass and the increase in breast tissue). Could it be that men's fear of aging in early modern France incorporates an anxiety of becoming more womanlike? Laura Levine, in her study of effeminization in early modern English theater, notes that "the epistemology men seek to construct is the opposite of what they fear."[95] This observation may be usefully applied to men's apprehension of aging in the texts we will consider as well. Male fears of emasculation and impotence, which are represented in images of withering female bodies, do not constitute an opposite epistemology, however, but rather an allaying of anxieties by projecting them onto another group. Although ostensibly the gendered body is the crux of the issue, could it also be that the female body serves as an embodiment of the social strictures that men understandably wish to avoid? These and other related questions will form the center of our investigations into the use of the body in its various forms as a measure of time.

To the query, "Is there such a thing as 'women's time' in early modern France?," I reply by posing another question: Is it plausible that women, consistently addressed as a category separate from men in contemporary philosophical, medical, and moral discourses, would conceive of time—both philosophically and practically—in the same ways as their masculine counterparts? A positive response to the latter question seems unlikely. Of course, just as no univocal temporal philosophy emerges among the humanist men included in this study, so there seems to be no single notion of "women's time" among writing women. Yet in these women's texts, differences of attitudes toward time—from subtle to strident—emerge.

The suggestion that sixteenth-century men and women had differing assumptions about the passage of time must of course be advanced with a number of qualifiers. Clearly, social position figured as a dominant force (as is still the case at the cusp of the twentieth-first century) in shaping attitudes toward time. A peasant laboring outside Petrarch's study window obviously thought very differently from the solitary scholar about the approach of evening, much less about the state of letters in three hundred years. (Similarly, the twentieth-century house cleaner and her executive employer no doubt perceive ten-hour workdays quite differently.) But beyond this obvious class distinction, I will argue that in the texts of early European men and women of the same social standing differing attitudes toward time emerge, and that we can come closer to an understanding of early modern mentalities by taking these differences into account.

Historical studies of time have largely ignored the problem of gender in general and women in particular for somewhat predictable reasons. As

Julia Kristeva has noted, "[W]hen evoking the name and destiny of women, one thinks more of the space generating and forming the human species than of time, becoming, or history."[96] Yet, as we will see, the sixteenth-century women poets examined here do indeed advance distinct temporal philosophies, and all of them (with the exception of Pernette du Guillet, who, probably because of her early death in her mid-twenties, left no explicit reflections on her own writing) see themselves or their texts as making a statement, as inscribing themselves or their ideas in the annals of literary history.

The reconceiving of temporality by the women poets included in this study often proves to be an audacious enterprise. All of these women reject to varying degrees the temporal ideology represented by the threats of the *carpe diem* tradition embodied in Ronsard's works and posit instead very different approaches to time. It is as if, to return to Rosso's fresco *La jeunesse perdue,* the symbolically charged young woman, at the moment when she was to be exchanged for water, had dismounted from the donkey and followed another path. Only through an examination of temporality through the women's eyes—in conjunction with the men's—can we begin to reconstruct the temporal landscape of early modern France.

2
Time in a Body: Ronsard's Corporeal Clock

>Ma douce jouvance est passée
>Ma première force est cassée
>J'ay la dent noire et le chef blanc. . . .
>—Ronsard (1555)

[My sweet youth has passed / My former strength is broken / My teeth are black and my hair silver. . . .]

>Non, Ronsard n'est point mort, la Muse est immortelle,
>Ou si Ronsard est mort, c'est un Phoenix nouveau,
>Qui n'ayant son pareil soy-mesme renouvelle,
>Et survit à sa cendre, animant son tombeau.
>—Claude Binet

[No, Ronsard is not dead, the Muse is immortal / Or if Ronsard is dead, he is a new phoenix, / Who, having no one to equal him, recreates himself, / And emerges from the ashes, giving life to his tomb.]

Two contradictory images have frequently emerged in depictions of Ronsard, both of which have contributed to the fashioning of a Promethean literary figure, a process that began with the publication of Binet's biography shortly after the poet's death.[1] The first of these portrays a highly successful court poet, seducing aristocratic ladies of his acquaintance in his youth and dominating the world of letters during the reign of Henri II and Henri III. The other depicts a sickly young man who turned to the tonsured life and to poetry when he could not pursue his intended diplomatic career, and who in later years, despite deafness and other serious physical ailments, still managed to devote himself to poetry.[2] In both cases, Ronsard is seen within this Renaissance mythology as ultimately transcending or sublimating the worldly and the physical in favor of poetic immortality, as illustrated in the often-cited verse of the last sonnet in the *Derniers vers:* "Ma plume vole au ciel pour estre quelque signe / Loin des appas mondains qui trompent les plus fins" (L.XVIII,180; P.II,1104) [My pen flies to the heavens to become a constellation / Far from the worldly enticements that beguile even the most discriminating].

The question of transcendence, troped as it is in terms of otherworldliness and timelessness, paradoxically provides an excellent point of departure for examining Ronsard's sense of time, which I will argue finds its most articulate elaboration in his treatment of the human body. Ronsard's texts often subvert the transcendence they claim, particularly in the *Amours*, by continually returning to the corporeal. The body mediates the poet's relationship to temporality; through it, Ronsard reads, measures, and imagines time.

Ronsard figures as the focus of this chapter not so much because he is prototypical as because his work reveals the most varied and most complex manifestation of temporal attitudes recorded by male poets in the middle of the sixteenth century. Like Petrarch, Ronsard expresses terror when faced with the passage of time, but, far more than Petrarch, he stages those fears through the depiction of the disintegration of the human body.[3] Like the ancient poets he imitates in his *Amours*, Ronsard illustrates time's ravages through the aging body of a spurning female lover, but much more than his models Ronsard explicitly personalizes the question, thus revealing his own attitudes toward the human life cycle, youth, and senescence.

Long before Mallarmé, Ronsard had stipulated in his posthumous preface to *La Franciade* that "les excellens Poëtes nomment peu souvent les choses par leur nom propre" (L.XVI, 333; P.I,1162) [Excellent poets rarely call things by their own names]. Time, indisputably one of Ronsard's greatest preoccupations, appears in a number of guises in his work: as a cosmic machine capable of destroying and creating a universal order, as an avenger, a scythe, and an old man.[4] Beyond these metaphorical manifestations, defying his own exhortation in the *Franciade*, Ronsard employs the word "temps" and its derivatives, according to Creore's *Word Index*, over five hundred times in his poetic corpus.

In addition to time's figuring as a central topos in Ronsard's work, the poet also develops three principal temporal motifs, each of which can be identified by a Latin designation: *exegi monumentum, carpe diem,* and *ubi sunt* (the latter being "where are," as in Villon's "Où sont les neiges d'antan?"). In nostalgically evoking a past that no longer is, or perhaps that never was, *ubi sunt* insists upon the distance between the dilapidated present and the idealized past.[5] This motif reveals quite interestingly the poet's linear notion of an irretrievable past, but it holds neither the prominence nor the force of the other two motifs. Ronsard's response to Virgil's fleeing time, given both the continually receding past and the ephemeral present, is to turn to the future, which, as I will attempt to show, is the domain of both *exegi monumentum* and *carpe diem*.

Figuring the Future: *Exegi Monumentum*

In his preface to the *Amours* of 1552, Ronsard proclaims both the motivation and the aspiration of his work: poetic immortality. In this initial sonnet, following Bembo,[6] the poet invokes the Muses, entreating them to inscribe verses in his honor in their temple:

> Plus dur qu'en fer, qu'en cuivre et qu'en metal,
> Dans vostre Temple engravez ces paroles:
> RONSARD, AFFIN QUE LE SIECLE A VENIR,
> DE PERE EN FILZ SE PUISSE SOUVENIR,
> D'UNE BEAUTÉ QUI SAGEMENT AFFOLE,
> DE LA MAIN DEXTRE APEND A NOSTRE AUTEL,
> L'HUMBLE DISCOURS DE SON LIVRE IMMORTEL,
> SON COEUR DE L'AUTRE, AUX PIEDZ DE CESTE IDOLE.
> (L.IV,4; P.I,19)

[Harder than in iron, copper, and metal, engrave these words in your Temple: so that the century to come, from father to son, will remember a beauty who discreetly wounds, Ronsard offers at our altar the humble words of his immortal book with his right hand, and with the other hand, his heart, beneath this image.]

Echoing his Horatian decree from the end of the fourth book of the *Odes* two years earlier, Ronsard clearly privileges the principles of *exegi monumentum* (by which I mean topoi and textual strategies that specifically focus on poetic immortality) as the motivating force of his writing. *Exegi monumentum* ("I have raised a monument," from Horace's ode "Exegi monumentum aere perennius") has been extensively analyzed by a number of critics, both ancient and modern.[7]

I will argue that Ronsard's conception of the future is almost inevitably associated with the human body, a conception that is revealed forcefully in his corporealizing the topos of poetic immortality. While the *exegi monumentum* motif by definition deprecates the mortal in favor of the immortal, Ronsard never fully transcends the human body in his use of the motif. Further, while initially it would appear that *exegi monumentum* has

2 / Time in a Body: Ronsard

no relationship to gender, upon closer examination it becomes apparent that gender does enter significantly into the functioning of the motif in Ronsard's work. These two problems converge in a prefatory poem to the *Amours*, which proclaims that words, longer lasting than if they were etched in metal, will outlive the poet's body. This introductory pronouncement holds an ill-defined future as its focal point: the poet writes for posterity ("le siecle à venir" [the coming century], "son livre immortel" [his immortal book]) in order to secure his lady's beauty, captured and frozen in the present, in the annals of literary history.

Ronsard thus opens his *Amours* with the principle that the poet alone has the authority to bestow immortality, a bequest that emerges in these verses as a specifically male prerogative. Female participation (in the form of the Muses, who here will accept Ronsard's book in their temple, or in the form of a model, here the unnamed Cassandre) is depicted in the text as essential for the purposes of the poet's creation, but only Ronsard, the single proper name inscribed in the poem, will produce the "livre immortel."[8]

The twin engraved portraits of Ronsard and Cassandre by either Jean Cousin or Nicolas Denisot,[9] which follow this preface and form the frontispiece of the first and subsequent editions of the *Amours*, serve as the iconographical replica of the liminary poem. The two images, depicting the poet and his mistress in profile face to face, are aligned such that eye contact seems to be established between them across the page.

Ronsard, crowned with a laurel wreath and draped in neo-Hellenic attire, looks at Cassandre with a lively eye. The Greek inscriptions of the 1552 and 1553 editions shown below were replaced in later editions by stanzas in French. Beneath Ronsard's image, a quatrain explains the triumphant gaze of the poet, whose double portrait is inscribed in the *Amours:*[10]

> Tel fut Ronsard, autheur de cest ouvrage,
> Tel fut son oeil, sa bouche et son visage.
> Portraict au vif de deux crayons divers:
> Icy le Corps, et l'Esprit en ses vers.

[Such was Ronsard, author of this work, such was his eye, his mouth and his face: living portrait from two different palettes: here his body, and his spirit in his verses.]

Cassandre, with bare breasts discreetly displayed among folds of material loosely draped from her shoulders, returns the poet's stare, but in a more reserved manner, as befits the poet's model. A string of pearls (symbolizing alternatively chastity and sexualized female beauty) encircles her forehead,

Ronsard and Cassandre from the 1552 edition of the *Amours*, Bibliothèque Nationale.

AN. 20.

Ὡς ἀπὸ ῥωνσαρδȣ
εἰς τὴν κασανδραν.
Φοιβάδα τὴν Κασανδραν, ἔρως τὸν ἕτερον ἐκείνης,
Φοιβομανῆ τεῦξεν φοῖβος ἐρωμανέων.
Ἡ δ᾽ ἄλλη Κασανδρὴ ἡ κιλπίδος, οὐκ ἔτι φοιβὰς,
Νῦν ἐμ᾽ ἐρωμανέα ῥέξ᾽ ἰδὲ φοιβομανῆ.
Ια. Αντω. Βαιφις.

and a few curls fall freely from her coiffure.[11] The quatrain below her portrait conjectures Cassandre's response to the poetry of her suitor:

> L'Art la Nature exprimant
> En ce pourtraict me faict belle
> Mais si ne sui-je poinct telle
> Qu'aux escrits de mon amant.

[Art as it translates Nature in this portrait makes me beautiful, but I am not at all so—except in the writings of my lover.][12]

Both the prefatory poem and the frontispiece establish not only the power of the male poet to record his lady's portrait for posterity, but also the primacy of terms that originate in the body as the genesis of the *exegi monumentum* motif. In the poem, the poet's right hand places his book on the Muses' altar, while his left hand lays his heart beneath Cassandre's portrait ("aux piedz" [at her feet]). In the quatrains, the poet's eye, mouth, face, and body prepare the terrain for the poet's "Esprit," which the verses promise to portray. Cassandre's physical beauty, mentioned in the first two verses of the quatrain, is revealed in the final two verses as having been created only by the power of the poet's writing.[13] As Marc-Antoine Muret remarks in his 1553 commentary on the *Amours,* "[Ronsard] feint pour amplifier la beauté de sa Dame" [To increase his lady's beauty, Ronsard is exaggerating].[14] According to the quatrain, Ronsard's physical portrait will be recorded only by the iconographical representation, but Cassandre's "amplified" beauty is seized both in the engraving and in the poet's verses. While the quatrains promise the foregrounding of Cassandre's beauty and the effacing of Ronsard's body in favor of his spirit in the verses, in fact the poet's own body remains prevalent throughout the different books of the *Amours*.

In a preface added to the 1584 edition of the *Œuvres*, Ronsard once again utilizes his own body as the central axis from which the book and its effects radiate, but here the temporal implications are more explicit:

> 7 ... Va, livre, va, desboucle la barriere,
> Lasche la bride, et asseure ta peur. ...
> Mais non, arreste, et demeure en ton rang,
> Bien que mon coeur bouillonne d'un beau sang,
> Fort de genoux, d'haleine encore bonne;
> 12 Livre, cesson d'acquerir plus de bien,
> Sans nous fascher si la belle couronne
> Du Laurier serre autre front que le mien.
>
> (L.IV,185; P.I,3)

2 / Time in a Body: Ronsard

[Go, book, break the barriers, let out the reins, and fear not.... But no, stop, stay put, even though my heart bubbles with excellent blood, I have sturdy legs and my breath is still strong. Book, let's stop seeking further riches, without worrying that the beautiful laurel crown might encircle a forehead other than mine.]

In these verses, the poet draws an implicit parallel between the relative youth and strength of his body (lines 10–11) and the strength of his refusal to let rivals' challenges interfere with the release of his book. While the poet appears resigned to competition (lines 13–14), he nonetheless maintains confidence in his ability to retain on some level the triumphant laurel wreath (hence his decision to publish). Here, the poet's body serves as a literary ally, but only fleetingly. Time's specter is clearly evoked in the phrase "haleine *encore* bonne," and readers of the 1550 ode "Quand je suis vingt ou trente mois" would be apprised of Ronsard's insistence on the condition of knees as a primary measure of the aging body.[15] In these verses, the linked notions of time passing and the urgency of publication converge in the chronometer of the poet's body.

The crucial role of physicality in Ronsard's employment of *exegi monumentum* can be further glimpsed through the optic of gender. The poet adopts a very different approach to the immortalization of the subject depending on whether the addressee is male or female, as two pieces from the first book of *Odes* reveal. Pindaric odes traditionally laud the power of song over all things mortal, and, under the guise of praising great rulers and victors of Olympic games, hail the poet's divine ability to extend their life cycle. It could be argued that because Pindar sang praises of male victors, such rhetoric was readily available to Ronsard, whereas the celebration of the accomplishments of a female addressee necessitated Ronsard's invention of a new laudatory vocabulary. But while the terms of male and female praise are indeed distinct, they appear so for predictable reasons of custom and social expectations. The poet celebrates the specifically masculine "valeureux courage" (L.III,5 [1550, var. 1584]; P.I,594) of Henri II, for example, whereas he praises the feminine beauty of Henri's daughters: "Chanteray-je vostre race, / Ou l'honneur de vostre face / D'un teint brun se colorant? [Shall I sing your race / Or the honor of your face / Of rich, dark complexion?] (L.VII,77; P.I,751). The difference is marked and important in the relationship that the poet establishes with the addressee within the ode. In his "Ode au Roy Henry II, sur la paix faicte entre luy et le Roy d'Angleterre, l'an 1550," the poet's Pindaric purpose is explicit from the beginning: the celebration of a great victory and the eulogizing of the king for posterity. Throughout the poem, Ronsard introduces four parallels, explicit or implicit, between King Henri and himself. First, he notes the fact that both were chosen by divine election to pursue their respective careers: "O Roy, par destin ordonné / Pour commander seul à la France" (L.III,4; P.I,593) [O King, alone ordained by destiny / to govern France].

The second commonality between the two men is that both the king and the poet accomplish a crucial function or "entreprise" in society:

> Quand l'âge t'animera,
> Alors ton bras s'armera
> Pour achever l'*entreprise*.
> (L.III, 13 [1550, var.1578]; P.I,597, my emphasis)

[When with maturity you are emboldened / Then you will put on arms / To accomplish the feat.]

In another ode addressed to Henri II, Ronsard describes his own mission using precisely the same term:

> ... Je suis tout prest
> De charpenter sa nef et dresser son apprest,
> Pourveu que ta grandeur Royale favorise
> A ton ayeul Francus, et à mon *entreprise*.
> (L.VII,10 [1555, var. 1560]; P.I,591, my emphasis)

[... I am completely willing to build the ship and get it ready, provided that your royal highness is favorable to your ancestor Francus and to my undertaking.]

The poet is further united with Henri II by his ability to bridge the gap among three generations of kings. Ronsard allies himself with Henri's father François I by their mutual appreciation of poetry:

> Mais le rond du grand univers
> Est plein de la gloire eternelle,
> Qui fait flamber ton Pere en elle
> Pour avoir tant aimé les vers.
> (L.III,34 [1550, var.1552]; P.I,603)

[But the circle of the great universe / Is filled with eternal glory, / Which inflames your father within it / For having loved poetry so much.]

Ronsard then praises Henri's current successes in both Italy and Spain, and establishes a generational link in the other direction, this time with Henri's son, by predicting the dauphin's future conquests:

> Avienne aussi que ton fils
> Survivant ton jour prefis
> Borne aux Indes sa victoire,
> Riche de gain et d'honneur,
> Et que je sois le sonneur
> De l'une et de l'autre gloire.
>
> (L.III,35; P.I,604)

[God grant also that your son, surviving your appointed day, extend his victory to the Indies, {becoming} rich in profit and honor, and that I be the bell ringer of both victories.]

Directly implying a brotherhood between the king and himself, Ronsard establishes an important connection with both Henri's father and his son. What Henri provides through heredity, Ronsard will achieve through his verses: a vital link between the royal generations.

The final connection between Ronsard and Henri is their mutual authority to conquer time, one by writing immortal odes and the other by being sung within them. Both men have a public to please, but Ronsard (not disinterestedly) makes the case for the superiority of the written word over evanescent compliments:

> Par trét de tens les flateurs meurent,
> Mais les beaus vers toujours demeurent
> S'enduricissans contre les ans.
>
> (L.III,33; P.I,603)

[Flatterers die by time's arrow, / But beautiful verses live forever, / Gaining strength against the years.]

Thus a camaraderie between the praiser and the praised is unequivocally established. Both men have accomplished heroic deeds, and both names will be recorded in the temple of immortality by the poet's writing: "mon petit Myrte ose attoucher le rond / Des lauriers, que la guerre a mis dessus ton front" (L.VII,8; P.I,590) [my little myrtle dares to graze the crown of laurels that war has placed upon your forehead].

Ronsard's "A Madame Marguerite, Soeur du Roy, Duchesse de Savoye" reveals the very different strategy the poet adopts in addressing a royal woman. In contrast to his articulating the likenesses between himself and Henri II, the poet here makes no attempt to construct a simulacrum of equality with the duchess. He praises Marguerite de France's victory over the personified "vilain monstre Ignorance" and acclaims her virtue and her merit.

But Ronsard establishes only one parallel between the duchess and himself near the end of the ode:

> Chanton donques Marguerite,
> Et celebron *son merite*,
> . . . .
> Respandon devant *ses yeux*
> *Ma musique* toute neuve,
> Et le Nectar dont j'abreuve
> Les honneurs dignes des Cieux,
> Afin que la Nymphe voye
> Que *mon luth* premierement
> Aux François monstra la voye
> De sonner si proprement,
> Et comme, imprimant *ma trace*
> Au champ Attiq' et Romain,
> Callimaq', Pindare, Horace
> Je déterray de *ma main*.
> (L.I,77–78 [1550, var. 1584]; P.I,612, my emphasis)

[Thus let us sing Marguerite's praises and celebrate her merit.... Let my all-new music and the nectar whose heaven-worthy honors I drink flow before her eyes, ... so that the Nymph will see that my lute was the first to show how it should be played, and {see} how I will unearth Callimachus, Pindar, and Horace with my own hands, making my mark in the Athenian and Roman field.]

Here the connection between the poet and the lady is limited to the fact that her excellence ("son merite") and her favor ("devant ses yeux") will contribute to the poet's song ("ma musique" and "mon luth"). For the last lines of the ode, in true Pindaric fashion, the third-person pronoun representing Marguerite disappears entirely in favor of the poet's first-person pronoun. Following the progression between "ses yeux" and "ma main," the reader is struck by the similarity in progression between this ode and Ronsard's love lyric, where the Petrarchan *innamoramento* brought on by the woman's eyes inevitably finds its way to the poet's hand, or pen. Despite the appreciable difference in context, in the ode to Marguerite of France, as in many sonnets of the *Amours* as well as the liminary poems examined above, the female model is depicted as vital to the poet's production but not complicitous with him or his project. Thus the female addressee, much like da Vinci's composite models, becomes the physical impetus for the composition as well as the body incarnated in the text.

The gender of the addressee is also strikingly germane in the body topos as it appears in Ronsard's *exegi monumentum* odes. In odes dedicated to women, Ronsard makes explicit reference to the body far more frequently than he does in odes dedicated to men—not only to the female body, but also to his own. In odes similar in subject and tone addressed to royal personages in books 1, 3, and 5 of the *Odes*, for example, the poet evokes the body and parts of the body at least twice as often when the ode is dedicated to a female as when it is dedicated to a male. In the odes addressed to Henri II in the first book, for example, 5 percent of the verses contain explicit references to body parts, whereas in those dedicated to "La royne sa femme" (Catherine de Médicis) or to Marguerite de France, his sister, 12 percent of the verses include such references. Similarly, in book three of the *Odes,* 5 percent of the verses of the ode addressed to Henri comprise allusions to the body, whereas the ode to the queen includes 10 percent. Finally, in book 5, approximately 3 percent of the verses in the ode to Henri II contain such citations versus 7 percent in the ode to Marguerite de France. This curious disparity could perhaps be attributed to a similar distribution of physical references in the poet's models—Pindar and Callimachus—but upon closer examination this seems not to be the case. Pindar's *Olympics* and *Pythics* are all dedicated to male victors, and in Callimachus's *Hymns* there is no appreciable difference in physical references between those dedicated to males and those dedicated to females.[16]

Enumeration and description of the female body in Ronsard's love lyrics can of course be traced largely to literary tradition, from Greek and Latin poetry to Petrarchism to the *Blasons anatomiques du corps féminin*. But no similar justification for the preponderance of references to the body in *exegi monumentum* odes addressed to women, particularly royal women, is immediately apparent. In only one case does the subject matter of the ode particularly invite an insistence on physicality, namely, in the second ode of the third book, "A la royne Catherine de Medicis, mère du roy" (L.VII,34–41; P.I,726–30). In this ode the poet cites a number of mythological examples that will contrast unfavorably with the regent queen's maternal practices in raising the dauphin François II. Unlike Rhea (Cybele), for example, Catherine will not exchange her son's body for a stone that Saturn devours; she will not hide him in a cave of Crete, as did Jupiter's mother. Thus, the question of newborns and mothers inspires such vocabulary as "gesine," "corps," "peau," "giron," and "sang."

But beyond this patent example, why do Ronsard's odes addressed to women make more frequent use of the vocabulary of the body? One obvious response could resolve part of this question: females, as evidenced both by the literary and iconographical examples mentioned above and by numerous other cultural examples, are defined by early modern—and postmodern—society more in terms of corporality than are men.[17] Ronsard would thus predictably be drawn to more frequent physical descriptions of women. But this answer is at best a partial one. What is particularly intriguing about these female addressees is not simply that they conjure up the topos of the female body in Ronsard's work but that they also invite the poet to evoke his own body. Does the imagined female reader serve as the stereotypical "good listener," emancipating the poet to bare, as it were, both body and soul? Such a conjecture meets with considerable resistance in Ronsard's text, however, because the camaraderie that Ronsard establishes with such male addressees as Henri, as we saw, is absent from the poems dedicated to females.[18] I would argue, rather, that if the male addressee becomes a "soul mate," the female functions as a "body double"; she is the locus of the physical, the other that through its difference paradoxically both magnifies and collapses the distance between the poet and his own body. In the case of Ronsard's aging body, for example, that distance is magnified by the poet's projection of his own fear of aging onto the other, and at the same time collapsed by the implicit comparison between his body and the addressee's.

The canonical sonnet "Quand vous serez bien vieille," dedicated not to a royal lady but to the resisting "belle Hélène," provides an excellent example of the complex rhetorical movement in Ronsard's text between the poet's body and that of the female addressee. This sonnet, frequently cited as a quintessential *carpe diem* poem, contains instead at its nucleus the *exegi monumentum* motif. Once again, the motif is inextricably linked with human bodies, and in this case Hélène's aging body is contrasted unfavorably with the poet's mortal remains. Time's power is again implacable, tamed only by the superior potential of poetry, which itself takes on a physical dimension in this sonnet:

>   Quand vous serez bien vieille, au soir à la chandelle,
> Assise aupres du feu, devidant et filant,
> Direz chantant mes vers, en vous esmerveillant;
> "Ronsard me celebroit du temps que j'estois belle."
>   Lors vous n'aurez servante oyant telle nouvelle,
> Desja sous le labeur à demy sommeillant,
> Qui au bruit de mon nom ne s'aille resveillant,
> Benissant vostre nom de louange immortelle.
>   Je seray sous la terre, et fantôme sans os
> Par les ombres myrteux je prendray mon repos;
> Vous serez au fouyer une vieille accroupie,
>   Regrettant mon amour et vostre fier desdain.

> Vivez, si m'en croyez, n'attendez à demain:
> Cueillez dés aujourdhuy les roses de la vie.
> (L.XVII,265; P.I,400–401)

[When you become old, sitting by the fire / In evening's candlelight, spinning and carding, / You'll say, in awe, as you sing my verses, / "Ronsard celebrated me long ago when I was beautiful." // There will not even be a maid, / Half asleep from her tedious work, / Who does not awaken to the sound of my name, / Blessing your name with immortal praise. // I will be under the earth, a boneless ghost, / And lying by the shadowy myrtle trees I shall rest. / You will be crouched by the fire, an old hag, // Regretting my love and your proud spite. / Live now, if you believe me, don't wait till tomorrow. / Gather life's roses today.]

The corporeal universe in which the sonnet plays itself out is essential to an understanding of the poet's temporal ideology. The disembodied dead poet, "fantôme sans os," is depicted in a more auspicious light than the aging body of Hélène, "une vieille accroupie," and the attitudes of the poem's characters reflect that opposition.[19] While the poet rests in the peaceful shade of the myrtle tree ("sans os" = "sans souci," no bones – no worries), Hélène is condemned to regret both the love of the poet and her proud disdain as she repetitively spins her destiny, turning the equivalent of Ixion's wheel. What will be recorded for posterity, according to the last line of the quatrains, is Hélène's name. The monument that the poet erects in this sonnet, however, is of course to the poet himself. The famous line "Ronsard me celebroit du temps que j'estois belle" paradoxically eclipses Hélène, whose name is evoked nowhere in the poem. Like Du Bellay's Rome,[20] which bears no resemblance to its eponym and functions rhetorically as an *antanaclasis* or a *ploce,* Hélène is presented as a phantom of her former self and is contrasted with Ronsard's prospering "fantôme." The materiality of Hélène's world—the candle, the fire, the spindle—creates the context for her physical effacement. All of these objects can be read as symbols of aging and death: the candle burns and is then extinguished, the fire consumes all, and the spindle evokes the Fates and the thread of life passing through one's hands.

Three sets of oppositions contribute to the paradox of Hélène's appearing to be more ghostlike than the dead poet. First, the ostensibly dead narrator has the power to affect ("esmerveiller," "resveiller"), whereas Hélène's body, much like the servant's, is on the brink of consciousness, slowly winding down her life at the spinning wheel. Second, the reversal of the two characters' life cycles is implied by the metamorphosis of the characters' sentiments according to a linear time sequence (Ronsard's past desire becomes the future regret of Hélène, whose former disdain becomes the poet's future triumph). Finally, the physical positions of the characters in the poem also serve to conjure up associations with age in the mind of the reader. Whereas Hélène's position huddling near the fire evinces her body's frailty and an ultimate sense of absence, the reference to Ronsard's remains resting under the shady myrtle tree denotes peace and plenitude. By virtue of its perpetual greenness, myrtle is associated with immortality.[21] (Read: Ronsard is still alive.) Further, myrtle leaves, an emblem of Venus because her Roman temple was surrounded by these trees, were used for medicinal purposes as an astringent and a stimulant. (Read: Ronsard still has the goddess of eroticism on his side.)

The substitution of the poet's body (the *corps* become *corpus*, the body become poetry) for Hélène's and vice versa, whereby her youthful characteristics become his and his aging becomes hers, suggests a double reversal. Hélène's and the poet's bodies are projected into a future where their positions on the time line are paradoxically reversed. At the same time, the sonnet oscillates between reflection (each character reflects the other's body; Hélène iterates Ronsard's song) and rejection (the poet's body is *not* Hélène's—his is at rest while hers toils, he is at peace while she regrets; the poet rejects the rejector). Further, the poet manages to place himself simultaneously at both ends of the life cycle by bypassing his own old age and portraying himself as dynamic even in death. But despite these reversals, the linearity of past and future clearly dominates the poem, as evidenced by the complete absence of the present tense until the last two lines of the sonnet, where the *exegi monumentum* motif briefly cedes to an exhortation of *carpe diem*.

Despite the frequency with which Ronsard evokes some version of *exegi monumentum*, and despite Ronsard's reputation as a proponent of literary immortality (as evidenced by his portrayal in Loys Le Caron's dialogue "Ronsard, ou De la poésie" and elsewhere), his attitude toward it remains equivocal.[22] This ambivalence surfaces both implicitly and explicitly at several moments in Ronsard's poetic career. In the "Elegie à Marie" of 1560, for example, the poet begins by casting his motives in traditional Horatian rhetoric:

> Marie, à celle fin que le siecle advenir
> De nos jeunes amours se puisse souvenir,
> Et que vostre beauté que j'ay long tems aimée
> Ne se perde au tumbeau par les ans consumée. . . .
>
> (L.X,238; P.I,244)

[Marie, so that the coming century / Will remember our young love, / And so that your beauty that I have loved so long / Not be lost in the tomb, consumed by years. . . .]

But the elegy soon turns to the poet's own physical desire, and Marie's "vertu," rather than inspiring immortal verses, arouses other sentiments entirely:

> O ma belle angevine, ô ma douce Marie,
> Mon oeil, mon coeur, mon sang, mon esprit et ma vie
> Dont la vertu me monstre un beau chemin aus cieux
> Je reçoy tant de bien quand je baise vos yeus,
> Quand je languis dessus, et quand je les regarde. . . .
> (L.X,238; P.I,244)

[Oh, my beautiful Angevine, my sweet Marie, / My eye, my heart, my blood, my spirit, and my life / Whose virtue shows me the way to heaven / I feel such delight when I kiss your eyes, / When I languish before them, and when I look at them. . . .]

The poet's vacillation in the elegy between the immortal future and the sexualized present, between the "aage de ce livre" and the poet's languishing body, implicitly calls into question Ronsard's unfettered devotion to the cause of poetic immortality. Similarly, in an elegy to Philippe Desportes, Ronsard returns again to the physical, and in this case the finite body explicitly takes precedence over infinite glory:

> Quant à moy, j'aime mieux trente ans de renommée,
> Jouyssant du Soleil, que mille ans de renom
> Lors que la rosse creuse enfouyra mon nom,
> Et lors que nostre forme en une autre se change.
> L'homme qui ne sent plus, n'a besoin de loüange.
> (L.XVIII, 250; P.II,418)

[As for me, I prefer thirty years of fame, / Enjoying the sunshine, than a thousand years of glory / When the deep trench buries my name, / And when our form changes to another. / He who no longer feels, does not need praise.]

Given these apparent contradictions, what are we to make of Ronsard's pronouncements on the principles of *exegi monumentum*? Isidore Silver argues that in the last sonnet of the *Derniers vers*, Ronsard triumphantly breaks away from physical bonds: "[I]t is with a sense of victorious abandonment of illusory terrestrial attachments that he writes 'Ma plume vole au ciel pour estre quelque constellation'" (L.XVIII,180; P.II,1104) [My pen flies to the heavens to become a constellation].[23] While such a coherent conclusion advancing Ronsard's subscription to the primacy of poetic immortality is attractive, it seems to me that in the *Derniers vers*, rather than arriving at a definitive conclusion, the poet advances a dialectic in which mortality and immortality, the physical and the metaphysical, and time and eternity remain in opposition.[24] What becomes clear is that the texts themselves challenge the poet's explicit claim of transcendence. The last tercet of the final sonnet seems to suggest the poet's imminent freedom from bodily attachments:

> Laissant pourrir çà-bas sa despouille de boüe,
> Dont le Sort, la Fortune, et le Destin se joüe,
> Franc des liens du corps pour n'estre qu'un esprit.
> (L.XVIII,180; P.II,1104)

[Leaving to rot there below his muddy remains, / Which Fate, Destiny and Fortune deride, / Freed from bodily bonds to become only a spirit.]

Yet throughout the seven sonnets of the *Derniers vers*, the poet evokes the disparity between youth and old age as well as his ambivalent attitudes toward dying, and the preponderance of corporeal references obverts the possible conclusion that the poet has completely transcended the physical. The famous "Je n'ay plus que les os, un squelette je semble, / Decharné, denervé, demusclé, depoulpé" (L.XVIII,176; P.II,1102) [I'm nothing but bones, a skeleton I seem / Without flesh, nerves, muscles, mass] of the first sonnet, for example, is immediately preceded by a meditation in the *Stances* on the pleasures of the youthful body, despite its evanescence:

> Le vray tresor de l'homme est la verte jeunesse,
> Le reste de nos ans ne sont que des hyvers
> ... ainsi qu'on voit fanir
> La rose par le chauld, ainsi, mal gouvernée,
> La jeunesse s'enfuit sans jamais revenir.
> (L.XVIII,175; P.II,1101)

[The true treasure of man is green youth, / The rest of our years are only winters / ... just as we see / The rose fading in the heat, so, if poorly lived / Youth escapes without ever returning.]

Here the alliteration of *j* and *s* in the last verse and the consonance of *f* and *v* in the last three verses accentuate the verbal sensuality of the last stanza. It is not corporality in toto that the poet spurns in the *Derniers vers*, but rather the specific physical suffering that his body continues to sustain:

> Pour chasser mes douleurs ameine moy la Mort.
> Hà! Mort, le port commun, des hommes le confort,
> Viens enterrer mes maux, je t'en prie à mains jointes!
> (L.XVII,178; P.II,1103)[25]

[To banish my sorrows, bring me Death, / Death the common port, men's comfort, / Come bury my afflictions, I beg you with my hands clasped!]

The interior rhyme "Mort"/"port" and the subsequent image of burying not the poet's body but his afflictions portray death specifically as an escape from pain rather than transcendence. Even the final sonnet that Silver cites as evidence for the poet's liberation from the physical begins with a nostalgic enumeration of the material pleasures the dying poet will leave behind: "... maisons et vergers et jardins, / Vaisselles et vaisseaux que l'artisan burine ..." (L.XVIII,180; P.II,1104) [houses and orchards and gardens, dishes and glasses that the artisan crafts].

In these examples drawn from the *Odes* to the *Derniers vers*, then, Ronsard corporealizes the traditionally disembodied *exegi monumentum* motif and attaches a decidedly physical dimension to the future. Further, in Ronsard's treatment of poetic immortality the presence of women—as addressee, object, or both—increases and concretizes physical references through a complex movement between speaker and addressee in the poem, as we have seen. Ultimately, even the most speculative of concepts, the *exegi monumentum*, finds a concrete elaboration in Ronsard. Much as the metamorphosed flea in "Ha, seigneur dieu" returns to the male body in order to reap the benefits of his intimate position, so Ronsard inevitably returns to his own body as an indicator, as a chronometer, as the sine qua non of his text in both its creation and its literary longevity.

CARPE DIEM REVISITED: RONSARD'S TEMPORAL PLOYS

> For women are as Roses, whose faire flowre
> Being once displaid, doth fall that verie howre.
> —*Twelfth Night*, 2.4.36–39

The *carpe diem* (pluck the day) motif, whose onomastic origins can be traced to Horace,[26] permeates not only classical Greek and Latin poetry but also lyric poetry from fifteenth-century Italy to sixteenth-century Spain to seventeenth-century England. Few students of English literature are unfamiliar with Herrick's "Corinna's Going A-Maying," Donne's "The Anagram," Shakespeare's Sonnets 1–17, or Marvell's "To His Coy Mistress." Similarly, in the Spanish tradition Garcilaso de la Vega's "En tanto que de rosa y azucena," Luis de Góngora's "Mientras por competir con tu cabello," Argensola's "Ojalá suyo así llamar pudiera," and Quevedo's "A una mujer afeitada" form part of a large corpus of *carpe diem* poems. But it is perhaps in early modern France in general, and in the Pléiade in particular, that the *carpe diem* motif evinces its greatest surge. As Laumonier humorously phrases it, "Le vieux thème est dans l'air, et l'air en est saturé"[27] [The old theme is in the air, and the air is saturated with it]. Ronsard figures prominently in this tradition, which he both embraces and transforms.

Construed traditionally as "a compliment and an invitation," and more recently as "an instrument of seduction," *carpe diem* has received much critical mention, but little sustained attention.[28] Perhaps this comparative dearth of scholarly scrutiny results from what appears to be a too obvious functioning of the literary motif. Even the most casual reader notes that the poet who invokes the *carpe diem* motif is attempting to convince the addressee, often through a comparison of the young girl to the ephemeral rose, that she should love him now, while the time is ripe. But what is the nature of this tactic? How does it function, both rhetorically and psychologically? Is the poet's ultimate message an epicurean exhortation to "gather rosebuds while ye may," or do other rhetorical elements in the poems obfuscate that reading? Ronsard's *carpe diem* poems reveal not only multiple responses to these questions but also the poet's own assumptions about time, the topos that is explicitly problematized by the motif.

Ronsard's complex and original adaptation of the *carpe diem* motif can perhaps best be illustrated by juxtaposing his texts with the classical sources that he sets out to imitate. When Ronsard began to adopt the *carpe diem* motif in the mid-sixteenth century, a number of Latin, Greek, and more contemporary models were available to him. The *Greek Anthology* had been published in Florence in 1494 by J. Lascaris and reprinted several times, including one printing in Paris by Josse Bade in 1531. J. Stobaeus's *Florilegium*, from which Ronsard borrowed many erotic-bacchic fragments,[29] was published in Venice in 1535 (Bartholomeo Zanetti Casterzagense), in 1543 in Zurich (Froschoverus), and again in Basel in 1549 (J. Oporinus). Horace's *Opera,* and specifically the *Carmina*, enjoyed a great popularity at the end of the fifteenth century and the beginning of the sixteenth, with numerous editions published in Venice, Florence, and Paris. In addition to these classical sources, the *carpe diem* motif experienced a rebirth in the late-fifteenth-century Italian poetry of the Petrarchisti, especially Lorenzo de' Medici and Poliziano.[30] Ronsard also read Johannes Secundus, which led him to other neo-Latins, notably Marullus, whose *Epigrammata et Hymni* had been published in Florence in 1497 and in Paris in 1529.

Many subtle differences exist among the various sorts of *carpe diem* poems, but the most prototypical form of the genre features the (older) male poet—with distinctly erotic designs—exhorting the (younger) female addressee to take advantage of the present moment. Propertius urges Cynthia to taste of life's pleasures now, for her kisses will fall like petals from a festive garland (*Elegies* 2.15). Ovid reminds a young Roman woman that years flow like water; she will regret having spurned her lover as she lies in her solitary bed in later years. She should gather the rose before it wilts and falls of its own accord (*Ars Amatoria* 2.5.59–80). In this representative form, three constitutive elements interact within the space of the poem, all conflicting with a diametric opposite and creating a tension that the poem proposes to resolve: the rose in its withered avatar clashes with its vigorous, youthful representation; the poet in most cases expresses an explicit or implicit contention with the addressee; and the menacing future (illustrated by the declining, aging body of the addressee) opposes the epicurean present (incarnated in the glowing, youthful body of the addressee).

I will argue here that Ronsard exploits these tensions in his *carpe diem* poems more explicitly than do his classical models, and that his staging of the tensions betrays certain of the poet's attitudes toward temporality, gender, and the body. Consider as a first example the paradigmatic sonnet "Je vous envoye un bouquet que ma main" (1572) with respect to its most frequently cited model, Rufinus's "To Rhodoklea,"[31] which follows:

> Here Rhodoklea
> is a garland
> a braid of delicate
> flowers laced
> by my own hands
> there are lilies
> roses
> moist anemones
> soft narcissus
> dark-gleaming violets
> wear it
> cease to be haughty
> both flowers and you
> will cease one day[32]

Here is Ronsard's version:

> Je vous envoye un bouquet que ma main
> Vint de trier de ces fleurs épanies:
> Qui ne les eust à ce vespre cuillies,
> Cheutes à terre elles fussent demain.
> Cela vous soit un exemple certain
> Que vos beautés, bien qu'elles soient fleuries,
> En peu de tems cherront toutes flétries,
> Et comme fleurs periront tout soudain.
> Le tems s'en va, le tems s'en va, ma Dame
> Las! le tems non, mais nous nous en allons,
> Et tost serons estendus sous la lame:
> Et des amours desquelles nous parlons
> Quand serons morts n'en sera plus nouvelle:
> Pour-ce aimés moi, ce pendant qu'estes belle.
>
> (L.VII,152; P.I,270)

[I am sending you a bouquet that my hand / Just picked among these blossoming flowers / Tomorrow they would have fallen / Had no one picked them today. / Let this be an unmistakable lesson to you: / Your beauty, although it is flourishing / In little time will be gone / And like flowers, it will suddenly perish. / Time is fleeting, time is fleeting, my Lady / Alas! Not time, but we are fleeting, / And soon we will lie under stone. / And of the loves we now speak, / There will be no more news when we are dead. / Thus love me now, while you are still beautiful.]

The tensions cited above generate the movement of both poems, but much more obviously in the case of Ronsard. Both poems insist on the flight of time and both compare the young addressee to freshly picked flowers. Both poets highlight their own authority: Rufinus's narrator emphasizes his role of weaving together the garland, and Ronsard's speaker underscores that it is his own hand that picked the flowers in full blossom. In both cases, the poet fully intends to reap benefits from the addressee's ephemeral beauty if she is so inclined. Rufinus's invitation, "wear it / Cease to be haughty," is the suggestive equivalent of Ronsard's "Pour-ce aimés moy." In contrast to the concise idea of Rufinus's poem, however, the elaboration and development of the motif in the French sonnet create a quite different message.

The images of both poems lead to the conclusion that the lovers must act before death sets in: "both flowers and you / will cease one day," "cheutes à terre elles fussent demain," "comme fleurs periront tout soudain," "tost serons estendus sous la lame."[33] Ronsard's speaker, unlike Rufinus's, rhetorically identifies with the lady in that both poet and addressee will someday die: "le tems s'en va, ma Dame / Las! le tems non, mais nous nous en allons." Yet the identification of the first-person-plural pronoun extends only to death, and not to the problem of aging. Given the paradigm of the older male poet/young girl, it is of course predictable that Ronsard would not conclude the sonnet with a reference to his own youth. The sonnet unfolds according to a principle of commonality, however, with one exception: both speaker and addressee will someday die, but within the rhetoric of the poem, only one of them will grow old. Five lines of the sestet proclaim the advent of death as the preeminent reason to love now; but the last line diverts the logical progression of the poem and substitutes the implication of the lady's eclipsed beauty ("while you are [still] beautiful") for their mutual death.

In Ronsard's sonnet, the poet is thus rhetorically connected to the addressee (through the use of the unifying first-person plural pronoun) and then distanced from her (through the pronounced shift back to the second-person pronoun). The subjective dynamics within the poem mirror this tension. The poet establishes a connection with the addressee both by the implicit suggestion of sexual attraction and by his evocation of their mutual destiny. A severance between the poet and the addressee takes place, however, when Ronsard evokes the lady's youthful beauty that will soon vanish. The shift from "nous" to "vous," from "quand serons morts" to "ce pendant qu'estes belle" is reminiscent of Tonto's quintessential "what do you mean 'we,' Paleface?" By rhetorically joining the lady (in their mutual expectation of death) and then separating himself from her (from her loss of youth), Ronsard manifests a more pronounced desire to gain mastery over both fleeting time and the lady's aging than does his classical model.[34]

The 1567 elegy "J'ay ce matin amassé de ma main" provides another clear example of the poet's insistence on the flower's atrophy and loss of beauty rather than its death, but this time the poet magnifies the fusion of the flower and the addressee to illustrate the lady's vanishing desirability. Thomas Greene notes in Ronsard "the tendency of a woman's body to become a landscape and conversely, of a landscape to become her body, a tendency so subtle and pervasive as almost to merit the term *Joycean*."[35] This reciprocity develops particularly in the beginning of the elegy where the earth's bosom has produced a bouquet worthy of the lady's breast. It is perhaps not coincidental that in this elegy Ronsard's speaker temporarily loses himself in a few uncharacteristically repetitive verses—"Elle est vermeille, et vous estes vermeille. / Sa blancheur est à la vostre pareille./ Elle est d'azur, vostre esprit et vos yeux / Ont pour couleur le bel azur des cieux. / Elle a le gris pour sa parure mise, / Et vous aimez la belle couleur grise" (L.XIV,148; P.II,353) [It is rosy and you are rosy. / Its whiteness is like yours. / It is blue, and your spirit and eyes are the beautiful blue of the skies. / It is wearing gray, / And you like the lovely color gray]. He insists upon the collapse of modifiers and linguistically coalesces the woman-flower so that the human and herbaceous qualities become interchangeable:

> Plus il ne reste à vous dire, maistresse,
> Que tout ainsi que ceste fleur se laisse
> Passer soudain, perdant grace et vigueur,
> Et tombe à terre atteinte de langueur,
> Sans estre plus des Amans desirée
> Comme une fleur toute desfigurée,
> Vostre âge ainsi verdoyant s'en-ira
> Et comme fleur sans grace perira.
>
> (L.XIV,148; P.II,353)

[It only remains to be said, my lady, / That just as a flower fades suddenly, losing its grace and vigor, / And falls, languishing, to the ground / No longer desired by any lovers, / Like a disfigured flower, / So your flourishing age will flee / And like a flower will perish gracelessly.]

In this elegy it is the anthropomorphic flower, not the lady (replaced by the substantive "âge"), that languishes, becomes disfigured, and fails to attract lovers. This referential indeterminacy that humanizes the flower also serves to dehumanize the addresse who "will perish gracelessly." But once again, while death punctuates the poet's comparison, it is in no way the central problem posed by the elegy. There are six specific mentions of the loss of attractiveness to lovers and the deterioration of physical beauty in the elegy, whereas death (in the form of the verb "périr") figures only once.[36]

Aging appears as a threat greater than death to the addressee in several of Ronsard's models as well,[37] but Ronsard both physicalizes and personalizes the temporal implications of the motif, thus emphasizing the poet's authority in setting the clock forward. Ronsard's imitation of an epigram by Julianus from the *Greek Anthology* corroborates this claim. The epigram is as follows:

Maria is proud; but do thou, mighty Justice, take vengeance on the hauteur of that arrogant lass,—not by death, O Queen, but on the contrary may she reach the grey hairs of age, may her hard face come to wrinkles. May the grey hairs avenge my tears: may her beauty suffer for the error of her soul, as it was the cause of it.[38]

2 / Time in a Body: Ronsard

Ronsard's imitation reads:

> Je ne veux point la mort de celle qui arreste
> Mon coeur en sa prison: mais, Amour, pour venger
> Mes larmes de six ans, fay ses cheveux changer,
> Et seme bien espais des neiges sur sa teste.
> Si tu veux, la vengeance est desja toute preste:
> Tu accourcis les ans, tu les peux allonger:
> Ne souffres en ton camp ton soudard outrager.
> Que vieille elle devienne, ottroyant ma requeste.
> Elle se glorifie en ses cheveux frisez,
> En sa verde jeunesse, en ses yeux aiguisez,
> Qui tirent dans les coeurs mille pointes encloses.
> Pourquoy te braves-tu de cela qui n'est rien?
> La beauté n'est que vent, la beauté n'est pas bien,
> Les beautez en un jour s'en-vont comme les roses.
>   (L.XVII,245; P. I,373)

[I do not wish the death of the one who holds / My heart in her prison. But God of Love, to avenge / My tears of six years, change the color of her hair, / And sow thick snow upon her head. // If you wish, vengeance is all ready. / You shorten the years, you can lengthen them as well: / Do not let your soldier be injured in your camp. / Make her old—grant my plea. // She glories in her curly locks, / In her green youth, in her sharp eyes / That pierce my heart with a thousand arrows. // Why do you play the gallant with something worthless? / Beauty is only wind, beauty is not a possession, / Beauties vanish in a day like roses.]

Ronsard's speaker, even while imploring Eros's aid, establishes his own voice from the outset ("je," "mon coeur," "mes larmes," "ton soudard"), which highlights his agency in the premature aging of the lady. The sixteenth-century poet insists more than does his Greek model upon the addressee's former beauty by furnishing concrete examples of the "before" as contrasted with the "after" ("cheveux frisez," "verde jeunesse," and "yeux aiguisez"), which are all revealed to be ephemeral. Maintaining his authority in the physical realm, Ronsard omits the moral dimension introduced by Julianus ("May her beauty suffer for the error of her soul"). Instead, Ronsard's speaker (still the "je" introduced in the first quatrain) concludes his sonnet by evoking the transitory nature of beauty, as illustrated by two physical images: wind and roses. The specific reference to time that he introduces, "six ans," alludes not to the object of the poem but to himself, thus emphasizing his own temporal chronology. Thus once again Ronsard's speaker rhetorically underscores his authority in the workings of time upon the lady and insists on time's devastation of her beauty more than does the classical model.

Why, in these poems and elsewhere, is aging depicted as a fate worse than death? Why does the threat of the aging body prove to be such a prominent rhetorical strategy for Ronsard, especially in comparison to his classical models? Female beauty in sixteenth-century France, as in fifteenth-century Italy, was a central preoccupation of artists and poets, to which the *Blasons anatomiques du corps féminin* and many other works attest.[39] Judging from observations of male contemporaries, beauty and youth are inseparable in the cultural sensibilities of early modern Europe. Vives's *Institution de la femme chrétienne* cites physical considerations as important factors in a man's choosing a wife, and first mentioned among those is age.[40] As we saw in chapter 1, early modern moralists urge girls to marry while they are still fresh and fair, and not to delay matrimony lest their perfect ripeness pass.[41] This ripe fruit apparently sours quickly, since aging women figure prominently as a subject of popular derision in sixteenth-century proverbs collected by Le Roux de Lincy, including "Temps pommelé, pomme ridée et femme fardée ne sont pas de longue durée" [Hazy weather, shriveled apple and painted woman do not last long].[42]

Thus it would appear that since youthful beauty is especially important to a woman in sixteenth-century France, at least from the perspectives cited, the threat of her losing that beauty by aging would be the most powerful of taunts. We could then agree with Henri Weber that in this poem Ronsard perhaps "a jugé que cet argument touchait plus directement l'orgueil féminin" [thought that this argument more directly touched feminine pride].[43] But that temptingly tidy conclusion fails to take into account the poet's terror about the future in general, and about the effects of time on his own body in particular. As early as 1555 in "Quand je suis vingt ou trente mois / Sans retourner en Vandomois" (P.I,806; L.VII,98), the poet at age thirty (to the bemusement of many twentieth-century readers) already laments that his youth is fleeting: "Mais tousjours ma jeunesse fuit, / Et la vieillesse qui me suit, / De jeune en vieillard me transforme" [my youth is continually fleeting, and old age follows me, transforming me from a young to an old man].

Ronsard's perennial consternation when faced with the problem of aging is corroborated in Creore's *Word Index*, which cites over six hundred references to forms of "vieux," and over eight hundred to forms of "jeune." The poet's anxiety about growing old translates first into his privileging the moment of youth, which finds one of its earliest expressions in "Dedans des Prés je vis une Dryade" in the first book of the *Amours:*

2 / Time in a Body: Ronsard

> Dedans des Prez je vis une Dryade,
> Qui comme fleur s'assisoyt par les fleurs,
> Et mignotoyt un chappeau de couleurs,
> Eschevelée, en simple verdugade.
>   De ce jour là ma raison fut malade,
> Mon cueur pensif, mes yeulx chargez de pleurs,
> Moy triste et lent: tel amas de douleurs
> En ma franchise imprima son oeillade.
>   Là je senty dedans mes yeulx voller
> Un doulx venin, qui se vint escouler
> Au fond de l'ame: et depuis cest oultrage,
>   Comme un beau lis, au moy de Juin blessé
> D'un ray trop chault, languist à chef baissée,
> Je me consume au plus verd de mon age.
> (L.IV,53 [1552]; P.I,55)

[In the meadow I saw a dryad / Sitting as a flower among flowers, / Sweetly donning a colorful hat, / Tousled, in a simple dress. // From this day forward my judgment grew weak, / My heart pensive, my eyes filled with tears, / I became sorrowful and slow. / Her gaze engraved such a heavy mark upon my liberty. // I felt a sweet venom fly into my eyes, flowing / Into the depths of my soul. And since this shattering event, // Just as a beautiful lily wounded by scorching rays in June / Languishes with its head bowed, / {So} I am wasting away in the prime of my youth.]

   This sonnet enumerates love's melancholic effects on the poet, with a conclusion highlighting the speaker's youth. Reflections on the budding beauty of the dryad in the form of a flower immediately give way to the poet's Petrarchan introspection regarding his own state, translated by the predominance of first-person referents: "*ma* raison," "*mon* cueur pensif, *mes* yeulx," "*moy* triste et lent. . ." The first tercet, troped in an *innamoramento*, elaborates the poet's condition brought about by the young dryad-flower.[44] The second tercet predictably exploits the image of the flower with its head down (recalling Virgil's description of the death of Euryalus in the *Aeneid,* 9.435–37); but, quite unpredictably, the flower in the last tercet represents no longer the dryad but the poet himself, languishing as he is consumed by melancholy in his youth. This insistence on the poet's youth is certainly not a commonplace within the tradition of *innamoramento* poems.[45] What is even more striking in the sonnet, and what distinguishes Ronsard from his classical models the most clearly, is this substitution of the poet for the lady as the referent of the metaphorical flower.[46]
   The woman-flower rhetorically metamorphosed into a man-flower

within the space of the poem signals a blurring of genders as well as of identities. The substitution of one flower for the other once again stages a complex connection between poet and addressee: the Other both represents and does not represent himself, as evidenced in "Je vous envoye un bouquet" above. The Other is she who in amatory terms conquers him and whom he seeks to conquer, either by causing her aging within the poem (as in "Je ne veux point la mort") or by seeking or pining over her affection and her favors (as in the poem under consideration here). This connection between speaker and addressee is often severed, however, within the register of Ronsard's *carpe diem* poems. The last line of the sonnet, completely focused on the poet's inner state (underscored by the reflexive verb form), insists on his separateness and summarizes his regrets about his own premature aging: in contrast to the "flower seated among flowers" who remains stable throughout the sonnet, the poet sees the "greenness" of his youth destroyed.

The attraction of youth for Ronsard lies not only in the promise of the future for the young poet (thwarted in the preceding poem), but also in an erotic proclivity for budding female sensuality in the aging poet:

> J'aime un bouton vermeil entre-esclos au matin,
> Non la rose du soir, qui au Soleil se lâche:
> J'aime un corps de jeunesse en son printemps fleury:
> J'aime une jeune bouche, un baiser enfantin
> Encore non souillé d'une rude moustache,
> Et qui n'a point senty le poil blanc d'un mary.
> (L. XVII, 326 [1569]; P.I,453)

[I like a ruby bud half-opened in the morning / Not the rose of evening, which is weary in the sun, / I like a youthful body in its blossoming spring / I like a young mouth, a childlike kiss / Not yet sullied by a rough mustache, / And which has never felt a husband's gray beard.]

This implicit fusion of the pure, pristine young woman and the unspoiled morning rosebud recalls *Les triumphes de la noble et amoureuse dame et l'art de honnestement aymer* (1535) by Jean Bouchet, who espouses the theory that, like flowers, a young girl's beauty fades if she is kissed or touched too much, "car le lys representant virginité pert incontinent sa beauté par attouchemens" [because the lily representing virginity quickly loses its beauty by being handled].[47] While, on the one hand, the poet in this context relishes the inexperienced lover, on the other, Ronsard's name has never figured among the advocates of preservation of female purity. Indeed, he chides the resisting Marie for despising nature (L.VII,254;

P.I,194), and for imagining honor "dedans son esprit sot" (L.VII,138; P.I,273) [in her foolish mind].

The second book of the *Sonnets pour Hélène* offers other examples of the poet's shunning societal strictures on sexual expression when such principles interfere with his erotic designs, as in the following 1578 sonnet:

> Cest honneur, ceste loy sont noms pleins d'imposture
> Que vous alleguez tant, sottement inventez
> De nos peres rêveurs, par lesquels vous ostez
> Et forcez les presents les meilleurs de Nature,
> Vous trompez votre sexe et lui faites injure. . . .
> (L.XVII,266; P.I,460)

[This honor and this law that you invoke so much are insidious, stupidly invented by our idle fathers. By {these limitations}, you abolish and constrain the best gifts of Nature, you deceive and abuse your sex. . . .]

Given Ronsard's unwavering adherence to orthodoxy in matters of state (as a fierce supporter of the kings he served) and religion (as a loyal Catholic), Ronsard's critique of contemporary sexual mores in this sonnet can be read as either exceptional or self-interested. I see evidence for both conclusions.

Challenging sexual strictures in a more comprehensive way, Ronsard launches a *boutade* in the *Continuation des Amours*, musing that if Petrarch didn't gain Laura's favors, the poet from Arezzo should never have continued his devotion to her for thirty years:

> Luy mesme ne fut tel: car à voir son escrit,
> Il estoit esveillé d'un trop gentil esprit
> Pour estre sot trente ans, abusant sa jeunesse,
> Et sa Muse, au giron d'une seule maitresse:
> Ou bien il jouissoit de sa Laurette, ou bien
> Il estoit un grand fat d'aymer sans avoir rien. . . .
> (L.VII,317; P.I,168–69)

[Judging from his work, / {Petrarch} had too fine a mind to be such a fool / For thirty years, wasting his youth / And his Muse, attached to the same mistress. / Either he was finding physical pleasure with his little Laura, or else / He was an idiot to love without getting anything. . . .]

In this passage Ronsard not only challenges Petrarch's inability to secure Laura's physical affection, but he also specifically deplores the loss of Petrarch's youth because of it.

In addition to Ronsard's unmitigated passion for youth, the poet's aversion to aging and the aged is revealed in countless poems. Some express more general psychological reservations: "[J]e porte en l'ame une amere tristesse, / Dequoy mon pied s'avance aux faubourgs de vieillesse" (L.XVIII,42; P.I,442) [My soul carries a bitter sadness because I am headed for the realm of old age].[48] Others convey the specific fear of physical debility: "tant de malheurs / Que la vieillesse apporte, entre tant de douleurs . . ." (L.XVIII,265–66; P.II,612) [so many misfortunes that old age brings, amidst so much pain . . .]. But nowhere does the anatomy of youth and senescence figure more pointedly than in the sonnet "Quand vous serez bien vieille," which we examined in the preceding section.

Several critics of Ronsard have concluded that the poet eventually rises above the questions of the flourishing or deteriorating physical body and accedes to a higher spiritual plane.[49] Indeed, in the first sonnet of a series devoted to the older "Sinope," Ronsard's speaker addresses her in a sanguine tone that seems initially to mark the poet's acceptance of aging and its effects:[50]

> L'an se rajeunissoit en sa verde jouvence,
> Quand je m'épris de vous, ma Sinope cruelle;
> Seize ans estoyent la fleur de vostre äge nouvelle,
> Et vostre teint sentoit encore son enfance.
>
> Vous aviez d'une infante encor la contenance,
> La parolle, et les pas; vostre bouche estoit belle,
> Vostre front, et voz mains dignes d'une immortelle
> Et vostre oeil, qui me fait trespasser quand j'y pense.
> . . . .
> Et si pour le jourd'huy voz beautez si parfaites
>   Ne sont comme autrefois, je n'en suis moins ravy,
> Car je n'ay pas égard à cela que vous estes,
> Mais au dous souvenir des beautez que je vy.
>
>   (L.X,87; P.I,277)

[The year was renewed in its fresh youth when I was taken with you, my cruel Sinope. Sixteen years were the flower of your new age, and your countenance seemed still in its childhood. You still had the look, the speech, and the step of a royal daughter. Your forehead, your hands (worthy of an immortal) and your eyes make me die just thinking about them. / . . . / And if today your perfect beauties are no longer as they were before, I am none the less thrilled, for I do not heed what you are, but rather the sweet memory of the beauties I saw.]

In this instance the poet disconcerts the reader by the *pointe* of the last line, rejecting any stoic acceptance of the effects of age. Deflecting the question of Sinope's diminishing beauty, the speaker retains instead the *image* of her more alluring youth. Sinope remains out of the poet's sight in her current, faded incarnation, displaced by the memory of her younger avatar. The poet thus in no way transcends through loftier considerations the loss of the young woman's beauty. On the contrary, he freezes in his mind the image of her former pulchritude by winding backward Mnemosyne's clock.

Here, as is so often the case in Ronsard's love lyrics, behind the problem of the Other looms the larger, more consuming question of the self. The fourth "Sonnet à Sinope" sheds considerable light on the poet's regrets about his own aging and his jealousy of a younger suitor:

> Or de vostre inconstance accuser je me doy,
> Vous fournissant d'amy qui fut plus beau que moy,
> Plus jeune et plus dispos, mais non d'amour si forte.
> (L.X,89; P.I,278)

[Now I must blame myself for your inconstancy, furnishing you with a lover more handsome, younger, and nimbler than I, but whose love was less strong.]

The poet consecrates the remaining sonnets to his loss of Sinope, culminating in the final poem where he renounces his quest: "C'est trop aymé, pauvre Ronsard, delaisse / D'estre plus sot, et le temps despendu / A pourchasser l'amour d'une maistresse . . ." (L.X,100; P.I,278) [You have loved too much, poor Ronsard, stop / Being a fool and wasting time / Chasing after a mistress's love]. Thus in light of the concluding sonnets of the cycle, the speaker's insistence on Sinope's declining beauty in the first sonnet can be glossed as a mask, a deflection, a substitute for the poet's discouragement about his own aging and his inveterate sense of loss.

What, then, is the relationship between Ronsard's apparent obsession with youth discernible throughout his work and the *carpe diem* poems? It seems clear from the preceding examples that the poet temporarily circumvents the question of his own aging (and of the alterity it represents) by projecting it onto the Other, incarnated textually in the female addressee.[51] The specific functioning of this projection is particularly apparent in Ronsard's 1550 "A Janne impitoyable," which imitates Horace's ode "Ad Ligurinum" (4.10).[52] The odes of both Ronsard and his model are concerned with time's control over physical as well as psychological human destiny. They address, both rhetorically and psychologically, the dimension of aging that divides the self from itself, a phenomenon that Montaigne describes succinctly: "moy à cette heure et moy tantost sommes bien deux" [myself now and myself a while ago are indeed two].⁵³ A commonplace in literary depictions of aging holds that the speaker does not recognize in the mirror his or her old face, which bears little resemblance to the "authentic" younger self. Horace's poet employs this image very convincingly when addressing the young Ligurinus:

> O crudelis adhuc et Veneris muneribus potens
> insperata tuae cum veniet pluma superbiae
> et, quae nunc umeris involitant, deciderint comae,
> nunc et qui color est puniceae flore prior rosae
> mutatus, Ligurine, in faciem verterit hispidam,
> dices "heu," *quotiens te speculo videris alterum,*
> "quae mens est hodie, cur eadem non puero fuit,
> vel cur his animis incolumes non redeunt genae?"
> (*Odes* 4.10.324, my emphasis)

[Ah, how cruel you are while you are still master of Venus's Gifts! / When your cheek of disdain comes to be plumed with an unwelcome down, / When cascades of your hair, falling in full waves to your shoulders now, / Start to thin and shed, when into rose-damask of fleshly tint / Harshness comes and a changed roughness of face, then, Ligurinus, then, / *As your mirror reflects someone unknown,* you will protest: "Alas!, / What I now understand, why did I not see as a lad? Or else, / May I not have again cheeks unimpaired, suiting what I know now?"]⁵⁴

Ronsard's ode threatens Janne with a similar fate:

> Jeune beauté, mais trop outrecuidée
> Des presens de Venus,
> Quand tu voirras ta peau estre ridée
> Et tes cheveux chenus,
> 5   Contre le temps et contre toy rebelle
> Diras en te tançant:
> "Que ne pensois-je alors que j'estois belle
> Ce que je vais pensant?
> Ou bien pourquoi à mon desir pareille
> 10   Ne suis-je maintenant?
> La beauté semble à la rose vermeille
> Qui meurt incontinent."
> – Voilà les vers tragiques et la plainte
> Qu'au ciel tu envoyras,
> 15   Incontinent que ta face dépainte
> Par le temps tu voirras.

2 / Time in a Body: Ronsard 79

>   Tu sçais combien ardemment je t'adore,
>   Indocile à pitié,
>   Et tu me fuis, et tu ne veux encore
>   20   Te joindre à ta moitié.
>   O de Paphos et de Cypre regente,
>   Deesse aux noirs sourcis!
>   Plustost encor que le temps, sois vengente
>   . . . .
>   25   Et du brandon dont les coeurs tu enflames
>   Des jumens tout autour,
>   Brusle-la moy, à fin que de ses flames
>   Je me rie à mon tour.
>   (L.II, 33–35; P.I,761–62)

[Young beauty, too proud of Venus's gifts, when you see your wrinkled skin and gray hair rebellious against time and you, you'll chide yourself, saying, "Why didn't I think what I do now when I was beautiful? Or why am I not as I wish now? Beauty, like the crimson rose, dies suddenly."—You'll exclaim these tragic jeremiads to the heavens, as you see your face quickly worn by time. You know how ardently I love you, {but} obstinate and unmerciful, you escape me, not wishing to join your other half. O queen of Paphos and Cyprus, goddess with black eyebrows! Even more than time, take revenge . . . and with the torch you use to ignite young girls' hearts, fire her up for me, so that I can have my turn to laugh.]

On a first reading, the poems appear to be identical in the relationship between poet and addressee: each poet desires the young addressee, who has not reciprocated his love; both poets taunt the young object of desire, threatening old age and regret. But significant differences in the poems arise in the poets' rhetorical strategies, and some of these differences are attributable to the fact that Horace's addressee is male whereas Ronsard's is female. Voltaire, in his epistle to Horace, "n'a pas osé lui parler de son Ligurinus" [didn't dare speak to him of his Ligurinus], and Laumonier expresses the same reservation.[55] Though the distinctions between the homoerotic lyric in Horace and the heterosexual lyric in Ronsard would be compelling to pursue, they extend beyond the scope of the present study.[56] What is of particular interest to us in this context are the techniques by which Ronsard once again establishes a semblance of connection with the addressee, only to replace it with a more detached stance, thus highlighting the sixteenth-century poet's mastery of the addressee and her time.[57]

The structure of the odes initially appears similar, in that both poems are predicated on an axis of when/then: *When* all these physical changes befall you, both poets stipulate, *then* you will see the light. Both addressees are made to speak of their moment of realization and cognition. As the poems progress, however, a significant structural difference between the two poems emerges. In the Horatian ode, the paternal speaker willingly relinquishes the power of speech to his son/lover so that youth articulates his own belated discovery. Ligurinus thus has the last word. In contrast, Ronsard's speaker frames the lady's words (almost identical to Ligurinus's) within his own discourse, providing an exegesis and an elaboration such that the concluding message remains the poet's own. The poet's voice further enters the ode more explicitly in the form of a monologue to the addressee in line 17, "Tu sçais bien combien ardemment je t'adore," and the speaker's voice continues to dominate the remainder of the poem.

The psychological underpinning of this form of *carpe diem*—the rhetorical aging of a lover who spurns the poet—functions similarly in the two poems in that both poets seek retribution for love refused. But Ronsard's ode far surpasses the Horatian ode in its depiction of difference and conflict. In the Horatian ode, the speaker details Ligurinus's present beauty in concrete terms, evoking his "cascades of . . . hair, falling in full waves" and his "rose-damask of fleshly tint," whereas Ronsard's speaker, apparently unwilling in this context to concede any semblance of complimentary language, describes the lady's beauty simply as "outrecuidée" [proud, haughty]. In "Ad Ligurinum," the relationship between the speaker and the addressee remains implicit, since the speaker is nowhere present in the poem, and the only concrete indication of the speaker's position emerges in the first words of the ode: "O crudelis. . . ." The mirror image in line 6 of the Horatian ode evinces a relationship in which both identity and alterity are suggested, and where, it could be argued, the *alter* (different one) resembles the aged speaker more than he resembles the youthful Ligurinus.

Ronsard's speaker, unlike Horace's, enters fully into the poem beginning in line 17, proclaiming his ardor, chastising Janne explicitly for fleeing his advances, and invoking Venus's vengeance upon her. Whereas in Horace, the conflict between narrator and narratee remains implicit, in Ronsard the poem becomes a battlefield in which the speaker-general triumphs, reserving for himself the last laugh. This last laugh adds a temporal dimension as well, since it transports the ode from the register of a future perspective of the present (the regrets of the young woman) back to the present ("Tu sçais combien ardemment je t'adore") and again the implied future of the imperative ("Brusle-la moy"), thus insisting even more on the tensions provoked by time's linear progression. Horace's ode, on the other hand, despite its insistence on fleeting time, remains rhetorically situated in the future. The Ronsardian ode thus stages the temporal tensions more dynamically both by its shift in time and by the intervention of the narrator. The sixteenth-century poet once again establishes his personal complicity with time and its powers more forcefully than does his classical model.

The tone Horace's poet adopts when directing a *carpe diem* poem to a male other than an elusive lover is, not surprisingly, even more complicitous than in his ode to Ligurinus. In the well-known "Aequam memento rebus in arduis," ("Remember, when life's path is steep," *Odes* 2.3), addressed to Dellius, the tone of the ode suggests a vital connection between poet and addressee as the first counsels the second to partake of wines and perfumes "while Fortune and youth allow."

Several of Ronsard's poems on the subject of savoring the present moment, replete with wilting roses, are also addressed to men (as friends and colleagues, ostensibly, not as elusive lovers like Ligurinus), and in those odes and sonnets the poet establishes a tone of camaraderie, as in "Verson ces roses en ce vin," dedicated to Aubert:

> La belle Rose du printemps,
> Aubert, admoneste les hommes
> Passer joyeusement le temps,
> Et pendant que jeunes nous sommes,
> Esbattre la fleur de nos ans. . . .
>
> (L. VII,190; P.I,841)

[The beautiful spring rose, Aubert, incites men to pass the time joyously, and while we are young, to relish the flower of our years. . . .]

The explicit identification of the poet with the addressee predicates a kind of shared history that nullifies the conflict present in the motif when the addressee is a spurning female lover. Predictably, in this context Ronsard's menacing depictions of old age vanish and his epicurean urgings become egalitarian and untainted by spite.

Does Ronsard ever identify with a female addressee when he writes of the ravages of time? To a limited degree, yes. In "Comme une belle fleur assise entre les fleurs," for example, the poet deplores "l'importune vieillesse [qui] nous suit" [importunate old age that follows us] and the tone reveals the poet's indisputable complicity with the female addressee. Yet it is love itself and not the human body that withers and grows old in this poem: "Amour et les fleurs ne durent qu'un Printemps" (L.XVII,224;P.I,364) [love and flowers only last a springtime]. In the 1550 ode "Nimphe aus beaus yeus," also, Ronsard's speaker allies himself with Cassandre by the first-person-plural pronoun: "Incontinent nous mourrons . . . Donc cependant que l'âge nous convie / De nous esbattre, esgayon nostre vie. / Ne vois-tu le temps qui s'enfuit, / Et la vieillesse qui nous suit?" (P. L.II,127-28;I,807-8) [Suddenly we will die.... So while age calls us to enjoy ourselves, let us make our lives merry./ Don't you see time fleeing / And old age following us?]. In both of these examples, however, time's devastation remains abstract; the reader will note the absence of references to the aging poet's own body in the context of his exhortation to pluck the day.

In his extensive study of time in Ronsard, Quainton concludes that for Ronsard, "human happiness and wisdom are seen to reside in a submission to the rhythmic variety of time and in a stoical acceptance of man's inevitable transience in the name of cosmic harmony."[58] But the poet writes in a multiplicity of registers.[59] I have argued that Ronsard's lyric poetry reveals an adamant attachment to youth and a pronounced terror of aging, neither of which is convincingly assuaged even in the *Derniers vers*. These attachments and fears, embodied in various corporal images throughout Ronsard's poetic corpus, find their most powerful expression in the *carpe diem* motif, which represents the poet's ultimate attempt to triumph over time and the aging body. Neither explicitly succumbing to Chronos's devastation of his own body nor stoically accepting it, as the above examples have illustrated, Ronsard in the *carpe diem* motif rhetorically masters the lady's time, ravishing her body by the ravaging of old age. Cassandre, Janne, and Hélène, all consigned at some point to a shriveled future within the poet's verses, function for Ronsard's speaker as his doubles, and their bodies enact the aging that the poet so forcefully dreads for himself elsewhere in his work.[60]

These physical projections into the future also reveal a paradoxical functioning of *carpe diem* in Ronsard's poetic corpus. While the motif's didactic message incites readers to relish the present moment, to round out, as it were, time's advancement, the repeated images contrasting youthful and aging bodies unfold in a mercilessly linear time frame. In *Physics*, Aristotle asserts that time is no more made up of instants than a line is made up of points. But as points can be established on a line, so Ronsard's employment of the *carpe diem* motif freezes in time fixed images of corporeal flowering and withering. Seizing textually not the moment but the human body, Ronsard, rhetorically if not epistemologically, takes time into his hands and makes it his own.

Temporality and the Other

As a poet of movement and of metamorphoses, Ronsard assumes endless incarnations in the *Amours,* changing identities with a subtle sleight of pen. Becoming alternately Narcissus, Ixion, Sisyphus, Tantalus, golden rain, a flea, and "cent metamorfoses" (L.V,109; P:I,45), the narrator is temporarily transported outside his own body and he gains a new perspective on the situation created in the poem (such as Cassandre's breast seen from a flea's point of view in "Ha Seigneur Dieu") (L.V,109; P.I,44 [1553]).[61]

Beyond these explicit metamorphoses, the identity of Ronsard's speaker becomes even more complicated when one takes into account the question of gender. As we have seen, the interchange between Ronsard's speaker and the female addressee reveals a sexual and textual dynamic that privileges the physical and involves a complex doubling between poet and addressee. Two recent studies have further prepared this fecund terrain of inquiry by problematizing the poet's masculine identity within Ronsard's corpus. Lawrence Kritzman finds that Ronsard's text challenges assumptions concerning the masculinity of the desiring subject in order to uncover "the phallocentric masquerade"[62] that is inscribed in the text. Daniel Ménager examines the female voice assumed by Ronsard in the characters of Hyante, Clymène, and Calypso, and he concludes that these female characters, who express both passion and sadness more convincingly than does Ronsard's masculine voice, serve to renew Ronsard's amorous discourse.[63] Beyond these interesting studies, there remains much uncharted territory in the domain of gender studies in Ronsard's work.

The Others in Ronsard's corpus—metamorphosed selves, degendered or feminized voices, female addressees—all seem upon first reflection to be situated principally in space. But the Other exists also in time. In Ronsard's temporal scheme, the movement from past to future unfolds so relentlessly that present itself becomes unreliable. The metamorphoses of his text most frequently occur not only elsewhere, but also in another time, as numerous examples illustrate. "Je voudroy bien richement jaunissant" (L.IV,23; P.I,34) and "Ha, seigneur dieu" (L.V,109; P.I,44), sonnets that are both governed by metamorphoses, take place in the conditional and future tenses. In "Mignogne, levés-vous, vous estes paresseuse," one of Ronsard's most explicitly sensuous poems, a description of future actions constitutes the concluding twist of the sonnet: "Je vois baiser cent fois vostre oeil, vostre tetin, / Afin de vous aprendre à vous lever matin" (L.VII,141; P.I,188) [I will kiss your eyes and breast a hundred times / To teach you to get up in the morning].[64] Moreover, when Ronsard refers quite obviously to "the fifth point in love," in "Ha! Belacueil, que ta douce parolle," he recounts the event in the past and concludes the sonnet in the future: "A ma jeunesse il fault donner la faulte; / En cheveux gris je seray plus rusé" (L.IV,132; P.I,113) [My youth must be blamed / With gray hair, I shall become more clever]. Thus even in the most immediate of circumstances, Ronsard represents the present as transitory.[65] In this respect, Ronsard's poetic expression of a temporal philosophy prefigures Montaigne's pithy formulation: "L'homme marche entier vers son croist et vers son descroist"[66] [Man grows and dwindles in his entirety.]

Given the impossibility of appropriating the present, the poet's temporal focus becomes the future. As Emmanuel Levinas argues, "[T]he future is what is not grasped.... Imagination and projection of the future are but the present of the future and not the authentic future. The other is the future."[67] This unknown future, the principal abstract Other against which Ronsard forges his poetic identity,[68] dominates the literary motifs that situate his text in time. Rather than simply perpetuating the *exegi monumentum* and *carpe diem* traditions bequeathed to him by his numerous models, Ronsard molds these motifs, assigning to them a physicality theretofore unseen. Thus, he insists upon their temporal intensity. In one case, the poet proposes to transcend the inevitable ravages of the future by raising a monument more powerful than time; in the other, he exploits images of an ominous future ostensibly to shed light on the present. In both instances, even while the poet confers immortality upon kings or prematurely ages spurning lovers, time's linear progression is measured, the intangible becomes tangible, and the unfathomable becomes substantial through the corporeal clock of the poet's body.

3

By Virtue of Their *Vertu:*
Amplified Time in Pernette du Guillet
and Louise Labé

> Il n'y aurait pas d'être séparé si le temps de l'Un pouvait tomber dans le temps de l'Autre.
>
> [There would be no separate being if the time of the One were collapsed into the time of the Other.]
> —Emmanuel Levinas

In this epigraph Levinas reminds us that without time there would be no difference, no self, no Other. In early modern France, as we have seen, time constitutes not only a central topos of literary discourse, but also a veritable obsession for most sixteenth-century poets who—consciously or not—espouse the idea of time shaped by human will. Time plays a crucial role in the social reconsiderations of the sixteenth century, as well as in the definition of virtue, especially women's virtue, for the contemporaries of Pernette du Guillet and Louise Labé. While the two poets' attitudes toward time do not appear to be identical, both women implicitly question a number of beliefs and literary commonplaces relating to temporality, particularly concerning the connection between virtue and the use of time.

Given the ambiguity of the word *vertu* in sixteenth-century France, and given the numerous current theories on what it means, it will be useful first to establish a working definition of *vertu* in the two poets and their critics. The ubiquity of the word in sixteenth-century texts in general, and in Pernette's work in particular, further obfuscates the question. Virtue for Scève and Pernette, according to the felicitous formulation of Ann Rosalind Jones, is "the power to achieve perfection in love and in poetry. In their dialect, it means amorous devotion, verbal brilliance, and high poetic style."[1] For François Rigolot, virtue in the sixteenth-century sense signifies "force of character,"[2] and for Françoise Charpentier, virtuous women are "dotées de 'virtù' poétique et créatrice, voire amoureuse" [graced with poetic, creative and even amorous power].[3] All of these definitions are derived from the Italian word *virtù* (from the Latin *virtus*, moral force and courage; *vir*, man).[4]

While neither Huguet's *Dictionnaire de la langue du 16ᵉ siècle* nor Cotgrave's *Dictionarie of the French and English Tongues* (1611) indicates virtue's link with chastity, and while Bloch, Wartburg, and Robert situate in the seventeenth century the first usage of the word *vertu* meaning chastity for women, it is clear that moral connotations of sexual purity in women began to creep into the language, at least by association, in the middle of the sixteenth century.[5] The high-minded character Oisille of Marguerite de Navarre's *Heptameron*, for example, extols chastity as the supreme moral principle. In her description of the chaste mule-driver's wife, who in the second novella dies a bloody death defending her sexual honor, Oisille uses the word *vertueuses* interchangeably with *chastes:* "Ainsy fut enterrée ceste martire de chasteté en l'eglise de Sainct-Florentin, où toutes les femmes de bien de la ville ne faillirent à faire leur debvoir de l'honorer autant qu'il estoit possible, se tenans bien heureuses d'estre de la ville où une femme si vertueuse avoit esté trouvée"[6] [Thus this martyr of chastity was buried in the church of Saint Florentin, where all the townswomen did not neglect their duty of honoring her as much as possible, considering themselves fortunate to be from the town where such a virtuous woman had lived].

Virtue for men and virtue for women are often depicted as different qualities, however, as evidenced in Charles Estienne's *Paradoxes* of 1553. Estienne, in ostensibly positing women's superiority over men,[7] equates masculine virtue with strength: "Combien de fois ont elles (si les anciennes et modernes histoires sont veritables) esté cause de grandes victoires? Et combien de fois ont elles courageusement resisté alencontre des troppes et esquadrons de la foible vertu des hommes?"[8] [How many times have women (if ancient and modern stories are true) been responsible for great victories? And how many times have they courageously resisted against troops and squadrons of weak men?]. But on the same page, he praises the "vertu" of Zenobie, Valasque, and other famous women of ancient times, whose primordial attribute is their sexual fidelity: "Qui est celuy qui les surmonte, ou (pour plus proprement parler) qui ne leur soit inferieur quand à la fidelité et constance?" [Who surpasses women or, to be more precise, who is not inferior to them in fidelity and constancy?]. The word *vertu* appears to retain its sense of physical or moral force when applied to men, but when applied to women, it becomes more ambiguous, sometimes taking on connotations of purity, as the preceding texts suggest.[9]

Beyond these etymological and philological distinctions lies an even more compelling social question. While numerous conduct manuals in the sixteenth century reveal that virtue for women is determined by their *activities* (what they do and specifically what they don't do), virtue for men appears to be considered a more inherent, essential quality. "Oysiveté" or "paresse" is seen as wasteful in the humanist tradition and sinful according to Christian doctrine, but the particular consequences of idleness for men remain ambiguous or unspecified.[10] Certainly, the reader of early modern educational treatises quickly discerns a growing insistence on the notion of "liberal arbitre" or "libre arbitre" (free will).[11] The presupposition governing Budé's *De l'Institution du Prince*, however, holds that much like François I, to whom the book is dedicated, noble men, when equipped with the necessary "Sapience" (wisdom), will make intelligent choices.[12] In the same vein, Jean Bouchet, in his *Panégyric du Chevalier sans reproche*, asserts that for virtuous men ("les gens de vertu"), ceasing activity for rest is valuable, whereas for the lazy, repose should be avoided, which implies the stability of virtuousness when men possess this quality.[13] Juan Luis Vives, whose *De institutio foeminae christianae (Institution de la femme chrétienne, A Very Frutefull and Pleasant Boke called the Instruction of a Christen Woman)* enjoyed an enormous influence not only in his own country (Spain), but also in France and England, makes an even more specific claim about men's inherent virtue. In a chapter entitled "L'office des marys," Vives clarifies that for good men, virtue is an inalterable state: "La vertu est tousjours preste, non oyseuse, mais en effect: pource aux bons est permanente."[14] [Virtue is always ready, not idle, but in action: because in good men it is permanent]. Idleness is therefore discouraged for all, but in these treatises a man's virtue is not determined by his activity—in good men, virtue remains an enduring quality.

A woman's virtue, on the other hand, proves to be contingent upon her use of time. The Huguenot Théodore de Bèze, writing of "Les vertus de la femme fidèle et bonne menasgere" in 1556, echoes his Catholic predecessor as he warns against women's misuse of time: "Et son pain point ne mangera / Avec oisiveté maudite"[15] [She will not eat her bread with accursed idleness]. Symphorien Champier, in his *La Nef des dames vertueuses* of 1503, had already disseminated Aristotle's exhortation to men seeking virtuous wives: "On doit prendre une femme diligente et qui ne quert point estre oyseuse et paresseuse. Car ne peult estre que la femme oyseuse ne pense a plusieurs maulx et cogitations illicites ainsi que dit Aristote au vii.

des politiques"[16] [One must take a diligent wife who in no way seeks to be idle and lazy. For the idle woman inevitably thinks evil and illicit thoughts, as Aristotle said in *Politics*].

Whereas nobility provides a firm foundation for masculine virtue in Machiavelli's prince, Castiglione's courtier, and Bouchet's knight, no precondition—not even noble status—can safeguard a woman's virtue. In *Enseignements à sa fille*, Anne de France, who as "the virtual ruler of France during the first eight years of the reign of her brother Charles VIII"[17] reflects the dominant ideology of the court in 1505, refers twice in two pages to her noble daughter's *acquiring* virtue by her activities.[18] Should a noblewoman not use her time wisely (and thus not become virtuous), Anne de France warns, inevitable consequences will result:

> Au surplus ma fille gardez vous d'estre oyseuse. Et en gardez bien voz femmes. Car oysivete est fille du dyable. Laquelle mainne l'ame à perdition. Elle n'engendre pas seullement le peche de la chair, ains tous les vices.[19]

> [Further, my daughter, avoid being idle. And make sure that your women servants avoid it as well. For idleness is the devil's daughter, who carries the soul to perdition. It engenders not only the sin of the flesh, but all vices.]

Thus the acquisition of virtue for a noblewoman is depicted as an ongoing enterprise, and the consequences of her failing are rendered most explicitly. A sixteenth-century proverb cited by Le Roux de Lincy sums up succinctly what the conduct manuals develop in dozens of chapters, illustrating that all women, noble or common, will be judged by the same criterion:

> Fille oisive,
> a mal pensive
> Fille trop en rue,
> tost perdue.[20]

[Idle girl / Evil thinking / Girl in the street too much / Soon lost.]

In all of these examples, women's recommended activities are understood not as useful in themselves but rather as buffers or barriers against the frivolous, illicit and evil thoughts that inevitably lead to a loss of virtue. In this sense, a woman's virtue is determined principally by what is *not* rather than by what is. According to these moralists, the desired absence of a certain kind of activity requires vigilantly filling time with almost anything else—some task to accomplish, however small.

Clearly, a woman's safeguarding her virtue is seen as a perilous enterprise. But beyond refraining from falling into disrepute through idleness, how, according to sixteenth-century sensibilities, should a woman best employ her time in order to remain virtuous? In this case, many of the widely circulated conduct manuals directly conflict with the humanist notions of women's education. According to Cornelius Agrippa, for example, only noble women should study, because if women of a lesser class read, they would lose interest in housework and their husbands.[21] Vives warns against women's reading of "fables et inventions de mensonges—composees par gens oyseux, ignorants ou vicieux"[22] [false tales and creations of lies— written by idle, ignorant or wicked people]. The reading of religious books should be encouraged, however, since they lead to virtue and a good moral foundation.[23] Similarly, later in the century, Beroalde de Verville specifies that women may read, but he notes that books should be chosen (presumably by men) with two specific goals in mind: sparing ever-evil idleness and teaching women to respect authority.[24]

Not all authors of conduct manuals proscribe serious reading for women, however. Erasmus, straddling the fence between the new humanism and traditional Christian dogma, holds that noble women should be taught Greek and Latin, and lower-class women should learn to read in their own language, provided that such studies never interfere with their religious duties.[25] Ultimately, Erasmus advises that women's instruction should be guided by their husbands:

> Car comme dans la génération une femme ne produit rien de parfait sans le concours d'un mari bien sain, & que sans ce secours elle ne produit que des moles informes, . . . de même si le mari n'a soin de cultiver l'esprit de sa femme, et de lui inspirer des sentimens bien sains, qu'en peut-on attendre?[26]
>
> [For, just as in generation a woman does not produce anything perfect without intercourse with a healthy man, and without this aid she only produces shapeless lumps of flesh, . . . so also if a husband does not take care to cultivate his wife's spirit, and inspire in her healthy sentiments, what else can one expect?]

Thomas Artus, in *Qu'il est bienséant que les filles soient sçavantes* [That it is fitting for girls to be learned], opts for the humanist position in maintaining that the virtuous woman will emulate not Lucrecia but Cornelia, who spent her days in the company of good books and learned people, "enseignant à la postérité que la science est bien seante à l'une et à l'autre sexe, quand ils en sçavent bien user" [teaching posterity that wisdom is suitable for both sexes, when they know how to use it well].[27]

Despite Artus's insistence on women's learning, the woman's virtue once again becomes entangled in questions of chastity in his text. Part of Cornelia's appeal to the author is no doubt her "pudicité fort exemplaire" [quite exemplary chastity] after the death of her husband Gracchus, since she resisted even kings who sought her hand in marriage or "pour autre dessein" [with some other intent]. Artus's conclusion reveals that a virtuous woman must be both chaste *and* learned, and the mutability of feminine virtue is once again underscored:

> Imitez-la donc, mes belles, en la vie, afin de recevoir pareille récompense en la mort. Et sans vous arrester aux sifflemens de ces langues venimeuses, *croissez toujours de vertu en vertu*, . . . fuyez l'ignorance comme le plus dangereux poison de la renommée, laquelle par la science vous conserverez florissante, au temple de l'immortalité.[28]

> [So imitate her, my ladies, in life, in order to receive a similar reward in death. And without heeding the hissing of these venomous tongues, always *grow from virtue to virtue* . . . flee ignorance as the most dangerous poison of fame, which you will keep flourishing by knowledge, in the temple of immortality.]

Thus, according to these sixteenth-century moralists, "virtue" for a woman, even a noble woman, constitutes less a state of being than a process of becoming, continually redetermined and renegotiated. Within the context of the perceived transitory nature of virtue for women as well as the codification of "women's time" by contemporaneous moralists, both Pernette du Guillet and Louise Labé reformulate in their works the relationship between virtue and time, and each poet proposes in some sense "a time of her own."

Pernette and the Perennial Present

Verdun Saulnier, in his lengthy and now canonical study of Pernette du Guillet, asserts that "pour Pernette, le temps n'existe pas" [for Pernette, time does not exist].[29] Certainly time in Pernette's text exists *otherwise* than it does for the male contemporaries who comment on her works (Maurice Scève, Antoine du Moulin, Jean de Tournes) and those who author moral treatises addressing human use of time (Juan Luis Vives, Jean Bouchet, Symphorien Champier). But the nature of time—its potential and its malleability—is nonetheless of considerable importance in Pernette's work.

In her temporal system, Pernette du Guillet unmistakably privileges the present. In this she distinguishes herself most decisively from her poetic mentor, Scève, in whose verses both the Petrarchan *innamoramento* (emphasizing the contrast between the poet's past and present states) and the notion of poetic immortality (insisting upon the future) assume preponderant roles. The present in Pernette's work appears not as a captured moment, but rather as a continuous process, revealed in the development of three conceptual leitmotifs in the *Rymes:* "vertu," "Jour," and "contentement." Moreover, the topos of immortality further illustrates Pernette's temporal schema not by its presence but, given the contextual parameters of the *Rymes*, by its remarkable absence from the collection.

PAR LA VERTU EN MOY TANT ESPROUVÉE . . .
(ELEGY 1)

Pernette du Guillet's *Rymes*, published by Antoine du Moulin in 1545, are framed by reflections on time, from the prefatory letter by the publisher to the epitaphs by a number of fellow poets following the *Rymes*. The attention accorded to fleeting time by these men is not surprising, given that the poems were published shortly after Pernette's death at the age of about 25.[30] Yet du Moulin's letter goes far beyond the predictable contemplations on death and the young poet's untimely demise. Indeed, the entire letter turns upon the axis of time, and specifically Pernette's relationship to time, both as a woman and as a poet. In his preface addressed to the "Dames Lyonnoizes," du Moulin situates Pernette's work as a perpetual reminder of absence or lack, where the present has meaning only insofar as it evokes the past and where the future consists only of unfulfilled promise. He acknowledges that the publication of Pernette's poems will rekindle the readers' regret, using the verb "renouveller" twice in two adjacent sentences. He further elicits, in a curious combination of sentimental and Neoplatonic terms, the temporal ambiguity of these poems, mementos of a promising future that was not to be: "[L]a Mort. . . nous a privez de la consummation, que par cest heureux commencement la felicité de son celeste engin nous promettoit" (*Rymes*, 2) [Death . . . prevented our enjoying what the felicitousness of her celestial spirit promised by this fortunate beginning]. But while du Moulin engages in these brief reflections on the abyss between Pernette's past and future, the editor reveals a greater interest in her use of time while she was alive:

[V]eu le peu de temps, que les Cieux l'ont laissée entre nous, il est quasi incroyable *comme elle a peu avoir le loisir*, je ne dy seulement de se rendre si parfaitement asseurée en tous instrumentz musiquaulx, soit au luth, Espinette, et autres, lesquelz de soy requierent une bien longue vie à s'y rendre parfaictz, comme elle estoit . . . : mais encores à *si bien dispencer le reste de ses bonnes heures*, qu'elle l'aye employé à toutes bonnes lettres, par lesquelles elle avoit eu premierement entiere et familiere congnoissance des plus louables vulgaires (oultre le sien) comme du Thuscan, et Castillan. . . et apres avoit jà bien avant passé les Rudimentz de la langue Latine aspirant à la Grecque. . . ." (*Rymes,* 2, my emphasis)

[{G}iven the short time that the Heavens allowed her stay among us, it is almost unbelievable *that she could find the time* not only to become such an accomplished player of all musical instruments, such as the lute, spinet, and others, which alone would require a long lifetime to reach perfection in them, as she did; but also *that she could employ the rest of her hours so fruitfully* in letters. She had complete and familiar knowledge of such vernacular languages (besides her own) as Italian and Spanish, . . . and she had already learned the fundamentals of Latin, aspiring also to learn Greek. . . .]

The structure of this praise uncovers significant information about du Moulin's own attitudes toward what might be called "women's time," or perhaps about his understanding of the audience's sensibilities and expectations on the subject. What is "almost unbelievable" in Du Moulin's formulation is neither Pernette's musical genius nor the quality of her humanist endeavors, but rather the fact that she found time ("le loisir") to accomplish them, and that she could make such good use of her time.

Du Moulin exhorts the women of Lyons to follow Pernette's example, "et tellement, que, si par ce sien petit passetemps elle vous a monstré le chemin à bien, vous la puissiez si glorieusement ensuyvre" (*Rymes,* 3) [and so that, if by this little pastime she showed you the path to goodness, you can gloriously follow her]. But the two levels of du Moulin's discourse here, as elsewhere in the preface, seem to contradict one another. At first glance, du Moulin's respectfulness toward Pernette appears to dominate the text, as evidenced by such expressions as "la dexterité de son divin esprit" [the dexterity of her divine wit] and "la felicité de son celeste engin" [the fortune of her celestial wisdom]. His elevated exposition is continually undermined and challenged, however, by terms denoting the inconsequential nature of the *Rymes*. Scattered throughout the preface are such diminutive epithets for the *Rymes* as "ce petit amas de rymes" [this little group of rhymes], "ce peu de commencement" [this little beginning], "ces petites, et louables jeunesses siennes" [these little, praiseworthy youthful poems], and, most significantly, "ce sien petit passetemps" [her little pastime]. Du Moulin's surprisingly apologetic apology of Pernette's *Rymes* ultimately reveals his conviction that while Pernette's work itself is not impressive, her consecration of time to music and letters has contributed to her "virtue" (a term that Du Moulin uses six times in the preface), and that other "virtuous" women of Lyons should follow in her footsteps. Du Moulin thereby suggests that a woman's virtue is determined by her activities—in short, by the way she spends her time.

Time is thus the driving force in du Moulin's preface: time as a fleeting, irrecoverable entity, time as the motivator of regret, time that both promises and deceives, time as that phenomenon over which literature seeks to triumph, and, finally, time (particularly the way women spend it) as the principal determinant of virtue. Significantly, despite the discernible nuances in their use of the word *vertu* (from industriousness to chastity), the authors of the prefaces and epitaphs surrounding Pernette's work cast the poet's virtue in relationship to time. Du Moulin allies Pernette's virtue with her efficacious use of her waking hours, and he acknowledges those readers who will strive ("s'*évertu*eront") to imitate Pernette's accomplishments. The printer Jean de Tournes associates the poet's virtue with the effects her poems will exert in the future, even after her death: "Quelle puissance Amytié puisse avoir, / Quand la vertu y est au vif empraincte, / Tu le pourras clerement icy veoir, / . . . /. . . elle peult cy, sans aucune contraincte, / (Maulgré la Mort) faire taire l'Envie" (*Rymes,* 7). [What power Love can have / When virtue leaves its fresh imprint there / You will be able to see it clearly here, / . . . / Here she can, with no constraints/ (In spite of Death) silence Envy.]

Maurice Scève's epitaphs following the collection also address Pernette's virtue in relation to temporality, both terrestrial and celestial. The first of these treats the long suffering that the poet's friends will endure in her absence; the second proposes Pernette's immortality with such terms as "Vertu vive et qui jamais n'empire" [live virtue that never lessens] and "son Nom avec immortel los" [her Name with immortal praise] (*Rymes,* 112) . For Scève, Pernette's virtue indelibly inscribes itself in her text, conferring upon her an immortality only accessible through literature.

Pernette's own poetry resists the link between virtue and the eternal as articulated by Scève. In three epigrams near the beginning of the collection (3, 4, and 6), Pernette praises her mentor's virtue(s), connecting in each case "vertu" with Scève's prowess as a writer and his eloquence.[31] Epigram 17 places the concept of *vertu* at both its physical and its epistemological center:

> Je suis tant bien que *je ne le puis dire,*
> Ayant sondé son amytié profonde
> Par sa *vertu,* qui à l'aymer m'attire
> Plus que beaulté: car sa grace, et *faconde*
> Me font cuyder la premiere du monde.
>
> (*Rymes,* 25, my emphasis)

[I am so happy that I cannot express it, / Having probed the depths of his friendship / By his virtue, which draws me to love him / More than beauty: for his grace and eloquence / Make me believe I'm the most fortunate woman in the world.]

Between Pernette's speaker's poetic *aporia* ("je ne le puis dire") and Scève's fine articulation ("faconde") lies the mediating force of the mentor's "vertu." Much like the Neoplatonic androgyne, this *demi-dizain* (the only one in the collection) begs the question of halves: the word "vertu" divides the epigram in two, the fourth syllable of the third line being the virtual center, given the necessary caesura of decasyllabic verse. The incantatory repetition of the nasal "on" occurs three times before the center and three times afterward. Mediating the opposition between "amytié" in line 2 and beauty in line 4 is once again "vertu" in line 3.

Whereas throughout Scève's *canzoniere*, Délie's virtue serves as a catapult for her (and the poet's) immortal glory, Pernette's mentor's virtue provokes in this epigram more immediate psychological consequences: the beloved's eloquence, linked with his profound "amytié," whose agent is virtue, inspires the poet's delight. The present once again dominates the poem, with the only past reference ("ayant sondé") attenuated, adjoining the domain of the present by its more active gerundive form. Thus, in this poem, as elsewhere in Pernette's oeuvre, virtue is an agent not of the putative future, but rather of the perceptible here and now.

Not only does Pernette's work call into question the link between virtue and the eternal, but it also reveals her rejection of the equation *virtue = busyness* promoted by her editor and the authors of moral treatises cited above. Of the twenty-some occurrences of some form of the word *vertu* in Pernette's work, several refer to the worthy characteristics of her mentor, often allied with his poetic verve and eloquence, as we have seen. Most occurrences, however, treat of virtue as an abstract quality. Pernette depicts virtue as a disposition that can be cultivated once present, but unlike such moralists as Vives and Théodore de Bèze, she manifests no anxiety about ensuring that every moment be filled to avoid idleness. On the contrary, the sustaining of virtue is described as a slow process:

> Car la vertu est d'une action lente,
> Qui tant plus va, plus vient à se nourrir.
>
> (Epigram 40, *Rymes,* 68)

[For virtue acts slowly / The more it advances, the more it is nourished.]

Only one occurrence of the word "vertu" refers unequivocally to the poet herself:

> C'est que de moy tant bien il se contente,
> Qu'il n'en vouldroit esperer autre attente,
> Que celle là qui ne finit jamais,
> Et que j'espere asseurer desormais
> Par la vertu en moy tant esprouvée,
> Qu'il la dira es plus haultz Cieux trouvée.
> (Elegy 1, *Rymes*, 52)

[He is so contented with me / That he harbors no other expectation / Than the one that never ends, / And that I hope henceforth to ensure / By the virtue abiding so strongly in me / That he will say it comes from the highest heavens.]

In this passage, "vertu" resides within the poet, yet it is a dynamic quality that is continually renewed. The movement of the expression "Par la vertu en moi esprouvée" is difficult to render in English, because the sixteenth-century sense of *esprouver* includes the notion of probing and proving—in Cotgrave's terms, "to assay . . . sound, looke, or search into."

Unlike the meaning of "vertu" in commentaries surrounding her work, then, Pernette's own use of the term, even when applied to herself, rarely suggests any connection with chastity,[32] nor does it tend toward the eternal. Upon a first reading of this passage, both the expression "[l'attente] qui ne finit jamais" [waiting that never ends] and "desormais" [henceforth] seem to indicate an infinite continuation. But the prolongation proposed is in fact the expectation of the beloved's "contentement," signaling a desire not to appeal to the future, but rather to extend the boundaries of the present. "Desormais," similarly, leads to the interplay of confidences in the last two lines, where the future verb is muted by the circularity of the lovers' mutual assurances.

Thus, within the parameters of Pernette's *Rymes* "vertu" mediates the relationship between lover and beloved in a temporal framework firmly dominated by the present. Pernette depicts virtue as a quality that develops within a time that is neither extremely devastating (as when women lose virtue by failing to employ hours wisely) nor extremely promising for the future (as when virtue inspires immortality and fame). It constitutes, rather, the quality sine qua non of both parties in the ideal "amityé." Moreover, the sense of "vertu" in Pernette's text, unlike in the conduct manuals cited above, seems to remain stable in that no discernible distinctions in usage exist when the term is applied to women or to men. Pernette thus implicitly posits the primacy of "equité" or equality in matters of virtue for both men and women and situates virtue's value within the context of the present.

SI M'ESJOUYS EN LA CLARTÉ PLAISANTE / DE MON CLER JOUR
(ELEGY 3)

Pernette's designation of her mentor, Scève, as "le Jour" functions metaphorically throughout the *Rymes* and reveals further aspects of the poet's temporal sensibilities. "Le jour" seems upon first consideration an obvious substitute for the sun, since both phenomena possess the identical properties of illuminating and renewing. Certainly Pernette's "Jour" manifests these qualities, as we shall see, but it is also worth noting that in the early modern period the day becomes an intellectual entity for the first time, and thus the temporal associations were doubtless more pronounced for contemporaneous readers than they are for readers today.[33] Further, "jour" in sixteenth-century usage is linked with human activity, as in the expression "il est jour" ("On est levé"), and as in the following example from Marot's *Epistres:* "une autre qui s'enqueste / S'il est jour ou non là dedans" [another who wonders / If anyone is up in there or not].[34]

Because Scève's magnum opus equates Délie with Diana (and metonymically, the moon), it seems befitting that Scève should become Pernette's "Jour" (and metonymically, the sun), capable of illuminating her heretofore tenebrous existence.[35] Within the logic of the poetic dialogue established between Pernette and Scève, such an equation seems irresistible. But Pernette does resist, and "la Délie se délie," breaking free from the homological model provided by Scève. Rather than incarnating Diana, the goddess whom Endymion begged for eternal life, the poet opts for a more earthly embodiment. Rather than assuming the role of the moon in her poems, she extends the metaphor of the Day/Lover by ascribing the day's double, "la journée," to herself.[36] A number of interesting interpretations of Pernette's designation of Scève as her *Jour* have appeared in recent scholarship, but most readers have not fully explored the question of Pernette's self-designation, insisting instead on the antithesis between day and night in the poems.[37]

How are we to interpret Pernette's juxtaposition of "jour" and "journée"? Several expressions in sixteenth-century usage indicate that the distinction between the two terms is not yet firmly established in the language. "A la journée," for example, signifies "au jour le jour," and "du jour à la journée" means "de jour en jour." Of particular importance to our analysis are the temporal connotations of the word "journée," which implies the passage of time more than its analogue, as Yvonne Bellenger has noted.[38] Huguet's examples of the sixteenth-century sense of the word all incorporate the sense of movement: "journée de marche, de navigation, de voyage." Pernette chooses an appellation for herself that implies the notions of process and motion, one that, in Montaigne's terminology, "paints the passage."[39] In designating herself as "journée" in the *Rymes*, then, the young poet appears to emphasize her evolving status.

Pernette's Chanson 9, the axiomatic exposition of the terms "jour" and "journée," provides an excellent point of departure for discerning Pernette's sense of time as it is reflected in her choice of these two metaphors. Robert Cottrell deftly reads this poem in terms of "an ontological and gnostic drama" that emphasizes within the poem's narrative context the poet's process of becoming.[40] He shows that the sense of becoming as distinguished from being is apparent in the evolution in the poem from the "fascheux sejour" in the first strophe to the "plaisant sejour" in last strophe. This movement has temporal implications, as well. The term "sejour" (from the Latin *subdiurnare,* meaning "to last a certain time") itself denotes an extended period, albeit not an indefinite one, since like the day it has both a beginning and an end. As in most of Pernette's poems, this chanson takes place not outside of time, but rather in the context of a time scheme created by the poet herself, in a temporal space that advances, as it were, from one sojourn to another. Yet the movement of the chanson works against a reading of clear, linear progression from point A to point B:

> Je suis la Journée,
> Vous, Amy, le Jour,
> Qui m'a destournée
> De fascheux sejour.
> 5   D'aymer la Nuict certes je ne veulx point,
> Pource qu'à vice elle vient toute appoint:
> Mais à vous toute estre
> Certes je veulx bien
> Pource qu'en vostre estre
> 10   Ne gist que tout bien.
> Là où en tenebres
> On ne peult rien veoir
> Que choses funebres,
> Qui font peur avoir,
> 15   On peult de nuict encor se resjouyr
> De leurs amours faisant amantz jouyr:

    Mais la jouyssance
De folle pitié
N'a point de puissance
    20 Sur nostre amytié,
Veu qu'elle est fondée
En prosperité
Sur Vertu sondée
De toute equité.
    25 La nuict ne peut un meurtre declarer,
Comme le jour, qui vient à esclairer
Ce que la nuict cache,
Faisant mille maulx,
Et ne veult qu'on sache
    30 Ses tours fins, et caultz.
La nuict la paresse
Nourrit, qui tant nuit:
Et le jour nous dresse
Au travail, qui duit.
    35 O heureux jour, bien te doit estimer
Celle qu'ainsi as voulu allumer,
Prenant tousjours cure
Reduire à clarté
Ceulx que nuict obscure
    40 Avoit escarté!
Ainsi esclairée
De si heureux jour,
Seray asseurée
De plaisant sejour.

[I am the Daytime / You, my friend, the Day / Who has turned me away / From an unfortunate stay. // Certainly I do not wish to love the Night / Because it leads directly to vice / Certainly I would love / To belong to you / Because in your being // Lies only good. / Where in shadows / Nothing can be seen / Save dismal things / Which frighten us, // At night some might delight in / Making their lovers find pleasure / But the bliss / Of passionate fervor / Has no power // Over our love, / Since it was founded / In prosperity / On Virtue probing / All equality. // Night cannot declare a murder / As can the day, which comes to illuminate / What the night conceals, / Causing a thousand evils, / And does not wish // Its cunning, shrewd schemes to be discovered. / At night laziness / Is kindled, which harms us. / The day spurs us / To work, which guides us. // O fortunate day, the one whom / You wished to illuminate must truly esteem you. / Always taking care / To bring back to the light / Those whom the dark night // Had estranged. / Thus enlightened by / Such a felicitous day / I will be assured / Of a favorable stay.]

The first four verses announce the central event described in the chanson, namely the poet's transformation brought about by the lover or the day. But rather than the "j'étais la nuict" that the reader might expect from a poem designed to recount the speaker's trajectory, already in the first line we see the poet's enlightenment: "Je suis la Journée." Throughout the chanson, the poet establishes not a depiction of her itinerary, but instead an alternation between two themes: first, the characteristics of the night (associated with both physical and moral shadows, vice, malevolence, laziness, and separation) versus those of the day (clarity, industriousness, and consolidation), and second, the equilibrium and reciprocity of lover and beloved. The first is manifested in lines 5–6, 12–16, 25–33, and the second in lines 7–10 and 17–24. Lines 35–40 formulate the poet's apostrophe to the Day and finally, the last quatrain echoes the first quatrain, with the poet's state now assured. Thus between the poet's "fascheux sejour" and her "plaisant sejour" in the chanson figures a poetic space where day and night are suspended in opposition, and where the friendship between lover and beloved, predicated as it is upon the reciprocal principle of "equité," itself evokes the movement of give-and-take, as in lines 7–10 and lines 23–24. With the exception of the first and last verbs of the chanson, Pernette's speaker introduces no tenses other than the present, which serves to underscore the state of suspended movement executed in the thematic structure. One could thus describe the temporality suggested in Pernette's presentation of the twin terms "Jour" and "Journée" as one of suspended animation—a time that, while it does not advance according to a linear progression (except insofar as states before and after the light can be discerned), remains in constant motion.

The poet's passage from the shadows of ignorance to the brilliant rays of enlightenment through the intervention of her "Jour" dominates a number of other poems in the *Rymes*, as well. Françoise Charpentier has characterized these antithetical states as "nuit-Pernette-ignorance" versus "jour-Amant-connaissance."[41] But again, Pernette's emphasis is less on the states themselves than on the space between them, less on the separate terms than on the antithesis. Unlike the Petrarchan *innamoramento* wherein the innocently bystanding poet is immediately transformed into the smitten lover, Pernette's passage from night/ignorance to day/knowledge is (re)enacted in the poems in a pliable temporal framework. Epigram 2, for example, fulfills the same introductory function in the collection as the liminary poems depicting the *innamoramento* in the *canzoniere* of Petrarch and Scève. Indeed, all signs point to the immediate transformation of the lover by the beloved. Predictably, Pernette's poet depicts her conversion in the preterite tense, underscoring both suddenness and change:

> La *nuict* estoit pour moy si tresobscure
> Que Terre, et Ciel elle m'obscurissoit,
> Tant qu'à *Midy* de discerner figure
> N'avois pouvoir, qui fort me marissoit:
> Mais quand je *vis* que l'*aulbe* apparoissoit
> En couleurs mille et diverse, et seraine,
> Je me *trouvay* de liesse si pleine
> (Voyant desjà la clarté à la ronde)
> Que *commençay* louer à voix haultaine
> Celuy qui feit pour moy ce *Jour* au Monde.
>
> (*Rymes,* 9, emphasis mine)

[The night was for me so dark / That it obscured Earth and Sky, / Even at noon I could discern no shape, / Which troubled me deeply. / But when I saw the dawn appearing / Serene, in a thousand diverse colors, / I found myself so filled with joy, / (Already seeing light on earth), / That I began to praise in an exalted voice / The one who brought for me this Day into the world.]

Still, the sweep is not entirely clean. "L'aulbe apparoissoit" denotes a breaking dawn that will continue. In the gerundive "Voyant desjà la clarté à la ronde," the action is depicted in process, and even the past historic "commençay" indicates prolonged activity, since the poet has only begun to sing her mentor's praises. Thus the poet's description of the past transformative moment assumes the value of the present and casts the Day in a more supple mold. Moreover, Pernette's metaphorization of the terms "nuict," "aulbe," "Midy," and "Jour" dislodges them from physical time and situates them within the poet's own chronological landscape.

The temporal dislocation of Pernette's "Jour" becomes even more obvious when we compare her Epigram 2 with Scève's first *dizain,* which treats of the *innamoramento* in the *Délie.* Both poets depict their transformations as taking place through the eyes, the locus of recognition of Beauty, where in the Petrarchan, Neoplatonic, and Anacreonic traditions the lover undergoes an unalterable change. Scève's poet is indeed smitten and overtaken by the "Basilisque":

> L'Oeil trop ardent en mes jeunes erreurs
> Girouettoit, mal cault, a l'impourveue:
> Voicy (ô paour d'agreables terreurs)
> Mon Basilisque avec sa poingnant' veue
> Perçant Corps, Coeur, & Raison despourveue,
> Vint penetrer en l'Ame de mon Ame.
>   Grand fut le coup, qui sans tranchante lame
> Fait, que vivant le Corps, l'Esprit desvie,

> Piteuse hostie au conspect de toy, Dame,
> Constituée Idole de ma vie.
>
> *(Rymes,* 5)

[My eye, too ardent in my young wanderings / Maladroit, was aimlessly searching / When (O fear of pleasant terrors) / My Basilisk with his piercing vision / Wounding body, heart, and reason, caught off guard / Penetrated the soul of my soul. // Immense was the blow that, without a cutting blade / Makes my spirit die while my body lives, / Pitiful host in your presence, Lady, / Ordained Idol of my life.]

For Scève's poet, the amorous transformation is charted in the language of battle, inflicting deep wounds to the body and soul ("*Perçant* Corps, Coeur, & Raison," "vint *penetrer* en l'Ame de mon Ame," "Grand fut le coup"). The basilisk's victory also establishes the beloved's immutable position vis-à-vis the poet ("*Constituée* Idole de ma vie"),[42] whose defenselessness is underscored by the complete absence of first-person verbs in the *dizain*. Pernette's text, in contrast, as we have seen, depicts not a sudden attack by an intruder but rather a continuing perception of the dawning Day by the lyric speaker and *actor* ("je vis," "*je* me trouvay," "[*je*] commençay louer"). Harbingers of the poets' temporal schemas, these two introductory poems set the stage for each collection: Scève's poet's ardor, like the beloved's "constituted" image, is depicted as indelible and eternal, while Pernette's speaker's amorous trajectory is punctuated by the periodic renewal of the Day.[43]

Because Pernette's Day dawns not every twenty-four hours, or even at regular intervals, the *Rymes* institute a further redefinition of a day's passage. In Elegy 3 ("La Nuict"), for example, the poet's "Jour," depicted as a deus ex machina, arrives at the propitious moment when the narrator has just completed an analysis of her nightmare:

> O miserable est la condition
> De nous, humains, laquelle est tousjours prompte
> A inventer nostre perdition.
> Mais sur ce point je voy l'aulbe, qui monte
> Chassant bien loing cette tourbe nuisante
> De Vaine gloire, Ambition, et Honte:
> Si m'esjouys en la clarté plaisante
> De mon cler Jour, que je veis apparoistre
> Pour esclarcir ma nuict tresmal plaisante,
> Comme il se faict assez de soy congnoistre
>
> *(Rymes,* 102)

[How miserable is our human condition, / Which is always ready / To cause our perdition. / But at this point I see the dawn rising, / Chasing away this harmful troop / Of arrogance, ambition, and shame; / Thus I rejoice in the pleasant light / Of my clear Day, whom I saw appearing / To brighten my disturbing night, / As he has made himself sufficiently known.]

Thus Pernette's metaphorical Day, unlike its physical counterpart, can be summoned within the temporal space of the poem, but like the natural phenomenon, it consistently returns, each time renewing the (rhetorical) landscape with its luminous intensity.

The Day's disjunction from physical time finds its most explicit manifestation in Epigram 8, where the Day continues to illuminate the poet's nights, if only figuratively:

> Jà n'est besoing que plus je me soucie
> Si le jour fault, ou que vienne la nuict,
> Nuict hyvernale, et sans Lune obscurcie:
> Car tout cela certes riens ne me nuit,
> Puis que mon Jour par clarté adoulcie
> M'esclaire toute, et tant, qu'à la mynuict
> En mon esprit me faict appercevoir
> Ce que mes yeulx ne sceurent oncques veoir.
>
> *(Rymes,* 16)

[I never need worry any longer / Whether light will be lacking or whether night will come, / Winter night, darkened by dearth of moonlight, / All that is of little concern to me, / Because my Day of gentle light / Illuminates everything for me, so much that even at midnight / He makes me perceive / What my eyes were never able to see before.]

Through her temporal metaphor of the Day-Lover, then, Pernette dislocates the temporality of the word "Jour" and redefines it according to an intricate poetic system. The day in Pernette's texts remains a light-bringing entity, but in her temporal scheme the day is expanded in both its duration and its powers. The poet's condition after the intervention of the Day remains in process, such that she becomes not "la nouvelle née," to borrow Colette Winn's lively epithet,[44] but rather "la nouvelle naissante."

EN NOZ ESPRITZ CONTENTEMENT DURABLE . . .
(EPIGRAM 13)

The word *content* figures prominently in the beginning of the *Rymes,* with some form of it appearing nine times in the first fifteen epigrams.

Lance Donaldson-Evans, in his analysis of the opening epigram, notes that the terms *heureuse* and *servie* are gendered not only by their endings, but by the situation they describe, as well: "[A] male author writing love poetry at this time in history is almost never *heureux*."[45] Pernette's texts do indeed enact, among others, the narrator's states of amorous radiance. But interestingly, none of the other occurrences of "heureux" in the entire *Rymes* refers to the poet herself. They refer, rather, to the beloved ("Comment il est en ses amours heureux," Elegy 1, *Rymes,* 52; "D'estre avec moy et heureux et content" Elegy 2, *Rymes,* 60), to something belonging to the beloved ("son heureux sçavoir," Chanson 6, *Rymes,* 54; "A te vouloir bien, et heureuse vie," Elegy 5, *Rymes,* 107) or to the amorous condition in general ("Heureuse est la peine / De qui le plaisir," Chanson 8, *Rymes,* 73). These examples are not meant to show that Pernette's speaker is unconcerned with her own fulfillment, but rather that "happiness" per se is incidental in Pernette's thought. The concept of "contentement," a state quite distinct from happiness in the rhetoric of the *Rymes*, occupies a far more central place in the collection, as evidenced not only by its frequent occurrence but also its function in the poems.

Pernette's notion of contentment doubtless originates in Leone Ebreo, who sees "Contentement des choses necessaires" along with "Suffisance" as the necessary components of virtue.[46] For Ebreo, contentment is allied with "continence" in the center of the spectrum between profligacy and avarice, thus representing the middle ground of "L'Amour moderé."[47] Huguet cites a considerable number of examples in sixteenth-century usage of the verb *contenter* (from the Latin *contenire,* to maintain or retain) conveying the meaning "to pay." By extension, *faire contente* (or *faire la contente*) signifies "to do justice." In both the philosophical and the etymological senses, then, *contentement* involves the notion of quid pro quo, maintenance or exchange.[48] In contrast, the adjective *heureux,* from the Latin *augurium* (presage or omen), by the sixteenth century signifies auspicious or happy, a state that comes by chance (as in the *innamoramento*) and that is, at least etymologically speaking, "maintenance free." Pernette's Epigram 9, when compared with Scève's Dizain 127, provides an excellent example of the different uses to which the word *heureux* is put by the two poets, as well as the functioning of the concept of *contentement* in Pernette's collection.

> L'esprit, qui fait tous tes membres movoir
> Au doulx concent de tes qualitez sainctes,
> A eu du Ciel ce tant heureux povoir
> D'enrichir l'Ame, ou Graces tiennent ceinctes

> Mille Vertus de mille aultres enceinctes,
> Comme tes faictz font au monde apparoistre.
> Si transparent m'estoit son chaste cloistre
> Pour reverer si grand' divinité,
> Je verrois l'Ame, ensemble et le Corps croistre,
> Avant leur temps, en leur eternité.[49]

[The spirit, which moves all your body / In the sweet harmony of your divine qualities, / Has received from Heaven the most fortunate power / To enrich the soul, where Graces hold / A thousand virtues enclosed within a thousand others, / As your deeds make apparent to the world. / If I were able to gaze into her chaste cloister, / To admire such great perfection, / I would see both soul and body reach, / Before their time, toward eternity.]

> Plus je desire, et la fortune adverse
> Moins me permect que puisse celuy veoir,
> A qui elle eust par mainte controverse
> Faict mainct ennuy, si ne fust son sçavoir
> Qui des Cieulx a ce tant heureux pouvoir
> De parvenir tousjours à son entente :
> Dont avec luy ce soulas puis avoir
> Que, luy content, je demeure contente.
>
> (Epigram 9, *Rymes,* 17)

[The more I desire, / The less I am permitted to see him / To whom adverse fortune through many trials / Would have brought many adversities, were it not for his knowledge, / Which from Heaven possesses the most fortunate power / Always to attain his objective. / With him I am able to have this pleasure: / His being content, I remain content.]

Line 3 of Scève's *dizain* is practically identical to line 5 of Pernette's *huitain*, incorporating the duplicate expression "ce tant heureux pouvoir." But the registers of the poems are strikingly different. Whereas the *dizain* is dominated by celestial terms ("sainctes," "reverer," "divinité," "Ame," "concent" [as in the harmony of the spheres]), the *huitain* employs a more psychological vocabulary ("desire," "entente," "soulas," "content," "contente"). As in a prayer of mortal man to immortal divinity, Scève's speaker remains reverent but distanced from the object. In contrast, even though the object's "sçavoir" occupies a pivotal point in the epigram, Pernette's poet concludes by establishing a vocabulary of equivalency. Both poems posit antithetical situations: in the *dizain*, the terminology of enclosure and hermetism ("ceintes," "enceintes," "cloistre") conflicts with the lexicon of transparency ("apparoistre," "transparent," "verrais"). In the resolution of Scève's poem, Délie's body and soul are projected before their time into eternity. For Pernette, "contentement" undercuts the initial antithesis ("Plus je desire, . . . Moins . . . puisse celuy veoir"), ending the poem with "luy content, je demeure contente." Thus Délie's "tant heureux pouvoir" in Scève's *dizain* introduces a hierarchy of lover and beloved that reaches its apogee in the concluding rhyme accentuating both her divinity and her immortality. The mentor's "tant heureux pouvoir" in Pernette's *huitain*, however, provokes very different circumstances: the initial hierarchy between lover and beloved collapses and is supplanted by reciprocal "contentement."

The temporality of each poem serves as a synecdoche of the movement reflected therein: Scève's *dizain* concludes in the conditional mood ("je verrais"), evoking a putative state beyond the present. Moreover, the final noun, "eternité," suggests the future of the divine addressee alone, as if to emphasize the mortal poet's distance from her. Pernette's *huitain*, in contrast, both begins and ends in the present tense, insisting upon the immediacy of the exchange established in the mirrored terms "content" and "contente" of the final verse. Thus whereas the "fortunate power" in Scève's *dizain* separates the lover and the beloved as it projects the beloved into the future, in Pernette's *huitain* it unites the two in a continuing exchange that unfolds in the present.

Scève's Dizain 136 of the *Délie*, written in response to Pernette's Epigram 13, provides a further illustration of the role of "contentement" in Pernette's temporal system. Using the rhetorical technique *contentio* or antithesis, both poets treat an identical theme: one soul, dying while living in sweet torment, in turn causes death in the other living soul. I. D. McFarlane, following Verdun Saulnier, holds that in Scève's response "we can see the poet trying to give greater clarity and balance to the themes initiated by Pernette."[50] Ann Rosalind Jones has persuasively demonstrated that these two poems in fact relay very different messages.[51] What is particularly striking for our purposes is the way in which, by shifting the emphases in his response, Scève significantly changes Pernette's temporal framing in the poem. Both Scève and Pernette end their poems with an apostrophe to personified love:

> Dieu aveuglé, tu nous as faict avoir
> Du bien le mal en effect honnorable:
> Fais donc aussi, que nous puissions avoir
> En noz espritz contentement durable!
>
> (*Rymes*, 21)

[Blind god, you have given to us / The suffering in pleasure that leads to honor. / Make us, as well, able to preserve / Long-lasting contentment, shared in our souls.][52]

> Dieu aveuglé tu nous as fait avoir
> Sans aultrement ensemble consentir,
> Et posseder, sans nous en repentir,
> Le bien du mal en effect desirable:
> Fais que puissions aussi long sentir
> Si doulx mourir en vie respirable.[53]

[Blind God, you have given to us / Without any other agreement or consent, / And let us possess without any regret, / The joy of suffering that leads to desire. / Let us sense, for just as long, / Such sweet death within the breath of life.][54]

In the final two verses, which form the *pointe* of both the epigram and the *dizain*, Pernette's grammatical insistence on the first-person plural, with "nous" and particularly "noz espritz," emphasizes the spiritual union of the lovers and the reciprocity of the lovers' contentment. "Contentement" thus serves once again as the explicit objective of Pernette's *contentio*. Though both poems are based on a parallel ("just as you, blind god, have made suffering respectable/desirable to us, so let us continue to have contentment/sweet death in life"), only Scève's establishes a temporal contingency: "Fais que puissions *aussi long* sentir. . . ." Scève's *dizain* thus shifts the emphasis of Pernette's epigram from circular reciprocity to a more linear notion of contingency.

Pernette's poet's repeated insistence on reciprocity as well as the recurring terms "Jour," "vertu," and "contentement" raise the question of repetition in Pernette's *Rymes*. Certainly Pernette was influenced by both the subtle and the not-so-subtle wordplays of the Rhetoriqueurs, as evidenced particularly by her Epigram 7, which constructs a sort of theme and variations on the letter *R*. But elsewhere, Pernette's vocabulary is also quite restricted and the structure of her poetry finely honed, as a number of critics have noted.[55] As Françoise Charpentier points out, the current critical fascination with the poetics of constraint and the efficacy of language has caused us to view in a different light what were once considered artistic limitations.[56]

Without repetition, of course, there would be no poetry. Gerald Manley Hopkins noted and Roman Jakobson developed the idea that "on every level of language the essence of poetic artifice consists in recurrent returns." This is true not only of repeated "figures of sound" but also of repeated "figures of grammar."[57] In a number of Pernette's poems, phonetic and structural repetition goes beyond a purely poetic function to reenact the reciprocity alluded to in the texts. Epigram 15, for example, provides a veritable labyrinth of repetitions that perform the circular drama inscribed in the text.

> Pour contenter celuy qui me tourmente,
> Chercher ne veulx remede à mon tourment
> Car, en mon mal voyant qu'il se contente,
> Contente suis de son contentement.
>
> (*Rymes,* 23, my underscoring)

[To satisfy him who torments me / I do not seek solace for my torment, / For seeing that in my suffering he is satisfied, / I am contented with his contentment.]

Upon a first reading this short epigram might appear to be a purely self-effacing if not masochistic statement on the poet's part. But as elsewhere in Pernette's poetry, the notions of reciprocity and exchange subtend the text, as the structure of the epigram demonstrates.[58] The two equal parts of the quatrain, the final word of each verse ("tourmente"/"tourment"; "contente"/"contentement") and the identical terminal consonances (*m, t, r, m* in verses 1 and 2; *s, c, t, t* in verses 3 and 4) all announce the mirrorlike nature of the poem. Syntactically, the final morphemes of verses 3 and 4 echo those of verses 1 and 2, with the reversal of pronouns and possessive adjectives in each case: "qui me tourmente"/"qu'il se contente"; "à mon tourment"/"de son contentement." Finally, the word "content" figures four times in the four verses, serving as both the introduction and the conclusion of the epigram, implicitly suggesting a da capo reading. Repetition thus enacts the dynamic state of reciprocity depicted in the epigram, and the four verbs in the present tense further emphasize the immediacy of the text as it remains suspended in the present.

Suspended time also exists in Scève's *Délie,* of course, as the poet crafts timeless formulations of both precise moments such as the *innamoramento* and imprecise moments such as waking consciousness, as well as Petrarchan enactments and reenactments of the lover's ratiocinations. Yet Scève's temporal schema, while not entirely situated in linear, "cursive" time (as Nietzsche called it), projects nonetheless Délie's *vertu* and the poet's literary prowess squarely into the realm of posterity.[59] Even in his two epitaphs for Pernette, presumably the most retrospective of all poetic forms, the future dominates. Scève's second epitaph following Pernette's *Rymes* predictably insists upon the recently deceased poet's ability to transcend physical death through her "Nom."[60] Lest we attribute these references simply to the rhetorical conventions of epitaphs, it should be noted that Scève's obsession with the immortal considerably predates Pernette's death. As early as Dizain 23 of the *Délie*, Scève sets a temporal stage whose wings include eternity:

> Doncques en vain travailleroit ma plume
> Pour t'entailler a perpetuité:
> Mais ton sainct feu, qui a tout bien m'allume,
> Resplendira a la posterité.[61]

[Thus my pen would work in vain / Endlessly to engrave you / But your sacred fire, which alights me to all goodness / Will be resplendent for posterity.]

Scève's framing of Dizain 136 further illustrates the preponderant role of the eternal in the *Délie*, as distinguished from Pernette's insistence on the present. At the end of Dizain 135, as in a number of examples throughout the *Délie*, Scève insists on death and Délie's power to transcend it through the immortality both of her *vertu* and of the poet's verses:

> J'espereray en seure indamnité . . .
> En Terre nom, au Ciel eternité.

[I shall expect with certitude . . . / glory on earth and in heaven, eternity.]

Foreshadowing the famous "Tu me seras la Myrrhe incorruptible / Contre les vers de ma mortalité" of Dizain 378 [You will the incorruptible myrrh for me / Against the worms of my mortality], Scève posits the "nom," that is, "renom" or Petrarchan *fama*, as the key to a victory over time.

Posterity, immortality, eternity—these are the notions that provide an escape from the recurring conundrums of the Petrarchan lover. Georges Poulet notes that Scève dreams of a time that would encompass virtually all times, *especially times to come*.[62] Indeed, although Scève's poet lives, relives, and languishes in the present, his temporal quarry remains the future.[63] Interestingly, even Scève's denial of his claim to immortality is based upon the principle of immortality, of life after death:

> Quant Mort aura, apres long endurer,
> De ma triste ame estendu le corps vuyde,
> Je ne veulx point pour en Siecles durer
> Un Mausolée ou une piramide.
> Mais bien me soit, Dame, pour tumbe humide

3 / Pernette du Guillet and Louise Labé

> (Si digne en suis) ton sein delicieux.
> Car si vivant sur Terre, & soubz les Cieulx,
> Tu m'as tousjours esté guerre implacable,
> Apres la mort en ce lieu precieux
> Tu me seras, du moins, paix amyable.[64]

[When death, after long endurance, / Stretches out the empty body of my sad soul / I do not wish a mausoleum or a pyramid / To last for centuries. / But I would be very pleased, Lady, / (If I am worthy) to have as a humid tomb your delightful breast. / For if living on earth and under the heavens / You always represented implacable war for me, / After death in this precious place / At least, for me you will become pleasant peace.]

Pernette, in contrast, explicitly excludes the projections into the future of her mentor and his associates. The absence of immortality in Pernette's texts is all the more conspicuous because virtually every other major theme in the *Délie* finds its dialogic counterpart in the *Rymes*.[65] As Jeffrey Masten has observed, absence of topicality in itself constitutes a topos.[66] Nowhere in Pernette's work does a hint of anxiety about the inexorable passage of time appear. In the whole of Pernette's poetic corpus, never does she use the nouns *immortalité* or *éternité*, and only twice the adjective *immortel*, both times simply to denote long-lasting: "immortel souci" (Chanson 8) and "propos immortel" (Elégie 5). Pernettian temporal vocabulary includes instead terms inscribing a continuing present: "joye continuelle" (Elegy 5), "perseverance" (Epigrams 34 and 38; Elegy 5), "longue patience" (Elegy 5), "durable" (Epigrams 10, 13, and 43). Even Pernette's expression for the longest possible duration, "toute ma vie" (Epigrams 19 and 28), is inextricably linked with the present, carrying no connotation of the eternal.[67] In Epigram 19, for example, Pernette, implicitly challenging her mentor's opprobrium, offers a witty apology for not honoring last night's promise:

> Je te promis au soir, que pour ce jour
> Je m'en irois à ton instance grande
> Faire chés toy quelque peu de sejour:
> Mais je ne puis: parquoy me recommande,
> Te promectant m'acquicter pour l'amande,
> Non d'un seul jour, mais de toute ma vie. . . .
>
> (*Rymes*, 27)

[I promised you last night that today / I would go, as you insisted, / Visit you for a short while. / But I cannot. So now I bid you farewell, / Promising you to absolve this debt, / Not one day, but all of my life. . . .]

This clever badinage gives way to a more serious use of "toute ma vie" in Epigram 28, which ends with "vostre ardeur me convye. . . . A demeurer vostre toute ma vie" [your ardor invites me . . . . to remain yours for all my life]. Once again, Pernette's poet replaces the notion of eternity championed by her literary interlocutor with a postulate of a different temporality, a dimension of time that maintains its roots in the human life cycle.

Pernette's most subtle questioning of Scève's notion of poetic immortality can be found in Elegy 2.[68] After disavowing her fantasy to transform Actaeon not into a "cerf" [stag] but into her "serf" [servant], Pernette's poet concludes the elegy with a final wish:

> Laissez le aller les neuf Muses servir,
> Sans se vouloir dessoubz moy asservir,
> Soubz moy, qui suis sans grace, et sans merite.
> Laissez le aller, qu'Apollo je ne irrite,
> Le remplissant de Deité profonde,
> Pour contre moy susciter tout le Monde,
> Lequel un jour par ses escriptz s'attend
> D'estre avec moy et heureux, et content.
>
> (*Rymes*, 59–60)

[Let him go to serve the Nine Muses / I must not insist on enslaving him to me, / As I lack both grace and merit. / Let him go; let me not anger Apollo, / Filling him with powerful divinity / So that he stirs up the whole world / Which, one day, expects through my love's writing / To be, along with me, blessed and content.][69]

It is evident in these verses, as elsewhere, that Pernette deprecates her own literary achievements while praising those of her Apollonian mentor, and in this sense she willingly submits to Scève's literary superiority. A number of recent critics have advanced theses to explain Pernette's poet's apparent subordination in this elegy, most of them concluding that her modest stance insists upon the importance of Scève's creativity.[70] Scève's continuing poetic production is indeed at issue in the poem, hence the elegiast's decision to allow Scève's return to serve the Muses. But it seems to me that the inducement for Pernette's sacrifice is neither simply Scève's poetic glory nor her own immortality in his verses. It is, rather, through Scève's writing that the world and specifically the poet herself will be content, and, as we have seen, "contentement" in the Pernettian sense is defined not as satisfaction, but as a Neoplatonically reciprocal and dynamic state. Pernette's desire is thus formulated as an expectation for herself as lover to be soon "blessed and content."[71] Although the desired state seems not to be attainable in the literal present ("un jour"), no future verb figures in the elegy, and the final impression is one of impending plenitude perceived in the present.

It is tempting to see in Pernette's embrace of the present a circular notion of time, anatomically female in its cyclical repetition as distinguished from Scève's phallic, linear projections.[72] But such a binary opposition of female and male attitudes toward time in sixteenth-century French poets, while arguably applicable to Pernette and her mentor, would be deceptively tidy. It also fails to account for other women writers' very different departures from the temporal ideology of their male colleagues, as we shall see particularly in the works of Louise Labé and Catherine des Roches. Ultimately, the pupil Pernette du Guillet subtly distances herself from her mentor Scève, redefining the terms of their literary commerce in her treatment of virtue, "contentement," and the temporal metaphor of the Day. Moreover, implicitly rejecting the concept of poetic immortality by the creation of a perennial present in her work, Pernette's poet shakes the foundations of her mentor's discourse with respect to time and prepares the terrain for other women poets' more radical ruptures with Ronsardian and Petrarchan temporal codes.

THE TEMPORALITY OF VIRTUE IN LOUISE LABÉ

Louise Labé, in her 1555 preface to the *Euvres*, situates herself firmly within the context of the debate over how women ought best to occupy their time. She seems at first glance to endorse Vives's and Lesnauderie's injunction that women should avoid idleness at all costs. In a justificatory phrase near the end of the preface, she assures readers that through writing she only sought a respectable pastime and a "moyen de fuir oisiveté" [a way to escape idleness].[73] Yet the rest of the preface boldly belies this apologetic aside. The question of idleness introduces two central paradoxes that emerge in Louise Labé's references to time throughout the preface. First, while the notion of avoiding idleness suggests that women potentially have too much time on their hands, all of Louise Labé's substantive references to time in the preface assume an economy of scarcity. The first four words, "estant le temps venu" (*Œuvres complètes,* 41) [the time having come], announce an urgency sustained by the poet throughout the preface. She also reveals that her devotion to "l'exercice de la Musique" regretfully left her little time to pursue studies. The second paradox surfaces as the poet claims to be writing simply to avoid idleness, yet she urges all women to undertake productive activities—studying, writing, and publishing—that will allow them to "passer ou egaler les hommes" (*Œuvres complètes,* 41) [equal or surpass men] in knowledge and virtue, thereby reconfiguring the intellectual hierarchy of early modern France. Thus what originates as an innocuous time-filler becomes transformed into a call to arms. Ultimately, Louise Labé's references to her writing as an escape from idleness serve to deflect potential protests against the audacity of her exhortations concerning the way women ought to spend their time.

Louise Labé's concept of virtuous activity is inextricably linked to the importance she accords to time, which can be elucidated not only by examining her own 1555 *Euvres*, but also by setting them against works by other poets in the Lyons-Chalon circle who write in a very similar register: Pontus de Tyard's *Erreurs amoureuses* (1549 and 1573)[74] and Olivier de Magny's *Gayetez* of 1554. The juxtaposition of these texts reveals a striking difference between Louise Labé's attitudes toward time and those of her male colleagues. Time in Louise Labé's works is characterized by its symbiotic relation to virtue, which Labé redefines in contrast to contemporaneous moralists, and by the privileging of the present, as distinguished from the insistence on the relentless progression from past to future so prevalent in Tyard and Magny.

On a first reading, the preface of Labé's *Euvres* and the dedicatory letter to the second edition of Tyard's *Erreurs amoureuses* appear remarkably similar. Both original works were published by Jean de Tournes in Lyons for a very specific Lyonnais audience steeped in the distilled poetry of Scève and accustomed to Italianate love lyrics. Both poets reiterate their initial resistance to being published, though both ultimately disclose a justification for allowing their works to go public. Both prefaces are dedicated to a young, "vertueuse damoiselle"—Catherine de Retz in the case of Tyard, and Clémence de Bourges in the case of Labé. And finally, both poets betray a preoccupation with temporality, addressing the relationship between their works and the passage of time.

The thematic resonance in the two works is so striking that the reader might suspect Tyard of imitating his colleague from Lyons, which is certainly conceivable, particularly given the two poets' geographical proximity, their knowledge of one another's work, and the success of Louise Labé's first edition. Alternatively, the resemblances could simply be attributed to the highly codified rhetorical convention of sixteenth-century prefaces.[75] In any event, given the identical themes of the two prefaces, it is all the more surprising that the same questions about the relationship among time, writing, and virtue yield radically different answers for the two poets.

Both Louise Labé and Pontus de Tyard incorporate in their prefaces carefully crafted protests about the publication of their work. Louise Labé recounts that friends came upon the collection of her poems "sans qu'[elle] ne susse rien" [without her knowing anything about it]. Despite the lady's protesting too much, the poet nonetheless succeeds in justifying her choice to publish—her work will inspire other virtuous young women to write and produce works that are, she argues, "mieus limé[s] et de meilleure grace" (*Œuvres complètes,* 43) [more refined and elegant]. In Louise Labé's vocabulary, then, virtue is inseparable from the problem of time and its productive use: she has spent her time writing poetry and now publishing, and she exhorts other "dames vertueuses" to do likewise.

Whereas in Louise Labé's preface virtue and temporality are symbiotically associated, in Tyard's preface virtue has no immediate link with time. Like Louise Labé, Pontus de Tyard discovers a pretext for publishing the collection despite his initial impulses to the contrary: he modestly (!) acquiesces to the appeals of his friends, acknowledging that the publication will show his "virtuous" readers the great strides French poetry has made during the past thirty years. For Tyard, virtue inherent in the readers will enable them more readily to judge the superiority of his recent poetry. Thus the two poets' avowed motives for publication focus on quite different aspects of time: in Tyard's case, the passage of time serves to record for posterity literary progress and achievement—time provides a *proof.* Louise Labé, on the other hand, insists on women's profitable use of time and the redefinition of "virtuous" activity—time becomes the space of an *exhortation.*

The poets' choice of dedicatee for their collections further reveals the different function that the topos of time assumes in the two works, in this case through the vehicle of youthfulness. When Louise Labé and Pontus de Tyard dedicate their works to virtuous young women, they are doubtless making explicit their projected appeal to the secular reading class in general and to young women readers in particular. But in Louise Labé's case, the young Clémence is called upon to serve as the poet's guide, "pource que les femmes ne se montrent volontiers en publiq seules" (*Œuvres complètes,* 43) [because women should not readily show themselves in public alone]. Accompanying this literary ruse is a much weightier proposition: that Clémence, as well as other young women, should study, write, and publish. The "virtue" (in the sense of force and resourcefulness) of the addressee thus provides the backdrop for Louise's plea that women use their time more productively and more honorably by becoming women of letters.[76]

Tyard's selection of the young Catherine de Retz as addressee, in contrast, serves by association to rejuvenate his "erreurs," whose freshness might otherwise seem questionable, given the advanced age of the poet at the time of their republication (advanced by sixteenth-century standards; he was fifty-two). Here the poet's allusions to virtue flatter his female readers—"en faveur de vous et des vertueuses, doctes et gentilles Damoiselles voz semblables" [in favor of you and other learned, gentle maidens like you]—and invoke them to convince their gentlemen friends to judge his work favorably as well.[77] Virtue is linked to temporality through the person of Catherine, as her youth and her virtue are the very qualities Tyard seeks to emphasize in his readership. The strategy of choosing a young, virtuous woman as addressee for the two poets thus evinces very different explicit motivations: for Tyard, once again, the woman's youth and virtue serve largely as a *comprobatio*, or a flattering common denominator for the readership he seeks to convince. Louise Labé challenges the established concept of what constitutes virtuous activity for women, choosing a young addressee who is capable of acting upon her exhortation. Thus while the temporal motifs serve as a proof, measure, or closure in Tyard's preface, they become an invitation or aperture in Labé's text.

Writing, Production, and the "Presentness" of the Past

Time in its relationship to writing occupies a prominent place in the prose prefaces of Tyard and Labé as well as in the poetic preface of Olivier de Magny's *Gayetez*, and the intermingling of the two themes reveals another dichotomy between Louise Labé and her male cohorts. Whereas for Tyard and Magny, literary achievement unfolds on a temporal continuum (from the past of inferior poetry to the future of excellent poets' immortality), for Louise Labé writing expands the present.

In Tyard's preface, temporality serves to establish a contrast between "then" and "now," illustrating a trajectory of the development of French poetry since he began to write thirty years earlier (although, as John McClelland notes, that figure is probably exaggerated by Tyard to assert his anteriority over Ronsard and Du Bellay).[78] Insisting on the passage of time, Tyard points to "la mutation du stile Poëtique" [the evolution of poetic style] and "le progrez et avancement qu'a fait nostre langage François depuis ce temps"[79] [the progress and advancement of our French language since that time]. He asserts that no one before him had published such elevated lyric poetry in French (Du Bellay had published *L'Olive* seven months earlier, but who's counting?).[80] Tyard argues that the rise of French poetry, begun by his generation in general and by himself in particular, has provided posterity with a good number of excellent poets to choose from.[81] Time thus serves in this preface to underscore the distance between the past and the present, and also to project his work's reception into the future.

Olivier de Magny, too, in his introductory poem to the *Gayetez*, situates his work within the tradition of *exegi monumentum*. He invokes the Muses, requesting that they bestow immortality concomitantly upon his book and his dedicatee Paschal:

> Et vous Pegaside Déesses,
> Et toy Dieu, qui ces Chanteresses
> Guides carollant en leur bal,
> Faictes que le nom de Paschal,
> Le nom de Paschal, et mon livre,
> Puissent d'age en age revivre,
> Si bien qu'exemptez de mourir
> Ilz ne puissent jamais perir.[82]

[And you, goddesses of Pegasus, / And you god, who guide these singers / Caroling in their dance, / Let the name of Paschal, / The name of Paschal, and my book, / Live from age to age / So that immune from death, / They can never perish.]

In contrast to Tyard's chronological depiction of time and Magny's Pléiadian projections into the future, Labé represents writing as recuperation of the past and an amplification of the present. As Gisèle Mathieu-Castellani has shown, Louise Labé's lyric work is born from a relationship to lost time.[83] The very process of writing as Louise Labé describes it centers on the interrelations of different moments of human experience. The pleasures derived from study and writing incorporate temporal aspects in that both activities enact a continuous intercourse between past and present. In contrast to the traditionally female activities and occupations that simply serve to pass the time, Louise Labé writes in her preface, the pleasures of reading and writing are longer lasting. By returning to a passage written earlier, she argues, an author can in some sense recreate past time:

Car le passé nous resjouit, et sert plus que le present: mais les plaisirs des sentimens se perdent incontinent, et ne reviennent jamais, et en est quelquefois la memoire autant facheuse, comme les actes ont esté delectables.... Mais quand il avient que mettons par escrit nos concepcions, combien que puis apres notre cerveau coure par une infinité d'afaires et incessamment remue, si est ce que long tems apres, reprenans nos escrits, nous revenons au mesme point, et à la mesme disposicion ou nous estions. Lors nous redouble notre aise: car nous retrouvons le plaisir passé qu'avons ù ou en la matiere dont escrivions, ou en l'intelligence des sciences ou lors estions adonnez. Et outre ce, le jugement que font nos secondes[84] concepcions des premieres, nous rend un singulier contentement. (*Œuvres complètes,* 42–43)

[The past delights us, and is more useful than the present, but the feeling of enjoyment escapes us immediately and never returns. Other pleasures are such that when we remember them, we can never recreate our frame of mind at that moment. Try though we might to imagine that state and record it in our heads, we know that it is only a shadow of the past tricking and misleading us. . . . But if it happens that we write down our ideas, how much more easily can we return to that point and to that state of mind, even though an infinity of changes have elapsed in the meantime. Our enjoyment is thus doubled; we find the past pleasure that we had in the subject we were writing about, or in the understanding of disciplines to which we were devoted. Beyond this, the judgment that our later ideas bring to earlier ones gives us singular satisfaction.]

The temporal allusions in this passage illustrate the multilayered "presentness" of the past in Louise Labé's conception. The pleasure of writing can be doubled by an author's bringing present judgments and reflections to a previously written text, where present and former selves (revived by the memory inscribed in the text) can enter into dialogue. As Deborah Lesko Baker notes, "Labé's model of memory finally privileges not the mere recall of feeling but the full and continuing capacity to re-experience it as a condition of life itself."[85]

Thus while Tyard's treatment of time in the preface forms a linear progression (thirty years ago/now/posterity), Louise Labé's traces a circle (recording of the moment/returning to the recording of the moment/writing as continuing pleasure). Both poets advance a political and literary cause in their prefaces: the advancement of French poetry in the case of Tyard and the importance of women writing in Labé. Yet in Tyard's preface, time marches relentlessly forward toward poetic posterity. Louise Labé's preface, in contrast, constitutes an invitation to circumvent time's progression by engaging in the process of writing.

A final instance of the nexus between time and writing can be found in Labé's celebrated Sonnet 14, "Tant que mes yeux pourront larmes espandre," which perhaps more than any other of her works portrays her complex attitudes toward time. While the preface depicts the "presentness" of the past, as we have seen, Sonnet 14 records the "presentness" of both the past and the future in the poet's temporal system:

> Tant que mes yeux pourront larmes espandre,
> A l'heur passé avec toy regretter:

> Et qu'aus sanglots et soupirs resister
> Pourra ma voix, et un peu faire entendre:
> 5 Tant que ma main pourra les cordes tendre
> Du mignart Lut, pour tes graces chanter:
> Tant que l'esprit se voudra contenter
> De ne vouloir rien fors que toy comprendre:
> 9 Je ne souhaitte encore point mourir.
> Mais quand mes yeus je sentiray tarir,
> Ma voix cassee, et ma main impuissante,
> 12 Et mon esprit en ce mortel sejour
> Ne pouvant plus montrer signe d'amante
> Prirey la Mort noircir mon plus cler jour.
>   (*Œuvres complètes*, 129)

[As long as my eyes still have tears to shed, / Regretting the happy moments spent with you, / And my voice, overcoming sobs and sighs, / Still has the power to sing, // As long as my fingers can touch the strings / Of the gentle lute in singing your graces / As long as my soul is satisfied / Seeking to comprehend nothing beyond you, // I do not yet wish to die. / But when I feel the tears dry on my face, / My voice broken, my fingers bereft of force, // And my spirit in this mortal dwelling / No longer showing signs of love / I shall pray death to darken my brightest day.]

The anaphora "tant que" of lines 1, 5, and 7 inscribes a temporal contingency that for the first nine lines of the sonnet is framed in the present. "Tant que" signals a rare French construction after which what might be called a "false future tense" is used—the future tense here denotes not an event to take place in the future, but rather *present* actions that continue.

The mention of lute playing in the second stanza further insists upon the present, recalling Sonnet 12, in which the poet proclaims the lute's function in Labé's poetic creation:

> Lut, compagnon de ma calamité,
> De mes soupirs témoin irreprochable,
> De mes ennuis controlleur veritable,
> Tu as souvent avec moy lamenté. . . .
>   (*Œuvres complètes*, 127)

[Lute, companion of my calamity, / Witness of my sighs, / True authority on my sorrows, / You have often lamented with me. . . .]

Louise Labé's accomplishment as a lutenist has been recorded both in contemporaneous accounts and in her own preface, where she acknowledges having devoted much of her youth to music. Music, especially in its connection to poetry, enjoyed a particular distinction from the 1550s through the 1570s in France, as evidenced by such events as the publication of Tyard's *Solitaire second, ou Prose de la musique* in 1555, the large number of poems written about music by members of the Pléiade (and often set to music by such composers as Janequin and Costelay), and the founding of the Académie de Poésie et de Musique in 1570.[86] In the Pléiade, music frequently figures as a metaphor for writing poetry, and, more specifically, the lute or the lyre represents lyric poetry (from the Greek λύρα). Within this elevated register, the poet almost inevitably broaches the future glory of his own poetry, as Ronsard's "Hymne de France" of 1549 illustrates. Ronsard begins by addressing his lute, "Sus, lut doré, des Muses le partaige, / Et d'Apollon le commun heritaige" (L.I,24; P.II, 647) [Arise, golden lute, attribute of the Muses, / and collective legacy of Apollo], and ends with an impassioned accolade to his own originality and *fama:* "Moy ton Poëte, ayant premier osé / Avoir ton los en rime composé..."(L.I.25; P.II,652) [I, your poet, having first dared to compose your praise in verse...]. Ronsard's lute thus figures as an image for the future glory of his poetry.

Olivier de Magny, too, in his *Gayetez*, employs the image of the lyre to advance his literary cause. François Rouget notes Magny's tendency to utilize objects as a means of "lyrical intercession," although paradoxically these images serve to maintain the poet's distance from the beloved.[87] In one of the first poems of the collection, Magny utilizes the lyre not as a link to his lady but rather as a springboard for his projections of poetic immortality:

> Sus donc Ronsard, Bellay, Jodelle,
> Accordez la lyre immortelle,
> Qui rend immortel vostre loz,
> Et d'un chant qui doucement sonne,
> Chantez ceste douce fellonne,
> Qui me brusle jusques aux os.[88]

[Then arise, Ronsard, Bellay, Jodelle, / Tune the immortal lyre, / That makes your praise immortal, / And with a sweetly ringing song, / Sing of this exquisite felon, / Who burns me to the bones.]

Seen in the light of these contemporaneous poets' use of the lute as an object of projection and glory, then, Louise Labé's hymn to her lute-companion appears all the more detached from contemporaneous poetic practice. While at least one recent critic has seen in Louise Labé's lute a phallic symbol over which the poetic subject gains power,[89] it seems to me that the poet's attitude toward her lute is more decidedly complicitous in both Sonnet 11 and Sonnet 14. Insofar as tension arises between the lutenist and her instrument ("Et si te veus efforcer au contraire / Tu te destens, et si me contreins taire" [And if I try to force you to play with joy / You come unstrung and reduce me to silence], the lute serves here as the embodiment of the poet's contradictory sentiments and the pretext for a dialogic exchange. By its status as companion, witness, and implied interlocutor, the lute in Louise Labé functions once again to amplify the sense of the present in her texts.

Lute playing constitutes but one of the contingencies enumerated in the first nine lines of Sonnet 14: *as long as* certain conditions are satisfied, the poet will resist death. In the remaining verses, the poet symmetrically enacts the consequences of a loss of each of these conditions. What is the specific nature of these conditions? All of them—the power to weep, sing, play, and desire—can be seen as metaphors for writing. Simply identifying these powers as metaphors, however, fails to explain their consequence not only in this sonnet but also in the whole of Labé's work. In his *Interpretation and Overinterpretation*, Umberto Eco proposes criteria for determining what he calls the *intentio operis*, or the intention of the text (as distinguished from the intention of the author or that of the reader). Foremost among these criteria is the plausibility of a given semantic isotopy.[90]

These terms prove useful for identifying at the center of Sonnet 14 the isotopy of *production*. Throughout the quatrains, the poet actively "produces" tears, singing, lute playing, and desire. In the last tercet, the dynamic verb "montrer" is set against the lugubrious "noircir," accentuating the contrast between the poet's current state of production and the hypothetical possibility of inertia. Seen in this light, the "signes d'amant" are not simply signs of love but rather "life signs"—the poet's existence depends upon her being capable of producing them.[91]

The words "Mais quand" in line 10 announce the turning point of the sonnet, signaling the existence of a future moment when the ability to produce, and by extension time, will stop. It is difficult to imagine a temporal stance more removed from the ideology of poetic immortality than this: the summum bonum for Louise Labé's poet can be found only in "presentness" of production, be it constructed by memory or formed by the extension of current time. Paradoxically, while both Tyard's and Magny's temporal environments are wider-reaching than Labé's (the progression from past to present to future versus the "presentness" of all time in Labé), time as a construct appears far more malleable and supple in Labé's temporal system.

Virtue Revisited: Temporality and Transgression

In what is arguably Louise Labé's most celebrated line, the poet exhorts young women to rise above their spindles and to pursue the practices of study and writing:[92]

> [J]e ne puis faire autre chose que prier les vertueuses Dames d'eslever un peu leurs esprits par-dessus leurs quenoilles et fuseaus, et s'employer à faire entendre au monde que si nous ne sommes faites pour comander, si ne devons nous estre desdaignees pour compagnes tant es afaires domestiques que publiques, de ceus qui gouvernent et se font obeïr. (*Œuvres complètes,* 41–42)

> [. . . I can only beseech virtuous women to raise their minds above their distaffs and spindles and to make the world understand that even if we are not made to command, we should not be disdained as participants in private or public affairs by those who govern and ensure that others obey them.]

Not only does writing appropriately take women into the public arena, Labé argues later in this preface, but it also brings glory, honor, and pleasure (*Œuvres complètes,* 42). In other activities (such as spinning), she notes,

> [Q]uand on en ha pris tant que lon veut, on ne se peut vanter d'autre chose, que d'avoir *passé le tems*. Mais celle de l'estude laisse un contentement de soy, qui nous demeure plus longuement. (*Œuvres complètes,* 42)

> [{W}hen you have done {those activities} as long as you wish, you can only say that you have passed the time. But study leaves you in a state of contentment, which is longer lasting.]

Thus Louise Labé opens her collected works by interrogating women's time, challenging the dominion of the distaff as anathema to women's critical vocation of writing. The dramatic implications of Louise Labé's call to action can be fully appreciated only within the context of the distaff's multiple manifestations—linguistic, social, and literary.

Serving as the quintessential emblem of women's occupation and thus social place, the "quenouille" denotes the female line in a succession as early as the sixteenth century. It metonymically represents women or "old wives," as in the collection of axioms entitled *Les Evangiles des quenouilles,* published in the late fifteenth century. "Quenouille" also appears in idiomatic expressions denoting women's potential power: "tenir de la quenouille," according to Cotgrave, means "to hold . . . his wife to be his Maister." The proverb "A la quenouille le fol s'agenouille" is echoed by its sixteenth-century English counterpart, "fooles kneele to distaves, weake men unto women" (Cotgrave). In iconographical representations, the distaff serves to denote the exclusively female domain as well: when a man is pictured with a distaff, he becomes burlesque and ridiculous.[93]

The distaff has received considerable critical attention of late, particularly as scholarly inquiry has established the parallel between misogyny and privatization, on the one hand, and nascent feminism and resistance to domesticity, on the other.[94] In a recent article on the iconography of spinning, Frances Biscoglio outlines the two traditions from which the image of the spinning woman emerges. In primitive myth and classical antiquity, the spinning woman represents the creator, life-giver, intermediary, and source of wisdom, as in the spinning Parcae who control human destiny. In the Judeo-Christian tradition, however, the spinner embodies the ideal woman, the *mulier economica* of Proverbs 31, a model of virtue who is charitable, industrious, and obedient.[95] The distaff of Louise Labé's preface figures firmly within this second context. In ironic contrast to the term "quenouille" implying female authority in the expressions cited above, the distaff in sixteenth-century French discourse fulfills the social function of keeping its mistress as far away from power as possible. Erasmus, for example, recommends spinning silk, weaving tapestries, or playing a musical instrument as a respectable activity to occupy a noblewoman.[96] A number of other humanist conduct manuals prescribe spinning as a safeguard against idleness because, as Vives warns, "s' elle pense seule, elle pense mal"[97] [if she thinks alone, she thinks evil]. Seen within the context of widespread public anxiety about the potentially pernicious use of free time by women, the distaff serves in these texts as an instrument of regulation and confinement.

In 1559, four years after Louise Labé's works appeared, Ronsard published in his *Second livre des meslanges* a poem entitled "La quenoille," in which the poet underscores the distaff's vital function: keeping his lady occupied. Marie stands in worthy company as Ronsard's poet establishes an equivalency between her and Pallas Athena, goddess of wisdom, and patron of the arts, peace, and war. Athena had as companion and friend a distaff, as will henceforth Marie. A brief examination of the poem reveals the purposes to which, in the eyes of the poet, Marie's distaff should be put: it will occupy the lady as she pines for the poet in his absence. Here the distaff offered by the poet ("cher present que je porte à ma chere Marie" [dear present that I offer to my dear Marie]) constitutes a rather demagogic gift to his lady:

> A fin de soulager l'ennuy qu'elle a de moy
> . . . .
> Quenoille je te meine où je suis arresté:
> Je voudrois racheter par toy la liberté.
>
> (L.X,122-23; P.I,236–37)

[To relieve her pining over me / . . . / Distaff, I am taking you where I am held captive; / Through you, I would like to regain my freedom.]⁹⁸

The "pointe" ending the poem magnifies the domestic object's grandeur in language worthy of a mock encomium: the distaff, offered by a "loyal amy," surpasses in its glory both scepters and crowns. Thus in this text the distaff serves to underscore Marie's place (and, synecdochically, women's place) as she engages in sheltered, sanctioned activity while the poet breaks away.

In Ronsard's often recited *Sonnet pour Hélène*, also, the domain of the distaff serves to remind Hélène of her subordinate status, as she wastes away, crouching by the fireplace, for having refused the poet's verdant love years before, "devidant et filant /. . . regrettant mon amour et vostre fier desdain" (L.XVII,265; P.I,401) [winding and spinning . . . regretting my love and your proud disdain]. In both cases the distaff represents a form of banishment for the female addressee, in the first example as a means of granting the poet's own freedom from Marie, and in the second as a punishment for Hélène's heartless rejection.

The contradiction between contemporaneous moralists and poets' enthusiastic championing of the distaff, on the one hand, and Louise Labé's pointed reference to rising above it in order to write, on the other, reveals the extent of Labé's transgressive stance regarding women's time. The poet's simple exhortation to put spinning aside, when seen as explicitly calling into question socially sanctioned women's work, and thus women's place, takes on a revolutionary quality. This is not to say, of course, that Louise Labé is the only sixteenth-century woman to interrogate the icon of the distaff: Hélisenne de Crenne assails it and Catherine des Roches, in her later poem "A ma quenoille," paradoxically glorifies it. In Catherine's poem, the exalted distaff serves as a subterfuge for her writing.⁹⁹ But Louise Labé's injunction to *rise above* the distaff declares a clear hierarchy between writing (discouraged for women, but desirable) and traditionally female work (encouraged, but undesirable) and thus constitutes the most devastating critique of all. In her bold preface not only does Louise Labé open herself to charges of arrogance, but she also goes beyond established boundaries by challenging a primary usurper of women's time and the most cherished icon of female subjugation in early modern Europe.

Another manifestation of Louise Labé's temporal transgression is evoked in her treatment of the amorous tropes of confession and repentance. The conceit of *erreurs* is significant not because Louise Labé employs it, but rather because she seems studiously to avoid it. On several occasions she grazes the motif, but in every case she subverts it, adapting it to her own very different ends. The conceit of *erreurs*, often figuring at the beginning of a collection of love lyrics, expresses for the most part the contrived repentance on the part of the poet for some past behavior, notably his youthful infatuation. Petrarch's allusion to his *giovenile errore* in the first sonnet of *Rime sparse* serves as a prototype for this tradition: "et del mio vaneggiar vergogna è'l frutto"[100] [and of my raving, shame is the fruit]. Similarly, Pontus de Tyard, in the last line of the first sonnet of his *Erreurs amoureuses*, proclaims himself "Prest d'endurer honteuse penitence / Pour les erreurs de ma jeunesse vaine"[101] [ready to endure shameful penitence / For the wanderings {errors} of my vain youth], and Scève, too, includes the notion of *erreurs* in the liminary *huitain* of the *Délie*. These disclaimer poems incorporate considerable ambiguity, however, given that they denote the will to repudiate manifestations of youthful, lusty thoughts while simultaneously preceding poems that record and thereby recreate those same thoughts. Yet within the poems themselves, the conceit stands unadulterated: the poet revisits past behavior and repents. Petrarch, Tyard, and Scève all trace an explicit temporal separation between the one who committed these "errors" in his youth and the now wiser writer reflecting upon them.

Given Louise Labé's clear affinity for Italian love poets and their French imitators,[102] the reader might reasonably expect to encounter references to *errore* early in her collection. Indeed, embedded in Louise Labé's first elegy are several verses that promise to state the poet's *erreurs:*

> Et meintenant me suis encor contreinte
> De rafreschir d'une nouvelle pleinte
> Mes maus passez. Dames, qui les lirez,
> De mes regrets avec moy soupirez. . . .
> (*Œuvres complètes*,108)

[And now I am constrained again / To revive with a new lamentation / The griefs of my past. You ladies who will read of them, / Sigh with me about my regrets. . . .]

But several lines later the poet clarifies her position that an apology is out of the question, since it is Cupid who "inflames" women. Women who fall prey to love's wounds should never be blamed, since the noblest souls are the most susceptible:

> N'estimez point que lon doive blamer
> Celles qu'a fait Cupidon inflamer.
> ... les plus nobles esprits
> En sont plus fort et plus soudain espris.
>
> (*Œuvres complètes*, 108)

[Do not imagine that those whom Cupid has inflamed should be blamed ... the noblest spirits are taken the most strongly and suddenly.]

I do not mean to imply, of course, that Louise Labé does not plead for the understanding and approbation of her critical cohorts, the "dames lyonnaises." On the contrary, winning the approval of her readers constitutes a central question in both the elegies and the sonnets. But rather than admitting to wrongdoing in the past, Labé justifies and explains her behavior in the present. Instead of "confessing" in the Petrarchan mode, the poet constructs a legal strategy in her own defense, explaining Cupid's continual seizing of "noble spirits."

Another case in point is what initially seems to be a confession of past wrongs at the beginning of Elegy 3. Assuming what appears to be the same rhetorical position as Petrarch, Tyard, and Scève, Louise Labé implores her readers not to condemn the loves of her youthful folly, but she then challenges the very definition of "erreurs":

> Quand vous lirez, ô Dames Lionnoises,
> Ces miens escrits pleins d'amoureuses noises,
> Quand mes regrets, ennuis, despits et larmes
> M'orrez chanter en pitoyables carmes,
> Ne veuillez pas condamner ma simplesse,
> Et jeune erreur de ma fole jeunesse,
> Si c'est erreur....
>
> (*Œuvres complètes*, 115)

[When you read, O ladies of Lyons, / These writings filled with amorous rumbling, / You will hear me sing in pitiful verses / Do not condemn my simplicity, / And the young wandering {error} of my foolish youth / If it is error....]

All signs point to a confession with the inclusion of the familiar words "jeune erreur." But the poet immediately subverts her own declaration: *si c'est erreur*. If the definition of "erreurs" is unclear, then so too is the determination of what constitutes virtue and vice, as the poem explicitly suggests. By whose definition are amorous exploits classified as "erreurs"?

Only by the reader's, it would appear, and the poet sets out to secure the reader's allegiance: "mais qui dessous les Cieus / Se peut vanter de n'estre vicieus?" [but who under the Heavens / Can boast of having no imperfections?]. She then proceeds to detail a compendium of true vice: "Mentir, tromper, et abuser autrui" (*Œuvres complètes*, 116) [lying, cheating, and abusing others]. But if despite the poet's reasoning to the contrary, the reader should continue to categorize sexual desire as a vice, the speaker offers yet another justification. Eros's deceptively simple workings are entirely responsible:

> Mais si en moy rien y ha d'imparfait,
> Qu'on blame Amour: c'est lui seul qui l'a fait.
> (*Œuvres complètes*, 116)

[But if there is anything imperfect in me, / Let love be blamed: it is he alone who did it.]

The *si* of "si c'est erreur" and "si en moy rien y ha d'imparfait" are reminiscent of the numerous ambiguous *sis* of Sonnet 24: "*si* j'ay aymé" [*if* I have loved], "*si* j'ay senti mile torches ardentes" [*if* I have felt a thousand burning torches], "*si* en pleurant, j'ay mon tems consumé" [*if* weeping I have spent my time], "*si* j'ay failli" [*if* I have failed]. The hypothetical "si" underscores that all experience can only be fully known and grounded in the individual body. In all these cases, the poet implies that although the reader might construe it otherwise, no one is immune from the vicissitudes of love, thus explicitly deflecting charges of malfeasance: "Et gardez vous d'estre plus malheureuses" (*Œuvres complètes*, 135) [And avoid being more miserable yourselves]. The poet's justification of her passion appears airtight: first, Eros is to blame, and second, love's pangs are both insuperable and universal. Despite the plaintive tone of both the elegy and the sonnet, the poet's syllogistic declarations eschew the notion of past "erreurs" and culminate in the triumph of her desire in the present.

A related rhetorical manifestation of the "erreurs" conceit is the use of the poetic devise *repentir* or retraction (from the Latin *retractare*, to draw back), which again involves a conceptual return to the past, however temporary, in order to repudiate what has just been written. The retraction, frequently used by Petrarch as well as his Italian and French imitators, is ubiquitous in sixteenth-century verse. Once again, the significance of this device in Louise Labé's poetry is not its presence, but rather its absence, particularly in the case of Labé's "O beaux yeux bruns, ô regars destournez," as set against her colleague and alleged lover Olivier de Magny's sonnet by the same title.[103] Both sonnets are imitations of Petrarch's "Oi occhi mei." Petrarch and Magny, unlike Labé, include a prominent retraction in their sonnets: "oi occhi miei (occhi non già, ma fonti)" and "O vous mes yeux, non plus yeux mais fonteines" [no longer eyes but fountains]. Labé's omission could perhaps be attributed to mere coincidence, were it not for the absence of retraction in the whole of Louise Labé's work.[104] Her rhetorical approach, in fact, seems to be quite the opposite: in what Ann Rosalind Jones calls Labé's "female takeover of the *basium*,"[105] there are certainly no retractions, and the explicit repetition underscores the boldness of her invitation:

> Baise m'encor, rebaise moy et baise:
> Donne m'en un de tes plus savoureux,
> Donne m'en un de tes plus amoureux. . . .
>
> (*Œuvres complètes*, 131)

[Kiss me, kiss me again and again, / Give me one of your most delicious ones, / Give me one of your most amorous ones. . . .]

Stylistically as well as psychologically, Louise Labé's poet resists returning to the past to revisit specific "erreurs" or to repent. She explains, implores, repeats, justifies, fantasizes, and cajoles, but she does not repent. Her transgression is therefore magnified: while on the surface Labé's speaker appears to be begging the "dames lyonnoises" to forgive her past actions, upon closer examination of the rhetoric it becomes apparent that she resists this formulation in favor of firmly standing her ground in the present.

* * *

In their attitudes to time and its connections with both virtue and writing, then, the poets from the *lyonnois* circle appear to distinguish themselves according to gender. While all of these poets write in a genre that privileges lyrical atemporality, Scève, Tyard, and Magny nonetheless posit time's movement in terms of progression, be it through the *exegi monumentum* motif, the measure of French poetry's advancement, or the contrast between youthful *erreurs* and present penitence. The imagery employed by Pernette du Guillet and Louise Labé, on the other hand, tends to insist upon a magnification of current time. The concepts of contentment and the moveable Day in Pernette as well as writing as a recurring enterprise and the dialogic lute in Labé all suggest the enactment of a continually mobile present. If these temporal conceptions could be imagined in geometric terms, the works of both Pernette du Guillet and Louise Labé seem to trace a three-dimensional figure in movement (such as a Klein bottle).[106] Disregarding time's linear progress, both poets create a more dynamic temporality in their texts.

Despite these apparently gendered distinctions, any attempt to reduce the temporal attitudes of the Lyonnais poets to a purely binary classification will inevitably meet with resistance. Scève reveals an obsession with literary immortality in the future, for example, yet he nonetheless creates in his *dizains* a lyrical present that embraces what might be termed "masochistic delectation." Moreover, while Louise Labé explicitly champions writing as a kind of subjective fusion of past and present for one's present edification, she also encourages women not to eschew the public honor and glory that accompany literary pursuits. Her insistence upon the present pleasures of writing clearly takes precedence over the question of glory ("désir," "plaisir," and "contentement" figure ten times in the preface, whereas "gloire" appears twice), but Labé's references to glory can also be read as a subtle manifestation of her concern for the favorable reception of her work in the future.

Ultimately, among the many antiphonal—and sometimes cacophonous—voices attempting to articulate women's virtue and its relationship to time in mid-sixteenth-century France, Louise Labé's emerges as the most comprehensive. While Vives, Bouchet, and Champier postulate "women's time" to be filled by virtuous activities that avoid idleness, Labé broaches ethical and psychological dimensions of temporality for writing women. Not only do women of letters contribute to the reputation of their sex by rising above jewels and spindles, she argues, but they also find pleasure for themselves in the discoveries that writing affords. By inviting female readers into the public domain as producers who will "surpass or equal" men, Louise Labé redefines what ought rightly to constitute "women's time," and indeed within sixteenth-century boundaries seeks to make such a consideration obsolete.

4

Temporal Enclosure in Anne de Marquets and Nicole Estienne

> And than whan she cometh to age, able to be maried, she is delyvered to the rule and governance of a jelous husband, orels she is perpetually shutte up in a close nounrye.
> —Agrippa, *Of the Nobilitie and Excellencie of Womankynde* (1542)

Historical studies have demonstrated the most prevalent socially sanctioned possibilities for a woman coming of age in early modern France: marriage, which is the preferable alternative, or the convent.[1] The character of both institutions in the sixteenth century suggests that women require an enclosed structure to protect (or to control) them—thus the bride's husband or the authority of the convent immediately replaces the young girl's family at the moment of the wedding or the taking of vows. In Erasmus's colloquy "A Girl with No Interest in Marriage," the character Eubulus tries to dissuade Catherine, who has announced her intention to enter a convent. He argues that she will relinquish the freedom she now enjoys and subject herself to the "servitude" of the cloister. As Constance Jordan notes, however, had Catherine remained at home under the jurisdiction of her parents, she would have been required to marry and live under the authority of her husband.[2] Seen in this light, life in a convent could be conceived as paradoxically liberating for a young woman, as she establishes new friendships and enters into a new social order. Yet both institutions depend for their functioning on an elaborately developed hierarchy.[3] As the two principal structures (and strictures) within which women lived in early modern Europe, the institutions of marriage and the convent constitute an excellent framework for viewing women writers' attitudes toward time.

The temporal perceptions articulated by women writing within the confines of these two institutions prove to be embedded not only in the topoi they address but also in the rhetorical structures and the forms they choose as vehicles. Time quite obviously takes on a different psychological pace for individuals according to such physical circumstances as schedules and work, and such psychological variables as the sense of servitude, freedom, hope, or despair. Both Anne de Marquets (from the vantage point of a nun) and Nicole Liébaut Estienne (from the point of view of a wife) broach the question of time directly in their poetry, and their temporal attitudes are further embedded in their texts.

ANNE DE MARQUETS: EMBODYING FEMININE CHRISTIANITY AND CONCRETE TIME

En MARQUEZ on remarque ung immortel honneur
—Album of the Maréchal de Retz

Anne de Marquets, who received enthusiastic critical acclaim from her contemporaries during the second half of the sixteenth century, has been relatively neglected by subsequent critics. In the twentieth century, one monograph was published in 1931 by Sister Mary Hilarine Seiler, and in recent years critical attention to Anne de Marquets has increased somewhat with several articles, a dissertation chapter devoted to her poetry, and, finally, a scholarly edition of *Sonets spirituels*.[4] Perhaps the hiatus in critical regard of several centuries can be explained by the exclusively devotional nature of her three collections of poetry,[5] or perhaps it is because there seems to be little extraordinary in her verses beyond the two traditions to which her work belongs—in terms of topoi and inspiration, she resembles Chassignet and Sponde, and in matters of form and style she clearly draws from the Pléiade. But particularly in the case of Anne de Marquets, *l'habit ne fait pas la nonne* (clothes don't make the woman). Beyond the lyric qualities of her spiritual meditations, her poetry abounds in indications and intimations of her attitudes toward several contemporaneous problems, among which figures the question of women and time.

When she was quite young, probably in the early 1540s, Anne de Marquets entered into the Dominican convent at Poissy for schooling and later took the veil there. La Royale Maison de Poissy[6] was, it should be noted, no ordinary convent. Since its foundation by Philippe le Bel in 1304, it had harbored not only such aristocratic women as Christine de Pizan, but also royal women, including Marie de Clermont (Saint Louis's granddaughter) and Marie de France (Charles VI's daughter).[7] As in all convents, life was highly regulated for the sisters of Poissy. In *Time, Work, and Culture in the Middle Ages*, Jacques Le Goff points out that the introduction of the clock into the work environment provided a tool to assert power over the masses.[8] Yet for centuries monasteries had already established a form of regulation by the bell that governed the daily existence of monks and nuns. "Es religions de ce monde tout est compassé, limité et reiglé par heures" [In the monasteries and convents of the world everything is measured, limited, and regulated by hours], Gargantua had complained as he banned all clocks and sundials from his utopian monastery.[9] Still, as convents go, Poissy afforded more freedom to the nuns (more individual choice of activity, more humanist studies, more involvement in the community) than most, no doubt largely because of the sisters' elite social status.[10] Seiler notes the "imposing architecture" of the convent, and with its luscious shady gardens and its "viviers très poissonneux" [well-stocked fish ponds], Poissy was also reputed to be one of the most beautiful convent sites in France.[11] When I refer to the "enclosure" from which Anne de Marquets writes, then, I mean less the geographically situated convent than the intellectual and social condition of a nun living in the sixteenth century.

Anne de Marquets became a well-known figure in the 1560s, garnering considerable acclaim from her literary colleagues both within and without the convent. Ronsard, in "Quelle nouvelle fleur apparoist à noz yeux?," a sonnet written as a liminary piece for *Sonets, prières et devises*, describes Anne in an extended metaphor as the "new flower":

> Son Printemps est le Ciel, sa racine est l'Eglise,
> Ses oeuvres et sa foy, ses feuilles et son fruict.[12]

[Her spring is the sky, her roots the Church, / Her works and her faith, the leaves and the fruit.]

Similarly, P. Cointerel praises her verses, "tableaux de chasteté / Dediés à l'honneur de la Divine essence / Enrichis des couleurs d'une docte eloquence / Et qui ont justement des lauriers merité" (*Sonets spirituels*, a4r; 82)[13] [paintings of chastity / Dedicated to the honor of divine essence, / Enriched with colors of learned eloquence / Which rightly deserved laurels]. Dorat calls her "monasteri gloria Pissiaci" [the glory of the monastery of Poissy] (*Sonets, prières*, a6v; *Sonets spirituels*, a3r; 79, signed "Io. Avrati").

Feugère concludes that Anne de Marquets found refuge in the monastery of Poissy because, as for many young noble women, the family did not succeed in arranging a marriage worthy of her.[14] Both her own poetry and all contemporaneous evidence, however, point to her having consciously chosen the cloistered life from an early age. An anonymous epitaph in the *Sonets spirituels* describes her voluntary entry into the convent:

> Une qui mesprisant dés son aage plus tendre,
> Le monde et ses appasts, à Poissy se vint rendre,
> Voüant sa liberté dans l'enclos de ce lieu,
> Ou l'on fait de son coeur un sacrifice à Dieu,
> Son amour qu'elle avoit gravee en sa pensee
> Monstre bien qu'en ses voeux elle ne fust forcee.
> (*Sonets spirituels*, 346; 373)

[She who from the tenderest age despised / The world and its lures, / Came to Poissy, / Pledging her freedom in the enclosure of this place, / Where hearts are sacrificed to God. / The love that she had inscribed in her thoughts / Clearly shows that she was not forced to take vows.]

Monsigot likewise insists upon Anne de Marquets's deliberate decision to become a nun: "Enclose de son gré dans un sainct Monastere / Elle feit le voeu triple à la Trine unité" (*Sonets spirituels*, a5r; 84) [Enclosed by her own will in a holy monastery, she made a triple vow to the Trinity]. While these might be construed as semihagiographic justifications for Anne's desire to become a nun, her own texts in no way suggest that she harbored any hesitation about her decision. The early modern literary historian Hilaron de Coste also notes Anne's conscious taking of the veil.[15]

Nonetheless, despite the relative freedom accorded to the noble nuns and despite Marquets's voluntary association with Poissy, the king's privilege signed by the councillor "Burgensis" (de Bourges) reminds readers of the tight surveillance of works emerging from the convent, and indeed of all religious works. Burgensis grants publishing rights for her translation (entitled *Divines poésies*) of Flaminio's *De rebus divinis carmina* along with her own works, "moyennant qu'elles soient visitees et approuvees par les docteurs de la faculté de Theologie de Paris"[16] [provided that they be scrutinized and approved by the doctors of the Paris Faculty of Theology].

Within what initially appears to be a very closed system (the author's writing from a convent religious texts that will be monitored by the theological masters of the Sorbonne), Anne de Marquets's texts effectuate a number of displacements or shifts in established hierarchy, both religious and literary. These displacements reveal the alternative temporal system underlying her work and result in the foregrounding of feminine religious experience as well as the concretization of temporality in her texts.

The most prevalent displacement in Anne de Marquets's religious verses is the shift in emphasis from an implicitly male to an explicitly female perspective. This shift can be seen most markedly in the attention the poet accords to Mary, both quantitatively (in the number of poems devoted to her) and qualitatively (in the nature of the believer's veneration). The insistence on Mary is not peculiar to Anne de Marquets, of course, because passionate devotion to the Virgin Mary and to women saints had flourished in the late Middle Ages, as Carolyn Walker Bynum and others have shown.[17] While Anne de Marquets avoids the former excesses of Marian devotion, her privileging of Mary not only serves as a point of departure for a broader feminization of the religious text, but it also posits Mary's use of time as a model for humanity.

Mary's role in sixteenth-century discourse, both in religious works and in the context of the "Querelle des femmes," was of course considerable. In his *De la noblesse et preexcellence du sexe foeminin*, published in French in 1529, Agrippa had advanced the feminist counterattack to the claim that women were inferior to men because men were created in God's image: Jesus, he argues, was the son not of a man, but of a woman.[18] In her *Sonets spirituels*, one of the first religious sonnet cycles written in France,[19] Marquets's partiality for Mary becomes immediately evident. Seiler notes that in the collection the number of sonnets varies according to the importance of respective Sundays and festivals in Dominican ritual—for example, twenty-six for Christmas, twenty-two for Pentecost, twenty for Easter, eight for the first Sunday of Lent, and so on.[20] But the relative importance of festivals cannot account for the fact that the poet devotes eighty-two sonnets to the festivals of the Virgin (Immaculate Conception, Annunciation, Assumption), whereas there are only fifty for all the other saints combined. The disproportionate number of poems dedicated to Mary seems somewhat explicable in the section devoted to Christmas, but even there the number of poems in honor of the Virgin appear out of proportion when compared with those celebrating the Christ child. Since Mary is often depicted as the one who offers Christ to humanity, Jesus figures in many of the sonnets devoted to Mary as well. Still, the sheer number of poems dedicated to the Virgin is significant.[21]

Part of the controversy between Catholics and Huguenots centered on the extent of Mary's relative importance in Christian devotion, since Huguenots accused Catholics of an idolatrous loyalty to the Virgin Mother.[22] This conflict provoked notable social consequences. While the Protestant opposition to Mariolatry has sometimes been associated with a desexualizing of society and therefore a certain liberation of women, Natalie Zemon Davis notes that, on the contrary, Protestant asceticism brought about the destruction of female saints as exemplars for both sexes.[23] Building upon Catholic tradition, Anne de Marquets clearly underscores Mary's exemplary status as a model of Christian devotion, but she also explicitly elevates the female qualities of the Virgin Mother. This privileging is particularly apparent when one juxtaposes her work with that of contemporaneous male religious poets.

In his *Entretiens spirituels*, for example, Antoine Favre defends the traditional Catholic adoration of the Virgin against Protestant challenges:

> Je ne puis endurer l'impudence heretique
> De nos sots reformez, qui feignants de vouloir
> Honorer un seul Dieu, enragent de nous voir,
> Saincte Vierge, t'offrir le salut Angelique.[24]

[I cannot bear the heretical impudence / Of our idiotic reformers, who, feigning a desire to / Honor God alone, are enraged to see us / Pray to you the Hail Mary, Holy Virgin.]

Despite Favre's highly orthodox position on the venerability of the Virgin, his sonnet cycle of 1602 provides an example of the ancillary role assigned to Mary in traditional Catholic discourse. While Jesus's mother is lauded as pure and holy, she remains consistently eclipsed by her son. Favre's *Entretiens spirituels*, like Anne de Marquet's *Sonets spirituels*, is a collection of sonnets devoted to meditation and celebration of Christian festivals throughout the year. Only a small number of the three hundred sonnets are devoted to Mary, and even in those beginning with the Virgin's praises, Jesus predictably takes precedence over his mother. At the moment in Favre's *Entretiens* when Jesus announces to Mary that he will be killed and bids her farewell, the poet first attempts to depict Mary's suffering. The suffering quickly gives way, however, to the reminder of Jesus's superior mission and Mary's subordinate destiny:

> Ah! ton coeur est percé: mais puis que tu scais bien
> Qu'il n'est moins Dieu pourtant, quel regret est le tien?
> Que pour le voir mourir, sa mere il t'a faicte estre![25]

[Ah! Your heart is pierced: but because you well know / That he is still no less God, what is your regret? / You know that you were made to be his mother in order to see him die.]

Anne de Marquets, in contrast, rarely insists upon Mary's theologically sanctioned secondary role, presenting instead the argument that all those who worship Jesus should also hold Mary in the highest esteem:

> Quiconque ha de Jesus l'amour au coeur escrit,
> Il doit incessamment par maint hymne et cantique
> Celebrer les vertus de la Vierge pudique,
> En qui ce doux Sauveur nostre humanité prit:

> Car il ne faut douter qu'à la gloire de Christ
> Ne redonde l'honneur qu'à sa Mere on applique,
> Et qu'ainsi cela soit, luy-mesme nous l'explique
> En maint passage et lieu de son divin escrit.
>
> Chantons donc et louons ceste Vierge honorée,
> Qui sur tous a esté par son Fils decorée
> De tout ce qui est beau, excellent et parfaict:
>
> Et si pour loüanger un si rare merite,
> Nostre style est trop bas, nostre voix trop petite,
> Qu'elle reçoive au moins le desir pour l'effect.
>
> (Sonets spirituels, 310; 334)

[All who have love for Jesus inscribed in their hearts, / Must ceaselessly, through hymns and songs of praise / Celebrate the virtues of the chaste Virgin, / In whom the sweet Savior took on our humanity. // For you must not doubt that the honor we attribute to Mary / Flows back to the glory of Christ. / That this is the case, He explains to us himself / In many passages in his divine writings. // So let us sing and praise this honorable Virgin, / Who above all was graced by her Son / With all that is beautiful, excellent, and perfect. // And if to glorify such rare merit, / Our style is too low, our voice too small, / Let her at least receive the intention as the result.]

This sonnet, while explicitly inviting readers to praise Mary as they praise Jesus, rhetorically elevates Mary, even vis-à-vis her son. While her son has "decorated" her with all things beautiful and perfect in the space of the poem, it is nonetheless Mary herself whom the poet bids readers to praise and celebrate ceaselessly. Given the disproportionate attention accorded to Mary in this collection, Marquets not surprisingly affirms the orthodox notion that in exalting Mary those who are faithful exalt Jesus.

Anne de Marquets's feminization of religious texts through the emphasis on Mary can be seen explicitly in the juxtaposition of strophes from two similar poems, one by Flaminio whose works Marquets translated in 1567 (published in 1568), and one by the poet herself. Flaminio writes:

> Tu es l'Evesque eternel et sublime,
> Qui pour nous peult appaiser promptement
> Le seigneur Dieu courroucé justement.
> O sainct enfant des humains l'asseurance!
> Qui du pere as receu toute puissance.[26]

[You are the eternal and sublime High Priest, / Who can quickly appease for us / God's justifiable anger. / O holy child, assurance of all humans! / Who have received all power from the Father.]

Marquets's version of the same theme reads:

> De Marie aujourd'huy le semblable on peut dire;
> Car voulant appaiser le Monarque des cieux,
> Justement courroucé contre les vicieux,
> Elle offre un don si beau qu'il n'y a que redire.
> Or ce riche present, plein de grace et bonté,
> C'est Jesus-Christ, par elle au temple presenté.
> (*Sonets spirituels*, 294; 314–15)

[We can say the same of Mary today, / Because wishing to appease the heavenly Monarch, / Justifiably angry with sinners, / She offers a gift so beautiful that one could desire no more. / This rich gift, full of grace and goodness / Is Jesus Christ, presented by Mary in the temple.]

In both poems, Jesus assumes the role of intercessor between humans and an angry God who is described identically (*justement courroucé/courroucé justement*). In Flaminio's poem, Jesus receives power from the Father he now seeks to placate and assumes the role of High Priest, intervening on humanity's behalf. This image serves not only to situate God as the locus of Jesus's authority, but also to validate the Catholic hierarchy (human priests simply emulate the true High Priest sent by God). In Anne de Marquets's version, however, despite the reference to the "heavenly Monarch," Mary functions as the impetus for God's forgiveness. Mary becomes the principal actor, instigating human absolution by offering the gift of Jesus, not unlike the poet herself, who offers through her text spiritual guidance to her readers.

Mary's importance in Anne de Marquets's works becomes even more striking when we consider the number of explicit and implicit parallels established in the text between the Virgin Mother and the poet herself. The most obvious of these parallels celebrated by sixteenth-century poets is both women's virginity, which assumes a crucial role not only because it describes the bodies of Mary and Jesus' followers, but also because it reflects the body of the church, as Vives describes:

> L'eglise est vierge et mere, et n'y a chose en quoy Dieu plus se delecte, qu'en Virginité seur des Anges. Il voulut avoir Mere vierge, Disciple vierge, L'eglise vierge. Les autres vierges il les espouse en foy, et entrent aux nopces avec luy.[27]

[The church is virgin and mother, and there is nothing God delights in more than in virginity, sister of the angels. He wished to have a virgin mother, virgin disciples, a virgin church. The other virgins He marries in faith, and they enter into marriage with Him.]

The poets who write the dedicatory poems in the *Sonets spirituels* celebrate Anne de Marquets's miraculous productions, implying a distinct parallel between her and the virgin mother:

> J'admire ces beaux vers de celeste origine
> Par miracle, ça-bas d'une Vierge enfantez,
> Qui pour estre conceus de semence Divine
> Meritent d'estre au ciel par les Anges chantez.
> (Monsigot, in *Sonets spirituels*, e1r; 83–84)

[I admire these beautiful verses of celestial origin / By a miracle, here on earth of a Virgin born, / Which, having been conceived by divine seed, / Deserve to be sung by the angels in Heaven.]

Evocations of the verses' celestial origin and the conception by divine seed ("semence") obviously suggest the analogy between the poet and Mary. Similarly, the verses signed "A. de Mont." (Antoine de Montchrestien)[28] rehearse the theme of the virgin bearing children, this time with the addition of God the husband, Anne the wife, and the immortality of their offspring. Note also the insistence upon the vocabulary of the Nativity ("miracle," "triumfans," "creature"), which establishes Anne's conflation with Mary:

> Comme a peu ceste Vierge enfanter des enfans
> Non subjects à la mort et du temps triumfans?
> Ce miracle vrayement est contre la nature.
> Son corps pourtant fut chaste et chaste son esprit:
> Prenant Dieu pour Espoux pour Espouse il la prist,
> Joignant le Createur avec la creature.
> (*Sonets spirituels*, e3r; 87)

[How could the Virgin give birth to children / Not subject to death and triumphant time? / This miracle is truly against nature. / Her body, however, was chaste, as was her spirit. / She took God as her Husband, and He took her as his Wife, / Joining the Creator with creation.]

Even more remarkable than these implicit parallels advanced by her contemporaries are the oblique comparisons between Anne de Marquets and the Virgin Mother established by the poet herself. The most frequent juxtaposition emerges once again in references to their mutual virginity and their shared decision to devote themselves to God, as evidenced in several passages of the *Sonets spirituels:*

> Maintes Vierges aussi la seconde [Marie] ont suivie,
> Se dedians à Dieu et d'esprit et de corps,
> Pour chanter nuict et jour, comme au ciel font les Anges,
> Et de coeur et de voix du grand Dieu les loüanges.
> *(Sonets spirituels*, 191; 312)

[Many Virgins have also followed Mary, / Dedicating themselves to God in body and in spirit, / To sing night and day, with hearts and voices, / Praises to the exalted God, as the angels do in Heaven.]

Also like Mary, Anne de Marquets is plagued by troublesome detractors, and although the poet does not explicitly mention her own Protestant critics in the following passage, the rhetoric resoundingly suggests a connection among Susanna (who triumphs over accusers in Daniel 13), Mary (who withstands false accusations from Jews and heretics regarding her chastity), and Anne de Marquets (who defends the Catholic Church against what she views as vituperative claims by the Protestants):

> Ainsi que Susanne eut deux faux accusateurs,
> Qui la deshonnoroient par tesmoignange inique,
> Ainsi le peuple Juif et la troupe heretique
> De la Vierge ont esté les calomniateurs:
>   Mais comme Daniel jugea les deux menteurs,
> Restituant l'honneur à Susanne pudique:
> Ainsi a condamné l'Eglise Catholique,
> De la mere de Dieu tous les blasphemateurs.
>   Pour lesquels démentir voicy ce qu'elle atteste,
> Nous croyons fermement que par l'esprit celeste,
> O Vierge, tu conceuz Christ nostre Redempteur.
>   Que ceux donc qui ont dict que Joseph fut son pere,
> Soient confus et remplis de honte et vitupere:
> Le deshonneur est deu à tout homme menteur.
> *(Sonets spirituels,* 181; 299–300)

[Just as Susanna had two false accusers, / Who dishonored her by wicked testimony, / Thus the Jewish people and the heretical flock / Were slanderers of the Virgin. // But just as Daniel judged the two liars, / Restoring chaste Susanna's honor, / So the Catholic Church has condemned / All the blasphemers of the mother of God. // To prove them wrong, the church says this:

/ We firmly believe that by the Holy Spirit, / O Virgin, you conceived Christ our Redeemer, // That those who have said Joseph was his father / Are troubled and filled with shame and reprehension. / Every liar deserves to be dishonored.]

The term "faux accusateurs" in the first verse recalls the Protestant challenges of the 1560s, to which Anne had responded in the "Epistre aux lecteurs" in the *Sonets, prières et devises, en formes de Pasquins* (to be examined below). Just as Susanna and Mary had emerged triumphant from the calumnies of their adversaries, so the Catholic Church (and by extension, Anne herself, who had been personally attacked for her ardent support of the bishops in 1561) would condemn all those who "blasphemed" (again, a word consistently associated with the Protestant rebellion). Finally, the expression "tout homme menteur" alludes equally to her Protestant detractor, whom she accuses in the "Epistre" of "peignant . . . comme il veult, et non pas comme il est" (*Sonets, prières*, D4r) [Depicting . . . as he wants to, not as it is]. Thus, the poem functions to predicate a connection between biblical conflicts (in which Christians prevail) and contemporary strife (in which Catholics triumph) as it simultaneously suggests the common condition of Mary and Anne, both of whom are ultimately vindicated.

Anne de Marquets's emphasis on the feminine perspective and the extended association between Mary and the poet are moderated by the humility topos, which figures prominently in Anne de Marquets's poems. Anne de Marquets's stance on humility (and its effects upon the publication of her works) reveals her underlying attitudes concerning the nonlinear nature of time. A trademark not only in the Christian tradition but also for early modern writers in general, the humility topos emerges many times in the *Sonets spirituels*.[29]

Mary consistently teaches the lesson of humility, as when the "venerable mother" deigns to visit Elizabeth in the sequence on the Visitation from the *Sonets spirituels*. Elizabeth speaks:

> Hé d'où me vient cet heur et gloire incomparable,
> Que du Seigneur mon Dieu la mere venerable
> Daigne tant m'honorer que de venir chez moy?
>   A sa servante helas vient la dame et maistresse!
> Qu'en elle chacun donc prenne exemple d'humblesse:
> Quiconque est humble il ha l'Esprit de Dieu en soy.
>   (*Sonets spirituels*, 189; 309)

[O where do this fortune and this incomparable glory come from, / That the mother of the Lord my God / Should deign to honor me by coming to my house? // To her servant, alas, the lady and mistress comes! / Let each one take her humility as an example: / Those who are humble have God's spirit within them.]

These references to Mary's humility in the Visitation sequence as well as in the Advent and Christmas poems are counterbalanced, however, by the notion of her divine power as intercessor and as "venerable mother." Anne de Marquets employs in the *Sonets spirituels* a host of metaphors to depict the Virgin Mother's powers: Mary is the vine that produces the blood of Christ/the sacramental wine (*Sonets spirituels*, 176; 293); a mystical lamp lighting the way for devout Catholics (300; 322); the burning bush who announces God's mercy (184; 303); the sacred earth cultivating the Christ child (185; 304); a fruit-bearing tree that heals humanity (186; 305); a flowing fountain offering the water of life, and a perfect garden imparting wisdom (308; 332). Set against Mary's humility, then, is the question of her triumph. The paradoxical problem arises: if the meek have inherited the earth, are they still meek? This is indeed one of the central Christian paradoxes, usually applied to Jesus: through his defeat, he (for humanity) experiences victory.

The same religious paradox cannot be evoked, however, to explain Anne's treatment of the humility topos in relation to herself. Once again, conspicuous parallels between the poet and Mary surface in Anne de Marquets's works, and here, also, the problem of humility is undermined within the text. Just as Anne de Marquets has Mary herself speak (unlike Marquets's contemporaries Flaminio, Favre, and Jodelle),[30] so the poet herself assumes a voice of authority in her writings, despite her explicit declarations to the contrary.

Each of Anne de Marquets's three poetic collections illustrates both the positing and the undoing of the humility topos. Marquets's first public writings were occasioned by the Colloquium of Poissy held in her convent in 1561. Hoping to avert threats to royal power, Catherine de Médicis, perhaps with the help of her chancellor, Michel de l'Hospital, or the Cardinal de Lorraine, had masterminded the colloquium. The royal mother had invited both Catholic and Protestant dignitaries to debate their differences, naively or peremptorily expecting that concessions could be made on both sides and order could be restored in the kingdom.[31] Anne de Marquets, who had attended the sessions, wrote verses praising the Catholic performance in the debate and particularly extolling the Cardinal de Lorraine's response to Théodore de Bèze's speech.[32] These poems were widely circulated in manuscript among Catholics and subsequently discovered by Protestants, who took them as an affront. The title of one extant Protestant response sums up the Protestant position: *Response aux Pasquins tirez de la Saincte Escriture, et destournez de leur vray sens par une Nonain de Poissy, en faveur des Prelats de France* [Response to the polemic poems based on the Holy Bible, and altered from their true meaning by a nun from Poissy, in favor of the prelates of France].[33] It is not known who decided to have the poems published, though it appears that the poet initially resisted their publication. Anne de Marquets grudgingly attaches an introductory letter to the Cardinal of Lorraine, insisting that it had never been her intention to have the work published:

> ... il n'avoit esté faict seulement,
> Que pour mon exercice et seul contentement:
> Non pour estre transcript, et beaucoup moins encore
> Pour estre publié et veu, comme il est ore:
> M'estant bien souvenu que la pudicité,
> Pour mieux se conserver en son integrité,
> Se doibt accompaigner d'une honte modeste,
> Et plustost se cacher, que d'estre manifeste.
> ("Epistre aux lecteurs," in *Sonets, prières,* D1r)

[... I wrote it only for my own exercice and contentment, not to be transcribed, and even less for it to be published and seen, as it is now. I remembered that purity, to be conserved in its integrity, must be accompanied by modest shame, and should be hidden, rather than disclosed.]

The structure of the poet's protest reveals at once her avowed humility and her obligation to assume such a position. The poet "remembers" (from past teachings) that she must demonstrate modesty. Furthermore, she predictably warns that her "opuscule" is unworthy of being read (D1r). She thus accomplishes her duty by including a modesty clause in her letter while at the same time begrudgingly allowing the collection to be published.

Her pointed counterresponse to the Protestant critic following the poems, however, contradicts her avowed hesitancy about having her work more widely circulated. The indignation and the authority of the poet's tone are unmistakable:

> Et comme donc, helas, eussay-je massacrée [*sic*]
> Ceste saincte doctrine et parolle sacrée,
> Que tant j'honore et prise, et que j'aime trop mieux,
> (Comme Dieu le congnoist) que ma vie et mes yeux?
> . . . .
> O Dieu respand sur Moy ta fureur et ton ire,

> Si de ta saincte voix j'ay faict un nez de cire,
> Pour la prendre et tourner selon ma volonté:
> Ou si j'ay entrepris d'un orgueil effronté
> D'assaillir ta grandeur jusqu'au throsne celique,
> Comme dict en ses vers ce causeur satyrique.
>
> *(Sonets, prières,* D1v-D2r)

[And how then, alas! would I have massacred / Our holy doctrine and sacred word / That I honor and cherish, and love more / (As God knows) than my own life and eyes? / . . . / O God, send your wrath and ire upon me / If I have distorted your holy voice / Taking it and turning it around for my purposes, / Or if I have undertaken, with impudent pride, / To challenge your greatness on the heavenly throne, / As the satirical babbler claims in his verses.]

Taking God as a witness ("Comme Dieu le congnoist" / . . . "O Dieu"), the poet defends her work, proclaiming herself innocent of all charges of falsifying Scripture, distorting God's holy voice, and manifesting hubris. In each negation, she aligns herself with the divine: "ceste saincte doctrine et parolle sacrée," "ta saincte voix," et "ta grandeur jusqu'au throsne celique." The cacophony of the words of the "satirical babbler" opposes the harmony of holy voices in this passage. In direct contrast to the poet herself, the Protestant challenger remains removed from divine reference, relegated to a godless position within the poem.

Marquets then exacerbates the controversy by adding her own accusations of the Protestant critic. The speaker depicts herself as a reasonable observer, as distinguished from the adversarial "luy":

> Car tout ce qui l'offence, et dont tant il mesdict,
> C'est pourtant que je n'ay, ainsi comme luy, dict
> Des Prelats et pasteurs mille maulx et injures,
> Aiant plustost choisi des sainctes escriptures
> Quelques tiltres d'honneur, que je leur ay rendus . . .
>
> *(Sonets, prières,* Dvr)

[For all that offends him and that he criticizes so much is that I did not, as he did, engage in a thousand accusations and insults against the prelates and pastors. I chose rather a few scriptures and several honorable titles, which I gave them. . . .]

Once again, the poet rhetorically associates herself with the "sainctes escriptures," whereas her verbal enemy antithetically produces "mille maulx et injures." In these verses, both the poet and her adversary figure as active subjects of verbs denoting speech, but while the Protestant is associated with the negative verb "mesdire," Anne paints her innocence through the verb denoting generosity, "rendre (les tiltres d'honneur)."

Finally, in a stanza that attempts to devastate her adversary, she reproaches him first on his own terms and then in comparison to the worthy bishops:

> Cest Anonyme donc eust il pas bien mieux faict,
> De deplorer soy-mesme et son propre meffaict,
> Que de mesdire ainsi contre sa conscience,
> De ceux à qui il doibt toute humble obeïssance?
> . . . .
> Et s'il dict, que j'ay Dieu par mes vers assailly,
> Regardez s'il a pas plus lourdement failly. . .
>
> (*Sonets, prières,* D3v-D4r)

[Wouldn't this anonymous man be better off / Deploring himself and his own misdeeds, / Than criticizing against his conscience / Those to whom he owes humble obedience? / . . . / And if he says that I assailed God in my verses, / Look to see if he himself didn't err more grievously.]

It is difficult to imagine that these patently polemic verses were not intended to be circulated. The vehemence of the tone ("deplorer soy-mesme"), the pointed jabs ("je n'ay, comme luy, dict . . . mille maulx et injures") and the incisive counteraccusations ("Regardez s'il a pas plus lourdement failly") certainly do not suggest that the work was written simply as an exercise and for Anne de Marquets's own purposes, as she claims in the passage cited above (D1r).

The poet further adopts and undermines the humility topos in her second collection of poems, *Les Divines poésies* (1568), a translation of Flaminio's *De rebus divinis carmina*. In her introductory letter addressed to "Madame Marguerite, soeur du Roy treschrestien, Charles IX," Anne assures her young patron that she is publishing only because the princess had requested a work from her, and she begs her addressee to consider the poet's good intentions rather than the quality of the work itself (*Les Divines poésies,* a3v). This collection consists of Anne's translation of Flaminio's Latin poems (which appear as marginalia), followed, as if an afterthought, by a collection of Anne's poems. Anne's own text, however, "hidden" by its absence from the main title of the book and by its placement in a secondary position, occupies sixty pages, whereas Flaminio's poems occupy only thirty-two! Her first words in the *Cantiques* ring out clearly—"je veux chanter, ô mon Dieu mon Seigneur, / Ta majesté excellente . . ." (*Les Divines poésies,* 33) [I want to sing, O my God, my Lord / Your excellent majesty . . .]—but she then returns to a humble stance: "Bien que je sois incapable et indigne / De telle office et d'un si grand honneur" [Although I am incapable and unworthy of such a position and such great honor]. Still, the voice that affirms her desire to sing does indeed do so for twice as long as the titular author of the collection.

Within her introduction, moreover, Marquets assumes an unmistakably authoritative tone as she addresses the princess, informing her (much as Rabelais informs his readers) that although the text may not be immediately accessible, if she seeks wisdom there, she shall find it:

> Si vous n'avez esgard (ô Roialle princesse)
> Qu'a l'imperfection, ignorance et rudesse
> De ces miens petits vers, dont je vous fay present,
> Vous n'y pourrez rien veoir qui soit bon ni plaisant,
> Et direz à bon droict qu'oeuvre si mal dressee
> Ne meritoit l'honneur de vous estre addressee:
> Mais tout ainsi qu'on voit, souvent caché dessous
> Quelque bien dure escorce, un fruict suave et doux,
> Ainsi j'ause asseurer que si vous prenez garde
> Au subject principal, qui concerne et regarde
> Une divine ardeur, une perfection
>
> . . . .
> Vous verrez bien alors, que sous la couverture
> D'une assez mal plaisante et indocte escriture,
> On peut facilement beaucoup de bien choisir,
> Avec un agreable et merveilleux plaisir.
>   *(Les Divines poésies,* a4v)

[If you do not heed, royal princess, / The imperfection, ignorance, and roughness / Of my little verses, which I present as a gift to you, / You will see nothing good or pleasing / And will rightly say that my badly presented work / Does not deserve the honor of being dedicated to you. / But just as we often see hidden beneath a hard covering, / A sweet and delicious fruit, / So I dare assure you that if you pay attention / To my main subject, which concerns divine love, perfection / . . . / Then you will see, that under the veneer / Of rather displeasing and unskillful writing, / You can easily find much good, / With agreeable and marvelous pleasure.]

This preface turns on an axis of if/then: *if* the princess overlooks the verses' flaws, and *if* the princess reads the text carefully, *then* she will find much good in it. The adjectives denoting the modest nature of Anne de Marquets's work ("imperfection, ignorance et rudesse") are ultimately overridden in the poem by the definitively positive phrases "beaucoup de bien" and "agreable et merveilleux plaisir."

Marquets further effaces the modesty she had established in relation to the young princess by offering sermonlike recommendations at the end of her introductory epistle:

> Dequoy je le [Dieu] supplie en fin vous faire part,
> Tres-illustre princesse, à qui tant il depart
> De ses plus rares dons: entre lesquels je prise
> Sur tout l'heur qu'il vous faict d'estre si bien apprise
> En tout ce qui conduit à *vertu et sçavoir:*
> Choses qu'on doit chercher et desirer avoir
> *Trop plus que les honneurs et richesses du monde.*
> (*Les Divines poésies,* e2v, my emphasis)

[So finally, I pray God to inform you, / Illustrious princess, on whom he bestows / His rarest gifts. Among them I cherish / Especially your good fortune of being so learned / In all that leads to *virtue and knowledge,* / *Things that we must seek and desire / More than worldly honors and riches.*]

Marquets's bidding God to teach the princess the importance of knowledge and virtue over "worldly honors and riches" evinces considerable boldness on the poet's part as she preaches simplicity and modesty to one of the wealthiest and most bejeweled families of her time. Even within the context of a humble nun's dedicatory epistle to a royal princess, replete with the obligatory humility clause, Marquets has the last word as she concludes with a minisermon that directly endorses Christian values as distinguished from those of the court.

Anne de Marquets's third and most important volume, the *Sonets spirituels,* contains no prefatory letter with the requisite humility clause on the poet's part because it was published posthumously in 1605. The circumstances of its publication remain mysterious. Marie de Fortia, who collected and published the manuscript, writes that Anne died "pendant qu'elle s'exerçoit sur le suject de ses loüanges" (a2r; 77) [while she was working on {God's} praises], yet the poet thanks God at the end of the volume for allowing her to finish ("achever") the work, thus revealing her own conviction that the cycle was complete (*Sonets spirituels,* 339; 365). In any event, the text was not published until seventeen years after her death. Marie de Fortia proclaims her devotion to the deceased sister manifested in the publication of the manuscript, but she neglects to explain the seventeen-year hiatus between the author's death and the publication of her work. "En fin," she notes elliptically in her prefatory letter to Madame de Fresnes, "je me suis souvenuë d'avoir en ma possession un ouvrage tel, que vous estant presenté de ma part, vous le pourriez juger capable de recompenser par son merite le deffaut, que je recognoissois au mien" (a2r; 77) [I remembered having in my possession a work of such value that, after I have presented it to you, you might judge worthy of making up for the mistake that I recognize as mine]. As Seiler points out, given the fact that the prefatory and concluding laudatory poems date from two different periods, it is likely that the poems were widely circulated in manuscript form, as were Marquets's two earlier collections.[34] Kirk Read conjectures, in fact, that Sister Marie de Fortia chose to guard the *Sonets spirituels* from public scrutiny to keep them within the convent among Marquets's ardent admirers and ex-students.[35]

All three of Anne de Marquets's collections were thus published under somewhat anomalous conditions. Despite the confidence of the author's voice in the texts themselves, the first two works include the author's explicit reservations about publishing and the third was not published during her lifetime. How are we to explain the apparent contradiction between the author's wishing to circulate her works, on the one hand, and her reluctance to publish, on the other? I believe that the response to this dilemma lies in the poet's formal choices from the outset.

Anne de Marquets seems consistently to privilege the processes of writing, meditating, and discussing over the finished product of the book, to which all three of her works attest. The *Sonets, prières et devises* of 1562 functioned less as a published book than as a pamphlet, stirring up discussion in Catholic and Protestant circles both before and after its publication. The *Divines poésies* was intended as a practical moral and spiritual companion for the princess Marguerite. In all likelihood, Marquets's liturgical poems of the *Sonets spirituels* were circulated in the convent and read to commemorate various holidays and to complement the meditations of her fellow nuns.

The importance of process can perhaps best be seen in Marquets's sonnets when they are juxtaposed with Antoine Favre's *Entretiens spirituels*, particularly since initially the collections appear quite similar. Favre's sonnet cycle, organized according to the three themes of divine love, the sacraments, and the holy rosary,[36] recounts in the last section a poetic narrative of Jesus's life from the Nativity to the Crucifixion. Marquets's sonnet cycle, while also addressing events of the Christian story, does not easily lend itself to closure. Celebrating the different Catholic festivals, the book at its conclusion implicitly invites readers to return to the beginning and start the cycle again. Much like the continuity inscribed in the Christian seasons themselves (Advent leads to Christ's birth, Christmas leads to Epiphany; even Easter, which a priori might bring a kind of conclusion to the Gospel story, is followed by Ascension, and so on), so each set of poems forms a link in the liturgical chain.

Just as Anne de Marquets displaces the male perspective in her text by privileging Mary, then, so she effectuates a shift in emphasis from the potentially closural, published text (temporally fixed) to the work-in-action (emphasizing the present)—be it the fomenter of debate, the literary gift functioning as a moral lesson, or the liturgical sonnet cycle. In all cases, the formal presentation of Anne de Marquets's works resists teleological closure in favor of open-endedness, and in all cases the works constitute an endorsement of the active use of the written word in the present.

The poet enacts a final displacement in her texts as she renders biblical passages not only more feminine but also more concrete, which again privileges the present. Anne de Marquets depicts Advent, for example, from the pregnant Mary's perspective as she walks through fields, inviting readers similarly to hold Jesus if not in their wombs, then in their hearts:

> La Royne des vertus, la princesse des cieux
> Humble va ce jourd'huy visiter sa cousine,
> Tous les monts et les champs par où elle chemine
> Produisent fleurs et fruicts et baumes precieux.
> Elle porte en son flanc le souverain des Dieux,
> . . . .
> Et ce divin fardeau la soulage et soustien:
> Car toujours ce bon Dieu fortifie et conforte,
> Et donne ayde et faveur à quiconque le porte.
> Heureux est donc celuy qui au coeur le retient.
>
> (*Sonets spirituels,* 188; 308)

[The Queen of virtues, the Princess of Heaven, / Will go humbly to visit her cousin today. / All the mountains and fields by which she walks / Produce flowers and fruits and precious balms. / She carries in her womb the sovereign God / . . . / And this divine burden relieves and sustains her, / For our good God always strengthens and comforts, / And gives succor and favor to her who bears him. / Blessed are those who keep him in their hearts.]

The poet also invites readers to share Mary's dignity by suckling the baby Jesus. Given these references to the female body, as in the preceding example, one would expect the poet to address an audience consisting exclusively of women, yet the following sonnet challenges such an assumption:

> Qu'heureuse est celle-là qui a vierge enfanté
> Le hault Dieu, le grand Roy, le Redempteur du monde;
> Et qui soigneuse l'a de son laict pur et monde,
> Comme son cher enfant, doucement allaicté!
>   Las! nous pouvons avoir part en sa dignité,
> Si continence en nous et foy sincere abonde,
> Et si par charité nostre ame estant feconde,
> Nous observons de Dieu la saincte volonté.
>   Car qui fait (disoit Christ) le vouloir de mon Pere,
> Cestuy-là est ma soeur, et ma mere et mon frere;
> La parenté charnelle est moins que celle-ci.
>   Soyons-luy donc ainsi mere spirituelle,
> Et l'allaictons souvent d'une double mammelle;
> C'est de l'amour de Dieu, et du prochain aussi.
>   (*Sonets spirituels,* 17; 107–8)

[Happy is she who as a virgin gave birth / To the exalted God, the great King, the Redeemer of the world / And who gives to him her milk, pure and pristine, / Like her sweetly suckled infant. // Ah! we can share in her dignity, / If in us we are filled with sobriety and sincere faith. / And if, our souls fecund with charity, / We observe the holy will of God. // For whoever does my Father's will, said Christ, / Is my sister, my mother and my brother. Relation of the flesh is less than this. // Thus let us be spiritual mothers, / And suckle Him often from both breasts, / Loving God and our neighbor as well.]

    The figuring of "frere" in the first tercet of the sonnet serves to broaden the intended readership and suggests that men, too, should imagine their relationship to Jesus and others through the vehicle of the female body. Caroline Walker Bynum notes the enthusiasm in the medieval period for the body as a means of religious access, particularly in female piety.[37] In Anne de Marquets's sonnets, the image of suckling the baby both physicalizes and feminizes the notion that by loving God and one's neighbor one can nourish Jesus, a lesson that appears more figuratively in the Gospel of Matthew: "insofar as ye have done it unto one of the least of these my brethren, ye have done it unto me" (Matt. 25:40). The best-known parable illustrating this principle, that of the Good Samaritan (Luke 10:29–37), has an exclusively male cast. Anne's invitation to all readers to become spiritual mothers and mimetically to assume Mary's role as suckler of Jesus, in contrast, frames the biblical injunction in terms of a privileged female (maternal) stance.

    Evoking the pathos of the relationship between mother and son at the Crucifixion had become a devotional commonplace at the end of the sixteenth century, as Terence Cave has noted.[38] In Renaissance religious verse, the reader is repeatedly invited to suffer along with Jesus during the Passion. While Mary's suffering is sometimes evoked as well, Anne de Marquets privileges this scene in concrete terms. Antoine Favre, for example, in his portrayal of the Crucifixion, rhetorically removes Mary from the painful scene:

> Ah! Vierge cache toy, retire toy de grace,
> Pour ne voir tant de maux que souffre ton cher fils. . . .[39]

[Ah! Virgin, hide, withdraw, I beg you, / So that you will not see the suffering of your dear son. . . .]

Anne de Marquets, on the other hand, places the reader in Mary's body at the very moment that she observes the spectacle of her son on the cross:

> Quel glaive de douleur transperça la saincte ame
> De la Vierge sacrée, alors qu'elle apperceut
> Que son cher et seul Fils, que Vierge elle conceut,
> Enduroit une mort si cruelle et infame?
> Voire et qu'on luy disoit mainte injure et diffame;
> Ce que sans grand' angoisse ouyr elle ne sceut:
> Et quand pour le Seigneur le serf elle receut,
> Lors qu'il dict de sainct Jean, voila ton fils, ô femme.
> Qu'elle luy eust donné volontiers la mamelle,
> Quand il crioit, j'ay soif, alteré du tourment:
> Elle eust peu dire alors, j'ay une angoisse telle,
> Que celle d'une femme en son accouchement:
> Car helas! j'oy et voy des choses si funebres,
> Que j'ay le cœur en pouldre, et les yeux en tenebres.
> *(Sonets spirituels,* 299; 320–21)

[What painful sword pierced the holy soul / Of the sacred Virgin, when she saw / That her dear and only Son, whom as a Virgin she conceived, / Was suffering such a cruel and infamous death? // Truly, they were insulting and disparaging him, / Which she could not hear without great anguish / And when she received a servant for the Lord, / As he said of St. John, "Here is your son, oh woman." // She would have gladly suckled him at her breast, / When he cried, "I'm thirsty," beside himself with torment. / She could then say, I feel the same anguish // As a woman in labor / For alas! I hear and see such deadly things / That my heart is in dust, my eyes in shadow.]

The reader's perspective of the Crucifixion seen through the mother's eyes, combined with evocations of such physical sensations as the anguish of childbirth, heighten both the physical and the psychological realism of the sonnet. Anne de Marquets reminds us of Mary's original role in giving birth and at the same time links her to a type of suffering many members of her audience would know. Further, the poet's naming the body parts "mamelle," "cœur en pouldre," and "yeux en tenebres" serves to enact Mary's suffering in its physical (and female) specificity.

Just as Marquets grounds the concept of suffering in the human body by placing the reader in Mary's body, so she renders concrete the more intangible construct of time. Time and space seem to exist symbiotically within Anne de Marquets's poetic system. The poet in fact replaces the word *temps* by *espace*.[40]

> Elle a porté par longue espace
> Dedans son ventre precieux
> Celluy qui la terre compasse,
> Qui tourne et gouverne les cieux.
> *(Divines poésies,* 42)

[She bore for a long time [space] / In her precious womb / Him who turns the earth / Who moves and governs the skies.]

In this passage Mary's consecration of time serves as the necessary condition for the Christ child's coming. But whereas Jesus is timeless as he encompasses and rules over the earth, Mary's role as "vessel" or incubator is firmly situated within finite, earthly time.

Not only does Mary's consecration of human time lead to the delivery of God's greatest gift, but Mary's use of time is also advanced as a model for humanity as her actions affect the here and now. Set against God's immutability and Jesus's immortality, Mary's temporal accessibility becomes even more apparent. Within the context of a list of Mary's admirable activities, the poet portrays Mary as mirror and example for humanity:

> Elle jeusne, elle veille, elle prie et contemple,
> La parolle de Dieu sans cesse elle rumine,
> Bien qu'en terre elle soit son coeur au ciel chemine,
> Et sa vie à tous sert de miroir et d'exemple.
> *(Sonets spirituels,* 178; 295-96)

[She fasts, watches, prays, and contemplates / God's word, ceaselessly pondering, / Although she is on earth, her heart reaches for heaven, / And her life serves as a mirror and example to all.]

Mary's power in this passage derives from her dedication of human time ("bien qu'en terre elle soit") as a link to the divine ("son coeur au ciel chemine"). As both a mirror (reflecting the reader's own human qualities) and a model (elevated, but not unattainably so), Mary's actions rhetorically supersede all others.[41] Here, as elsewhere in Anne de Marquets's works, the virgin mother is depicted as acting in the present. Mary is not, of course, the only character in the *Sonets spirituels* for whom this is the case. Indeed, the present tense governs most of the sonnets, largely because of the liturgical nature of the sonnet cycle.[42] But Anne de Marquets's particular insistence on Mary—both as exemplary (as a model for human use of time) and as comparable to the poet herself—distinguishes her poetry from that of other contemporaries. Metaphorically represented throughout Anne de Marquets's texts as a fountain offering the water of life, a fruit-bearing tree healing humanity, and a burning bush announcing God's mercy, Mary's consecration of human time is accorded a kind of materiality throughout the collections.

Anne de Marquets's concrete depictions of temporality appear even more striking when her poems following the *Divines poésies* are set against Flaminio's treatment of the same subject, their future beatitude in heaven. Flaminio's vision includes a disembodied soul:

> Finalement, o Dieu, je te supplie
> Que ta bonté de ce corps me deslie,
> Et que mon ame en pure integrité
> Regnant aux cieux par immortalité,
> Incessamment te confesse et te louë,
> Pareillement qu'elle adore et advoue
> Le pere sainct, et l'eternel esprit.
>
> (*Divines poésies*, 17)

[Last, O God, I beseech you / That your goodness release me from this body / And that my soul, in pure wholeness, / Reign in Heaven in immortality / Ceaselessly confessing and praising you, / While it adores and proclaims / The holy father and the eternal spirit.]

Marquets's depiction, in contrast, is more corporeal:

> Qui me don^roit [*sic*] des aisles pour voler
> Plus vistement que tout oiseau de proie,
> Afin que j'aille au lieu d'heur et de joye
> Mon doux espoux sainctement accoler?

> M'a il pas faict en son livre enroller,
> A ce qu'au ciel avecques luy je soie,
> Et que sans fin je le contemple et voie?
>
> (*Divines poésies*, 78)

[Who would give me wings to fly / More quickly than a bird of prey / So that I might go to the place of fortune and joy / And reverently embrace my sweet husband? // Didn't he inscribe my name in his book / So that I could be in Heaven with him / And without ceasing behold and contemplate him?]

Both poems evoke the endless association in heaven between the speaker (or the speaker's soul) and God. The "incessamment . . . loué" in Flaminio corresponds to "sans fin je le contemple" in Marquets. But while Flaminio's speaker begs to be delivered from his body, leaving his soul in "pure integrity," Marquets's poet imagines herself with wings, flying faster than a rapacious bird to embrace her husband (God). The verb *accoler* (*col* = *cou* [neck]) projects the image of the woman throwing her arms (or wings!) around the husband's neck as they embrace. The representation of heaven's roll book bearing the poet's name adds further materiality to the description of eternal life. Thus, while Flaminio's heaven remains ethereal and disembodied in the implied future, Marquets's future paradise appears more immediate and present by the physical references to flying, embracing, wings, the neck, and the book.

A final comparison between Flaminio and Marquets reveals the nun's vision of plenitude in the present moment. A commonplace in devotional poetry, the "illness poem" constitutes a meditation prompted by physical suffering or discomfort. In both texts, the poets are awakened in the night and contemplate God's perfection in contrast to their weakened state. The final strophes of Flaminio's long poem and Marquets's sonnet illustrate significant differences in two poets' emphases. Flaminio writes:

> *Pour invoquer Dieu en longue et griefve maladie*
> . . . .
> Le bon Jesus tresaimable et doux
> Qui a souffert si cruels maux pour nous,
> Est tousjours prompt à donner allegeance
> A ceux qui sont en misere et souffrance:
> Repoulse donc, o mon ame, de toy
> Crainte et angoisse, et t'asseure par foy
> Invoquant l'aide et le nom favorable
> De ton seigneur et prince desirable

> Car de tous ceux qui s'addressent à luy
> Il est la tour de deffence et l'appuy.
>
> (*Divines poésies*, 15)

[*Calling upon God during a long and serious illness* / . . . / Good Jesus, beloved and sweet / Who suffered such cruel afflictions for us, / Is always quick to soothe / Those who are in misery and suffering / Take away, o my soul, / Fear and anguish, and be assured by faith, / Invoking succor and the auspicious name / Of your Lord and felicitous prince / Because for those who come to him, / He is the tower of defense and support.]

Marquets addresses the same subject:

> *Estant malade et ne pouvant dormir*
> Puis que du corps le repos m'est osté
> Ayant perdu ma santé tant aimable,
> Fay que je soye, ô seigneur pitoyable,
> Recompensée en un autre costé:
>   C'est que l'esprit contemple ta beauté,
> Ton excellence et pouvoir admirable:
> Et que mon coeur en plaisir incroyable
> Puisse gouster ta douceur et bonté.
>   Lors je seray si contente et ravie,
> Que plus n'auray de reposer envie,
> Encore moins de vivre longuement:
>   Car ayant beu de ceste source vive,
> Et contemplé ceste beauté nayve,
> Je ne vouldray autre contentement.
>
> (*Divines poésies*, 63–64)

[*Being ill and unable to sleep* / Because rest is taken away from my body / Having lost my beloved health, / O merciful Lord, let me be / Rewarded in another way. // Let my spirit contemplate your beauty, / Your excellence and admirable power: / And may my heart in unfathomable pleasure / Taste of your sweetness and goodness. // Then shall I be so contented and ravished / That I will no longer want to rest / And even less to live long. // For having drunk of this living source, / And contemplated this natural beauty, / I will desire no other contentment.]

Both poets invoke God's succor, and in both poems the speaker identifies the divine comfort that will be sent, which, however, does not arrive within the space of either poem. But whereas Flaminio, using the martial metaphor of the tower, emphasizes God's defense and the support that will aid the suffering poet, Marquets imagines instead substituting a new state of pleasure and contentment. The remarkably sensual description of tasting sweetness, drinking from the fountain, and gazing upon natural beauty belies by its virtual reality (so to speak) the three future verbs in the sonnet. This poem crystallizes both Marquets's tendency to render abstractions concrete and her depiction of plenitude in the present (or in this case, a time that is made to resemble the present).

Anne de Marquets thus presents temporality, often through the optic of Mary, as immediate and tangible. I am not suggesting that Anne de Marquets is the only poet to concretize religious experience, or that only women poets engage in this practice. It is my intention, rather, to show in Anne de Marquets's works the convergence of factors, both rhetorical and formal, that reveal a marked privileging of a recurring present—a time made palpable in her texts most notably by the repeated mothering of Mary (who mothered Jesus and continues to nurture humanity). This recurrence escapes stasis because each repetition, much like liturgical or ritualistic activity, brings a sense of renewal and re-creation.

Ultimately, then, Marquets's writings, while not entirely breaking out of the "enclosure" of their author's monastically defined literary space, do nonetheless effectuate some significant apertures. A lack of closure, often figured in circles and cycles, characterizes the poet's choice of genre and the nature of the collections themselves. Marquets's prizing of Mary beyond the call of Catholic duty and her obvious identification with Mary's actions (described in the present) contribute to an insistence not only on the feminine but also on the human aspects of religious experience in her texts. Further, by emphasizing the present, Marquets's experimentation with the work-in-progress implicitly contradicts the humanist aspiration to poetic immortality. As we have seen, in Marquets's work, feminist challenges remain relatively discrete and attenuated. Nicole Liébaut Estienne's *Les misères de la femme mariée*, on the other hand, directly confronts the entire institution of marriage and its usurping of women's time and lives.

NICOLE ESTIENNE: TELLING STORIES, TELLING TIME

Mariages qui se font par amourettes finissent par noisettes.

[Marriages made by dalliance end up in quarrels.]
—Brantôme

In a letter written circa 1373, Petrarch articulates the hierarchy between intellectual offspring and physical offspring, which to his mind is indistinguishable from the hierarchy between men and women:

> We shall extend our name into the future, God willing, by intellect not marriage, with the aid of books not children and through virtue not wives. You will not have a bright and long-lasting name unless you get it for yourself. This is the work of manhood, not women. How much fame would Plato and Aristotle, Homer and Virgil have today if they had thought to possess it through matrimony and offspring?[43]

This passage tellingly reveals an intellectual bias against women in general and against marriage in particular that extends both geographically and temporally beyond fourteenth-century Italy into much of early modern humanist discourse. A corollary to Aristotle's notion that women furnish the matter of children and men provide the "motive principle,"[44] Petrarch's aspiration, unquestionably assumed to be identical to that of his reader, is *fama* or poetic immortality for the male writer rather than biological progeny. The four binary oppositions involving the institution of marriage in Petrarch's letter all portray marriage (and women) as anathema to the serious work of writing for posterity. The antitheses intellect/marriage, books/children, virtue/wives, and fame/matrimony (and offspring) dominate the passage, illustrating the deleterious effect of women on literary endeavors. For Petrarch, the most beautiful children are metaphorical: the perfect reproduction can only be found in literary imitation, which should resemble the original work as a son resembles his father: "[S]eeing the son's face, we are reminded of the father's, although if it came to measurement, the features would all be different, but there is something subtle that creates this effect."[45] In Petrarch's autochthonous fantasy, fathers give birth to (literary) sons without the participation of mothers, which is of course similar to the ideal of a humanist education.

Unlike Petrarch and his humanist descendants, who denigrate marriage in theory because it usurps time that could be consecrated to higher pursuits, Nicole Liébaut Estienne assails marriage in practice, as observed and experienced by a Parisian wife in the second half of the sixteenth century. Her collection of thirty-five stanzas entitled *Les Misères de la femme mariée, où se peuvent voir les peines et tourmens qu'elle reçoit durant sa vie* [Adversities of the married woman, where the suffering and torment she undergoes in her lifetime can be seen] was not the first to critique the wife's position in marriage, but it is the work devoted the most exclusively to challenging marriage from the woman's point of view in sixteenth-century France.[46] Hélisenne de Crenne, in her invective letters published in Paris in 1560, had also protested against women's plight in marriage, in the context of the ills men inflict upon women. Her references to the "superabondance de mes cruelz travaulx"[47] [superabundance of my cruel labor] and other marital woes appear within the context of a multifaceted and voluminous work, however, and therefore lack the singleness of purpose discernible in Estienne's collection.

Before examining *Les Misères de la Femme mariée*, it will be useful to situate these poems within the context of marriage as it was imagined and practiced in the sixteenth century. Contemporary conduct manuals give us some indication of opinions on the raison d'être of marriage as well as the recommended roles for wife and husband, although, as Heather Dubrow points out, the extent to which readers were influenced by these pronouncements on marriage is not entirely clear.[48] Still, among the somewhat heterogeneous discourses, discernible patterns emerge. Vives summarizes the purpose of marriage succinctly in a chapter of the *Institution chrétienne* on the origin and utility of marriage.[49] Unlike Petrarch, Vives sees women as beneficial to men's daily lives. If it weren't for the institution of marriage (and the responsibilities women assume therein), who would take care of worldly concerns?

> Qui soustien droit telz labeurs, et anxietez journellement advenans? coucher, lever, garder et alimenter enfans . . . ? de quel vouloir ilz seront, si n'estoit ce sacrement de mariage?[50]

> [Who would undertake these tasks and daily cares? Awakening, keeping, feeding, and tucking in the children . . . ? What kind of disposition would [the children] have, if it weren't for the sacrament of marriage?]

Similarly, in 1523 Pierre Lesnauderie notes as a principal argument in favor of marriage that the man will be able to accomplish much more if he has a wife to assume the mundane responsibilities of daily life:

> Item quant vous aurez femme vous pourrez seurement aller dehors a voz affaires et laisser vostre maison: car elle y prendra bien garde.[51]

> [When you have a wife, you can safely tend to your affairs and leave your house: for she will take good care of it.]

Other contemporary moralists echo Vives's insistence on the myriad duties the wife must accomplish. According to Pierre Charron in *De la sagesse*, in addition to maintaining the household and caring for the children, the wife should wash her husband's feet.[52] Readers of these treatises cannot fail to notice the sheer volume of married women's responsibilities, often described in terms of repetitive tasks to be accomplished.

Thus women's work, which includes the day-to-day negotiation of family life, is seen as rooted in the terrestrial passage of time as distinguished from the male humanist's calling, which involves creating timeless works. In the public imagination, the wife is associated with what might be called the worldly time span or *durée* not only because of her ability to bear children but also because she serves as the manager of family life, as Billon articulates in *Le Fort inexpugnable de l'honneur du sexe feminin:*

> Consideré, en premier lieu, que sans la Femme aucune maison et chose domestique ne peult avoir durée, veu qu'a faute d'elle, ne s'étend progenie . . . et aucun nom de famille ou Pere de famille ne sauroit estre attribué à l'homme, qui (sans elle) outreplus, ne peult former l'ordre requis de ménage. . . ."53
>
> [Considering that, in the first place, without the woman no household and domestic entity could last, given that without her, there would be no progeny . . . and no family name or father would be attributed to man, who furthermore (without her) could not manage the household. . . .]

In addition to the considerable labor expected of married women, the young age of brides, particularly in comparison to the age of their husbands, served to exacerbate the imbalance of power between marital partners, as we saw in the introductory chapter. The difference in age between spouses was both observed in practice and recommended in theory. Louise de Savoie, for example, was married at age twelve to the count of Angoulême, who was "proche de la trentaine" [close to thirty] at the time of their union; and similarly, her granddaughter Jeanne was twelve when she married the duc de Clèves.54 The youngest wives were among the court nobility, but in other social classes, the disparity between women's and men's ages at marriage existed as well. Barbara Diefendorf shows that among the children of city councillors in sixteenth-century Paris, the median marriage age for women was nineteen and for men almost twenty-eight.55 Parents apparently condoned this system because it allowed sons to be more self-sufficient while protecting daughters' chastity and desirability.

The authority of the husband over the wife was thus assured by the difference in age and experience between newlyweds as well as through the juridical status of the wife as "L'Éternelle mineure."56 While the son of an affluent family typically spent his twenties in sexual adventures, completing his education and beginning a career, his young wife came into marriage directly from a protective family whose role had been specifically to shield her from those same worldly experiences.57 This practice of coupling an older man with an inexperienced young woman, presumably designed to ensure wives' docility, of course gave rise to negative social consequences as well, as Nicole Liébaut Estienne details in her *Misères de la femme mariée*.

While the stanzas of *Misères de la femme mariée* doubtless do not describe the lives of all married women in sixteenth-century France, the publication of a second edition of the text suggests that considerable numbers of contemporary readers found at least some resonance in it.[58] It is well documented that husbands were often assumed to have power of correction over their wives and sometimes resorted to beating them.[59] Moderate beatings appear to have been legally condoned, but wives' retributive actions were nonetheless on the rise. Natalie Zemon Davis cites several cases of wives who retaliated with violence, including Marguerite Vallée, who in October 1536 picked up the ax that her husband had hurled at her and proceeded to give him two or three deadly blows. Similarly, in May, 1540, as Bonne Goberde was slaughtering chickens for dinner, her husband attacked her and during the beating "rencontra ledit cousteau" [met the knife]. Both women were granted a royal pardon by François I, who declared that they had acted in self-defense.[60]

Nicole Estienne, though apparently not as mistreated as Vallée and Goberde, seems to have undergone hardship in her own marriage. Few biographical details have survived, but her existence was not as privileged as one might expect, given her origin. In terms of public history, her life appears to have been largely influenced by three men: her father, her presumed fiancé, and her husband. The daughter of printer Charles Estienne, third son of printing genius Henri (I), Nicole was born into one of the most influential printing families in early modern Europe. As Evelyne Berriot-Salvadore notes, printing, the symbiosis of art and sciences, is the very symbol of the Renaissance,[61] and this was the milieu of Nicole's childhood. But while Nicole's father's history began rosily, it had a less-than-happy end. Because of his superb knowledge of Latin and Greek, he was chosen to be the preceptor of Jean-Antoine de Baïf.[62] Charles later published over one hundred volumes, including scientific treatises on diverse subjects from anatomy to botany to geography, and he collaborated in the encyclopedic *Dictionnaire historique et poétique des nations, hommes, lieux, fleuves, montagnes,* which he published in 1553. He also wrote and published in 1553 the clever imitation of Ortensio Lando's *Paradossi, Paradoxes ou propos contre la commune opinion*. Despite this modest success in publishing, financial failures and a number of poor business decisions led to his imprisonment for debt in 1561 in the Châtelet, and he died there in 1564. Neither contemporaries nor later biographers depict Charles Estienne in hagiographic terms. Michaud cites a letter to Scaliger from Jean Maumont, who describes Charles as "un homme avare et emporté, jaloux de ses confrères et même de ses neveux, qu'il cherchait à desservir dans toutes les occasions" [an avaricious and moody man, jealous of his colleagues and even his nephews, whom he sought to harm at every turn].[63]

The poet Jacques Grévin, the second important masculine figure in Nicole Estienne's development, published his *Olimpe* in 1560. Nicole's identity as the eponymous heroine is corroborated within Grévin's own work by the anagram "SIEN EN ELECTION" [hers by choice],[64] and was noted by both La Croix du Maine and Colletet. In *Olimpe*, Grévin addresses his amorous declarations and *blasons* to Nicole, who was about seventeen at the time of the work's publication.[65] The presumed engagement of Nicole and Grévin was broken and hypotheses for this rupture are numerous, ranging from the religious to the financial. Lavaud conjectures that Grévin's conversion to Protestantism may have dissuaded Estienne, who seems to have remained a faithful Catholic.[66] Alternatively, Grévin could have renounced the marriage because the financial situation of Charles Estienne was so unfavorable. Whatever the reasons may have been, Nicole Estienne and Jacques Grévin went their separate ways. Because of his strident Huguenot apologies, Grévin was forced to leave France and was eventually offered protection by Marguerite de France in Turino. Grévin acquired the title of "médecin ordinaire" [personal physician] to the princess and became so close to her that when he died at age thirty-two Marguerite assumed responsibility for his young wife and child.[67] At the time of Grévin's death in 1570, Estienne had already been married to Jean Liébaut for a number of years.

Nicole's husband Jean Liébaut (sometimes spelled Liébault) appears to have had at least as troubled a history as that of her father, a fact that would no doubt be revelatory to pursue in psychoanalytic terms. From the frying pan to the fire, Nicole was associated with two brilliant humanists who accumulated tremendous debts and died destitute.[68] A regent of the Faculté de Médecine of Paris, Jean Liébaut worked with Charles Estienne and published several works with him including a book of Hippocratic aphorisms and an augmented version of Estienne's own *Agriculture et maison rustique*. Given what appears to be Liébaut's antifeminist stance, it might first seem anomalous that he published a book on women's health—*De sanitate, foecunditate et morbis mulierum* (1582)—which met with some success, as evidenced by a French translation published the same year. But his statement cited by Lavaud reveals his belief that women are feeble creatures and are therefore in greater need of health care than men: "[L]a femme n'est animant mutile ny imparfaict, mais foible et maladif"[69] [{W}oman isn't a defective or imperfect being, just weak and sickly]. Despite his relative success in publishing and as a doctor (having been the personal physician of Catherine de Navarre, Henri IV's sister), his father-in-law's financial misfortunes befell him as well.[70] Michaud succinctly describes Liébault's grim death:

> [I]l passa sa vie dans un état voisin de l'indigence et mourut le 21 juin 1596, à Paris, sur une pierre où il avait été contraint de s'asseoir dans la rue Gervais-Laurent.[71]

> [{H}e spent his life in a state of near indigence and died on 21 June 1596 in Paris, on a stone where he had been forced to sit in Gervais-Laurent Street.]

Nicole Estienne's *Les Misères de la femme mariée* appears to be inspired by her own marriage to Jean Liébault, although as we will see, it extends beyond the boundaries of an autobiographical collection in a number of ways. It was published by Pierre Mesnier in Paris, probably around 1587. Though the booklet is undated, Renouard notes that 1587 was the earliest possible date of publication, since Mesnier moved to a new porte Saint-Victor address that year.[72]

Les Misères de la femme mariée has received mostly favorable, though somewhat mixed, critical reviews both by Nicole Estienne's contemporaries and by twentieth-century readers. Lavaud unconvincingly conjectures that Estienne wrote poetry to atone for her lack of physical beauty:

> Assez peu jolie (un crayon conservé à la Bibliothèque nationale nous le prouve, et elle l'avoue elle-même dans ses vers), Nicole Estienne comptait peut-être sur son talent poétique pour remédier aux imperfections de son visage et pour assurer à son nom une réputation qui le fît passer à la postérité.[73]

> [Rather homely (a charcoal drawing at the National Library proves it to us, and she admits it herself in her verses), Nicole Estienne was perhaps counting on her poetic talent to remedy the imperfections of her face and to ensure that the reputation of her name would survive into posterity].[74]

This interesting reaction could be a defensive response on the part of Lavaud: the beautiful woman is the object of poetry, whereas the homely one is the subject who writes it. But beyond that, it is true that Estienne rejects flattering Petrarchan descriptions of herself, as evidenced in a response to poems on her signature anagram "J'estonne le ciel" [I astound heaven]: ". . . vous avez erré, me faisant si parfaicte; / Pour chanter mes beautés ne faut point de trompette. / Le Ciel m'a départi ses faveurs chichement"[75] [. . . you have erred, in making me so perfect, / No fanfare is necessary to sing my beauties. / When it came to me, Providence was abstemious with its favors]. Ostensibly, then, Estienne is simply articulating modesty about her appearance. But in the second "Reponce par Madame Liebaut" in the manuscript, Estienne reveals why physical beauty should be of little consequence:

> Bien que le nom s'accorde à la chose nommée,
> Comme on peut remarquer et veoir assez souvent,
> Ce n'est pas toutesfois ung si fort argument:
> La vertu seulle rend la personne estimée.
>   Si j'estonne le ciel, ne faictes jugement
> Que je suys de beauté divinement douee,
> Ou que toute vertu s'est en moy retirée,
> Ou que j'ay le bien dire à mon commandement.
>   Ce n'est point qu'à Pallas en faveur je ressamble,
> Ce n'est poinct que les Dieulx en moy mirent ensamble
> Tout ce qu'ils réservoient de rare et plus prisé;
>   Mais c'est tant seullement par une patience
> Qui me rend comme ung roch, lequel faict resistance
> A la rigueur des flotz et jamais n'est brisé.[76]

[Although the name goes with the mentioned object / As you can see fairly frequently, / Still, it isn't a strong argument: / Only virtue makes a person worthy. // If I astonish heaven, do not judge / That I am gifted with divine beauty, / Or that all virtue is lodged in me / Or that I have all eloquence at my disposal. // It is not that I resemble Pallas / Or that the gods saw in me / All the rarest and most worthy qualities // But rather by patience / Which makes me like a rock, resisting / The strengths of the waves, never breaking.]

Since for Estienne virtue, strength, and patience—not beauty—determine a person's worth, the physical beauty both created and sung by the Petrarchan poets loses its commanding presence in her work. This is not to say, of course, that other commentators ignored Estienne's attractiveness and its alleged effects. After this poem in the manuscript, written in a different pen and different script, the following comment appears: "[I]l est de l'histoire qu'apres tant de discours faits sur la rencontre de cest Anagramme que quelque medisant luy demanda si cest anagramme ne vouloit point parler du ciel de son lict"[77] [{O}ne story tells that after so much commentary on this anagram, some slanderer asked her if the anagram wasn't referring to the canopy {pun on "ciel"} of her bed].

Although Lavaud gets sidetracked by the question of Estienne's beauty, he nonetheless acknowledges the writer's real talent despite her small corpus: "[S]on oeuvre est mince; du moins n'en subsiste-t-il presque rien, assez toutefois pour nous faire entrevoir une figure curieuse et un talent indiscutable"[78] [{H}er work is slim; at least almost nothing has survived, but enough nonetheless to allow us to see a curious figure of undeniable talent]. Du Verdier, in the *Bibliographie française* of 1772, praises Estienne's "grâce de bien dire" [gift of eloquence].

Estienne's contemporaries and late-twentieth-century readers have in common the interpretation of *Les Misères* as an intensely personal work in which the poet bemoans her own unfortunate marriage. In the Pléiade edition of the *Poètes du seizième siècle*, for example, Albert-Marie Schmidt attributes Nicole Estienne's dissatisfaction in marriage to her regret at not having chosen the poet Jacques Grévin, who had been her fiancé:

> [E]lle finit par préférer [à Grévin] le médecin dijonnais Jean Liébaut. D'ailleurs, juste vengence des Muses outrées, elle regrette toute sa vie son choix imprudent et se distingue par la rancune qu'elle nourrit contre les obligations matrimoniales, ainsi qu'en témoignent les stances vives et sarcastiques qu'elle intitule: *Les Misères de la Femme mariée*.[79]

> [{S}he ends up choosing the Dijonnais doctor Jean Liébaut over Grévin. Furthermore, as sweet revenge for the outraged Muses, she regrets her unwise choice all her life and distinguishes herself by the spite that she harbors against marital obligations, to which the lively and sarcastic stanzas of *Les Misères de la Femme mariée* attest.]

To my mind, there are two dangerous repercussions to Schmidt's conclusion. First, there is nothing in Estienne's own text or contemporary sources indicating that she regrets not marrying Grévin. Certainly, her stanzas imply dissatisfaction and disillusionment in her own marriage, since grammatically and logically the numerous references to "nous" and "la femme" include the poet herself. But nowhere in the stanzas does the poet express the idea that all would be different had she married another man. Second, because her grievances are registered not against an individual but against a group of tyrannical husbands, her avowed mission extends beyond the personal and into the social, political arena. To put it another way, if these verses could be represented in twentieth-century legal terms, Estienne would not be simply filing for divorce but rather launching a class-action suit. The conclusion that Estienne's work is simply the product of her remorse over having chosen the wrong man denies the very real cultural and social importance of the collection.

In her introduction to the stanzas reproduced in *Misères et grandeur de la femme au XVIe siècle*, Ilana Zinguer acknowledges the social potential of Estienne's work, but she regrets that the poet does not propose concrete suggestions for women to reject their servile condition and adopt a plan for women's education: "Elle s'est tournée vers les muses, que leur demande-t-elle? d'être écoutée, d'être plainte! Elle aurait pu profiter de cette fiction et s'en servir pour émettre des voeux même cocasses, utopiques, audacieux"[80] [She turned to the muses, and what does she ask them? To be heard, to be pitied! She could have benefited from this fiction and used it to express even amusing, utopian, audacious wishes.]

One could indeed read Estienne's project according to a late-twentieth-century feminist vision, or, alternatively, one could consider Estienne's feminism on its own terms, that is, within the context of the accepted sixteenth-century dogma on marriage cited above. Seen in this light, Estienne's device of imploring the Muses (and by extension, her readers) to listen to her complaints constitutes an important step in making women's voices heard on this heretofore male-dominated subject. The first stanza immediately brings readers into the writer's explicit intention, namely, to describe the horrors of marriage as she has known it:

> Muses qui chastement passez vostre bel aage,
> Sans vous assujettir aux lois de Mariage,
> Sachant combien la femme y endure de mal
> Favorisez moy tant que je puisse descrire,
> Les travaux continus, et le cruel martyre,
> Qui sans fin nous tallonne en ce joug nuptial.[81]

[Muses who are chastely enjoying the prime of life / Without being subjected to marital laws, / Knowing how much woman endures adversity, / Honor me by allowing me to describe / The continuous labor and cruel martyrdom / That ceaselessly spurs us in this marital yoke.]

Here Estienne calls on the Muses for guidance, as does Ronsard, but rather than seeking transcendence of the human condition through poetic immortality, she proposes solely to describe the married woman's life.

In addition to alerting readers to the writer's project, stanza 1 announces the principal leitmotifs that recur throughout the stanzas: enclosure and domination ("assujettir," "cruel martyre," "joug nuptial"; "chastement" underscores a quality attributed to the Muses that is denied the poet), continuity and repetition ("endure," "sans fin," "travaux continus") and women's time—bodily time ("vostre bel aage"), time as it is perceived by wives, and the collapse of time as the promise of the future becomes the deception of the present (both iterated in expressions of continuity and circularity).

The introductory stanza sets the collection against a temporal backdrop: the Muses, expressly established as living in the prime of life unattached by constraining bonds, contrast with the timelessness of the "travaux continus" and the endless martyrdom of the married narrator. Stanza 2 similarly posits the wife's repeated suffering against the temporal measurement of the sun's passage:

> Du Soleil tout-voyant, la lampe journalière
> Ne scaurait remarquer en faisant sa carrière
> Rien de plus miserable, et de plus tourmenté,
> Que la femme subjette à ces hommes iniques,
> Qui despourvueuz d'amour, par leurs loix tiraniques
> Se font maistres du corps, et de la volonté.
> (*Les Misères,* a4r; 32)

[The all-seeing sun, daily light / In crossing the sky could observe nothing more tormented, / Than the woman subjected to these wicked men, / Who, depraved of love, by their tyrannical laws / Make themselves masters of our bodies and our wills.]

The terms "journalière" and "carrière" rehearse the movement of the sun's repeated journey, which in turn insists upon the speaker's misery and torment observed by the sun during its daily course. The use of the singular "la femme" as distinguished from the plural "hommes iniques" and "maistres" has the effect of focusing on the isolated woman/wife, who, having been deprived of her own subjectivity by the loss of both body and will, no longer has an identity separable from "femme." By this Estienne suggests the universality of the wife's isolation and subjection—in short, her essentialization—as observed by the cyclic movement of the sun.

A host of other stanzas review the continuity and circularity of the married woman's existence as well. The verb "endurer" recurs throughout the collection, and such terms as "immortelle gesne" (*Les Misères,* b1r; 34) [immortal torture], "à jamais en peine et en misère" (b1r; 34) [always in pain and misery], "à tout jamais ensemble" (b1v; 35) [forever together] establish the repetitive nature of time in the married woman's existence. Interestingly, much of Estienne's language is reminiscent of the Petrarchan-Pléiadian vocabulary of endless suffering. In the sonnets of Grévin's *Olimpe* addressed to Nicole Estienne, the poet "endures" martyrdom, torment, and pain caused by the rejection of his lady.[82] The semantic similarities between the two works are sometimes striking, as the following sonnet from the *Olimpe* illustrates:

> Encore que je soy vostre esclave, Maistresse,
> Et que d'un seul clin d'oeil vous puissiez foudroyer
> Ce pauvre langoureux qui ne fait qu'employer
> Ses ans pour addoucir vostre grande rudesse,
> Encor que je prévoye une rigueur, si est-ce
> Que je suis toujours prest d'attendre et d'espier
> Mille et mille moyens qui me pourront lier
> Et délivrer ès mains de la cuisante angoisse.[83]

[Although I am your slave, Love, / And though with a simple wink you can strike with a thunderbolt / This poor languorous lover who only devotes / His years to sweetening your harshness, / Although I foresee resistance, / I am still ready to wait and to seek / Thousands of ways that could tie me up / And deliver me into the hands of stinging anguish.]

Whereas Grévin's speaker declares himself the addressee's slave, Estienne notes the slavery inherent in marriage, "esclaver son coeur sous le joug d'Hymenee" (*Les Misères,* b2v, 38) [to enslave one's heart under Hymen's yoke]. Grévin notes the lady's "rigueur," and in Estienne's text, the husband transforms peace into "rigueur" (b3v; 33). While Grévin's suffering poet seeks "mille et mille moyens" [thousands of ways] to be linked to his lady, Estienne's couple suffers "mille discensions" (b1v; 35) [a thousand disagreements].

At first glance, the identical vocabulary used to portray Grévin's lover's torment and Estienne's wife's suffering seems to refer to two completely unrelated phenomena. One critic argues, in fact, that despite the semantic similarity between the two poets, Estienne transforms the Petrarchan terms because in her text they translate real suffering.[84] While one cannot deny in the poems two distinct semantic isotopies (to use Umberto Eco's term),[85] it seems to me that the striking resemblance between the vocabularies of torment in the two texts evinces a deeper ideological connection between them than first meets the eye. The Petrarchan sufferer-turned-torturer and the cruel lady-turned-victim prove to be cut from the same cloth. To put it another way, the master/slave relationship conserves the same characteristics even when the roles of master and slave are reversed. The male suitor's deceptively subordinate rhetorical stance with regard to his lady in fact establishes the context for the husband's authoritarian power over the wife. Estienne's linking the deceit employed by lovers in ensnaring their prey to the tyrannical behavior of husbands unveils her conviction that the feigned suffering of lovers leads directly to the actual suffering of wives:

> A peine maintenant sommes-nous hors d'enfance,
> Et n'avons pas encor du monde congnoissance

> Que vous taschez déjà par dix mille moyens,
> Par presens et discours par des l'armes [sic] contraintes
> A nous embarasser dedans vos labyrintes,
> Vos cruelles prisons, vos dangereux liens.
>
> (*Les Misères*, a4v; 33)

[We are scarcely out of childhood / And have yet no knowledge of the world / When you attempt by a thousand methods, / By presents and speeches with forced tears, / To capture us in your labyrinths, / Your cruel prisons, your dangerous webs.]

The paronomasia suggested by the misprint "l'armes" is telling: tears ("larmes") constitute the lover's arms or weapons that ultimately win his war and imprison the beloved.

While this imprisonment in itself would suffice to cause the wife's distress, her disillusionment brought about by the lover's deception exacerbates her plight, as depicted in the stanza cited above and the five following it (stanzas 6–11). In each case, the cunning and counterfeit of the lover lead to the wife's high expectations, and in each case she is caught in the web that the lover has spun. Stanza 7 introduces the image of the conniving bird-catcher:

> Et comme l'Oiseleur pour les oiseaux attraire
> En ses pipeuses rhets sçait sa voix contrefaire
> Aussi vous par escrits cauteleux et rusés
> Faites semblant d'offrir vos biens [sic] humbles services
> A nous, qui ne sçachant vos fraudes et malices
> Ne pensons que nos cœurs soient ainsi desguisées.
>
> (*Les Misères*, a4v; 33)

[And as the bird-catcher knows how to disguise his voice / To attract the birds into his treacherous net, / Likewise by your deceitful and cunning letters / You pretend to offer your humble services / To us who, not suspecting your fraud and malice, / Cannot imagine our own hearts so disguised.]

Here the bird-catcher serves as a simile for the lover ("comme" . . . "ainsi"). Just as the bird-catcher projects an altered voice, so the lover projects altered sentiments, in both cases to beguile their unsuspecting prey.

Estienne develops a final image of enclosure or entrapment in stanza 8, where rings and necklaces become the enticement for women's interest, much like bait for fish:

> Nous sommes vostre coeur, nous sommes vos maitresses
> Ce ne sont que respects, ce ne sont que caresses

> Le Ciel, a vous oüir ne vous est rien au pris:
> Puis vous sçavez donner quelque anneau, quelque chaîne,
> Pour nous reduire après en immortelle gesne
> Ainsi par des appas le poisson se sent pris.
>
> *(Les Misères,* b1r; 34)

[We are your hearts, your beloved ones, / You are full of consideration and caresses, / To hear you, not even the sky's the limit. / Then you give us some ring or necklace / Only to have us end up in immortal torture, / Just as a fish is trapped by bait.]

The repetition of "nous sommes," "ce ne sont," and "quelque" in the first three verses underscores the lover's belabored flattery. Further, the explosive *p,* which figures four times in the last verse, creates an intense, syncopated rhythm suggesting the force of the capture. Finally, regarding the term "chaîne," as Deborah Lesko Baker notes in her study of Louise Labé, "the same gold chains that make women into the showpieces of male success underline their enslavement within the traditional patriarchal system."[86]

Thus, these metaphors of enclosure—labyrinths, prisons, webs, nets—depict in a figural way a temporal stasis for the women imprisoned within them. Estienne also describes time's passage for the married woman more literally by enumerating the myriad activities she must accomplish. The most abhorrent couple, to the poet's mind, is a very young woman and an old man. Not only do the young bride's tasks prove to be overwhelming, as Estienne describes them, but also the old man won't let his wife out of his sight:

> La femme prend le soin d'apprester les viande [*sic*]
> Qui au goust du vieillard seront les plus friandes,
> Sans prendre aucun repos ny la nuict ny le jour,
> Et luy se souvenant de sa folle jeunesse,
> Si tant soit peu sa femme aucune fois le laisse,
> Pense qu'elle luy veut jouer un mauvais tour.
>
> *(Les Misères,* b1v-b2r; 36)

[The wife takes care to prepare the dishes / So that they will be just to the old man's taste / Without resting day or night / And he, remembering his wild youth, / If she leaves him for even a moment, / Thinks that she wants to play a trick on him.]

Estienne's portrait of the wife who works relentlessly, devotes all her efforts to pleasing a tyrannical old man ("un vieillard remply de cruauté,"

4 / Anne de Marquets and Nicole Estienne 167

stanza 14, 1bv, 35), and has her movements restricted confirms the dynamic between spouses of greatly differing ages noted above. Indeed, the older man's licentiousness in his youth and his subsequent worries about his young wife come alive in Estienne's depiction:

> Luy qui avoit coustume auparavant follastre
> De diverses amours ses jeunes ans esbattre,
> Entretenant sa vie en toute oisiveté,
> Se sent or'accablé de quelque mal funeste,
> Qui, mal gré qu'il en ait dans son lict, le moleste
> Assez digne loyer de sa lubricité.
> (*Les Misères,* b1v; 35)

[He who was used to living it up, / Dallying with various lovers / Idly taking things as they came, / Now feels overwhelmed by an ominous thought / That haunts him, even though he has in his bed / A just reward for his lasciviousness.]

The old man's free and idle youth (rendered more colorful by such words as "follastre" and "esbattre") contrasts starkly with the young wife's forced labor, in whose life every moment must be accounted for. Stanza 26 enumerates the young wife's burdensome responsibilities with even greater force. Here, the broken rhythm of the verse serves to underscore the lady's repeated actions:

> ... hélas: qui pourrait dire
> La honte, le mespris, le chagrin, le martyre
> Qu'en son pauvre mesnage il luy faut endurer?
> Elle seule entretient sa petite famille,
> Esleve ses enfants, les nourrit, les habille
> Contre gardant son bien, pour le faire durer.
> (*Les Misères,* b3r; 38)

[... alas!—who could describe / The shame, the disdain, the sorrow, the martyrdom / That she must endure in her household? / She alone keeps her small family, / Raises the children, feeds them, dresses them, / Tending to her possessions, to make them last.]

The structure of the stanza links two categories in lines 2 and 6: the wife's feelings, separated by commas without any conjunctions (shame, disdain ...) counterbalance her daily activities, also separated by commas without conjunctions (raises the children, feeds them ...), implicitly connecting the wife's recurring misery to the repeated tasks she performs.[87] The adjectives "pauvre" (occurring twice in six lines) and "petit" suggest the perceived inconsequence of her work.

To return to the nature of Estienne's project announced in the first stanza, what is the point of Estienne's text? Why simply *describe* married women's woes? Claude Le Villain, who wrote the preface to the *Misères*, proposes one response to this question in his dedication of the work to the nun "Madame de Médine." In his view, the stanzas will fortunately discourage people from marrying. Marriage, he opines, remains the domain of men, "ne differans en beaucoup de choses des bestes brutes que de la seule parole" (*Les Misères,* a2r; 29) [only differing from beasts by speech]. Seizing the opportunity to advance church doctrine, Le Villain evokes the Pauline assertion that while marriage is acceptable, the decision not to marry is even better (1 Cor. 7:1–9). Le Villain ultimately champions the contemplative life, no doubt in honor of his veiled dedicatee, and he recommends celibacy and retreat to the convent—a conclusion obviously quite different from Estienne's own.[88]

Set against the widespread injunction against complaining of marital woes, the bold political statement of Estienne's *Misères* comes more clearly into focus. Other than Hélisenne de Crenne, women publishing in the sixteenth century before Estienne had systematically avoided or downplayed the taboo subject of domestic violence, particularly in first-person narratives.[89] The relative sparseness of this topos is not surprising, given the received idea that wives should graciously accept (or pretend to accept) their marital fate, however egregious. François d'Amboise's *Dialogues et devis* of 1581 corroborate this opinion via the interlocutor Beatrice:

> Je vous ay dit voiment qu'une femme doit aimer son mary, ses enfans et sa famille, et que si elle ne le peut faire de bonne et aggreable volonté (comme il est aucunesfois impossible, pour l'extreme, mauvais et cruel traictement d'un mary) si faut il qu'elle se gouverne si sagement, que le mary pense n'estre point hay, mais aimé. Car outre que nostre commun proverbe dit, Que là où est la chevre attachee, il faut qu'elle broute, c'est à dire que le mal qu'on a avec son mary, est domestique et necessaire: que pourroit servir à une femme une demonstration de mescontentement et inimitié evidente? ou au contraire, sa patience forcee et sa dissimulation volontaire, la garderont d'estre desestimee des estrangers, et qu'on ne face des contes de risee de sa maison.[90]

> [I told you certainly that a woman must love her husband, her children, and her family, and that if she cannot do so willingly (as is sometimes impossible, in the case of extremely bad and cruel treatment of a wife by her hus-

band), she must behave so well that the husband does not believe he is hated, but loved. Because as the proverb says, "Where the goat is attached, there it must graze," which is to say that the trouble a wife has with her husband is domestic and unavoidable. What good would it do her to demonstrate obvious unhappiness and enmity? Whereas, on the contrary, her affected patience and her voluntary dissimulation will keep her from being disrespected by strangers, and will avoid others' making a mockery of her household.]

Similarly, Claude Mermet, in his *Le temps passé, Contenant le bon droict des femmes* of 1585, assures wives that it is best to acquiesce to beatings (and remain silent), since he who loves his wife will punish her:

> Si tous les jours comme insensé il crie,
> Tempestatif, colere, sans repos,
> Faisant mestier de battre à tous propos,
> Endure tout; bien ayme qui chastie.[91]

[If every day he screams like a madman / Ceaselessly tempestuous and angry, / Finding occasion to beat you at every turn, / Endure it all; for he who loves, punishes.]

Given this context of restricted speech, the deliberate undertaking of "describing" the wife's existence divulges the author's belief in the importance of language and its powers. In addition to heightening public awareness of the wife's unfortunate treatment, Estienne also uses language to construct a new hierarchy between traditionally male and traditionally female characteristics. Near the end of the collection in stanza 27, Estienne effectuates a dramatic reversal of roles, creating a sort of *monde à l'envers* wherein she valorizes women's traditional functions and assigns normally masculine qualities to the woman:

> Et toutes fois encore l'homme se glorifie
> Que c'est par son labeur que la femme est nourrie,
> Et qu'il apporte seul ce pain à la maison.
> C'est beaucoup d'acquérir, mais plus encore je prise
> Quand l'on scait sagement garder la chose acquise:
> L'un despend de fortune et l'autre de raison.
> (*Les Misères*, b3r; 38)

[And still the man boasts / That it is by his labor that the woman is fed, / And that he alone brings bread home. / It is considerable to acquire, but I value even more / When someone knows how to keep wisely what has been acquired. / One depends on fortune, the other on reason.]

Two oppositions dominate the stanza: acquisition/maintenance and reason/fortune. In the first opposition, the husband stereotypically acquires and the wife maintains or oversees acquisitions. Estienne here affirms the stereotype but contradicts the values it represents: how one manages is more important than what one has. In the second opposition, Estienne substitutes reason for Virtus (always portrayed in sixteenth-century iconography as masculine), which contrasts with Fortuna (usually portrayed as feminine), but here she reverses the stereotype itself. Feminine reason is thus accorded the highest value in this stanza, supplanting the stability and wisdom generally attributed to men. Masculine fortune, on the other hand, here suggests the capriciousness principally attributed to women.

In addition to asserting women's capabilities in particular, these oppositions serve the function of questioning hierarchy in general. What determines, for example, whether men's or women's work is deemed superior? In this passage, Estienne does not hesitate to select women's work as the higher good, because, as already mentioned, maintenance is much more significant than the initial acquisition. Upon first consideration, this stanza appears to insist on preservation for posterity, yet the future figures nowhere in the stanza (or in any of the surrounding stanzas). "Keeping wisely what has been acquired," the woman's time remains that of the present.

The defense of women's work and the apparent belief in the promise of the present come not from the *femme mariée*, of course, but from the text itself. Both the language and the structure of *Les Misères* enact the circularity and continuity of the wife's temporal system. Within the stanzas, repetition is underscored by frequent alliteration, and the semantic field appears to be purposely limited as well: the terms "tourment," "endure," "cruel" "fascheux," "fraude," "jeunesse," "vieillesse," and "à jamais" recur intermittently throughout the collection (note the repetition of words denoting repetition). On a structural level, all the stanzas are symmetrical, with alexandrine *sizains* (aabccb) respecting the caesura after the sixth syllable. The collection as a whole also forms a circular structure, with the opening and closing stanzas including an apostrophe to the Muses. At first glance one might note the ironic significance of someone who is apparently committed to change espousing circularity, but upon reflection it becomes clear that the poet's accomplishment lies precisely in reenacting the wife's repetitive stasis.

An examination of the striking distinction between the pronouns "nous" and "je" reveals another example of Estienne's attention to the powers of language in the *Misères de la femme mariée*. In every case where the author describes the predicament, treatment and suffering of the married woman, she employs either the third-person-singular "la femme" (illustrating the essentialized wife, as noted above) or the second-person-plural "nous" (implying the common condition and solidarity of married women and including herself). The pronoun "je," on the other hand, denotes exclusively the self as writer: "favorisez moy tant que *je* puisse descrire" (*Les Misères,* a4r; 32), "*Je* pense qu'il faudroit une torche bien claire. . ." (b2r; 37); "*Je* n'aurais jamais fait si *je* veux entreprendre / O Muses par mes vers . . ." (b4r; 40). Within the context of the stanzas, then, the wife is subsumed with countless others under the rubric of "nous." The "je," however, is consummate and the author's identity becomes realized in the first-person singular only in her role as interpreter and writer.[92]

The distance separating the "je," actor and author, from the third-person "elle," object and victim, manifests itself most clearly in stanza 34:

> Je laisse maintenant l'incroyable tristesse
> Que cette pauvre femme endure en sa grossesse,
> Le danger où elle est durant l'enfantement,
> La charge des enfants si pénible et fascheuse.
> Combien pour son mary elle se rend soigneuse
> Dont elle ne reçoit pour loyer que tourment.
>
> (*Les Misères,* b4r; 40)

[I'll leave aside for now the unbelievable sadness / That this poor woman endures during her pregnancy, / The danger she undergoes during childbirth, / The onerous and deplorable burden of the children. / How helpful she is to her husband! / And what does she receive as compensation? Nothing but torment.]

In this stanza the "je" is established as the only entity capable of recording the wife's affliction. Nowhere in the collection does the figure of the wife speak. The first person's declaration that she will not depict the woman's suffering with children, followed paradoxically by a description in toto, serves to signal the power of the writer (and of the "je") to produce actively, as distinguished from physical reproduction that is here described as passive. The fricative sound *s,* repeated eight times in the first two verses of the stanza, creates a phonetic tension echoing the distress of the woman depicted therein. The tormented wife "elle" remains notably distinct from the narrator and producer "je," as if to insist once again upon the potential powers of language and of the first-person speaker who employs them.

While in her "description" Estienne does not explicitly propose in her verses revolutionary solutions to the problems of marriage, she does nonetheless proffer implicit suggestions for ameliorating the institution. Acknowledging marriage to be what the historian Jean-Louis Flandrin calls a "social cement,"[93] the poet calls for a new model in which the spouses' dispositions would be taken into consideration. In stanza 13, she laments in the choosing of mates the lack of attention paid to what the twentieth century would call compatibility:

> Encore maintenant pour faire un mariage
> On songe seulement aux biens et au lignage
> Sans cognoistre les moeurs et les complexions
> Par ainsi ce lien trop rigoureux assemble,
> Deux contraires humeurs à tout jamais ensemble,
> Dont viennent puis apres mille discensions.
>
> (*Les Misères,* b1v; 35)

[These days to make a marriage / They only think of wealth and lineage / Without understanding habits and dispositions. / This is how two contrary temperaments / Are inextricably linked forever, / From which a thousand disagreements arise.]

Not holding the original institution itself at fault, the poet describes marriage at its conception as gracious, pleasurable, and sacred.[94] What has led the institution astray, to her mind, is the development of significant inequality between the spouses (exemplified by the tyranny of "presumptuous man"):

> O bien heureux accord, ô sacrée alliance,
> Présent digne des Cieux, gracieuse accointance
> Pleine de tout plaisir, de grâce et de douceur:
> Si l'homme audacieux n'eust à sa fantaisie
> Changé tes douces loix en dure tyrannie,
> Ton miel en amertume et ta paix en rigueur.
>
> (*Les Misères,* a4v; 33)

[O fortunate accord, o sacred alliance, / Present worthy of Heaven, gracious association / Filled with all pleasure, grace, and sweetness, / If presumptuous man had not recklessly / Changed your sweet laws into hard tyranny, / Your honey into bitterness and your peace into severity.]

In the union as God intended it, according to Estienne, power and dominion were to be divided between spouses, whereas instead women have been deprived of their liberty:

> [eux pleins de malice] usurpans tous seuls à tort la seigneurie
> Qui de Dieu nous estait en commun despartie
> Nous ravissent, cruels, la chère liberté.
>
> (*Les Misères,* b3v; 40)

[{those full of malice} wrongly usurping for themselves all power / That God had divided between us, / Cruel {husbands} rob us of our liberty.]

Seen within the context of sixteenth-century conceptions of women's place within marriage and the injunction against speaking out discussed above, then, Estienne's description of the "miseries" of the married woman appears all the more forceful. As if to respond to Petrarch's contention that "intellect not marriage" will ensure the male poet's literary longevity, the writer embodied in Estienne's "je" proclaims in *Misères de la femme mariée* the very different end to which she devotes her own intellect. Like Petrarch, Estienne writes for a cause beyond herself, though her focus is both terrestrial and immediate. In rehearsing the wife's current plight, she indirectly and directly lobbies for fundamental changes in the institution of marriage that would end the husband's "tyranny" and bring greater equality to the spouses.

The present is thus the central temporal reality for the beleaguered wife in Estienne's stanzas. The poet adroitly depicts in a number of ways the circular qualities of time for women in the marital "prison," as we have seen. Through her challenging of the married woman's repetitive existence, Estienne suggests the possibility of reconfiguring "women's time," which would render the institution of marriage, as she believes it was intended, a "présent digne des cieux" (*Les Misères,* av4; 33) [a present worthy of heaven].

* * *

Anne de Marquets's and Nicole Estienne's works, in addition to their appeal as important literary and social artifacts of the sixteenth century, raise the broader question of both the possibilities and the limitations of subversion. They invite us to navigate beyond the Scylla of assigning feminist motives to every text written by a woman, and the Charybdis of failing to recognize such motives when they are present, often because of the unremarkable rhetoric in which these motives are embedded. While Estienne's stanzas explicitly address a notion of "women's time," Marquets sonnets do so obliquely, through the poet's insistence on Mary's physicality and on the present.

The two poets have in common their "enclosure" in the two principal institutions for women in early modern France. Nicole Estienne herself articulated the similarities between the two institutions, both of which involve leaving home and family for a husband, figurative or literal, "pour à votre vouloir pauvreté consentir" (*Les Misères,* b1r; 34) [to consent to poverty according to your will]. The relative status of these women within the institutions in question of course proves to be radically different. Anne de Marquets, a highly educated noblewoman, holds a privileged position both within the monastery and in the world of letters, whereas Nicole Estienne, a bankrupt printer's daughter, laments women's inferior status within the marital hierarchy. Yet as we have seen, both writers argue for the valorization of women and for a feminizing of a particular institution, explicitly in the case of Nicole Estienne and implicitly in the case of Anne de Marquets.

The temporal implications of these poets' challenges are manifold: both emphasize the present, in contrast to the humanist claim to poetic immortality. Again, by accentuating the present, both writers suggest the importance of connectedness (in these cases, with other women subsumed under the pronoun "nous") as well as the immediacy of political action.[95] Finally, both writers appear to recognize a cyclic, circular concept of time as seen from the enclosure of their institutions, yet both authors escape solipsism and stasis in their works by what might be called textual "fissures"—displacements in the case of Marquets and challenges in the case of Estienne. Through these fissures, Anne de Marquets and Nicole Estienne reveal their powers to introduce apertures, however subtle, in the temporal framework of the institutions that in many ways sought to confine and define early modern women. By creating a temporal space that is rendered immediate and tangible, by telling stories and telling time, these two poets insist upon the present as a locus of human engagement, possibility, and transformation.

5

Le temps retrouvé:
Exemplarity and the Temporal Body in Catherine des Roches

In her *Œuvres* of 1555 Louise Labé had eloquently urged women to rise above the spindle and take up the pen. Catherine des Roches, whose writing began to be published twenty-four years later, was the first to embrace fully Labé's exhortations, articulating and elaborating the raison d'être of the scholarly and literary woman. Indeed, des Roches is the first well-known woman in French history to have rejected all offers of marriage explicitly in order to devote herself exclusively to letters.[1]

Catherine's social environment doubtless contributed to the independence that ultimately allowed her to carve out a unique space for herself in sixteenth-century society: neither wife, nun, nor widow, she nonetheless acquired a respected position both in her native Poitiers and in contemporary French letters.[2] Despite hardships sustained in the religious wars, the des Roches's finances remained for the most part stable. Catherine's mother, Madeleine Neveu, was raised in the milieu of the *bourgeoisie de robe* and remained there in her marriages, first to the procurer André Fradonnet and then to the lawyer and city councillor François Eboissard.[3] She maintained a relatively high standard of living for herself and her daughter.[4] After the death of her second husband, Madeleine proved to be entirely self-sufficient, not only managing the family's investments but also defending them in a number of lawsuits.[5] These sometimes lengthy battles principally involved unpaid debts by various parties to the des Roches during the difficult times following the siege of Poitiers by Coligny's army in 1569.[6]

To appreciate the extent to which Catherine's household was particularly gynocentric, one need only begin by her name. Des Roches, the name adopted by both mother and daughter, comes from Madeleine's family, which possessed a house and land called des Roches, just east of Chatellerault. In addition to the ennobling preposition of the adopted name, Madeleine's onomastic attachment shifts from a male ancestor to the maternal familial terrain.[7] Also very unusual in early modern society, Madeleine continued to educate Catherine well beyond the period normally permitted for a mother's instruction, initiating her into the culture of philosophy, history, and letters.[8]

Given this humanist education with an emphasis on such moral historians as Plutarch (the most frequently cited source in Catherine's work),[9] it is not surprising that in her writing Catherine crafts moral examples of her own. These exemplary figures, almost exclusively women (again, not surprisingly, given her feminist surroundings) either derive more or less accurately from historical, mythological, and biblical texts, or they emerge as fictional characters of Catherine's creation. But juxtaposed with these purportedly timeless models of human comportment, the notion of a woman as a temporal, physical entity also figures in Catherine's texts. For Catherine, the central ethical question concerning concrete time—how ought one best employ the passing hours?—is closely linked to the question of the body, as expressed both in her own voice and in that of her characters. Catherine's attitudes toward time prove thus to be enmeshed in the dichotomy between the timelessness of exemplars and the heightened temporality inherent in the topos of the human body. Through her treatment of both exemplars and the human body, in contradistinction to contemporaneous moralists and *carpe diem* poets, Catherine proposes her own model for imagining women's time.

The Woman as Exemplar

Timothy Hampton has described the original function of exemplarity in humanist culture, noting that "the words, deeds and texts of antiquity [serve] as sources of value for all men at all times."[10] Stored in the name of the exemplar are a host of great deeds from the heroic figure's life, which, when "opened up,"[11] transmit to the reader an exhortative ideological message intended to move him to virtuous action. While through his relationship to exemplary figures "the Renaissance schoolboy grows into the garments prepared by family and society,"[12] I would argue that the Renaissance girl, schooled quite differently from her masculine counterpart, begins to compress herself into the *verdugade* (corset) prepared by the same entourage.

Yet the authority of exemplary figures during the sixteenth century becomes progressively more ambiguous. As Terence Cave notes, "[I]f venerable texts are to be fragmented and eventually transformed by the process of rewriting, it becomes visibly less necessary to regard them as closed and authoritative wholes."[13] Hampton argues that both ideological anxiety and epistemological skepticism bring about the decline of ancient exemplars.[14] The historicism characterizing much of humanist discourse, Hampton points out, undermines the faith in ancient exemplars, which are conspicuously absent in seventeenth-century moralist texts such as those of La Fontaine and La Bruyère.[15] What is particularly fascinating about Hampton's analysis for our purposes is the way in which the progressive introduction of historical references situated in time question ipso facto the principle of timeless universality.

Catherine des Roches's refashioning of traditional exemplars for a female (and, to a lesser extent, male) readership problematizes humanist assumptions in a very different way. Her recasting of ancient models challenges previous notions of exemplarity for women, the universality of which is obviously undermined by their having been heretofore proposed almost exclusively by men, with the notable exception of Christine de Pizan. Rather than shifting away from ancient exemplary figures as do the seventeenth-century moralists, in other words, Catherine des Roches creates instead feminist exemplars of her own. Insisting not upon their timeless qualities but rather upon their accomplishments and endeavors, she highlights these women's reappropriation of time for laudable purposes. In her *Œuvres* Catherine portrays three principal female prototypes that illustrate varying degrees of exemplarity, determined largely by the ways in which they apportion their time: the *mesnagere or mulier economica*, the Amazon, and the humanist woman.

COMPAIGNE ET SERVANTE ET AMIE
(*ŒUVRES*, 328)

Of the exemplary figures in Catherine's work, the *mesnagere* or the *mulier economica* poses the largest critical difficulty. At least one of the literary origins of the exemplar is easily traceable: Placide, the ideal humanist father in Catherine's *Dialogue de Placide et Severe,* recommends to the misogynist brute Severe, somewhat ironically, that if he allowed his daughter to read, she could learn some behavioral lessons from Xenophon.[16] The resurgence of popularity of Xenophon's *Oeconomicus* in sixteenth-century France emblematically reflects a growing public concern for the moral education of women. The catalog of the Bibliothèque Nationale de France alone lists eight Greek and eleven Latin editions of Xenophon's complete works published during the sixteenth century, as well as sixteen editions of the *Oeconomicus (La Mesnagerie)*.[17] In contrast to the plethora of possibilities for men in the social sphere, women were enjoined, through what Evelyne Berriot-Salvadore calls "the discursive erasure of [their] social existence,"[18] to withdraw to the confines of the house and remain occupied but silent. Yet quite obviously, a significant number of women in early modern France dismissed this injunction, not only by managing households, property, and business during and after the religious wars but also by the act of writing.

How are we to read these eloquent praises of the housewife written by a poet who specifically rejected the life she describes? While ostensibly providing a prototypical, timeless exemplar, the depictions of the housewife implicitly raise the question of women's time in its most concrete manifestation. While through the figure of the *mulier economica* Catherine appears to applaud the value of traditionally female work, in every case the exemplum is subtly undermined in the same text or elsewhere in Catherine's *Œuvre*. This phenomenon is most clearly manifest in "La femme forte descritte par Salomon," a rewriting of the Old Testament passage portraying the ideal woman in early Jewish culture (Prov. 31:10–31).[19] Like the biblical text, Catherine insists on the woman's resourcefulness in terms of manual labor, care for others, and financial profit (she is worth more than pearls, Prov. 31:10;[20] she acquires fields, v. 16; she sells cloth she has woven, v. 24; she should receive a share of what she has produced, v. 31). While retaining both the framework and the details of the biblical passage, Catherine's poet feminizes the text, according to it a subjectivity absent in the original and assigning to the housewoman qualities more frequently associated with the humanist woman than with the *mulier economica*. Whereas Théodore de Bèze entitles his contemporaneous paraphrase of the same passage "Les vertus de la femme *fidele* et bonne menasgere"[21] (my emphasis) [Virtues of the *faithful* woman and good homemaker], Catherine not coincidentally retains "forte" as the primary qualifying adjective in her title. While the woman in Proverbs speaks according to a "pious doctrine" (v. 26), Catherine's character manifests "perfect eloquence" and "true wisdom," demonstrating, contrary to the claims of a number of contemporary treatises on women, that "un bon propos surpasse le silence" (*Les Œuvres,* 331) [good speech is better than silence].[22] Like the biblical text as well as de Bèze's translation, Catherine stresses the importance of utilizing every waking moment. Following the guidelines sketched in the conduct manuals considered in chapter 3, Catherine's strong woman fills her day with useful activity, beginning with the sun's first rays. But unlike her models, Catherine's character draws pleasure from her salutary work, a sentiment suspiciously reminiscent of the Horatian *dolce utile* so extensively promulgated by the Pléiade.[23]

> Ell' se leve au matin, premier que le soleil
> Monstre ses beaux rayons, et puis faict un ouvrage,
> Ou de laine, ou de lin, pour servir son mesnage,
> Tirant de son labeur un utile plaisir.
> (*Les Œuvres*, 328)

[She rises in the morning, when the sun first shows its beautiful rays, and then does some spinning, wool or linen, to serve her household, drawing from her labor useful pleasure.]

In addition to the humanist leanings of Catherine's housewife, she also receives public recognition within the community. In an interesting role reversal, whereas the husband of the biblical housewife is a well-known citizen in his own right, in Catherine's version he is admired uniquely because of his wife:

> Son mary est prisé en tous lieux de la ville
> Pour estre possesseur de femme si gentille.
> (*Les Œuvres*, 331)

[Her husband is honored everywhere in town / For having such an affable wife.]

Near the end of the poem, Catherine's poet celebrates this traditionally unsung woman with the lexicon normally reserved for glorious war victors:

> Mais la femme qui ayme, et qui craint le Seigneur,
> Merite recevoir un immortel honneur.
> Sus doncques! rendez-luy la gloire meritée!
> Sa loüange ne soit de bornes limitée.
> Faictes-luy voisiner la grand' voute des Cieux,
> Puisqu'elle est en ce monde un miracle à voz yeux!
> (*Les Œuvres*, 331–32)

[But the woman who loves, and who fears God / Deserves immortal honor. / Arise, then! Give her the glory she deserves. / Let her praise be boundless. / Place her in the great dome of the Heavens, / Because in your eyes she is a miracle in this world.]

Perhaps the lady doth praise too much. Or perhaps Catherine's laudatory rhetoric is convincing precisely because her "femme forte" is subtly revealed as stronger, more eloquent, and more influential than the *mulierem fortem* of Proverbs. In either case, the discord between the simplicity of the traditional housewife and the ennobling, lofty rhetoric used to praise her signals the potentially problematic nature of Catherine's position in this poem. While the conflicting registers could be read as fertile ground for a false encomium, it seems, rather, that Catherine genuinely praises the woman of Proverbs by refashioning her in her own image, according her the intellectual and "writerly" qualities of "vraye sapience," "esprit divin," and "parfaicte eloquence" (*Les Œuvres,* 331).

The valorization of female manual labor also figures in Catherine's *Dialogue de la main, du pié et de la bouche,* but once again it is undermined, this time by the superior position accorded to the voice of wisdom. In the dialogue, the Hand (of course feminine), depicted as always industrious and always occupied, challenges her masculine counterpart, the Foot: "Ha mignon! que tu parles bien à ton aise, cependant que je travaille tous les jours à filer la laine ou la soye, dont tu es vestu, ou bien à descouper les escarpins, dans lesquels tu fays les caprioles devant les Dames" (*Les Œuvres,* 219) [Hey, fellow! You just talk as much as you want, while I work every day spinning wool or silk, which you're dressed in, or else cutting shoes, which you dance around in for the ladies]. The point of the dialogue seems at first glance to be the value of women's work metaphorically posited through the triumph of the Hand. Yet the debate is resolved by neither the Hand nor the Foot, but rather by the wise, reconciling, feminine voice of the Mouth, a humanist interlocutor who enjoins the body parts to work in concert for the good of all.[24] Thus wisdom and eloquence again ultimately prevail over the traditional female work ostensibly being praised in the dialogue.

Perhaps the most subtle undermining of the *mulier economica* in Catherine's work unfolds in the image of the distaff, the icon par excellence of women's subjugation in early modern Europe.[25] Catherine's sonnet to the distaff, "A ma Quenoille," treats the duality of literary and domestic pursuits:

>Quenoille mon souci, je vous promets et jure
>De vous aimer tousjours, et jamais ne changer
>Vostre honneur domestic pour un bien estranger,
>Qui erre inconstamment et fort peu de temps dure.
>   Vous ayant au costé je suis beaucoup plus seure
>Que si encre et papier se venoient aranger

> Tout à l'entour de moy; car pour me revanger
> Vous pouvez bien plustost repousser une injure.
> 　　Mais quenoille m'amie, il ne faut pas pourtant
> Que pour vous estimer, et pour vous aimer tant
> Je delaisse du tout cest' honneste coustume
> 　　D'escrire quelquefois; en escrivant ainsi,
> J'escri de voz valeurs, quenoille mon souci,
> Ayant dedans la main, le fuzeau, et la plume.
>
> 　　　　　　　　　　　　　　(*Les Oeuvres*, 292–93)

[Distaff, my care, I promise and swear / To love you always and never to exchange / Your domestic honor for another / Who wanders aimlessly and lasts but a short time. // Having you next to me, I am much more secure / Than if I had paper and ink spread out / All around me; because to avenge me / You are much better at warding off an affront. // But distaff, my friend, I mustn't, / Just because I value and love you so much, / Forgo this legitimate practice // Of writing sometimes; in writing like this, / I record your merit, distaff, my care, / Holding in my hand both my distaff and my pen.]

Recent critical response to this sonnet in which Catherine explicitly argues *in utramque partem*, or at least on both sides of the fence, has been varied. Anne Larsen and Colette Winn, from different perspectives, read this poem as a salutary fusion of the two poles of Catherine's existence.[26] Tilde Sankovitch, on the other hand, reads the sonnet as an exposition of Catherine's polarization: "Torn between the pen and the spindle, between the female muse and the male-originated conventionality, both of which represent, torturingly, herself and not-herself, Catherine seems here mutilated and alienated, whether she opts for one or the other."[27] Finally, Ann Rosalind Jones argues that for Catherine the distaff serves as a "shelter against insult and infamy,"[28] thus resolving "an apparently irreconcilable ideological opposition."[29]

The question of women's time forms the nucleus of this sonnet: is it possible for a woman to inhabit the domain of the distaff and still undertake the humanist enterprise of writing? Catherine explicitly answers in the affirmative. Yet while she does indeed make the case for a kind of "mixed life"[30] in this sonnet and elsewhere, the scales in her work are heavily weighted in favor of intellectual pursuits over domesticity. Consider, for example, the coyly phrased verses in which the poet assures the distaff that she will not leave it for something "qui erre inconstamment et peu de temps dure" (*Les Œuvres*, 292) [that wanders erratically and lasts a short time]. This quatrain implies that the poet could, however, abandon her distaff in favor of writing, which figures elsewhere in her work as an enduring activity.[31]

Rather than echoing Hélisenne de Crenne's assailing of the distaff or prefiguring Marie de Gournay's sweeping repudiation of it,[32] Catherine more subtly but deftly adapts the distaff to her own political purposes. To my mind, then, the distaff poem constitutes a subversion under the guise of reconciliation.

Just as in social terms the des Roches' widespread reputation for being excellent homemakers served to sanction or exonerate their intellectually daring salon and publications, so in rhetorical terms the distaff functions as a subterfuge for Catherine's poet.[33] But while Catherine ascribes both personal and social merit to her distaff, the ideological underpinnings of her assignations differ considerably from those articulated in many other contemporaneous texts. As we saw in chapter 3, Erasmus recommends spinning as a respectable activity to occupy a noblewoman,[34] and Ronsard proposes the distaff to keep his lady busy while he breaks free (L.X,122–23; I,236–37).

The social function Catherine proposes for the distaff repudiates the confining purpose of both Erasmus's and Ronsard's designs. Well before Mahatma Gandhi, Catherine argues that the spindle and the distaff are capable of contributing to the social good. Had Achilles used them rather than his weapons, she opines, much violence could have been spared:

> Achille feit tort à ses mains,
> Quittant le fuseau pour l'espee:
> L'un file la vie aux humains,
> De l'autre la vie est coupee.[35]

[Achilles dishonored his hands, / Abandoning the spindle in favor of the sword: / One spins human life, / By the other life is severed.]

This depiction of the spindle's social worth serves here to broaden the base of the housewoman, with whom the textile tools are inextricably associated. Yet elsewhere in Catherine's work, the distaff has nefarious social consequences, constituting both a means of subjugation (*Œuvres*, 291) and a masculine strategy for keeping women apart (336). The proverbial strong woman, obeying all injunctions for female behavior,[36] of course takes up the distaff, but Catherine's description figures in the negative: "En ne refusant pas de prendre la quenoille, . . ." (330) [Not refusing to take up the distaff, . . .]. Since the passage in Proverbs is written in the positive verb form, this negative construction obviously begs the question of why the housewife would refuse, implying that a truly independent woman might indeed resist participating in the socially sanctioned female activity of spinning.

The exemplar of the domestic woman is thus explicitly undermined on several occasions in Catherine's text, as we have seen. The *mesnagere*, simultaneously glorified and problematized much like the distaff that represents her, thus fulfills a complex function in Catherine's work. While the housewoman initially appears to represent an ideal, as she does in extensive contemporary exegesis of the biblical text, the contradictions we have examined call into question the value of women's time spent exclusively in domestic pursuits. Ultimately, the *mulier economica* fails to be entirely convincing as an exemplar in Catherine's texts, particularly in comparison to the Amazon and the humanist woman.

BRAVANT LES PLUS GLORIEUX / PAR NOSTRE PRUDENCE / ET NOSTRE VAILLANCE
(*ŒUVRES*, 291)

A familiar mythical figure from Scythia, the Caucasus, or Asia Minor, notorious for being a ferocious warrior, murdering or mutilating male babies, and pillaging for a living, the Amazon takes on a decidedly tame character in Catherine's poetry. The Amazonian theme enjoyed considerable popularity in the late sixteenth century, as evidenced by records of contemporary court celebrations, including a tournament in Bayonne in 1562 where Henri III and his brothers disguised themselves as Amazons.[37] Jacqueline Boucher suggests that Catherine might have written the "Mascarade des Amazones" and the "Chanson des Amazones" for the court as it traveled through Poitiers.[38] But while according to Boucher the image of the Amazon served in the court as a force symbolically reconciling masculine valor and feminine chastity, for Catherine it appears to represent less problematically female strength and independence.

In her depiction of the Amazons, Catherine insists on a number of characteristics that render the women worthy of becoming exemplary figures: their valor, their chastity, their transgression, and their social and political power. "Pour une mascarade d'amazones" recounts the victory song in the first-person plural, which, in addition to rendering the account more immediate, implies the author's identification with her heroines. Through the reference to the Apollonian laurel, Catherine highlights the implicit connection between her (or between writing women) and the Amazons, since both poets and military victors were crowned with laurel wreaths:

> Par les traits de noz yeux, et l'effort de noz lances,
> Nous rapportons en main les Myrthes et Lauriers.
>
> (*Les Œuvres*, 289)

[By the arrows of our eyes and the strength of our lances, / We bring back in our hands myrtle and laurel.]

The "arrows of [the women's] eyes," traditionally depicted as the source of the male poet's suffering, here become the agents of the women warriors' conquest.

In her edition of the Dames des Roches, Larsen proposes that "Pour une mascarade d'amazones" may have been inspired by Ronsard's "Le trophée de l'amour" and "Le trophee de la chasteté" (*Les Œuvres,* 289 n. 1). If this is the case, the poems provide an excellent illustration, as do the pieces on the distaff considered above, of the strikingly different purposes to which an identical topos may be put. Ronsard wrote "Le trophée de la chasteté" as an interlude for a court comedy by Ariosto. While the poem is presented as a first-person narrative, and while the speaker manifests the same resistance to passion and the same victory over Cupid, Ronsard's and Catherine's poems ultimately sketch very different portraits of the legendary women.

Ronsard's allegorized Chastity speaks in the first-person singular, explaining that she employs her icy exterior as a shield for Amour's arrows. Presumably unable to oppose the adversary of her own accord, she requires the aid of a shield, insinuating the difficulty she encounters in rising above the winged cherub:

> Pour resister à ce Prince animé,
> D'un fort bouclier l'estomac je m'armé,
> Fait de constance et de perserverance. . . .
>
> (L.XIII,220; P.II,239)

[To resist this lively Prince / I armed my stomach with a strong shield, / Forged with constancy and perseverance. . . .]

Not surprisingly, Catherine's representation of chastity, couched in terms of both alacrity and force, insists upon the will of the Amazons to remain celibate and to rely on their own power when faced with the enemy:

> L'amour audacieux, desirant que ses flames
> Alentissent du tout la vertu de noz ames,
> Elançoit dens noz coeurs mille flambeaux ardans;
> Mais nostre chasteté qui gardoit cette place
> Changeoit incontinent les ardans feux en glace,
> Empeschant que l'amour ne logeast au dedans.
>
> (*Les Œuvres,* 289)

[Audacious love, wishing that its flames / Would mollify the virtue of our souls, / Cast a thousand burning torches in our hearts; / But our chastity that was standing guard / Suddenly changed these ardent fires to ice, / Thwarting love's settling therein.]

Catherine's Amazons, like Ronsard's Chastity, employ ice as a weapon against Amour, but rather than simply deterring arrows, this chastity actively transforms one substance to another (fire to ice) in their hearts. Both poems describe chastity's victory, but the Amazons' defeat of Cupid (depicted as "dechassé" [chased away]) is self-propelled in Catherine's work, whereas Ronsard's Chastity requires armaments to protect her.

Finally, Ronsard's poem concludes with a clever twist reminiscent of the *Roman de Renart*, which leaves the reader with a final impression of the Amazons' vengeance and ruse. Chastity makes Amour her prisoner, and the one who is destined to be vanquished becomes the conqueror, as the last verse spells out: "C'est bien raison que le trompeur on trompe" (L.XIII,220; P.II,239) [It is fitting that the deceiver be deceived]. The conclusion of Catherine's poem, on the other hand, praises the power of the Amazons, and especially the queen, Otrera, whose female lineage is evoked in a final strophe filled with praise for her prowess:

> Son nom est Otrera, fille de Martesie,[39]
> Qui tient pour la servir cette trouppe choisie,
> Voulant par sa proüesse eterniser son nom;
> Elle retient du tout le souverain empire
> De la grande cité nommée Themyscire,
> Enceinte par les bras du fameux Thermodon.
>
> (*Œuvres*, 290)

[Her name is Otrera, daughter of Martesia, / Who keeps this chosen troop to serve her, / Wishing to immortalize her name by her prowess, / She retains the sovereign empire / Of the great city named Themyscire / Encircled by the arms of the famous {river} Thermodon.]

Thus while both sets of Amazons manifest the identical results of conquering masculine enemies, Catherine's poet clearly assigns to the women of Themyscire an exemplary value that is absent in Ronsard's interlude. The cunning betrayers of Ronsard's verses become in Catherine's work the heroines who succeed in gaining glory through valor and political power.

The "Chanson des amazones" furnishes another significant example of Catherine's original depiction of these exemplary legendary figures. Interestingly, the power of the women is illustrated here in a reversal of the principal activity of the *mulier economica:* spinning. The first two strophes announce the admirable qualities ensuring the women's victory: prudence, bravery, virtue, purity, and chastity (*Les Œuvres,* 291). In the last strophe, Catherine's poet describes the punishment of the captives, which involves their forced participation in a traditionally female activity:

> Nous tenons les hommes,
> Des lieux où nous sommes,
> Tous empeschez à filer....
>
> (*Les Œuvres,* 291)

[We hold the men down where we are, forcing all of them to spin....]

The image of a male hostage's spinning can doubtless be traced to the Hercules story recounted in Ovid's *Heroides* (9.30ff.) But Catherine's depiction is radically different from that of the classical source and reveals once again her distinct vision of these mythological heroines. In the *Heroides,* Deianeira, Hercules' wife, describes her husband as perpetually absent, constantly pursuing monsters while she remains a widow at home making chaste wishes ("Ipsa domo vidua votis operata pudicis"; 9.30–35). After having claimed that she will refrain from mentioning in detail Hercules' adulterous liaisons, all the while citing each one of them (9.50), Deianeira chastises Hercules for his submission to Omphala, queen of Lydia. Dressed like a licentious woman ("lascivae more puellae," 9.65), he spins as much as his lover desires (9.75–80). Significantly, Omphala's domination over Hercules is sexual, which obviously puts quite a different spin, so to speak, on the nature of her power when compared with that of Catherine's Amazons, whose victory is described as both chaste and valiant (*Les Œuvres,* 291).

The chaste Amazonian figure who fulfills the highest exemplary function in Catherine's work is indisputably Agnodice, the eponymous heroine of Catherine's allegory treating the importance of access to reading and writing (and by extension, to a humanist education) for women.[40] In this epic poem, Envy strikes men who are jealous of the knowledge of their wives, following which the men forbid books and learning to their spouses. These women, deprived of "pleasures of the soul" (*Les Œuvres,* 335), fall desperately ill. Agnodice, seeing their suffering, dresses as a man, studies medicine, and returns to care for the women, but upon observing her success, Envy strikes again, and the men condemn Agnodice to death. To reveal her identity, Agnodice bares her breasts, lowers her gaze, and explains that her motivation was not to trick the men, but rather to render what rightfully belonged to the women:

> . . . le desir qui la faict desguiser
> N'est point pour les tromper mais pour authoriser
> Les lettres qu'elle apprist voulant servir leurs Dames.
> (*Les Œuvres,* 339)

[. . . the desire that made her disguise herself / Is not to deceive them but to authorize / The knowledge she acquired wishing to serve their ladies.]

The men take pity on her, begging her forgiveness, and in her triumph Agnodice once again utilizes the opportunity to urge that the men allow their wives to study. But the poem nonetheless ends with a caveat: Envy, seeking vengeance against Agnodice who defeated her, still pursues learned women who are as virtuous as Agnodice.

The androgynous figure of Agnodice takes on an overtly exemplary character within the rhetoric of the epic poem as the first-person plural attempts to assimilate narrator and readers in a common eulogy:

> Aymons ce qui nous reste, honorons sa prison,
> Le feu s'en est volé, gardons bien le tison.
> (*Les Œuvres,* 335)

[Let us love what remains for us, let us honor her prison, / The fire has fled, let us preserve the brand.]

A number of other expressions reveal the importance of collectivity throughout the poem and by extension the political intentions of its author. The lamentable circumstances in which Agnodice initially finds the women, for example, include the women's being separated from one another: "Les femmes (o pitié!) n'osaient plus se mesler / De s'aider l'une l'autre" (*Les Œuvres,* 336) [The women (alas!) no longer dared to be together, to help one another]. While Agnodice's assuming a masculine identity allows her to study and to accomplish an important role in society, the burning question throughout the text remains the right of *all* women to a humanist education, for the enlightened society should "faire estudier / Les Dames du pays, sans envier la gloire / Que l'on a pour servir les filles de Memoire" (*Les Œuvres,* 339) [have the women of the country study, without envying the glory that one acquires by serving the daughters of Memory {Mnemosyne}].

The Amazon's strength, much like the *mesnagere*'s, thus derives less from qualities normally associated with the exemplar than from her humanist formation. Unlike the original Amazons who dominate by the brute force of muscles and weapons, Catherine's Agnodice triumphs through a sharp brain and a generous heart. Agnodice's brazen acts (cross-dressing, practicing a man's trade, and petitioning the men in favor of the women) are all justified and attenuated by the humanist principle she represents, namely, the prerogative of women to study and to write.

L'HONNEUR ET LE PROfit D'UNE AGREABLE ÉTUDE
(*SECONDES ŒUVRES,* 55R)

The humanist woman emerges as the summum bonum of Catherine's exemplary figures. As we have observed in *L'Agnodice*, reading and writing, the primary tools of the humanist, constitute the foundation of both happiness and agency for the women in Catherine's works. All of Catherine's heroic figures contain some characteristics of the humanist woman (such as the wisdom of "la femme descritte par Salomon" and the eloquence of the Amazonian Agnodice), and indeed the humanist woman in Catherine's system figuratively coalesces the modest industriousness of the housewife with the glorious exploits of the Amazons. The lively and highly educated Pasithée,[41] much like Catherine herself, serves as the exemplar who embodies this intermingling of qualities.[42] The reader first glimpses Pasithée obliquely in the *Dialogue de Placide et Severe*, in which two fathers are discussing the education of their daughters. Severe—absurdly misogynistic and thus an ideal candidate to launch the debate—opens the dialogue with a lamentation on the ignorance of women in general and of his wife and daughter in particular:

> O la grand [*sic*] peine que c'est d'avoir Femmes, ou Filles a gouverner! Vray-ment je ne m'estonne point, dont un renommé Philosophe, pense les devoir tenir au rang des Animaux sans raison. Et si jamais pauvre homme s'est trouvé affligé de leurs importunitez, je suis ce miserable. (*Secondes œuvres*, 35r)

> [What trouble it is to have wives or daughters to manage! It really doesn't surprise me that a well-known philosopher believes they should be considered as animals without reason. And if ever a poor man has found himself suffering from their annoyances, I'm the one.]

In response to Severe's complaint, Placide suggests that Severe should allow his wife and daughter to read and study, but Severe protests vigorously that women would profane the authors in question even by pronouncing their names (*Secondes oeuvres,* 36r).[43] Severe then reveals that his daughter refuses to stay at home: "[E]lle est a la fenestre, a la porte, en la rüe, en visite, elle n'a point de repos, ny moy non plus" (36r) [{S}he is at the window, at the door, in the street, out visiting—she gets no rest, and neither do I]. When Severe asks what Placide's daughter is doing, the latter responds that she is in her room. "Alone?" asks Severe. "Non, elle est avec des ames sans cors, et des cors sans ames . . ." [No, she's with souls without bodies and bodies without souls . . .], the first category being her lute and viol, the second her Plutarch and Seneca (36r). The reader soon discovers that this learned daughter is Pasithée, whose father continues his apology of women's education throughout the dialogue.

Placide emerges as a hero in his own right as he attempts to use psychological finesse to convince the obtuse Severe. At the beginning of the dialogue Severe avers his belief that all education of women is dangerous, since a woman only needs to know how to honor her husband and keep house, "et non pas a frequenter les livres. Il ne luy faut autre Docteur que ma voix" (37r) [and not to be spending time with books. She needs no other teacher than my own voice]. But Placide retorts that if she read Xenophon's *Menagerie*, she would do her duties more readily (37r).[44] Similarly, he argues for women's study of biblical texts not so that women will preach to the multitudes, but in order to cultivate subservience to their husbands (37v). Women should also study law, which could be to their husbands' benefit.

[Une Femme] doit elle renoncer au Droit Velleien[45] sans l'entendre? Héé, ceux qui ont Femmes riches en ce pays, leurs [*sic*] font bien sçavoir qu'elles peuvent donner leurs meubles et acquestz, avec le tiers de leurs heritages aux maris sur-vivans: pource que la loy de la coutume le permet. (*Secondes œuvres,* 38r)

[Should a wife reject the Velleien Law without understanding it? Those who have rich wives in this country certainly let them know that they can leave their furniture and belongings, with a third of their inheritance, to surviving husbands: because common law permits it.]

Near the end of the dialogue Severe recites a poem whose last strophe sums up concisely his apparently implacable position, vividly illustrating the intransigence of the unenlightened character:

> Fuiez donc la Femme sçavante,
> Recherchez plustost l'ignorante,
> L'une pourroit vous mespriser,
> L'autre se laisse maistriser.
>
> (*Secondes œuvres,* 39r)

[Thus flee the learned woman, / Seek instead the ignorant, / One could hold you in disdain, / The other lets you be the master.]

But in the last exchanges of the dialogue, Placide's arguments concerning the power of books to conquer lascivious thoughts (41r) appear to have won over the interlocutor, who concedes that with education his daughter might improve her behavior: "[P]eut étre qu'a vostre persuasion elle sentira un heureux change" (41v) [{P}erhaps with your persuasion she will experience a positive change].

The dialogue between Severe and Placide might initially be read as an exposition of the belief that women's learning ultimately serves patriarchal interests.[46] Yet the dialogue following it in the *Secondes Oeuvres, Le dialogue d'Iris et Pasithée*, reveals the crucial link between women's education and their freedom—both freedom from the burdens of demanding suitors and freedom to pursue their own intellectual interests.

Le dialogue d'Iris et Pasithée continues the topos of women's learning in a discussion between the daughters of Severe and Placide. Gently challenging the capricious, untutored Iris, Pasithée introduces the crucial question of how women ought best to employ their time. Just as her father Placide had inserted several arguments intended to appeal to his traditionalist interlocutor (as well as to a number of similar readers), so Pasithée discusses the subject that most interests Iris—her beauty—and then proceeds to subvert it:

> C'est pourtant dommage que vostre beauté de face n'est accompagnée de quelque gentillesse d'esprit, qui dure plus long tans qu'elle. (*Secondes œuvres*, 45r [misprinted as 40])

> [It's a shame, however, that your face's beauty isn't accompanied by some cultivation of the mind, which lasts longer].

On a lighter note, Pasithée discloses an unexpected purpose for the study of literature for young girls. Iris remarks that her suitor would be afraid to visit Pasithée because she is a "sçavante" (scholar), which prompts the following rejoinder from the young humanist:

> Ha ha, vraiment je l'en dispence, luy et tout autre qui le resemble. Je ne pense point que les letres soient en vain aprises par les filles, puis qu'elles donnent la chasse à telz galans. (*Secondes œuvres*, 53r)

> [Ha, ha, really I can do without him, him and anyone else who resembles him. I don't think girls learn letters in vain, since literature chases away such suitors.]

5 / *Le temps retrouvé:* Catherine des Roches 191

Pasithée in this dialogue fulfills the role of a "metahumanist" whose discourse is more pedagogical than intellectual, and it is evident that she functions as the author's mouthpiece, illustrating that humanistic wisdom brings with it a reasoned judgment beyond the unschooled Iris's grasp. The poised and eloquent Pasithée contrasts patently with the befuddled Iris. To exemplify Iris's inability to express herself, Catherine includes a humorous passage near the end of the dialogue. After having played a song on her lute for Iris to dance to, Pasithée requests Iris's opinion:

Pasith. Et bien Iris qu'en dites vous? est elle aisee à dancer?
Iris. Nenny pas beaucoup Pasithee, il m'est advis qu'elle est trop, la je ne sçay comment: Elle n'est pas assez.
Pasith. Voulez vous dire qu'elle n'est pas assez gaie?
Iris. Ouy, ouy, c'est cela mesme.
(Secondes œuvres, 51r-v)

[*P.* Well, Iris, what do you say? Is it easy to dance to? *I.* No, not really, Pasithée, I think that it's too—oh, I don't know—I don't think it's enough. *P.* Do you mean that it's not lively enough? *I.* Yes, yes, that's it.]

In response to Iris's distress about her lover, Pasithée relativizes such concerns throughout the dialogue by insisting on the greater importance of the life of the mind.[47] The mentor's recommendations to Iris, *grosso modo*, include taking pleasure in reading, writing well, and perfecting her speech (49r-v). Pasithée exerts even more influence over her interlocutor than did her father on Severe, and the dialogue concludes with optimism about Iris's future in her newly found mentor's company, even though the pupil's suitor interrupts their lesson:

Mon Dieu que vous dites bien Pasithee! Je viendrois tous les jours à votre école, si j'avois loisir.[48] Je prends tous les plaisirs du monde a discourir aveques vous. Il faut toutefois que je prenne congé, car Eole m'apelle, et puis il est tard. Je vous baise les mains Pasithee.
(Secondes œuvres, 53r)

[My goodness, you speak well, Pasithée! I'd come every day to your school if I had the time. But still I have to leave, because Eole is calling me, and it's late. I kiss your hands, Pasithée.]

Ultimately, Pasithée represents less the timeless exemplum than a practical paradigm for the intelligent use of a woman's time. As the dialogue between Pasithée and Iris illustrates, Catherine's humanist woman spends her time not only becoming learned in her own right but also engaging in a pedagogy that is both witty and personal. And the larger didactic message is specific: by consecrating herself to letters, Iris—and by extension, any woman, since Iris is a priori the least likely of candidates—will perfect her spirit (49v), finding both pleasure (47r) and virtue (48v).

Catherine's models of the *mesnagere*, the Amazon, and the humanist woman thus enact a reclaiming of women's time, breaking away from the temporal apportionment recommended by the moralists discussed in chapter 2. Through these models Catherine des Roches reveals her subscription to a kind of "mixed life," combining the two not easily compatible activities of traditionally female domestic occupation, on the one hand, and bold literary accomplishment, on the other. This sort of tension, in addition to suggesting several important late-twentieth-century questions concerning the lives of individuals,[49] is borne out in a number of examples drawn from literary history. Perhaps the most striking conflict emerges in the New Testament story of Mary and Martha, who represent the oppositional poles of the mixed life: contemplation and good works.[50] Similar tensions arise in the secular world, as in the conflict between public and private lives or between public service and letters. Thomas More deplores the tension between his legal career and family, on the one hand, and writing, on the other ("When doo I wryte, then?"),[51] and Montaigne argues for the preservation of one's private "arriere boutique" (back shop [of the mind]) against the invasion of the public sphere.[52] While the resolution of any of these personal conflicts contains some political element, Catherine des Roches's defense of her choice to live the humanist life rather than to marry takes on far more immediate social consequences.[53] Montaigne, for example, in a description of his withdrawal from public life to the tower library,[54] shows no indication that his right to make such a choice might be challenged (and even if it were, the reader understands that for the essayist the challenge would be a moot point). Catherine des Roches, on the other hand, justifies her decision to write throughout the *Oeuvres*, and her refusal to marry in favor of pursuing letters did indeed trouble at least some members of her entourage, as Estienne Pasquier's letter to his friend Pithou suggests:

> Il n'y a qu'une chose qui me desplaise en ceste maison, qu'estant la fille belle en perfection, tant de corps que d'esprit, riche de biens, comme celle qui doit estre unique heritiere de sa mere, requise en mariage par une infinité de personnages d'honneur, toutesfois elle met toutes ces requestes sous pieds.[55]

> [The only thing I do not like in this household is that the daughter, beautiful to perfection both in body and in spirit, wealthy as the single inheritor of her

mother, sought in marriage by an infinite number of honorable men, still firmly rejects all offers.]

By virtue of their positions, of course, Montaigne is under no obligation to represent anyone but himself, whereas Catherine des Roches, as a woman whose literary career illustrates the triumph of the pen over the spindle, speaks not only for herself but also ipso facto for all women who wish to write in sixteenth-century France.[56]

Seen in the light of Catherine's own exemplary status, her recasting of the Amazon and the *mulier economica* in a more humanistic mold takes on even greater significance. Catherine's "humanizing" of exemplary figures (rendering them both more human and more humanistic) removes them from the atemporal, eternal realm of the traditional exemplar and situates them within a more concrete, practical time as women live it. Catherine's reclaiming of temporality for women is perhaps most evident in her particular treatment of the human body.

THE WOMAN AS BODY

"Exemplarity," Hampton argues, "aims at exhorting the reader to move from words to deeds, from language to action. Thus it is no accident that the surface on which much attention is focused in writing on exemplarity is the surface of the body—the surface that lies at the frontier of word and deed, the zone that both acts and signifies. Just as the words and deeds of the heroic ancient function as signs of his excellence, so too the image of his body, held up to the reader, functions as a text to be read, as a surface on which are inscribed the signs of heroism."[57] Quite obviously, in the case of Catherine des Roches's exemplars, the human body, this time markedly female, fulfills an even more complex function than do the bodies of the male heroes Hampton describes. Two opposing forces motivate her depiction of women exemplars. On the one hand, because moral discourse in late sixteenth-century France situates the female body primarily as the locus of sexual transgression, and because both the Reformation and the Counter Reformation insist upon the containment of that potential source of evil,[58] Catherine's poet's own ambivalence toward the body ensures public acceptance and thus a wide readership (which we know was of interest to her).[59] On the other hand, since the exemplars she creates are decidedly women rather than sexless moral guides, and since the female body serves to mark that particularity, the necessity remains to focus on the body in some way. Through an examination of the erotic body and the body as a measure of time in Catherine's work, I will argue that the poet ultimately resolves her equivocal stance concerning the body by diminishing the importance of material being in her work. She nonetheless navigates with considerable grace between the Scylla of showcasing the female body and the Charybdis of obliterating it.

The Erotic Body

A preliminary question to be posed in examining Catherine's poet's attitudes toward the body is whether she, like her forebear Christine de Pizan, deplores her status as female. In *La Cité des Dames*, before analyzing a number of authorities who have been the roots of her oppression, Pizan initially accuses God of having condemned her to a female fate: "Hélas, mon Dieu! pourquoi ne pas m'avoir fait naître mâle afin que mes inclinations aillent à ton service? . . . En ma folie je me désespérais que Dieu m'ait fait naître dans un corps féminin"[60] [Alas, my God! Why did you not make me born male so that my good intentions could be devoted to your service? . . . In my madness I despaired that God had me born in a female body]. But unlike Christine de Pizan, Catherine des Roches never rejects the female body in particular, even for rhetorical purposes. On the contrary, she depicts it in a positive light in several contexts. When the cross-dressed Agnodice bares her breasts, revealing her gender first to the women and then to the men, for example, her female body serves her well in both cases. Catherine describes Agnodice's physique in elegiac terms:

> Agnodice, voyant leur grande chasteté,
> Les estima beaucoup pour ceste honnesteté;
> Lors descouvrant du sein les blanches pommes rondes,
> Et de son chef doré les belles tresses blondes,
> Monstre qu'elle estoit fille, et que son gentil cueur
> Les vouloit delivrer de leur triste langueur.
>
> (*Les Œuvres,* 337)

[Agnodice, seeing their great chastity, / Admired them very much for this goodness; / Then revealing the round white apples of her bosom, / And the beautiful blond braids of her golden head, / She showed that she was a girl, and that her kind heart / Wished to deliver them from their languishing.]

The women, now drawn to trust Agnodice in her feminine avatar, are themselves not impervious to her physical beauty, which Catherine describes in terms befitting a *blason:*

5 / *Le temps retrouvé:* Catherine des Roches

> Les Dames admirant cest honte naïsve,
> Et de son teint doüillet la blanche couleur vive,
> Et de son sein poupin le petit mont jumeau,
> Et de son chef sacré l'or crepelu tant beau,
> Et de ses yeux divins les flammes ravissantes,
> Et de ses doux propos les graces attirantes,
> Baiserent mille fois et sa bouche et son sein,
> Recevant le secours de son heureuse main.
>
> *(Les Œuvres,* 337)

[The women admiring this natural shame / And the lively white color of her soft complexion / And the small twin mountain of her lovely breast / And the beautiful wavy gold of her beloved head, / And the ravishing flames of her divine eyes / And the becoming graces of her sweet speech, / Kissed her mouth and bosom a thousand times, / Receiving succor from her favorable hand.]

Similarly, when Agnodice reveals her female identity to the husbands who have condemned her to death, she uncovers her "sein beau, aggreable sejour / Des Muses, des vertus, des graces, de l'amour" (*Les Œuvres,* 338–39) [beautiful bosom, pleasant harbor of the Muses, virtues, graces and love]. This description, neither as lengthy nor as elegiac as the one in which Catherine reveals Agnodice's identity to the women, seems implicitly to call into question the notion of the female body as the locus of the male (erotic) gaze, eulogizing instead Agnodice's physical beauty as it corresponds with her "sweet speech" and her moral goodness.[61] Note also that Agnodice is revealed not to be a "femme," but rather a "fille," which again serves to mitigate the erotic potential of the poem. The passage further suggests the appreciation of the female body by other women, and expands the message of the epic poem by advocating the importance of women's community.

Catherine's poet's appreciation of the female body can also be glimpsed in the *Dialogue d'Iris et Pasithée* in the *Secondes œuvres*. Even the quintessential humanist Pasithée recognizes and commends the young Iris's beauty (*Secondes œuvres,* 45r, 48r). Pasithée recites a poem that represents perfectly her interlocutor's physical state:

> Vous resemblez un dous printans,
> Orné de fleurs et de feuillage,
> Ainsi la fleur de vos beaux ans
> Luit en vostre mignard visage.
>
> *(Secondes œuvres,* 44v)

[You resemble a sweet spring, / Adorned with flowers and leaves, / Thus the flower of your beautiful age / Glows in your lovely face.]

Pasithée also seems to draw pleasure from Iris's dancing, proposing to accompany her on the lute and seeking a lively song with a danceable rhythm (49v-51r).

A final example of Catherine's favorable depiction of the female body occurs in "La femme forte decritte par Salomon," where, as Ann Rosalind Jones notes, Catherine, like Alberti, "eroticizes domestic energy"[62] as she describes the housewoman:

> Vous la verriez parfois r'accourcir sa vesture,
> Troussée proprement d'une forte ceinture,
> Et revirer apres ses manches sur les bras
> Qui paroissent charnus, poupins, douïllets et gras:
> Car il ne faut penser que la delicatesse
> Se trouve seulement avecques la paresse.
>
> *(Les Œuvres,* 329)

[You would sometimes see her take up her dress, / Nicely tucked with a wide belt, / And roll up her sleeves, showing her arms / Which seem fleshy, lovely, soft, and plump / For you must not think that delicacy / Comes only with idleness.]

Significantly, in all of these descriptions, the female body is first eroticized but then in some way desexualized, as if to attenuate the force of the purely physical image. While the description of Agnodice's dauntless act of exposing her breasts reveals a dazzlingly attractive body, the heroine remains ashamed (*Les Œuvres,* 337, 339) and honorable (339), betraying a virginal blush (339). Catherine's poet also intercepts the gaze of both female and male observers, encoding in her text the chastity of the women gazing at Agnodice's body, on the one hand, and the pity of the men to whom the heroine reveals herself, on the other (337, 339). Similarly, the description of Iris's body in the *Dialogue d'Iris et Pasithée* serves to set the stage for a dialogic lesson on the importance of the spiritual, thereby calling into question the consequence of Iris's physical beauty. Catherine's poet's sensuous description of the "femme forte" is also followed by a reneging: "La beauté se flestrist . . . ce n'est qu'une fable" (331) [Beauty wanes . . . it is only a fable]. Rather than repudiating the female body per se, then, Catherine's poet celebrates it up to a certain point, taking care nonetheless to deflect its erotic possibilities.

We have examined the way in which Catherine's narrator sexualizes and immediately desexualizes the female body in nonerotic contexts. How, then, does she write about the female body when the topos at hand is inextricably linked with corporality, such as in amorous discourse? Catherine's treatment of the erotic body manifests itself not only by what is present in the text but also by what is omitted. As Evelyne Berriot-Salvadore has noted,[63] nowhere in her work does Catherine give homage to Louise Labé, despite the Lyonnais poet's pioneering efforts in publishing and exhorting other women to write. This absence is all the more conspicuous because of Catherine's extensive use of Labé's dialogues as a source for her own.[64] But again, given the public moral climate in 1579 and the very real possibility that even a single reference to the name Labé would conjure up lascivious images in the minds of contemporary readers, it is not surprising that Catherine erases the name of the person whose influence can nonetheless be discerned in her work.

Catherine's oeuvre provides a number of angles from which to view what might be called the poet's sublimation of the physical. In her refusal of suitors within the text, Catherine's poet foreshadows the methods of the Précieuses, who steadfastly turn lovers away with a clever turn of phrase, a pertinent pun, or an elaborate verbal obstruction. Catherine's style occasionally suggests that of the Précieuses in its "recherche de la rareté" [search for rarity],[65] an acute example of which occurs in an excruciatingly extended wordplay between Catherine and Pasquier published in his *Œuvres complètes*. The two poets establish a mock rivalry around puns on the words "roche" and "serre"; Catherine begins:

> Vostre ame sans fin Amoureuse
> De Serrer est tant desireuse,
> Que plustost que de ne serrer,
> On vous pourroit vif enterrer.
> Encore estant dessous la terre,
> Je ne croy point qu'elle vous serre,
> Que vous espris de son Amour
> Ne la serriez à vostre tour.[66]

[Your endlessly loving soul / Desires to embrace so much / That rather than not embracing / It would prefer to be burned alive. / But even with your being under the earth, / I don't believe the earth could embrace you / Without your being taken by her love / And embracing her in return.]

Pasquier responds:

> De tant serrer je n'auray le reproche,
> Comme en François m'en donnez le blason:

>SERRE en Gascon est un mont, une roche,
>Et il me plaist vous respondre en Gascon.
>Si je tenois toutes choses en SERRE,
>J'enserrerois, et vos affections,
>Et gravirois (ô ma Roche) la serre,
>Et au sommet de vos perfections.[67]

[I have nothing against all the embracing, / As in the French *blazon* you have written for me; / EMBRACE in Gascon is a mountain, a rock, / And I am pleased to answer you in Gascon. / If I held all these things captive / I would store all your affections / And I would both climb (O my Rock) where you are held / And scale to the summit of your perfections.]

In the *Dialogue de Sincero et de Charite*, on the other hand, the language appears less precious than do the premises. Even though Charite explicitly advocates a Neoplatonic or reciprocal love, the exchanges emerge as a sort of game in which the winner takes or refuses all. The codification and rhetorical hoops through which the interlocutors jump timidly announce the amorous topography of Mlle. de Scudéry's "Carte du Tendre."[68] Also similar to the Précieuses, the des Roches's salon stages a matriarchal world, where, much like Catherine's "A ma quenoille," the public domain is coupled with the private, and where women govern the conversation, both philosophical and amorous. Pelous describes the comportmental code for a courted woman in the precious salons of the seventeenth century: "A l'égard de l'amour, . . . il lui faut résister, se dérober . . . et répondre aux déclarations si respectueuses soit-elles par une fin de non recevoir" (*Les Œuvres,* 58) [With respect to love, she must resist, escape, and respond to declarations, no matter how respectful, by refusing.] Here, however, Catherine's character's resistance differs significantly from that of her seventeenth-century literary descendants, because the art of the Précieuses consists of unleashing the passions while simultaneously keeping them out of reach. While Charite's resistance to Sincero's amorous proposals is both playful and witty, and while it may at first appear that she refuses simply for the sake of refusal, as the dialogue advances, and especially in the sonnets following the dialogue, Charite reveals the logic behind her opposition. In rebuking Sincero's enraptured rhetoric, for example, Charite injects not only humor but also a good measure of the reality principle:

>*Sincero.* Madame, je persevere tousjours en mes premiers propos, et ma requeste premiere, demandant à voz graces, puisqu'il leur plaist bien quelquesfois de me conduire au Ciel, qu'elles ne desdaignent non plus de me guider en terre.

Charite. Puisque vous ne pouvez encore vous guider en terre sans ayde d'autruy, comment vous mettez-vous à vouloir rechercher le Ciel?
Sincero. Vous en estes cause, Madame, car j'y suis conduit par vous, et vous par moy.
Charite. Si n'ay-je point souvenance d'y avoir jamais esté; mais possible m'en ferez-vous revenir la memoire me disant ce que j'aperceu de plus esmerveillable en ce voyage.

(Les Œuvres, 253)

[*S.* Madame, I am still insisting on my first topic, and my first request, asking that your graces, since sometimes they transport me to Heaven, deign to guide me on earth as well. *C.* Since you cannot yet guide yourself on earth without someone's help, how is it that you wish to seek Heaven? *S.* You are the cause, madam, for I am transported there by you, and you by me. *C.* I don't recall ever having been there. But it's possible that you'll make it come back to me by telling me what I found the most remarkable about the trip.]

Throughout the dialogue, Charite critiques the courtly "fable" (254) concocted by Sincero. In the subsequent sonnet sequence Charite changes tone somewhat as she betrays an interest in her suitor, but she imposes a number of precise conditions concerning his behavior and especially his fidelity, revealing her considerable skepticism about the trustworthiness of poetic palaverers. The first sonnet outlines in *blason*-like fashion a number of admirable qualities that her suitor does not possess, but that he ought to (kindness, prudence, eloquence, intelligence, modesty): "Voilà, qu'en le voyant, je *desire* de voir" (272, my emphasis) [This is what I *want* to see when I look at him].

The obverse of the courtly lady, Charite further articulates specific contingencies for her sentiments. In short, her fidelity will extend only as far as Sincero's. In her most impetuous challenge, Charite suggests that if Sincero cannot be faithful to her, the solution lies simply in each seeking a new partner:

> Si vous m'estes constant, je vous seray constante,
> Si vous voulez changer, hé bien j'en suis contente,
> Cherchez une autre amie et moy un autre amy.

(Les Œuvres, 278)

[If you are faithful to me, I will be faithful to you, / If you wish to change, that's fine with me, / Seek another love and I will do the same.]

Thus in these texts Catherine creates a poetic dialogue that, like the rhetoric of the Précieuses, insists upon the power of the woman in an amorous exchange. Unlike the Précieuses, however, Catherine deflects the embers of eroticism rather than stoking them. In the penultimate sonnet, Charite once again downplays the physical, advising Sincero to consider love as an activity to be pursued only in leisure, and even then not to dwell on it:

> Je vous sçauray bon gré, s'il vous plaist, de choisir
> Le temps le plus commode aux oeuvres serieuses;
> Mais ne me racontez voz plaintes amoureuses
> Sinon quand vous serez aux heures de loisir.
> La plus grand part du temps demeurez à l'estude. . . .
> (Les Œuvres, 280)

[I would be grateful, if you would be so kind as to choose / The most fitting time for serious work; / But do not tell me your amorous complaints / Except in moments of leisure. / Spend most of your time in study. . . .]

Catherine's poet declines to assume the role of the lover not only in order to assert her own authority but also as a means of preserving independence. Catherine's frequent depiction of love as a prison capable of usurping freedom initially seems to echo the Pléiade and other Petrarchan poets. But unlike her lyric predecessors, she insists on the loss of freedom of both lover and beloved. In her *Dialogue d'Amour de Beauté et de Physis*, for example, the poet unmasks Amour as the culprit who makes men fall prey to feminine beauty. Depicted in a very negative light, Catherine's Cupid makes men believe that beauty alone has enraptured them, and in Catherine's dialogue it is the woman who bears the troublesome consequences. Here Beauty, in an apostrophe to Cupid, describes men's desire for vengeance against her:

> Pour ce faire, prenant les traicts que vous leur avez tirez, ils me les rejettent, les uns empennez de papier escrit, les autres de courtoises parolles, les autres qui ont la pointe dorée plus persante que le fer ny l'acier: et toutes ces malicieuses cautelles leurs sont enseignées par vous [*sic*]. (*Les Œuvres,* 244–45)

[To do this, they take the arrows you have shot and throw them at me, some of them adorned with inscribed paper, others with galant speech and others with a golden point more piercing than iron or steel: and you are the one who taught them all these malicious ruses.]

According to this model, both lover and beloved become prisoners of an amorous system in which the man is battered by Cupid's arrows and the woman then besieged by invasive amorous discourse. Hélisenne de Crenne, writing in the 1540s, had also lamented masculine vindictiveness faced with feminine beauty. In her second invective letter, Hélisenne has the husband echo a sentiment similar to the one Beauty describes: "O que malheureuses sont voz beautez, fardz et aornemens, dont tant de malheurs s'ensuiyvent"[69] [Oh how unfortunate are your beauties, cosmetics, and ornaments, from which so many afflictions follow].[70] Much like Catherine's character Beauty, Hélisenne challenges the woman's responsibility therein: "Et pourtant deporte toy de blasmer la corporelle beauté en femme. Car je t'asseure qu'elle n'est perilleuse pour les hommes, ausquelz consiste vertu"[71] [So stop accusing physical beauty in women. I assure you that it is not perilous for men in whom virtue resides].

The negative consequences of erotic love's imprisonment of women are also manifest in Catherine's dramatic poem *Tobie*, where Sarra describes her attachment to Tobie as tantamount to her loss of liberty:

> De ses gentils propos l'agreable douceur
> A desrobé du tout ma liberté premiere,
> Et mis en son pouvoir mon ame prisonniere.
> *(Les Œuvres,* 369)

[The pleasant sweetness of his speech stole my former freedom, holding my soul captive in his power.]

Interestingly, although Catherine depicts Sarra's devotion to Tobie in a positive light, the marriage nonetheless causes Sarra's definitive separation from her beloved mother. Not coincidentally (given Catherine's fierce attachment to her own mother),[72] the passage describing Sarra's departure from her mother, filled with uncharacteristic passion and pathos, is much more forceful than those describing her love for Tobie:

> Ma mere, je m'en vais, et m'en allant d'icy
> J'emporte la douleur, la peine, et le souci.
> Mil et mille regrets ores me font la guerre.
> Helas! j'ay si grand deuil de laisser nostre terre
> . . . .
> . . . vous perdant de veüe,
> Je pers tout mon tresor, et vous laisse mon cueur
> Pour vous porter amour, reverence, et honneur.
> Je prends congé de vous, he mon Dieu! je me pasme
> Dans votre sein aimé.
> *(Les Œuvres,* 380–81)

[Mother, I am leaving, and going away from here / I carry with me grief, sadness, and worry. / Thousands of regrets are now at war in me. / Alas! I grieve at leaving our land / . . . / . . . losing sight of you, / I lose all my treasure, and leave you my heart / To bring you love, reverence, and honor. / I am leaving you, O my God! I languish / In your beloved bosom.]

In this passage Catherine clearly downplays conjugal love, which holds Sarra hostage and carries her far from her mother and homeland. In a telling twist, Sarra applies the language of erotic poetry (the lover's suffering equated with war, languishing, leaving one's heart) not to her spouse but to her mother, suggesting an emotionally superior bond. A loss of self is suggested as Sarra explicitly surrenders both her treasure and her heart.

Whereas in the first instance, the woman represents the unwilling object of the man's captivation and in the second, the woman reluctantly abandons family and country for her husband, a final example shows the woman's outright refusal of amorous imprisonment by making a mockery of the man's infatuation. In the *Sonnets de Sincero à Charite,* Sincero, an overly zealous Petrarchan devotee, writes to his lady enraptured verses describing his imprisoned state: "Je veux mourir cent fois en ma douce prison, / Laissant ma liberté, ma vie, et ma raison / Dans voz yeux, dans vos mains, et vostre blonde tresse . . ." (*Les Œuvres,* 262) [I want to die a hundred deaths in my sweet prison, / Abandoning my freedom, my life, and my reason / To your eyes, your hands, and your blond braid]. In the dialogue between Charite and Sincero preceding the sonnet sequence, Charite has already humorously ironized the lover's passion:

Charite. Eh bien donc, comme à mon prisonnier, je vous commande de vous taire pour recommencer à parler une autre fois.
Sincero. Puisqu'il vous plaist, Madame, je m'en vays honorer le silence par luy-mesme.

(*Les Œuvres,* 257)

[C. Well, then, as {I would do to} my prisoner, I order you to be quiet. You can speak another time. / S. Since it pleases you, madam, I shall honor silence by observing it.]

The celibate body, which incarnates in Catherine's work the refusal of love's imprisonment, thus becomes the guardian of the humanist woman's potential. This "militant chastity"[73] serves to insist upon female authority, self-sufficiency, and intellectual industriousness. Catherine's championing of the celibate body, stridently feminist within her rhetorical system, paradoxically met with public acceptance and admiration,[74] since her stance also served the patriarchal interest in women's chastity, albeit with very different ends in mind. As Margaret King has observed, "[C]hastity was expressive of the learned woman's defiance of the established natural order, and of the learned man's attempt to constrain her energies by making her mind the prison of her body."[75] The politics of chastity, as we have seen, occupy a pivotal position in Catherine's work, as do the social consequences of writing about the female body as a measure of passing time.

THE BODY AND TEMPORALITY

In late medieval and sixteenth-century iconography, time was often represented as a winged old man, scythe in hand, flying above Roman ruins and pulling behind him several cherubs. Old age, on the other hand, was allegorized as a woman, and as we saw in chapter 1, this image, building on a long medieval tradition, incarnated both the grotesque and the satirical. Catherine, in her *Dialogue de Vieillesse et Jeunesse*, takes the stereotypical depiction of old age as a point of departure and then, in true dialogic fashion, challenges the foundations of the portrait of Vieillesse she has sketched. The dialogue opens with Vieillesse observing the frolicking of the "jeune folastre" Jeunesse, who, adorned with a crown of flowers, is dancing, singing, and playing the lute. Jeunesse perceives Vieillesse and describes her in the most traditional of terms:

> O Dieu! Qui ameine vers moy cette vieille decrepite avec le front de damas, et les yeux de verre? Il ne luy paroist aucunes dens en la bouche, le rhume les y a toutes fauchées. (*Les Œuvres,* 187–88)

> [Oh God! Who is bringing me this decrepit hag with a leathery forehead and glassy eyes? It looks like she has no teeth—disease has made them all fall out.]

After taunting Vieillesse, reminding her of her approaching death and calling her a "vieille hideuse" (190) [hideous hag], Jeunesse boasts that she, youthful and attractive, pleases everyone, whereas people find Vieillesse odious. Taking a more distanced, philosophical tone, Vieillesse defends herself:

> Il est vray que je suis penible à quelques-uns, pource qu'ils ont mal usé de vous, en vous donnant pour compaignie les voluptez desordonnées, qui sont causes dont ils souffrent apres les extremes douleurs pour lesquelles je reçoy blasme, sans en estre coupable. Voilà donc l'origine de leurs maux et des

miens; s'ils eussent eu la jeunesse moderée, ils sentiroient la vieillessse paisible. (*Les Œuvres,* 192)

[It is true that I am bothersome for some, because they used you {Youth} badly, giving you for company wild, sensuous pleasures, which are later the cause of extreme suffering, for which I receive the blame without being guilty. Here, then, is the origin of their troubles and mine: if they had had a more moderate youth, they would enjoy a peaceful old age.]

Throughout the dialogue Vieillesse insists on the importance of cycles and continuity in time, assuming the role of a wise arbitrator. When Jeunesse compares herself to the radiant spring and Vieillesse to cruel winter, the elder ripostes that both spring and winter are necessary, describing her own role in the human cycle as a positive one. Just as Noah enclosed animals in the ark so that they could perpetuate themselves after the flood, so winter must envelop the earth:

[A]insi j'enclos au sein de la terre durant la rigueur du froid, les semences de ce qu'elle doit produire en une autre saison: et si pour un temps je ne la rendoy espargnante, elle ne pourroit apres estre liberalle. (*Les Œuvres,* 193)

[{S}o I enclose in the folds of the earth during the adverse cold weather the seeds of what the earth must produce in another season: and if for a while I didn't make it sparing, it could not be bounteous thereafter.]

The sexual terms "sein" [breast] and "semences" [sperm] embedded in Vieillesse's discourse on the earth's barrenness linguistically rehearse the continual generation of Nature's cycle. Perhaps the most syncretic, collaborative gesture of the dialogue occurs when Jeunesse continues to insist upon her status as beloved in opposition to Vieillesse's position as pariah. Vieillesse responds:

Mon Dieu, que vous avez de gloire! Et en sçavez-vous pas bien que nous sommes creatures d'un mesme Createur, qui nous a faict venir au monde toutes deux pour mesme fin? (*Les Œuvres,* 194)[76]

[My God, you're arrogant! And don't you know that we are creatures of the same Creator, who brought both of us into the world for the same end?]

Near the end of the dialogue, Vieillesse's authority reaches its apogee as she justifies in alexandrine verses her place in the universe, suggesting the quieting discourse of Ecclesiastes 3:

> Je derobe sans fin les beautez et la grace
> Que je rends à nature affin qu'elle en reface
> Et maintiene le monde en son ordre ancien.
> Pour mille fois mourir et mille fois renaistre,
> Rien pourtant ne se perd, toute chose a son estre. . . .
> *(Les Œuvres,* 198)

[I endlessly steal beauties and grace / Which I return to nature so that she can remake / And maintain the world in its former order. / A thousand times dead and a thousand times reborn, / Nothing however is lost, everything has its own being.]

Here Vieillesse, much like the Roman divinity Genius, retains sovereignty over generation, birth, life, and destiny—time's cycle is thus vindicated. It is interesting to note that while Catherine's philosophical stance regarding the mutability of all things appears to recall certain of Ronsard's poems on the same subject,[77] Ronsard never depicts the allegorization of Old Age in a favorable light.[78] Here Catherine's wise old woman, on the contrary, shatters the stereotype of old age represented as a witchlike shrew. While like in earlier literary depictions Vieillesse is physically decrepit and "horribly ugly" (197), she nonetheless shows compassion toward her young interlocutor (194–96) and ultimately speaks with the voice of reason in the dialogue. In the final scene, Jeunesse avows that she has learned a secret from Vieillesse and debates with herself whether or not she should reveal it to other women (198–200). Even though in medieval fashion no clear victor emerges in the debate, the wisdom of Catherine's Vieillesse clearly prevails, mitigating her physical decrepitude.

Catherine, much like the carefree, dancing youth of the *Dialogue de Vieillesse et Jeunesse,* receives warnings of her imminent aging, but in this case the harbinger is not an allegory of old age but rather male poet-suitors who address *carpe diem* poems to their young colleague. Graced with considerable "avantages extérieurs" (as Michaud puts it),[79] charming, unattached, and resistant to all advances, Catherine was in many ways the ideal addressee for the *carpe diem* motif. Judging from a series of forty-five poems entitled "Responces" in her *Secondes œuvres,* Catherine indeed received many such poems. In these "Responces," Catherine explicitly rebuts the seductive verses of several unnamed admirers, among whom potentially figure Claude Pellejay, Caye-Jules de Guersens, and Estienne Pasquier, whose devotion is humorously immortalized in *La Puce de Madame des Roches* (1583).[80]

The ubiquitous motif *carpe diem* or *carpe florem,* in depicting the vibrant bud metamorphosing into a withered rose, simultaneously signals an explicit confidence in the present moment and an implicit terror concerning the future, as we saw in chapter 1. Privileging physical beauty, the prototypical *carpe diem* poem threatens the young woman addressee with the literal or implied portrait of her withered old age, which is presented as the alternative to her loving the poet now, while she is still beautiful.

Catherine formulates both philosophical and psychological objections to the temporal ideology inherent in the *carpe diem* motif, often within the context of her rejection of the rhetorical aim of that motif (the woman's seduction). Her philosophical notions concerning the passage of time are less nostalgic than those of her predecessors of the Pléiade, reflecting rather traces of certain Greek and Roman writers in her stoic acceptance of time's relentless pace. In Response 9, for example, Catherine reveals a Heraclitean consciousness of time's power to change all things.[81] Establishing a parallel between aging and change in all of nature, the poet describes the passage of time as a succession, rendered circular by the reference both to waves and to the sun:

> Ainsi que l'onde pousse l'onde,
> Que la nuit va suivant le jour,
> Le soleil ornement du monde,
> Chasse les ombres à son tour.
> . . . .
> Voions nous un plaisant visage
> Changer son vermeil en palleur?
> Nature bonne mere et sage
> En va metre un autre en valeur.
>
> (*Secondes œuvres,* 63v-64v)

[As one wave sends off another, / As night follows day, / As the sun, the world's embellishment, / Chases away shadows in turn. / . . . / Do we now see a lovely face / Changing to pale from rose-red? / Nature, good and wise Mother, / Will make another one beautiful in its stead.]

The Senecan notion that all progresses according to a natural order, that one face should lose its luster and pass it on to another, underlies these verses. Dismissing physical beauty as an ephemeral quality, and therefore unworthy of lovers' attention, Catherine recommends instead the attraction of lovers by beauties found in the soul. Such an affinity, she argues, is both healthier and more enduring:

> Il ne faut seulement represanter les faces
> De qui les dous atraitz tirent hors de leurs places,
> Par les sens trahissans les volages espris.

> Mais toutes les beautez demeurant en vostre ame
> Vous alumez aux cueurs une celeste flame,
> Et plus sain est celuy qui plus en est epris.
>
> *(Secondes œuvres,* 62r-v)

[Do not represent only the faces whose sweet attractions, by untrustworthy senses, draw fickle minds from reason. But given all the beauties of your soul, you ignite in hearts a celestial flame, and happier is he who is taken with them.]

Catherine further repudiates the *carpe diem* motif by directly rebuffing her literary suitors, with varying psychological twists. Unlike Pernette, whose female poet gladly participates as muse in the male poet's immortality if in so doing there results "contentement" for both parties, Catherine's speaker refuses to be the object of the male poet's amorous fiction. In one case she accomplishes this feat by outright rejection, chastising the male poet for his incessant literary pursuit:

> Si est-ce que la Renommee
> Ne peut chanter vos vers tant dous,
> Que moy par leur Grace animee
> Ne vole au ciel avecques vous.
> Et plus vous me voiez indigne
> De tant de belles fictions,
> Et plus vostre Muse divine
> Est riche en ses inventions.
>
> *(Secondes œuvres,* 64v)

[Fame can no more / Sing your sweet verses / Than I can fly to the heavens with you because of them. / And the more you see me indignant / At such fancy fictions / The more your divine muse / Is rich in her inventions.]

In Response 41, Catherine adopts a quite different tactic, turning the image of her own youthful beauty topsy-turvy, thereby throwing the ball back into the opponent's court. Flattering her flatterer, Catherine argues that it is not her face, a constantly declining entity, that should be compared to a flower, but rather her addressee's own soul:

> Prenant pour argument une face fanie
> Qui s'en va chécun jour declinant d'un degré.
> Un Jardin plein de fleurs n'est pas si diaprè,
> Que vostre Ame paroit de Graces embellie.
>
> *(Secondes œuvres,* 77v)

[Taking as proof a faded face / That declines a bit each day. / A garden filled with flowers is not as colorful / As your soul appears embellished by grace.]

In addition to writing responses to *carpe diem* poems, Catherine also treats the *carpe diem* motif extensively in her *Dialogue d'Iris et de Pasithée* (*Secondes œuvres,* 43v ff.). As we saw above, in this dialogue Pasithée tutors Iris, who has just received a *carpe diem* poem from her penultimate flame, Nirée. As if to distance herself more emphatically from the fictional writer of the *carpe diem* poem, Catherine has the character Iris read aloud Nirée's verses. The poem might be called a "second-stage" manifestation of the *carpe diem* motif; its theme, as in Ronsard's "Quand vous serez bien vieille," remains the centrality of the woman's desirability and its loss, which is rhetorically linked to her spurning of the male lover. But here the lover, weary of being enslaved to the lady, proclaims his love to have been as evanescent as her youthful beauty:

> Si j'ay fait autre-fois,
> Cruel Amour, a ton pouvoir hommage,
> Or' je quite tes loix
> M'afranchissant de ton fâcheux servage.
> . . . .
> A Dieu fleur de Printans
> Qui commandiez a mes jeunes pensees,
> Je voi au fil des ans,
> Et vos beautez, et mes amours passées.
>   (*Secondes œuvres,* 47v-48r)

[If, Cruel Love, I praised your power long ago, now I am leaving your laws, freeing myself from this tiresome slavery. . . . Farewell, spring flower, who commanded my young thoughts. I see vanishing with the passing of the years, both your beauty and my love.]

Iris's amusing account of Nirée's insulting description of her is significant, because it shows the evolution of Nirée's *carpe diem* threat into a worst-case scenario:

> Il me compare a cete Iris qui paroist en l'air: disant qu'elle denote la pluie, et moy les pleurs, qu'elle est courbe, et moy mal-droite, qu'elle se tient opposée au Soleil, et moy a la Raison, qu'elle est changeante, et moy variable, que ses beautez sont fauses, et les miennes faintes. . . . (*Secondes œuvres,* 45r)

5 / *Le temps retrouvé:* Catherine des Roches

[He compares me to the iris in the air, saying that she indicates rain, and I tears; that she is bent and I malformed; that she is opposed to the sun and I to reason; that she is changing and I flighty; that her beauties are false and mine fake. . . .]

Pasithée, in fine psychological form, presents the counterpoint to Nirée's defamation of Iris: "Et vraiment je croy que cét homme audacieux ne vous a point assez veüe pour vous connoistre, ou quelque dépit luy a fait tenir ce propos" (45v) [Truly I believe that this audacious man has not seen you enough to know you, or spite makes him say that].

The young Iris evokes the potential psychological force of the *carpe diem* motif when she avows her distress at the thought of having lost her beauty so quickly, but Pasithée assures her that either Nirée's eyes have gone bad or he's lying ("il dement le veritable temoignage," 48r). In response to Iris's query about what she should do next, Pasithée, here a wise mentor as distinguished from Tyard's wise acolyte,[82] responds economically, "vous devez lire" (49r) [You must read]. Study and research calm the spirit, chasing away vain and frivolous thoughts, Pasithée assures her student. But since Pasithée recognizes that Iris's principal desire is not to become a scholar but rather to attract faithful lovers, the mentor concludes the dialogue by presenting her message in terms Iris can understand: "Chécun veut aimer ce qui luy ressemble. . . . Embellissez donc vostre ame, si vous desirez d'être uniquement aimée par un Amy sage, accort, et sçavant" (49v) [Everyone seeks to love another who resembles him. . . . So embellish your soul, if you wish to be loved by a wise, clever, and knowledgeable suitor]. Thus, according to Pasithée the young woman must reject not only the threat of lost beauty but also any suitor-poet who would formulate such a threat. And once again, the alternative proposed to fretting about lost physical beauty through the passage of time is simply to turn one's thoughts to the more enduring beauties of the soul. Here the poet Nirée's desire to dominate his young addressee by describing the lost beauty of her body is subverted by Pasithée's Neoplatonic championing of the soul, the human entity most immune to the vicissitudes of time.

The acquisition of wisdom through reading, writing, and study is far preferable to preoccupation with physical beauty, according to Catherine's poet, but the most long-lasting quality of all is "vertu."[83] Pasithée ultimately sets up a clearly delineated hierarchy of the spiritual or mental and the physical, with "vertu" surpassing all spiritual qualities, and "la face," synecdoche of the aging body, representing the physical:

> Belle ne craignez point de tomber a mépris,
> Bien que plusieurs hivers vous ternissent la face,

> Decorez vostre Esprit de Vertus et de Grace,
> Car la Vertu retient ce que les yeux ont pris.
> <div align="right">(<i>Secondes œuvres,</i> 48v)</div>

[Young beauty, do not fear contempt, / Though several winters will tarnish your face, / Adorn your soul with virtues and grace, / For virtue retains what the eyes have taken in.]

In Response 34, Catherine further privileges virtue as the primordial quality that endures beyond the spring of a human life cycle:

> Si la Beauté, la richesse,
> Le sçavoir, la gentillesse,
> Decorent vostre Printans,
> Faites que la Vertu sage,
> Soit dedans vostre courage,
> Fleur de la Fleur de vos ans.
> <div align="right">(<i>Secondes œuvres,</i> 75v)</div>

[If beauty, wealth, / Knowledge and kindness, / Adorn your spring, / Keep wise virtue in your heart, / Flower of the flower of your years.]

Finally, in Response 12, "vertu" is also associated with "la parole" and by extension with the enterprise of writing:

> Ce n'est point le tans qui s'envole
> C'est la douce Fleur des beaux Ans,
> Mais par l'air de vostre parole
> La Vertu triomphe du Tans.
> <div align="right">(<i>Secondes œuvres,</i> 64v-65r)</div>

[Time is not flying away, / But rather the sweet flower of beautiful years, / Yet by the grace of your word / Virtue triumphs over Time.]

Thus for Catherine, as for the *carpe diem* poets, one of time's primary characteristics is its physical destruction, and specifically the toll it takes on the human body. But she continually subverts the power both of bodily deterioration itself and of the poets who use it as a threat by minimizing the importance of physical beauty in comparison with the nobler quality of "vertu," exemplified, as her character Pasithée explains, by the practice of reading and writing.[84]

Catherine's work thus radically rewrites the notion of women's time underlying both the *carpe diem* poets and such moralists as Erasmus, Vives, and Bouchet. Rejecting the terror of lost time inherent in the *carpe diem* motif and replacing the insistence upon the negative consequences of idleness by the advocacy of extensive study for women, Catherine reclaims time as an entity to be shaped and exploited in the present. More than any other writer I have examined, Catherine explicitly addresses time as a resource that, like the talents of the New Testament, must be cultivated and developed in order to flourish. The exemplars of the "femme forte," Agnodice and Pasithée, despite the different levels of importance accorded to them by Catherine in her work, all accomplish their feats through the careful consecration of time. Agnodice and Pasithée, having devoted themselves to a humanist education, also exercise an important public role, Agnodice as the more political representative of women's rights and Pasithée as an engaged pedagogue.

In the end, however, both the human body and the ostensibly timeless exemplars fail to provide a model for eternity in Catherine's work. While the future exists for Catherine as the domain of continuing knowledge during her lifetime and of a readership that will extend beyond it, the author nonetheless insists upon the thoughtful utilization of human time, particularly for women. Certainly, in Catherine's milieu, a passionate commitment to the best possible use of time is not unique. Pasquier's letter to Monsieur de Marillac reveals his own particular obsession with time, as he attempts to point out the advantages of the city over the country: "Voulez-vous passer vostre temps sur les herbes? Et qui est celuy qui ne sçache qu'un Pline, Dioscoride et Mathiole m'en apprendront plus en une heure que tous vos jardins en dix ans?"[85] [Do you want to spend your time on plants? Who doesn't know that Pliny, Dioscorides, and Mattioli will teach me more in an hour than all your gardens in ten years?]. But Catherine continually polemicizes the question by singling out notions of women's time that had been heretofore neglected in humanist discourse.

I have argued that for Catherine, "le temps retrouvé," rather than residing principally in timeless models or in the longevity of literature, constitutes a repossession of the women's time potentially "lost" to the threat of aging in *carpe diem* or to the temporal dictates of the moralists. In Catherine's vision as it is sketched throughout the *Œuvres*, this repossessed time, when consecrated by women to humanist endeavors, is capable of changing lives in both theory and practice. As Catherine concludes in a letter to an unnamed suitor, "[I]l me suffira bien si la vertu daigne me commander, la fortune m'accompagner, et les lettres me servir, pour exprimer ce qui est en mon ame..."[86] [I will be satisfied if virtue guides me, fortune accompanies me, and letters serve me to express what is in my soul...].

Epilogue:
The Bridges of Chronos

Le temps est cette distance perpétuellement comblée entre soi et soi.

[Time is the perpetually filled distance between the self and the self.]
—Françoise Joukovsky

In the preceding chapters I have argued that in early modern France men and women appear to conceive of time in perceptibly different ways. That women should imagine time quite distinctly from men is hardly surprising, given that for the most part women's lives were radically different from those of men in the bourgeois and aristocratic classes from which all these writers emerge. Louise Labé, Pernette du Guillet, and Catherine des Roches participated in literary circles that undoubtedly broadened their horizons beyond the experiences of most contemporaneous women, but because of societal expectations and exigencies in the early modern period, even learned women operated largely within the private, domestic sphere. Nicole Estienne decries the domestic domain as a cruel prison, recreating the repetitive sense of time characterizing the married woman's existence. Anne de Marquets, in contrast, writes within the enclosure of the convent, yet her poetry creates an open-ended temporal structure distinct from that of other contemporaneous religious poetry. The most sophisticated response to the dilemma of "women's time" within the domestic sphere comes from Catherine des Roches, whose work transcends domesticity in the guise of publicly embracing it.

Both male and female poets in early modern France attempt to capture time: indeed, this constitutes the raison d'être of writing. Yet as we have seen, notions of temporality are tempered by the gender of the writing subject. As literary objects of bodily temporality, women frequently represent youthful beauty followed by decay, as the engraving *Le miroir de la vie et de la mort* embodies in a single image.

As literary subjects, however, the women included in this study advance their own attitudes toward the passage of time, the female body, and aging. While these women poets do not advance a single female ideology of time in Renaissance France, they effectuate nonetheless a significant departure from their male counterparts, as we have seen. The temporal discourses of Ronsard, Scève, Tyard, and Magny, while not identical, share an insistence on time as a relentlessly progressive phenomenon. I do not mean to suggest that sixteenth-century male poets never depict circular or lyric time; on the contrary, Ixion, wheels, and rings are common images not only in Tyard's Neoplatonic verses but also in a number of other works by the Pléiade poets. Scève's collection of *canzoniere*, too, records the repeated enactment of specific moments in the amorous poet's consciousness. But ultimately, these poets return to a linear projection of one sort or another: at the end of *Delie,* for example, Scève recalls the promise of *exegi monumentum;* the concluding sonnets of Tyard's *Erreurs* refer to immortality; most forcefully, in the *Sonnets pour Hélène,* Ronsard foresees his poetic immortality in contrast to Hélène's rapidly disintegrating body.

Unlike Scève and the Pléiade, the women poets we have examined challenge the notion of an antagonistic time to be conquered. The female body, locus of both youthful beauty and decaying senectitude in Ronsard's poetry, serves rather to champion women's strength in Catherine des Roches's *Agnodice* and to render Christian experience both more female and more immediate in Anne de Marquets's collections. In imploring her fellow "Lyonnoises" to become educated rather than preoccupied with such superficialities as jewelry, Louise Labé suggests that the body's adornment pales in comparison to the life of the mind. Finally, in an ultimate repudiation of the philosophy subtending the *carpe diem* motif, Catherine challenges the threats of lost physical beauty by positing the quintessential beauty of the soul, which should be cultivated by reading, learning, and writing.

Compared to their male colleagues, then, the women poets included in this study accord a much less prominent role to the inevitable march of Chronos in their works. The future, in their consideration, holds neither the inalterable promise of Scève's "myhrre incorruptible"—that is, the assurance of *exegi monumentum*—nor the menacing terror of aging inherent in the *carpe diem* motif. Works by Louise Labé, Pernette du Guillet, and Catherine des Roches, as distinguished from those of their male colleagues, ultimately evince a temporal philosophy that seeks to acclaim the enduring qualities

Le miroir de la vie et de la mort, anonymous engraving, Musée Carnavalet.

of the present, be it through desiring amorous plenitude or through undermining the importance of time's power to destroy the human body. This is not to say, of course, that these women humanists disavow the future to such an extent that they have no ambitious designs for a positive reception of their work, and in Catherine des Roches's case, for a readership that will continue well after her death. But these women poets reject visionary versions of the future, preferring to conceive of it, whether articulated in terms of Du Guillet's Neoplatonism, Labé's sensuality, or des Roches's stoicism, as the continuing evolution of the present.

Given a certain consonance among these positions, the inevitable question arises: why should it be specifically *women* writers who raise "alternate visions" of temporality in early modern poetry? Is it simply that female poets use the lyric form in a more traditional "lyric" mode or recreate more consistently what Thomas Greene terms the "iterative present"?[1] Or that male writers, largely because of societal expectations and constraints, more imperatively formulate projects and projections into the future? Or that the female anatomy, emmeshed as it is in circles and cycles, forms the point of departure for a Renaissance *écriture féminine?* Or that French women of the sixteenth century, bearing fewer public responsibilities than their male counterparts, have the leisure—or the obligation—to concentrate more on the present moment? However we resolve these rhetorical, psychoanalytic, and historical dilemmas, it is clear that gender has become a crucial category of analysis as we read these early modern texts. Whether they are constructed, deconstructed, or revisionistically reconstructed, notions of gender will doubtless continue to inform our literary and cultural inquiries in fruitful ways.

Perhaps the most surprising aspect that this study uncovers is the resonance between the conflicting attitudes toward time addressed in the early modern authors we have considered and the very similar controversies surrounding the question of time at the turn of the twenty-first century. While Jeremy Rifkin and Stephen Hawking raise certain questions beyond the scope of the imaginable for sixteenth-century scientists, some of the fundamental queries remain unchanged.[2] The current cultural obsession with the computer and other technological "time-saving" devices, for example, is curiously reminiscent of Gargantua's doubling or tripling activities.[3] The emphasis on youthful beauty in the West, now culminating in all possible means to avoid or camouflage senescence, recalls Ronsard's continual preoccupation with aging, both his own and that of the young women he addresses in his sonnets. The immortality so sought after by the Pléiade poets resurfaces literally in current research on cloning and cryonics, and more figuratively in contemporary literary works (despite Woody Allen's claim to the contrary: "I don't want to achieve immortality through my works. I want to achieve it through not dying."). Whence arises a central paradox: there is nothing more timeless than the preoccupation with time.

Just as the early modern women poets we have examined provide what might be termed countercultural positions for a number of temporal commonplaces, so counterdiscourses abound today as well, although they appear as broadly cultural rather than specifically gendered phenomena. Exhortations in the media to "simplify" and to "return to nature," as well as a growing Western fascination with Eastern mystical practices, suggest a vision quite distinct from the dominant cultural tendency to encourage maximum accomplishment within a minimum time span.

The temporal landscape of early modern France thus includes the roots of some of today's conflicting discourses on time as well as a number of other complex temporal landmarks that make sense only within the context of the sixteenth century. As this study has attempted to demonstrate, the early modern temporal terrain proves to be richer and more variegated than literary historians have previously assumed, a terrain that can be glimpsed more clearly by reading men and women writers concurrently. Much like Agrippa, who at the end of his treatise on "la noblesse et preexcellence du sexe foeminin" of 1529 launches a collaborative call for additions to his arguments,[4] I too invite other "curieux" to interrogate further the significance of time and its relationship to gender in early modern culture. And much like the women poets whose works in many ways engendered this book, I contend that it may indeed be possible, in the present, to create "world enough, and time."

Notes

Prologue

1. On literature's powers to explicate historical and social reality see Stanley Chojnacki, "Comment: Blurring Genders," *Renaissance Quarterly* 4, nos. 3–4 (1987): 744ff.; Ann Rosalind Jones, *The Currency of Eros: Women's Love Lyric in Europe, 1540–1620* (Bloomington: Indiana University Press, 1990), 1–10; Natalie Zemon Davis, *Fiction in the Archives: Pardon Tales and their Tellers in Sixteenth-Century France* (Stanford, Calif.: Stanford University Press, 1987). Frank Kermode warns against a potential cultural domination of literary studies in "Changing Epochs," in *What's Happened to the Humanities?*, ed. Alvin Kernan (Princeton: Princeton University Press, 1997), 162–78; the conflict between literary and cultural studies is debated by a number of scholars in *PMLA* 112 (March 1997): 257–86.

2. Myra Jehlen, "The Paradox of Feminist Criticism," in *Feminisms*, ed. Robyn R. Warhol and Diane Price Herndl (New Brunswick, N.J.: Rutgers University Press, 1991), 87.

3. Chojnacki, "Comment: Blurring Genders," 745.

4. Joan W. Scott, "Gender: A Useful Category of Historical Analysis," *American Historical Review* 91 (1986): 1056.

5. Thomas Laqueur, *Making Sex: Body and Gender from the Greeks to Freud* (Cambridge: Harvard University Press, 1990), 8.

6. Jacques Ferrand, *Traité de l'essence et guérison de l'amour, ou De la mélancholie érotique* (Toulouse: J. and R. Colombiez, 1610), 16.

7. Erasmus, *Le mariage chrétien* (Paris: François Babuty, 1714), 23. For an extended analysis of this treatise, see Constance Jordan, *Renaissance Feminism: Literary Texts and Political Models* (Ithaca: Cornell University Press, 1990), 29–64.

8. François de Billon, *Le Fort inexpugnable de l'honneur du sexe feminin* (Paris: Ian d'Allyer, 1555), 21r.

9. Juan Luis Vives, *Institution de la femme chrétienne*, trans. Pierre de Changy (Lyon: S. Sabon, n.d. [1541–49]), 220.

10. Pietro Bembo, *Les Azolains,* trans. Jan Martin (1545), in *Le Miroir des femmes,* ed. J. P. Guillerm, L. Guillerm, L. Hordoir, M. F. Piejus (Lille: Presses Universitaires de Lille, 1983), 1:135–42.

11. Pierre Lesnauderie, *La Louange de mariage* (Paris: F. Regnault, 1523), 1v. See also Vives, *Institution de la femme chrétienne*, 158.

218   Notes to Chapter One

12. See, for example, Richard Glasser, *Time in French Life and Thought*, trans. C. G. Pearson (Manchester: Manchester University Press, 1972), 133.

Chapter 1. Forging Temporal Codes

1. See S. Béguin, O. Binenbaum, A. Chastel, W. M. Johnson, S. Pressouyre, and H. Zerner, *La Galerie François Ier au Château de Fontainebleau* (Paris: Flammarion, 1972), 59. Another version, wherein humans are being granted eternal youth as a reward for their fidelity to Zeus over Prometheus, is recorded in L. Ricchieri in *Antiquarum lectionume libri* (1542), cited by Pierre and Françoise Joukovsky in *A Travers la Galerie François Ier* (Paris: Champion, 1992), 34. Compare Kurt Kusenberg, *Le Rosso* (Paris: Albin Michel, 1931), 53–59.

2. I do not mean to suggest that sixteenth-century culture is unique in its insistence on the female body as a literary site for measuring the passage of time, as authors from Horace to Villon to Queneau illustrate. What is particularly striking, however, is the ubiquity of this topos in early modern French texts, both poetry and prose.

3. Glasser, *Time in French Life and Thought*, 134.

4. Ricardo J. Quinones, *The Renaissance Discovery of Time* (Cambridge: Harvard University Press, 1972), 3.

5. Cited by Lucien Febvre, *Le problème de l'incroyance au XVIe siècle* (Paris: Michel, 1962), 427.

6. F. C. Haber, "The Cathedral Clock and the Cosmological Metaphor," in *The Study of Time*, ed. J. T. Fraser and N. Lawrence (New York: Springer-Verlag, 1975), 2:401.

7. Ibid.

8. See Michel Picard, *Lire le temps* (Paris: Minuit, 1989), 59. Lucretius's *De natura rerum*, which was published in Paris by Josse Bade and Jean Petit in 1514, demonstrates the importance of time in Epicurean thought. The Bibliothèque Nationale catalog lists a total of twenty editions published in Europe (six in Paris) in the sixteenth century, which suggests an important readership. For further exploration of Epicurean influence in the sixteenth century, see Françoise Joukovsky, *Montaigne et le problème du temps* (Paris: Nizet, 1972), 61ff.

9. François Rabelais, *Le Tiers livre*, ed. Pierre Michel (Paris: Livre de Poche, 1966), 315.

10. See, for example, Ronsard's "Hynne de la mort" and Pontus de Tyard's *Discours du temps*.

11. Pontus de Tyard, *Discours du Temps, de l'an et de ses parties. Discours philosophiques* (Paris: Abel l'Angelier, 1587), 335v.

12. Joachim Du Bellay, *L'Olive*, ed. E. Calderini (Geneva: Droz, 1974), 162–63.

13. Joachim Du Bellay, *Poètes du Seizième Siècle*, ed. Albert-Marie Schmidt, Bibliothèque de la Pléiade (Paris: Gallimard, 1953), 431.

14. Terence Cave, *Devotional Poetry in France, 1570–1613* (Cambridge: Cambridge University Press, 1969), 149.

15. The *L.* refers to the Laumonier edition of the *Œuvres complètes* (Paris: Société des Textes Français Modernes, 1914–75), and the *P.* to the more recent Pléiade edition, edited by Jean Céard, Daniel Ménager, and Michel Simonin, 2 vols. (Paris: Gallimard, 1993–94). These abbreviations will be used henceforth in the text for reference to Ronsard's works.

16. On this transition, compare Georges Matoré, "Le temps au seizième siècle,"

L'Information Grammaticale 32 (1987): 5. See also Daniel Poirion, "Le temps perdu et retrouvé... au seizième siècle," *Revue des sciences humaines* 183 (1981): 71–84. Georges Poulet points out that during the Renaissance, God is no longer conceived as the transcendent cause but rather the internal power that upholds the universal movement within which people and things accomplish their temporal destiny. See *Mesure de l'instant*, vol. 2 of *Etudes sur le temps humain* (Paris: Presses Pocket, 1990), 5ff.

17. For another reading of the relationship between the macrocosm and the microcosm in sixteenth-century thought, see Michel Foucault, *Les mots et les choses* (Paris: Gallimard, 1966), 46ff.

18. Ovid, Seneca, Cicero, and Augustine, for example, all treat time as it relates to human experience.

19. Aristotle, *Physics*, trans. Edward Hussey (Oxford: Clarendon, 1983), 52 (= *Phys.* 4.14.223a). For an interesting and succinct exposition of Aristotle's sense of time, see Paul Ricoeur, *Le temps raconté* (Paris: Seuil, 1985), 30ff.

20. Augustine notes that time exists in the soul in bk. 11, xxvi–xxxi, of the *Confessions*, trans. Henry Chadwick (Oxford: Oxford University Press, 1992), 239–45. Françoise Joukovsky explores these and other early notions of time as they affect Montaigne's work in *Montaigne et le problème du temps*, 72–102. On Augustinian temporal theory and its limitations, see Ricoeur, *Le temps raconté*, 21ff.

21. Bk. 24, Letter 1, of *Letters from Petrarch*, ed. Morris Bishop (Bloomington: Indiana University Press, 1966), 201–2.

22. Leone Battista Alberti, *Opere Volgari*, ed. D. A. Bonucci (Florence: Galileiana, 1844), 2:243: "Ora avete voi figliuoli miei, le operazioni dell'animo, il corpo, e il tempo, tre cose da natura vostre proprie; e sapete quanto le siano preziose e care" [Now, my sons, you have the workings of the soul, the body and time, three things that belong to you; and you realize how precious and dear they are to you].

23. *Letters from Petrarch*, ed. Bishop, 291.

24. Gabriel Meurier, *Thresor de sentences dorees, proverbes et dicts* (Lyons: Jean d'Ogerolles, 1577), 19.

25. François Premier, *Œuvres Poétiques*, ed. J. E. Kane (Geneva: Slatkine, 1984), 99.

26. Michel de Montaigne, *Essais*, ed. Maurice Rat (Paris: Garnier, 1962), III,13; 2:572. The first reference denotes the standard numbering for Montaigne's *Essays*; the second indicates the volume and page number in the Rat edition. Subsequent references to Montaigne will follow this pattern.

27. Donald Frame, *Montaigne's Essays and Selected Writings* (New York: St. Martin's Press, 1963), 445.

28. Considerations of the proper season for everything are frequent in literary history (see, for example, Ecclesiastes 3), but they become much more prevalent in the early modern period.

29. The ancient debate regarding the appropriate gestation period to establish the legitimacy of a child was rekindled in the 1530s in France. For a synopsis of these legal and medical debates, see François Rabelais, *Gargantua*, ed. Ruth Calder and Michael Screech (Geneva: Droz, 1970), 32 n. 20.

30. Ambroise Paré, *Les Œuvres* (Paris: G. Buon, 1585), 32.

31. Symphorien Champier, *La Nef des dames vertueuses* (Lyon: J. Arnollet, 1503), k4r.

32. François Rabelais, *Gargantua*, ed. Gérard Defaux (Paris: Librairie Générale Française, 1994), 239.

33. Ibid., 241.
34. Ibid., 255–59.
35. Rabelais, *Pantagruel*, ed. Gérard Defaux (Paris: Librairie Générale Française, 1994), 163.
36. Rabelais, *Gargantua*, 443.
37. Ibid., 475–75.
38. *L'hystoyre et plaisante cronicque du petit Jehan de Saintré*, ed. Guichard (Paris, 1843), cited by Glasser, *Time in French Life and Thought,* 183.
39. Nicholas de Cholières, *Les Neuf Matinées* (Paris: J. Richer, 1585), 298.
40. Ibid., 289–91.
41. Quinones, *Renaissance Discovery,* 3–4.
42. Marguerite de Navarre, *L'Heptameron*, ed. Simone de Reyff (Paris: Flammarion, 1982), 45–48.
43. "Cette fraze ordinaire de *passe-temps* et de *passer le temps* represente l'usage de ces prudentes gens, qui ne pensent point avoir meilleur compte de leur vie que de la couler et eschapper, de la passer, gauchir et, autant qu'il est en eux, ignorer et fuir, comme chose de qualité ennuyeuse et desdaignable. Mais je la cognois autre, et la trouve et prisable et commode . . ." (*Essais*, II,13; 2:572) [This ordinary expression "Pastime" or "pass the time" represents the habit of those wise folk who think they can make no better use of their life than to let it slip by and escape it, pass it by, sidestep it, and, as far as in them lies, ignore it and run away from it, as something irksome and contemptible. But I know it to be otherwise and find it both agreeable and worth prizing . . ."] (Frame, *Montaigne's Essays,* 445–47).
44. Robert Mandrou, *Introduction à la France moderne, 1500–1640* (Paris: Albin Michel, 1974), 221–28.
45. François de Sales, *Introduction à la vie dévote* (1609), chaps. 33–34; cited by ibid., 224.
46. Jacques Tahureau, *Les Dialogues non moins profitables que facétieux* (1565), ed. Max Gauna (Geneva: Droz, 1981), 64, 71ff. For a more extended treatment of the connections Tahureau establishes between women and wasting time, see my "The Dialogic Delusion: Jacques Tahureau's *Dialogues* and the Rhetoric of Closure," in *The Dialogue in Early Modern France, 1547–1630: Art and Argument*, ed. Colette Winn (Washington, D.C.: The Catholic University of America Press, 1993), 169–76.
47. Le Seigneur de la Motte-Messemé (François Le Poulchre), *Le Passe-temps* (Paris: Jean Leblanc, 1595), 1v.
48. Similarly, building upon the close association between women and pastimes for men, Diane de Poitiers's nineteenth-century editor describes her as the "intendante des passe-temps" of Henri II. Diane de Poitiers, *Lettres inédites*, ed. Georges Guiffrey (1866; reprint, Geneva: Slatkine, 1970), lxv.
49. Bonaventure Des Periers, *Œuvres* (1544), ed. Louis Lacour (Paris: P. Jannet, 1856), 1:168.
50. Hélisenne de Crenne, *Epistres invectives*, in *Œuvres* (1560) (Geneva: Slatkine, 1977), M3v; Pernette du Guillet, *Rymes* (1545), ed. Victor Graham (Geneva: Droz, 1968), 3; Louise Labé, *Œuvres complètes* (1555), ed. François Rigolot (Paris: Flammarion, 1986), 43; Catherine des Roches, "Epistre à ma mère," in *Les Œuvres,* by Madeleine des Roches and Catherine des Roches (1579), ed. Anne R. Larsen (Geneva: Droz, 1993), 183. For useful analyses of these prefaces, see Deborah Lesko Baker, *The Subject of Desire: Petrarchan Poetics and the Female Voice in Louise Labé* (Lafayette, Ind.: Purdue University Press, 1996), 11–40; Anne R. Larsen, "'Un honneste passetems': Strategies of Legitimation in French

Renaissance Women's Prefaces," *L'Esprit Créateur* 30 (1990): 11–22; Deborah N. Losse, "Women Addressing Women: The Differentiated Text," in *French Women Writers: French Texts/American Contexts*, ed. Anne R. Larsen and Colette H. Winn (Detroit: Wayne State University Press, 1994), 23–37; Kirk D. Read, "Louise Labé in Search of Time Past: Prefatory Strategies and Rhetorical Transformations," *Critical Matrix* 5 (1990): 63–88; Kirk D. Read and François Rigolot, "Discours liminaire et identité littéraire: Remarques sur la préface féminine au XVIe siècle," *Versants* 15 (1989): 75–98; François Rigolot, "La préface à la Renaissance: Un discours sexué?" *Cahiers de l'association des études françaises* 42 (1990): 121–36; and Colette Winn, "La femme écrivain au XVIe siècle: Ecriture et transgression," *Poétique* 21 (1990): 435–52.

51. *Histoire des femmes en occident, XVIe–XVIIIe siècles,* ed. Georges Duby and Michelle Perrot, vol. 3, ed. Natalie Zemon Davis and Arlette Farge (Paris: Plon, 1991), 13. Of course, much like today, the extent to which women were occupied or consumed by menial tasks depended largely upon their social class.

52. Richard Bonney, *The European Dynastic States: 1494–1660* (Oxford: Oxford University Press, 1991), 365. Robert Muchembled notes that in sixteenth-century France, a fully accomplished life, like that of Jesus Christ, was considered to be thirty-three years. See *Popular Culture and Elite Culture in France, 1400–1750*, trans. Lydia Cochrane (Baton Rouge: Louisiana State University, 1985), 27–31.

53. These figures are based on studies of Beauvais in the seventeenth century, but Fernand Braudel includes them as indicative of the ancien régime between 1400 and 1800 in *The Limits of the Possible*, vol. 1 of *Structures of Everyday Life* (New York: Harper and Row, 1981), 90–92.

54. See Henri Chamard, *Histoire de la Pléiade* (Paris: Didier, 1939–40), 1:30.

55. *Lettres de Marguerite d'Angoulême* (Paris: Jules Renouard, 1841), I, ltr. 54, 221.

56. Marguerite de Navarre, *L'Heptameron*, ed. Simone de Reyff (Paris: Flammarion, 1982), Nouvelle 35, 308–9. Ronsard also complains of old age when he is thirty, but literary manifestations of aging in the sixteenth century describe the female body far more frequently than the male body, as will become evident during the course of my analysis.

57. Meurier, *Thresor de sentences dorees*, 15.

58. Paré, *Les Œuvres*, 9.

59. Erasmus, *Colloquies*, trans. Craig R. Thompson (Chicago: University of Chicago Press, 1965), 104.

60. Estienne Pasquier, *Lettres familières*, ed. D. Thickett (Geneva: Droz, 1974), 408.

61. Paré, *Les Œuvres*, 985.

62. Ibid.

63. See E.-V. Telle, *L'œuvre de Marguerite d'Angoulême, reine de Navarre, et la querelle des femmes* (1937; reprint, Paris: Slatkine, 1969), 74.

64. Estienne Pasquier, *Œuvres complètes* (Geneva: Slatkine, 1971), 1:68–70.

65. See Louis Flandrin, *Families in Former Times: Kinship, Household, and Sexuality in Early Modern France*, trans. Richard Southern (Cambridge: Cambridge University Press, 1979), 58; Barbara Diefendorf, *Paris City Councillors in the Sixteenth Century: The Politics of Patrimony* (Princeton: Princeton University Press, 1983), 181; and Bonney, *European Dynastic States*, 366.

66. Diefendorf, *Paris City Councillors*, 183.

67. Paré, *Les Œuvres*, 940.

68. François Barbaro, *Deux livres de l'estat du mariage*, trans. Claude Joly (Paris: Guillaume de Luyne, 1567), 29–30.

69. Diefendorf, *Paris City Councillors,* 183.

70. See, for example, *Poètes du seizième siècle,* ed. Albert-Marie Schmidt (Paris: Gallimard, 1953), 271. Compare also the lady from Pampelune in Marguerite de Navarre's *Heptameron,* who marries a man of almost fifty when she is twenty-three (Nouvelle 26, p. 258).

71. Cholières, *Les Neuf matinées,* 258ff.

72. Ibid., 241–42.

73. Ibid., 242.

74. Gratien du Pont, *Les controverses des sexes masculin et femenin* (Toulouse: J. Colomies, 1534), 116r.

75. Cholières, *Les Neuf matinées,* 246, 260.

76. Several stories of Marguerite de Navarre's *Heptaméron* also portray marriage from a woman's point of view, but in a fictional mode.

77. Véronique Nahom-Grappe, "La Belle femme," in *Histoire des femmes en occident,* ed. Davis and Farge, 3:108.

78. Clément Marot, *Œuvres poétiques,* ed. Gérard Defaux (Paris: Bordas, 1993), 2:243.

79. Gratien du Pont, *Controverses,* 116r.

80. Brantôme [Pierre de Bourdeille], *Œuvres complètes,* ed. Ludovic Lalanne (Paris: Jules Renouard, 1864–82), 2:387.

81. Vives, *Institution de la femme chrétienne,* 184.

82. Braudel, *Limits of the Possible,* 90.

83. Jean Lemaire de Belges, *La Concorde des deux langages,* ed. Jean Frappier (Paris: Droz, 1947), 26.

84. Montaigne, too, considers youthful, viril energy the supreme physical good: see especially *Essais,* III,5 and III,13.

85. *Essais,* III, 12.

86. Ibid., 2:509.

87. Frame, *Montaigne's Essays,* 810.

88. Ibid.

89. For example, Alessandro Piccolomini, *Instruction aux jeunes dames, en forme de dialogue, par laquelle les dames apprendront comme elles doivent se bien gouverner en amour* (1571), ed. Concetta Menna Scognamiglio (Fasano: Schena, 1992); François d'Amboise's adaptation, *Dialogues et devis des damoiselles pour les rendre vertueuses et bienheureuses en la vraye et parfaicte amitié* (Paris: V. Norment, 1581). Joyce Miller insightfully compared these different versions in a paper given at the Sixteenth Century Studies Conference, San Francisco, 27 October 1995.

90. Amboise, *Dialogues et devis,* 9v.

91. Marcel Françon, *Notes sur l'esthétique de la femme au XVIe siècle* (Cambridge: Harvard University Press, 1939).

92. Cited in Diane de Poitiers, *Lettres inédites,* lxxii.

93. At the end of her first elegy, Louise Labé uses the figure of the "povre vieille" who did not profit from her youthful beauty and attempts unsuccessfully to recapture it when she falls in love in her old age. Labé, *Œuvres complètes,* ed. Rigolot, 107–10. It seems, however, that rather than revealing a fear of lost beauty, Labé is using this literary commonplace to justify her own amorous involvement in her youth. She expresses no anxiety about her own aging either here or in any of the first-person sonnets (see chapter 3 below).

94. Diane de Poitiers, *Lettres inédites,* lxxxiii.

95. Laura Levine, *Men in Women's Clothing: Anti-theatricality and Effeminization,*

1579–1642 (Cambridge: Cambridge University Press, 1994), 2. For a fascinating treatment of the fear of effeminization and the irrational belief that costume could alter the gender beneath, see 3–25.

96. Julia Kristeva, "Women's Time," trans. Alice Jardine and Harry Blake, *Signs* 7 (1981): 15.

Chapter 2. Time in a Body: Ronsard

1. The term "Ronsard" poses obvious problems. By this designation I will mean "Ronsard's poetic voice" or "Ronsard the lyric subject" as I examine notions of temporality that emerge in the poetry itself. Occasionally, I have included pertinent details from the life of Ronsard the individual, and in so doing I have attempted to distinguish between the two. Gisèle Mathieu-Castellani sums up the problem eloquently: "*Je* a plusieurs référents. . . . Est-ce moi, Ronsard en tant qu'individu? Moi, locuteur, tenant *hic et nunc* un discours séducteur? Moi, Ronsard-poète? Ou moi, métonyme de mon livre?" ["I" has several referents. . . . Is it I, Ronsard, as an individual? I, speaker, holding a seductive discourse here and now? I, Ronsard the poet? Or I, metonymy of my book?]. Gisèle Mathieu-Castellani, "La main dextre et l'autre, ou la rhétorique détournée," in *Sur des vers de Ronsard, 1585–1985*, ed. Marcel Tetel (Paris: Aux Amateurs de Livres, 1990), 89.

2. These are obviously schematic descriptions. For particular biographical details on these points, see *Les Amours,* ed. Jean de Bonnot (Paris: Jean de Bonnot, 1980), 18ff., 30–53; Henri Longnon, *Pierre de Ronsard, essai de biographie . . .* (1912; reprint, Geneva: Slatkine, 1975), 115ff., 312ff.; Jacques Davy Du Perron, *Oraison funèbre sur la mort de Monsieur de Ronsard* (1586), ed. Michel Simonin (Geneva: Droz, 1985), 82–84, 93, 104–49; Philippe Desan, "The Tribulations of a Young Poet: Ronsard from 1547 to 1552," *Renaissance Rereadings*, ed. Maryanne Horowitz, Anne Cruz, and Wendy Furman (Urbana and Chicago: University of Illinois Press, 1988), 184–202. Ronsard creates his own amorous mythology in boasting to Olivier de Magny of his countless lovers in "Conte d'un rang premierement, / Deux cens que je pris en Touraine" (L.VI,256; P.I,958) [First count / the two hundred I had in Touraine].

3. Petrarch does address the question of his own aging body, though not graphically, as when his mirror reflects the poet's aging body in Poem 361 of the *Rime sparse* in *Petrarch's Lyric Poems*, ed. and trans. Robert M. Durling (Cambridge: Harvard University Press, 1976), 370.

4. Françoise Joukovsky notes that in the *Hymnes* time has two faces, both destroyer and creator (or preserver) of a universal order. "Temps et éternité dans les *Hymnes*," in *Autour des 'Hymnes' de Ronsard*, ed. Madeleine Lazard (Paris: Champion, 1984), 61. Other metaphors include the avenger (L.II, 33-35; P.I,761–62), the old man ("Hymne de l'esté," L.XII,35ff.; P.II,553ff.), and the scythe (L.X,105; P.II,839).

5. The most obvious example of an extended development of this motif is Du Bellay's work, both the *Antiquitez* and the *Regrets*. On Ronsard's dialogue with the past, see Elizabeth Armstrong, *Ronsard and the Age of Gold* (Cambridge: Cambridge University Press, 1968); and Madeleine Lazard, "La France en Arcadie: La pastorale politique du XVIe siècle," in *Vérité et illusion dans le théâtre au temps de la Renaissance*, ed. M. T. Jones-Davies (Paris: Touzot, 1983), 27–39.

6. Pietro Bembo, "Piansi e cantai," in *Rime* (Venice: G. A. de Nicolini da Sabio, 1535), A2r, vv.5–8.

7. At the end of the fourth book of the *Odes* of 1550, Ronsard had already translated line for line Horace's famous poem from which the term originates (*Carmina* 3.30, in Horace, *The Odes and Epodes*, ed. C. E. Bennett, Loeb Classical Library [Cambridge: Harvard University Press, 1968], 278):

> Plus dur que fer j'ai finy cest ouvrage,
> . . . .
> Sous le tombeau tout Ronsard n'ira pas,
> Restant de luy la part qui est meilleure.
> (L.II,152–53; P.I,926)

[Stronger than iron, I have finished this work, /. . . / Under the tomb Ronsard will not go, / The best part of him remaining.]

For an overview of the *exegi monumentum* motif, see Ernst Curtius, *La littérature européenne*, trans. Jean Bréjoux (Paris: Presses Universitaires de France, 1986), 2:285–91; Chamard, *Histoire de la Pléiade*, 1:291–93, 1:356–58, 2:274–75; Laumonier, *Ronsard, poète lyrique: Etude historique et littéraire* (1923; reprint, Geneva: Slatkine, 1972), 346–77. At least one critic considered the study of poetic immortality exhausted long ago: "The pro-glory convictions of this school are too familiar to students of the Renaissance to merit further amplification here. Almost every critic who has written on the mid-century poetic theory has noted this banal motif." Robert J. Clements, *Critical Theory and Practice of the Pléiade* (Cambridge: Harvard University Press, 1942), 51.

8. In "La Lyre" of 1569, Ronsard clarifies the distinction between children of the body and children of the soul:

> Le grand Platon en ses oeuvres nous chante
> Que nostre Esprit comme le corps enfante
> L'un, des enfans qui surmontent la mort,
> L'autre, des filz qui doibvent voir le port.
> (L. XV,21; P. II,691)

[The great Plato sings in his works / That our Spirit, like the body, gives birth. / From one, children who transcend death, / From the other, children who must see the port.]

Compare Diotima's reply to Socrates: "Those who are pregnant in the body only betake themselves to women and beget children. . . . Their offspring, as they hope, will preserve their memory and give them the blessedness and immortality which they desire in the future. But souls which are pregnant—for there certainly are men who are more creative in their souls than in their bodies—conceive that which is proper for the soul to conceive or contain. . . . Who, when he thinks of Homer and Hesiod and other great poets, would not rather have their children than ordinary human ones? Who would not emulate them in the creation of children such as theirs, which have preserved their memory and given them everlasting glory?" Plato, *Symposium*, trans. Benjamin Jowett (Indianapolis: Bobbs-Merrill, 1956), 208–9.

9. Chamard notes that opinions on the matter are divided (*Histoire de la Pléiade*, 1:257), and Laumonier opts for Denisot (Ronsard, *Œuvres complètes*, ed. Laumonier, 3:182, 4:v).

10. These portraits are reproduced in the Laumonier edition (4:2–3) with the Greek epigrams by Baïf that appeared in the 1552 and 1553 editions. The Weber edition reproduces the portraits with the French epigrams that replaced the Greek epigrams. *Les Amours*, ed. Henri Weber and Catherine Weber (Paris: Garnier, 1963), 15–16. Cassandre's portrait disappears entirely in the 1560 edition, but it returns in later editions.

11. On the ambiguous iconography of pearls, see Edy de Jongh, who argues that pearls are used in art to symbolize the divine, chastity, and virginity, on the one hand, and sexualized female beauty, on the other. "Pearls of Virtue and Pearls of Vice," *Simiolus* 8 (1975–76): 73–85. Cassandre is depicted as less sensuous and more regal the following year in Olivier de Magny, *Les Amours* (Paris: Estienne Groulleau, 1553), A2r.

12. Compare the sonnet "Chacun me dit, Ronsard, ta Maistresse n'est telle / Comme tu la descris. Certes je n'en sçay rien . . . ," (L. XVII, 317; P. I,454–55) [Everyone tells me, Ronsard, your Mistress is not as you describe her. Really, I don't know anything about it . . .].

13. Cassandre's words could be regarded simply as a requisite "modesty clause," but the question of Cassandre's invented beauty has a controversial critical history. Henri Chamard comments: "Est-ce que Cassandre était belle? Cette mauvaise langue de Brantôme insinue qu'elle ne l'était pas autant que dit Ronsard" (*Histoire de la Pléiade*, 1:257) [Was Cassandre beautiful? That gossip Brantôme insinuates that she wasn't as pretty as Ronsard said she was.]. Compare Brantôme: "Mais Ronsard me pardonne, s'il luy plaist; jamais sa maistresse, qu'il a faite si belle, ne parvint à ceste beauté. . . . Mais il est permis aux poëtes et peintres de dire et faire ce qu'il leur plaist" [I beg Ronsard's pardon, but his mistress, whom he described as beautiful, didn't achieve this beauty. . . . But poets and painters are permitted to say and do whatever they want.]. *Recueil des Dames, poésies et tombeaux*, ed. Etienne Vaucheret (Paris: Gallimard, 1991), 405.

14. Marc-Antoine de Muret, *Commentaire au premier livre des Amours de Ronsard*, in *Les Œuvres de Pierre de Ronsard* (1622), ed. Jacques Chomarat, Marie-Madeleine Fragonard, and Gisèle Mathieu-Castellani (Geneva: Droz, 1985), 2.

15. The relevant part of this ode is reproduced above, chapter 1, p. 43.

16. A brief analysis of Callimachus's hymns dedicated to Zeus, Apollo, Artemis, and Demeter shows that in poems dedicated to males, 8.5 percent of the verses contain references to the human body. In those dedicated to females, 8.1 percent of the verses include such references. I am indebted to Anne Groton and Andrea Ursprung for their verification of the Greek texts.

17. For a contemporary theory of the notion of women as visual spectacles, see Laura Mulvey, *Visual and Other Pleasures* (Bloomington: Indiana University Press), 1989.

18. I have, however, encountered an exception to this principle, which I address below, pp. 81–82.

19. Tom Conley reads this sonnet in terms of signs: "The letter appears to be a fragment of the body, a remainder of the poet transformed into a corpse of ossified signs." *The Graphic Unconscious in Early Modern French Writing* (Cambridge: Cambridge University Press, 1992), 106. Donald Stone, in contrast, concludes that the poem represents the poet's implicit triumph over both love and death. *Ronsard's Sonnet Cycles: A Study in Tone and Vision* (New Haven: Yale University Press, 1966), 21ff.

20. I am thinking of Rome's role in the *Antiquitéz*, particularly in "Nouveau venu, qui cherches Rome en Rome," "Qui voudra voir tout ce qu'ont peu nature," and "Telle que dans son char la Berecynthienne," Joachim Du Bellay, *Les Antiquitéz de Rome* and *"Songe,"* in *Poètes du Seizième Siècle*, ed. Albert Marie Schmidt, Bibliothèque de la Pléiade (Paris: Gallimard, 1953), 419–21.

21. See Maurice Pillard-Verneuil, *Dictionnaire des symboles* (1897; reprint, Geneva: Slatkine, 1981). In Virgil (*Aeneid* 6.443–44), myrtles provide a resting place for lovers in hell. See also the chanson "Plus estroit que la Vigne" (L.XVII,235; P.I,458) and the "Elegie à Marie" (L.X,238; P.I,244). I. D. McFarlane shows how grass and water, the symbols of continuity, surround the poet in death in "De l'élection de son sepulcre." "Yet," McFarlane qualifies, "as in so many cases of Ronsard's fundamental imagery, the margin between enveloping and engulfing and therefore destroying is a very thin one." "Aspects of Ronsard's poetic vision," in *Ronsard the Poet*, ed. Terence Cave (London: Methuen, 1973), 34.

22. See Louis Le Caron, *Dialogues* (1556), ed. Joan Buhlmann and Donald Gilman (Geneva: Droz, 1986), 262.

23. Isidore Silver, *Ronsard's Philosophic Thought*, vol. 3 of *The Intellectual Revolution of Ronsard* (Geneva: Droz, 1992), 164.

24. Françoise Joukovsky examines the distinctions between time and eternity in Ronsard's *Hymnes* in "Temps et éternité dans les *Hymnes*," in *Autour des "Hymnes" de Ronsard*, ed. Madeleine Lazard (Paris: Champion, 1984), 53–82.

25. Compare also the sonnet from *Les amours diverses*, "Ma Dame, je me meurs abandonné d'espoir" (L.XVII,329;P.I,410) [My lady, I am dying, bereft of hope].

26. From the ode to Leuconoë: "Carpe diem, quam minimum credula postero" [Reap the harvest of today, putting as little trust as may be in the morrow!]. *Carmina* 1.11 in Horace, *Odes and Epodes,* trans. Bennett, 32–33.

27. Laumonier, *Ronsard, poète lyrique*, 587.

28. Stone, *Ronsard's Sonnet Cycles,* 6; Elizabeth Berg, "Iconoclastic Moments: Reading the *Sonnets for Helene*, Writing the Portuguese Letters," in *The Poetics of Gender.* ed. Nancy K. Miller (New York: Columbia University Press, 1986), 208. In their monumental studies of Ronsard and sixteenth-century poets, both Laumonier and Weber each devote a section to the *carpe diem* motif in the *Amours*. Laumonier, *Ronsard, poète lyrique,* 581–91; Henri Weber, *La Création poétique au XVIe siècle en France* (Paris: Nizet, 1955), 333–56. Ricardo Quinones's excellent study of time in the Renaissance refers to *carpe diem* as an exhortation never to waste time, but there is no consideration of the motif as a rhetorical device. Richard Glasser mentions *carpe diem* as an indication of the changing attitudes toward time (*Time in French Life and Thought,* 143) and as the antidote to Ronsard's philosophy of the eternal: "Only that which resisted time was valuable and genuine" (168). See also Yvonne Bellenger's "Le vocabulaire de la journée et des moments dans la poésie du XVIe siècle," *Revue Belge de Philologie d'Histoire* 55 (1977): 760–84; Conley, *Graphic Unconscious*, 106ff.; Malcolm D. Quainton, *Ronsard's Ordered Chaos: Visions of Flux and Stability in the Poetry of Pierre de Ronsard* (Manchester: Manchester University Press, 1980), 121–26.

29. For further development of these borrowings, see Laumonier, *Ronsard, poète lyrique,* 596–98 and Chamard, *Histoire de la Pléiade,* 70.

30. Lorenzo de' Medici, *Poesie volgari* (Venice: Aldo, 1554); Agnolo Poliziano and Lorenzo de' Medici, *Canzone* (Florence: Giunti, 1568).

31. A number of other influences can be cited: Petrarch's "I' mi vivea," and more generally erotic epigrams from the *Greek Anthology* including Asclepiades, Agathias, and Rufinus. See Laumonier, *Ronsard, poète lyrique,* 585–91; Weber, *La Création poétique,* 341–50; and James Hutton, *The Greek Anthology in France* (Ithaca: Cornell University Press, 1946), 350–74. In most cases, Ronsard does not imitate a single, indisputable work, but rather he conflates several sources. In this chapter I have chosen to work with the most

obvious models, which lend themselves best to close readings when juxtaposed with the Ronsardian texts. But other classical sources that I have consulted also support the theses I advance here. For a very useful study of the phenomenon of multiple sources in Ronsard, see Edwin M. Duval, "Ronsard's Conflation of Classical Texts," *Classical and Modern Literature* 1, no. 4 (1981): 255–66.

32. *Anthologia Palatina* 5.74, in *The Greek Anthology*, trans. Alan Marshfield, ed. Peter Jay (Oxford: Oxford University Press, 1973), 306. I am indebted to Anne Groton for her help in verifying that the arguments presented here in reference to the English translations hold for the original Greek poems.

33. Quainton shows the progression of rhyming words of the octet and its depiction of the destruction wrought by time and the movement from life to death: "epanie," "demain," "fleuries," "flétries," "soudain" (in full bloom, tomorrow, flowering, wilted, suddenly). *Ronsard's Ordered Chaos,* 122.

34. Compare also the 1569 "Dame au gros cœur, pourquoy t'espargnes-tu?" (L.XV,121; P.II,885), which Hutton calls a "mere translation" (*Greek Anthology in France,* 361) of an epigram by Asclepiades (5.85). Indeed, the idea of the two poems is identical, except that Ronsard adds a dimension of physical aging absent from the original ("cependant que tu es jeune et belle"). Compare also "Douce beauté, meurdriere de ma vie" (L.VI, 219; P.I,92).

35. Thomas M. Greene, *The Light in Troy: Imitation and Discovery in Renaissance Poetry* (New Haven: Yale University Press, 1982), 205. See also François Rigolot, who notes that in "Mignonne, allons voir" Ronsard alternatively dresses his lady as a rose and his rose as a lady, according to the rhythm of the stanzas. "Rhétorique de la métamorphose chez Ronsard," in *Textes et Intertextes: Etudes sur le seizième siècle pour Alfred Glauser,* ed. Floyd Gray and Marcel Tetel (Paris: Nizet, 1979), 152; Compare Edmund Husserl, "En révélant les deux aspects de la réversibilité, le chiasme de la métamorphose permet de restituer une puissance de signifier" [In revealing the two aspects of reversibility, the chiasmus of metamorphosis allows signifying power to be restored], cited by M. Merleau-Ponty, *Le visible et l'invisible* (Paris: Gallimard, 1964), 203.

36. As Leonard Johnson cleverly points out, however, "with death once is enough" (note on the manuscript).

37. See Horace, *Carmina* 4.10; Propertius, *Elegies* 3.25; and Meleager (Hutton, *Greek Anthology in France,* 147).

38. *Anthologia Palatina* 5.298, in Hutton, *Greek Anthology in France,* 372.

39. See Elizabeth Cropper, "The Beauty of Women: Problems in the Rhetoric of Renaissance Portraiture," in *Rewriting the Renaissance: The Discourse of Sexual Difference in Early Modern Europe*, ed. Margaret Ferguson, Maureen Quilligan, and Nancy Vickers (Chicago: University of Chicago Press, 1986), 175–90; Ruth Kelso, *Doctrine for the Lady of the Renaissance* (Urbana: University of Illinois Press, 1978), 136–209; Nancy Vickers, "Diana Described: Scattered Woman and Scattered Rhyme," *Critical Inquiry* 8 (1976): 265–79; Alison Saunders, *The Sixteenth Century Blason Poétique* (Bern: Peter Lang, 1981); and my *"A la recherche du corps perdu:* A capstone of the Renaissance *Blasons anatomiques,"* *Romance Notes* 26 (1986): 135–42.

40. Vives, *Institution de la femme chrétienne*, 225. A part of Vives's text can also be found in *Le miroir des femmes,* ed. Guillerm et al., 1:86.

41. Erasmus, *Colloquies*, 104; Pasquier, *Lettres familières,* 408.

42. *Le Livre des proverbes français et leur emploi dans la littérature du Moyen Age et de la Renaissance* (Paris: A. Delahays, 1859), 1.220. For other examples of this phenomenon, see Jacques Bailbé, "Le thème de la vieille femme dans la poésie satirique du 16[e]

siècle et début du 17ᵉ siècle," *Bibliothèque d'Humanisme et Renaissance* 26 (1964): 98–119.

43. Compare Laumonier's summary: "C'est le rappel de la déchéance rapide des charmes extérieurs, auxquels le beau sexe tient le plus" (*Ronsard, poète lyrique,* 579) [This recalls the rapid decline of external charms, to which the beautiful sex is the most attached].

44. See also Petrarch's *Rime Sparse* 159 in *Petrarch's Lyric Poems*, ed. Durling, 304.

45. Compare, for example, Petrarch, *Rime Sparse,* 36–39, 138–39; *Delie* 1–30, in Maurice Scève, *The "Délie" of Maurice Scève*, ed. I. D. McFarlane (Cambridge: Cambridge University Press, 1966).

46. Henri Weber notes simply that the lily referring to the poet joins and completes the evocation of spring flowers in the first quatrain. *La Création poétique*, 248. The sonnet "En vain pour vous ce bouquet je compose" (L.XV,212; P.I,243–44) also includes a final image of the pining poet as wilting flower: "Comme je suis fany pour l'amour d'elle" [I am wilted out of love for her], whereas the epigram by Meleager on which it is based (5.143) limits the flower image to the addressee Heliodora. A comparison between the poet and the rose carries a different meaning in "Pren ceste rose aimable comme toy" (L.XV,204; P.I,72–73), where the poet's life of suffering, unlike that of the rose, is seen to have no end.

47. Jean Bouchet, *Les Triumphes de la noble et amoureuse dame, et l'art de honnestement aymer* (Paris: Galliot du Pré, 1535), 21r.

48. Other passages are far too numerous to develop here. See, for example, "Epitaphe de Feu Monseigneur d'Annebault" (L.XIII,182–83; P.II,917); "Celuy qui est mort aujourdhuy" (L. VII,281; P.I,785); "Voicy le temps, Hurault, qui joyeux nous convie" (L.XVII,380; P.II,340).

49. See Silver, *Ronsard's Philosophic Thought*, 158ff.; Quainton, *Ronsard's Ordered Chaos*, 93ff.; and Yvonne Bellenger, "Temps mythique et mythes du temps dans les *Hymnes* de Ronsard (*Hymnes* de 1555–56 et de 1563)," in *Le Temps et la durée dans la littérature au Moyen Age et à la Renaissance*, ed. Y. Bellenger (Paris: Nizet, 1986).

50. Bellenger in fact reads this poem as a confirmation of Ronsard's privileging love over beauty. "Temps mythique," 178.

51. See Jean Laplanche and J.-B. Pontalis's definition of projection: "Le sujet attribue à autrui les tendances, les désirs, etc., qu'il méconnaît en lui" [The subject attributes to others tendencies, desires, etc., that he fails to recognize in himself]. Jean Laplanche and J.-B. Pontalis, *Vocabulaire de la psychanalyse* (Paris: Presses Universitaires de France, 1976), 345.

52. Compare also Horace, *Carmina* 1.25.9–19 and 3.26.

53. Montaigne, *Essais,* III,9; 2:403; idem, *Essays*, ed. Frame, 361. For a contemporary psychoanalytic reading of this question, see Kathleen Woodward, "The Mirror Stage of Old Age," in *Memory and Desire: Aging-Literature-Psychoanalysis*, ed. Kathleen Woodward and Murray Schwartz (Bloomington: Indiana University Press, 1986).

54. The English translation is by Charles E. Passage, in *The Complete Works of Horace* (New York: Frederick Ungar, 1983), 328.

55. Laumonier, *Ronsard, poète lyrique,* 581.

56. Ehsan Ahmed has recently noted, for example, how Ronsard plays parodically with the homoerotic Horatian subtext (reset as a heterosexual dilemma) through the name Janne. See Ahmed, "'Quel genre de querelle?' Pierre de Ronsard and Janne," *Romance Notes* 38 (1998): 255–61.

57. Compare also Horace's "Ode to Lyce" (*Carmina* 4.13), a post–*carpe diem* apostrophe addressed to the now aged former lover. Here the poet is distanced from the female

addressee throughout the ode, and the speaker's presence in the text is limited to two first-person references: "Qudiuere, Lyce, di mea uota" [The gods, O Lyce, have heard my imprecations] and ""Quid habes illius, illius, / quaespirabat amores, / quae me surpuerat mihi" [What remains now of that beauty that our love breathed, that overtook me]. On the poet's distance from himself and his own youth, see Michael C. J. Putnam, *Artifices of Eternity: Horace's Fourth Book of Odes* (Ithaca: Cornell University Press, 1986), 227.

58. Quainton, *Ronsard's Ordered Chaos,* 127

59. Jean Céard, Daniel Ménager, and Michel Simonin, in their introduction to the Pléiade reedition of Ronsard's works, note Ronsard's ability to "se multiplier," in this case by his borrowing from other authors without engaging in servile imitation. Ronsard, *Œuvres complètes,* ed. Céard, Ménager, and Simonin, 1:xxvi.

60. In a different context, Michel Simonin has demonstrated the importance of the notions of *la gémellité* (twinship) and of the double in the *Sonnets pour Hélène*. "Hélène avant Surgères: Pour une lecture humaniste des *Sonnets pour Hélène,*" in *Sur des vers de Ronsard,* ed. Tetel, 127–43.

61. This particular example obviously figures in the tradition of paradoxical encomia. See Rosalie L. Colie, *Paradoxica Epidemica* (Princeton: Princeton University Press, 1966); Annette H. Tomarken, *The Smile of Truth: The French Satirical Eulogy and Its Antecedents* (Princeton: Princeton University Press, 1990); Cathy Yandell, "Of Lice and Women: 'La Puce de Madame des Roches,'" *Journal of Medieval and Renaissance Studies* 20 (1990): 123–35. On Ronsard's metamorphoses, see Kathleen Perry, who argues that in Ronsard's work metamorphosis is "a denial of the physical, a flight from the material, into a world governed by the imagination, and its fluidity demonstrates the elusive quality of what men call reality." *Another Reality: Metamorphosis and the Imagination in the Poetry of Pierre de Ronsard* (New York: Peter Lang, 1990), 1; and Ann Moss, "Ronsard et son Narcisse," in *Poétique et narration: Mélanges offerts à Guy Demerson* (Paris: Champion, 1993), 215–23.

62. Lawrence Kritzman, "Le corps de la fiction et la fiction du corps chez Ronsard," in *Sur des vers de Ronsard,* ed. Tetel, 71.

63. Daniel Ménager, "L'amour au féminin," in *Sur des vers de Ronsard,* ed. Tetel, 105–16.

64. Interestingly, as his own death was approaching, Ronsard substituted the present for this future tense in the 1584 edition.

65. Claude Blum notes the link between incompleteness in Ronsard's representation of love and time beyond the present: "Le lieu d'incomplétude qui se définit au centre de la représentation de l'amour à l'oeuvre dans la poésie de Ronsard n'est perceptible, bien entendu, qu'au regard d'un au-delà du présent où l'amour serait accompli" [The locus of incompleteness that is defined at the center of love's representation in Ronsard's poetry is only perceptible, of course, by scrutiny outside of the present where love is accomplished]. "Peinture de la souffrance et représentation du moi dans la poésie amoureuse de Ronsard," in *Sur des vers de Ronsard,* ed. Tetel, 31.

66. Montaigne, *Essais,* III, 2; 2:237. Trans. Frame, 914.

67. Emmanuel Levinas, *Time and the Other and Additional Essays,* trans. Richard Cohen (Pittsburgh, Pa.: Dusquesne University Press, 1987), 76–77.

68. Stephen Greenblatt argues that in the early modern period, "'self-fashioning' is achieved in relation to something perceived as alien, strange, or hostile. This threatening Other—heretic, savage, witch, adulteress, traitor, Antichrist—must be discovered or invented in order to be attacked and destroyed. There is always more than one authority and more than one alien in existence at a given time." *Renaissance Self-Fashioning* (Chicago:

University of Chicago Press, 1980), 9. As we have seen, the female addressees of Ronsard's verses serve as physical Others against whom the poet defines himself.

Chapter 3. Pernette du Guillet and Louise Labé

1. Jones, *Currency of Eros,* 83.
2. Rigolot in Labé, *Œuvres complètes*, ed. Rigolot, 9.
3. Françoise Charpentier, "Les Voix du désir: *Le Debat de Folie et d'Amour* de Louise Labé," in *Le Signe et le Texte: Etudes sur l'écriture au XVIe siècle en France*, ed. Lawrence D. Kritzman (Lexington, Ky.: French Forum, 1990), 28.
4. Ascertaining a single definition for the Italian word "virtù," however, is also problematic. Consider, for example, one of the versions of Castiglione's *Il Libro del Cortegiano* that Pernette's contemporaries were likely to have read: *Le Courtisan*, trans. Jacques Colin (Lyon: François Juste, 1538). On the one hand, the courtier should be born a gentleman since nobles are more prone to virtue, which here seems to signify a fundamental moral quality: "car noblesse est ainsi qu'une claire lampe qui manifeste et faict veoir les bonnes, et mauvaises œuvres et allume et incite a vertu" (22v) [for nobility is like a clear light that illuminates good and bad works; it kindles and incites virtue]. On the other, virtue is depicted elsewhere in the same text as a kind of savoir faire: "Aulcunesfoys pour faire des argus et facetieux en la presence des dames honorables, ilz se mettent a dire des parolles ordes et deshonnestes les adressant souvent aux mesmes dames. . . et quant plus ilz les voyent rougir, tans plus ilz se tiennent pour bons courtisans, et rient tousjours, et sont bien ayses d'avoir une si belle vertu, comme il leur semble qu'ilz ont. . . ." (99v) [Sometimes in the presence of honorable ladies they begin to direct dirty and dishonest remarks to these ladies . . . and the more the men see the ladies blush, the more they consider themselves good courtiers, laughing and reveling in the savoir faire they think they have . . .]. Warner Berthoff points out that in Florence at the beginning of the sixteenth century, a civil crisis overtook the word *virtù* itself; it began to signify a "circumstance-mastering force." *Literature and the Continuance of Virtue* (Princeton: Princeton University Press, 1985), 43.
5. Verdun Saulnier notes that the word is problematic, given its varying senses in Christian, Neoplatonic, and Italian Renaissance traditions. "Etude sur Pernette du Guillet et ses *Rymes*," *Bibliothèque d'Humanisme et Renaissance* 4 (1944): 92. Jan Boney argues that Pernette exploits this duality of meanings of *vertu*, particularly as it applies to the poet herself and to Scève. Boney, "Ardeur de veoir: Reading Knowledge in Pernette Du Guillet's *Rymes*," *L'Esprit Créateur* 30, no. 4 (1990): 54–55.
6. Marguerite de Navarre, *L'Heptameron,* 21.
7. The "declamation" is entitled "Pour les femmes/Que l'excellence de la femme est plus grande que celle de l'homme" [For women/That woman's excellence is greater than man's]. This is, of course, presented as a paradox, which in the sixteenth century often meant, as Estienne's subtitle indicates, "propos contre l'opinion commune" [statements against popular opinion]. It figures in the company of such other worthy "paradoxes" as "Pour la prison," "Pour l'infirmité du corps," "Pour le desir de mourir," and "Pour le bastard."
8. Charles Estienne, *Paradoxes* (Paris: Charles Estienne, 1553), 149.
9. Claude de Taillemont, in his *Discours des Champs faez à l'honneur et exaltation de l'Amour, et des Dames* (Paris: Galiot du Pré, 1571), employs *vertu* in the humanist, Italian sense (8v, 9r, 38r), but he also rails against what he sees as the double standard inherent in the distinctions between expectations of male and female virtue: "Mais pour autant qu'ils

cuident vertu en eux ce qu'ils estiment vice en autry, comme s'ils estoient seuls dispensez de mal faire, ils rejettent tout le mauvais sus vous autres pauvres femmes, et vous jugent par leurs propres demerites" (62r) [But insofar as they believe to be virtue in themselves what they consider vice in others, as if they were the only ones to be free from wrongdoing, they unload all the evil on you poor women, and judge you according to their own deficiencies].

10. For the humanist position, see Petrarch, *Letters on Familiar Matters: Rerum Familiarium Libri IX–XVI*, trans. Aldo S. Bernardo (Baltimore: Johns Hopkins University Press, 1982), bk. 15, letter 1, 240–51; Leone Battista Alberti, *Opere Volgari*, ed. D. A. Bonucci (Florence: Galileiana, 1844), 2:360–61; Leone Ebreo, *De l'Amour*, trans. Pontus de Tyard (Lyon: Jean de Tournes, 1541), 19; and Guillaume Budé, *De l'institution du Prince* (Paris: J. Foucher, 1547), 53r. The Christian notion of idleness is outlined in Jean Benedicti, *Somme des Pechez* (Paris, 1601), 401; and Erasmus, *Le mariage chrétien*, 121, 375–76. Erasmus warns of the possibility that both women and men might fall into debauchery (121–22), but throughout the treatise chastity is considered not only desirable but also indispensable for the marriageable woman (e.g., 106, 118–19, 375–76). For Erasmus, the risks of idleness for men pale in comparison to those for women: "Car il y a des hommes qui n'ont besoin que de leur esprit pour les plus grandes affaires. A moins que celui des jeunes filles ne soit retenu par quelque occupation, il se porte aussi-tôt au mal" (106) [For there are men who need only their minds to accomplish great things. Unless the minds of young women are retained by some occupation, they turn immediately to evil]. Budé comes closest to defining virtue in men by their good use of time. He notes that time unwisely spent could occasionally lead men to financial ruin, but in the same sentence he appeals to princes who are *naturally* good to set an example: "ainsi en doibvent faire tous hommes, et principalement les princes, au moins ceulx qui ont les moyens par nature . . ." (53r) [Thus all men should do, and especially princes, at least those who have the means by nature . . .]. In cautioning against procrastination, Budé further implies the innate goodness of certain men: "[U]n homme de cœur, et de cervelle ne se doibt poinct tirer à la chancellerie de procrastination" (53v, my emphasis) [{A} man of good heart and good brain should not resort to procrastination].

11. See, for example, Guillaume Budé, *De l'institution du Prince* (Paris: J. Foucher, 1547), 7v.

12. Ibid., fol. iir.

13. Jean Bouchet, *Panégyric du Chevalier sans reproche* (Poitiers: Jacques Bouchet, 1527), 118v.

14. Vives, *Institution de la femme chrétienne*, 232.

15. Théodore de Bèze, "Les Vertus de la femme fidele et bonne mesnagere" (1556), in *Le Miroir des femmes*, ed. Guillerm et al., 1:22.

16. Symphorien Champier, *La Nef des dames vertueuses* (Lyon: J. Arnollet, 1503), i8r.

17. René de Maulde La Clavière, *The Women of the Renaissance: A Study of Feminism*, trans. George Herbert Ely (New York: Putnam, 1901), 25 n, cited by Jordan, *Renaissance Feminism*, 97.

18. Anne de Beaujeu (Anne de France), *Les enseignements d'Anne de France à sa fille Suzanne de Bourbon* (Lyon: Le Price, n.d. [ca. 1521]), A5r, A5v.

19. Ibid., C7r.

20. Le Roux de Lincy, *Le livre des proverbes français et leur emploi dans la littérature du Moyen Age et de la Renaissance* (1858; reprint, Geneva: Slatkine, 1968), 1:233.

21. Henricus Cornelius (Henri Corneille) Agrippa, *De la Noblesse et Preexcellence*

du sexe fœminin (Paris: Denys Janot, n.d. [1529]). For a concise exposition of sixteenth-century ideas on women's education, see Madeleine Lazard, *Images littéraires de la femme à la Renaissance* (Paris: Presses Universitaires de France, 1985), 95–114.

22. Vives, *Institution de la femme chrétienne*, 235.
23. Ibid.
24. Beroalde de Verville, *Les aventures de Floride* (1594), in *Misères et grandeurs de la femme au XVIe siècle*, ed. Ilana Zinguer (Geneva: Slatkine, 1982), 83.
25. Erasmus, *Le mariage chrétien*, 234–35.
26. Ibid., 237. The idea of women furnishing the matter and men providing the "motive principle" originates in Aristotle: *The Generation of Animals*, trans. A. L. Peck (Cambridge: Harvard University Press, 1943), 1184 (= *Gen.An.* 4.1.765b1).
27. Artus, *Qu'il est bienséant que les filles soient sçavantes,* 28r. The discussion is reproduced in *Misères et grandeurs,* ed. Zinguer, 80, where the transcription "fiante" should be replaced by "seante."
28. Artus, *Qu'il est bienséant que les filles soient sçavantes,* in *Misères et grandeurs,* ed. Zinguer, 80; my emphasis.
29. Saulnier, "Etude," 72. Saulnier is to Pernette as Köchel is to Mozart: it was Saulnier who first assigned the genres and numbers to her poems that we systematically use to refer to them.
30. The year of Pernette's birth had been established as 1520, but since two of her poems were set to music and published in Paris in 1540, several scholars have questioned this late date. See ibid., 8 n. 2; Pernette du Guillet, *Rymes* (1545), ed. Victor Graham (Geneva: Droz, 1968), xv. Subsequent references will be to this edition.
31. For further development of the question of writing and virtue, see Jones, *Currency of Eros*, 83ff.; and Boney, "Ardeur de veoir," 54–58.
32. One example, however, appears ambiguous. In the much-analyzed Elegy 2, where Pernette's speaker dreams of swimming naked in the company of her observing addressee, she prefaces the encounter with an apparent disclaimer:

> . . . Que ne craindrois, sans aucune maignie,
> De me trouver seule en sa compaignie:
> Que dy-je : seule? ains bien accompaignée
> D'honnesteté, que Vertu a gaignée
> A Apollo, Muses, et Nymphes maintes,
> Ne s'adonnantz qu'à toutes œuvres sainctes.
>
> (*Rymes,* 58)

[. . . What would I fear, without any company, / To find myself alone in his presence . . . / What am I saying? Alone? No, accompanied / By honesty, which Virtue won / Over Apollo, the Muses and many nymphs, / Giving herself only to holy works.]

Here Virtue appears serves as the poet's shield in defense of her sexual purity, for fear that her fantasy might be taken too literally.

33. See Richard Lock, *Aspects of Time in Medieval Literature* (New York: Garland, 1985), 9–10. On the fascination with measuring time, see above, chapter 1, pp. 24–25 and 29–34.
34. Edmond Huguet, *Dictionnaire de la langue française du seizième siècle* (Paris: Champion, 1925), 4:726, s.v. "jour."

35. Paul Ardouin insists on the light of the Day and its transforming effects on the poet in *Maurice Scève, Pernette du Guillet, Louise Labé: L'amour à Lyon au temps de la Renaissance* (Paris: Nizet, 1981), 57–66.

36. For an interesting exploration of contemporary women poets' transformation of traditional imagery, see Alicia Ostriker, "Body Language: Imagery of the Body in Women's Poetry," in *The State of Language*, ed. Leonard Michaels and Christopher Rickes (Berkeley: University of California Press, 1980), 247–63.

37. Jones qualifies Pernette's epithet for herself as "the terrestrial materialization of [Scève's] spiritual power" (*Currency of Eros*, 95). Yvonne Bellenger argues similarly that "Journée" denotes a terrestrial and human order (duration, work, war and travel) in distinction to the celestial "Jour," in *Le jour dans la poésie française* (Tübingen: Gunter Narr Verlag, 1979), 22. For further development of the "Jour," see Françoise Charpentier, "Projet poétique, travail poétique dans les *Rymes* de Pernette Du Guillet: Autour de trois quatrains," in *Poétique et narration: Mélanges offerts à Guy Demerson*, ed. François Marotin and Jacques-Philippe Saint-Gérand (Paris: Champion, 1993), 147; Ann Rosalind Jones, "Pernette du Guillet: The Lyonnais Neoplatonist," in *Women Writers of the Renaissance and Reformation*, ed. Katharina Wilson (Athens: University of Georgia Press, 1987), 220ff.; Saulnier, "Etude," 87ff.; Colette H. Winn, "Le chant de la nouvelle née: Les *Rymes* de Pernette du Guillet," *Poétique* 20 (1989): 212ff.

38. Bellenger, *Le jour dans la poésie française,* 22.

39. Frame, *Montaigne's Essays,* 805.

40. Robert D. Cottrell, "Pernette du Guillet's *Rymes:* An Adventure in Ideal Love," *Bibliothèque d'Humanisme et Renaissance* 31 (1969): 564.

41. Charpentier, "Projet poétique," 147.

42. Scève, *The "Délie,"* 5. McFarlane notes that "constituée" contrasts with "girouettoit" and denotes permanence (367 n. 10).

43. This "Idole constituée" recalls the sun's continuity in Emblem VI of the *Délie*.

44. Winn, "Le chant de la nouvelle née," 207.

45. Lance Donaldson-Evans, "The Taming of the Muse: The Female Poetic Voice in Pernette Du Guillet's *Rymes*," in *Pre-Pléiade Poetry*, ed. Jerry C. Nash (Lexington, Ky.: French Forum, 1985), 90.

46. Ebreo, *De l'Amour,* 21.

47. Ibid., 22.

48. Compare with Estienne Pasquier, who also employs "contentement" with this meaning. *Œuvres complètes,* 2:14.

49. Scève, *The "Délie,"* 94.

50. Ibid., 411; Verdun-L. Saulnier, *Maurice Scève* (Paris: Klincksieck, 1948), 1:260.

51. Ann Rosalind Jones, "Assimilation with a Difference," *Yale French Studies* 62 (1981): 143–45; idem, *Currency of Eros,* 92–93.

52. Translated by Ann Rosalind Jones in "Pernette du Guillet," 225.

53. Scève, *The "Délie,"* 193.

54. The translation is by Jones, "Pernette du Guillet," 231 n. 3, with the exception of the last two lines, which I have translated to reflect more explicitly the temporal reference present in the original.

55. Marian Rothstein, "Pernette du Guillet," in *French Women Writers: A Bio-Bibliographical Source Book*, ed. Eva Martin Sartori and Dorothy Wynne Zimmerman (New York: Greenwood Press, 1991), 146; Joyce Miller, "In the Margins of Amatory Discourse:

The *Responces* of Pernette Du Guillet," *Sixteenth Century Journal* 24, no. 2 (1993): 351–68; Anthony Perry, "Pernette du Guillet's Poetry of Love and Desire," *Bibliothèque d'Humanisme et Renaissance* 35 (1973): 368.

56. Charpentier, "Projet poétique," 152.

57. Roman Jakobson, *Language in Literature*, ed. Krystyna Pomorska and Stephen Rudy (Cambridge: Harvard University Press, 1987), 124.

58. In his edition of the *Rymes*, Victor Graham notes the affinity between this poem and Ebreo's *Dialoghi d'Amore* (23). Two short anonymous poems in the *Fleur de Poésie Françoyse* of 1543 also play upon the words *content/tourment* (81, 96). A brief examination of these poems evinces the more important role accorded to the principle of "contentement" by Pernette's poet as well as the far more intricate and finely crafted structure of her quatrain.

59. Julia Kristeva provocatively presents cursive time and monumental time in relationship to gender in "Women's Time," trans. Alice Jardine and Harry Blake, *Signs* 7 (1981): 13–35. For a more extensive study of Scève's poet's complex treatment of the problem of immortality, see Deborah Lesko Baker, *Narcissus and the Lover: Mythic Recovery and Reinvention in Scève's Délie* (Saratoga, Calif.: Anma Libri, 1986), 132ff.

60. Scève, *The "Délie,"* 112.

61. Ibid., 21.

62. Georges Poulet, *Mesure de l'instant*, vol. 2 of *Etudes sur le temps humain* (Paris: Pocket, 1990), 11, my emphasis.

63. See, for example, Dizains 11, 22, 23, 90, 135, 153, 240, 284, 325, 368, 390, 407, 417, 442, 445, 446. Occasionally, but less frequently, life after life only serves to prolong the lover's suffering: "Tousjours vivant, tousjours aussi sans vie" [Always living, also always without life] (Dizain 279 in Scève, *The Délie*, 192) and "Tousjours mourant je ne meure jamais" [Always dying I never die] (Dizain 281, in ibid., 194).

64. Dizain 307, in Scève, *The "Délie,"* 277.

65. In addition to the questions examined in this chapter, a number of others come immediately to mind: the nature of love, death, Neoplatonic philosophy, light and darkness, vision, jealousy, etc.

66. Jeffrey Masten, "What is a Topic? Lady Mary Wroth and Current Events," paper delivered at the MLA Convention, San Francisco, 29 December 1991.

67. Saulnier contends that Pernette avows to Scève "une fidélité éternelle" ("Etude," 62), yet the examples he cites, rather than evoking eternity, address enduring love in more immediate terms: "amour durable" (Epigram 10), "toute ma vie" (Epigrams 19 and 28), "ma ferme asseurance" (Elegy 1).

68. This is probably Pernette's most analyzed poem. See Robert D. Cottrell, "Pernette du Guillet's *Rymes*: An Adventure in Ideal Love," *Bibliothèque d'Humanisme et Renaissance* 31 (1969): 553–71; JoAnn DellaNeva, "Mutare/Mutatus: Pernette Du Guillet's Actaeon Myth and the Silencing of the Poetic Voice," in *Women in French Literature*, ed. Michel Guggenheim (Saratoga, Calif.: Anma Libri, 1988), 47–55; Donaldson-Evans, "The Taming of the Muse," 84–96; Jones, *Currency of Eros*, 100–103; Lawrence D. Kritzman, *The Rhetoric of Sexuality and the Literature of the French Renaissance* (Cambridge: Cambridge University Press, 1991), 24–28; Gisèle Mathieu-Castellani, "Parole d'Echo? Pernette au miroir des *Rymes*," *L'Esprit créateur* 30, no. 4 (1990): 61–71; T. Anthony Perry, "Pernette Du Guillet's Poetry of Love and Desire," *Bibliothèque d'Humanisme et Renaissance* 35 (1973): 259–71; Kirk D. Read, "Poolside Transformations: Diana and Actaeon Revisited by French Renaissance Women Lyricists," in *Renaissance Women Writers: French Texts/American*

Contexts, ed. Anne R. Larsen and Colette Winn (Detroit: Wayne State University Press, 1994), 38–54; and Colette Winn, "Le procès du même et de l'autre: Pernette du Guillet et le mythe ovidien de Diane et Actéon," in *Les représentations de l'Autre du Moyen Age au XVIIe siècle,* ed. Evelyne Berriot-Salvadore (Saint-Etienne: Publications de l'Université de Saint-Etienne, 1995), 263–71.

    69. I have changed only line 3 from Jones's translation, "Pernette du Guillet," 230.

    70. Lance Donaldson-Evans writes, for example, that Pernette's "submission to Scève is partial and voluntary and is accepted in the name of a higher purpose: the continuance of his poetic creativity" ("The Taming of the Muse," 95). Robert Cottrell concludes that Pernette "abandons her dream of perfect terrestrial happiness for the sake of an *oeuvre* that will be admired long after she and Scève are gone," but he also acknowledges the "note of self-confident serenity" concluding the poem ("Pernette du Guillet's *Rymes,*" 570). JoAnn DellaNeva offers another reading: "That Du Guillet's elegy ends with this apparent failure is, of course, ironic, since the text itself bears witness to her obvious assumption of the poet's role" ("Mutare/Mutatis," 55).

    71. Both Kirk D. Read and Lawrence Kritzman conclude, as I do, that Pernette's poet gains by her submissive stance, but for slightly different reasons. Read convincingly argues that "keeping [the lover] alive and unbound in her poetry perpetuates the conditions that occasion *her* poetic work as well" ("Poolside Transformations," 43). Kritzman notes that "the illusion of subordination paradoxically allows du Guillet to empower Scève and thus realize her own sense of autonomy through the recognition of his: a creative talent that will immortalize the object of his desire" (*Rhetoric of Sexuality,* 28).

    72. Compare Gisèle Mathieu-Castellani, who, admitting the difficulty of her enterprise, seeks out "les marques du féminin" in Louise Labé's sonnets. She warns against falling back into former stereotypes of female territory: "le fluide, le flou, le mou, l'humide, le flux incontrôlé, l'affectif" [what is fluid, vague, soft, wet, uncontrollably changing, emotional]. "Les Marques du féminin dans la parole amoureuse de Louise Labé," in *Louise Labé: Les voix du lyrisme,* ed. Guy Demerson (Saint-Etienne: Institut Claude Longeon; Paris: CNRS, 1990), 190.

    73. "Je ne cherchois autre chose qu'un honneste passetems et moyen de fuir oisiveté" [I was only seeking an honest pastime and a way to avoid idleness]. Louise Labé, *Œuvres complètes* (1555), ed. François Rigolot (Paris: Flammarion, 1986), 43; subsequent text references to Labé's *Œuvres complètes* are to this edition.

    74. The ensuing analysis of Tyard's references to time in relationship to virtue and writing is by no means intended to include Tyard's complex cosmographical reflections on time in his *Discours du temps, de l'an et de ses parties* of 1556 and his *Ephemerides octavae spherae* of 1562. On these subjects, see Eva Kushner, "Le rôle de la temporalité dans la pensée de Pontus de Tyard," in *Le Temps et la durée dans la littérature au Moyen-Age et à la Renaissance* (Paris: Nizet, 1986), 211–30.

    75. A number of recent studies have raised useful and provocative questions about the nature of women's prefaces in the sixteenth century. See above, chapter 1, p. 223 n. 50.

    76. Rilke saw in Labé's work less an incitement of the young Clémence de Bourges to write than a promise that suffering would open up a wider universe to her ("elle lui promit la douleur comme un univers agrandi" [cited by Rigolot in Labé, *Œuvres complètes,* ed. Rigolot, 253]). Although Rilke's highly romanticized reading of suffering in Labé's texts conflicts with late-twentieth-century sensibilities, it is nonetheless significant that the textual enactment of suffering Rilke identifies in Labé emphasizes the present. While the topos of suffering does not figure in my analysis, it serves to further my thesis that Louise Labé privileges the present moment.

77. Tyard, *Les Erreurs amoureuses*, ed. John McClelland (Geneva: Droz, 1967), 92. The quotation is from p. 89.

78. Ibid., 89.

79. Ibid., 90.

80. "[N]'ayant aucun devant moy qui en François eust publié Poëmes respondans à l'elevation de mes passionnées conceptions . . ." (ibid.) [{T}here having been no one before me who had published poems in French reflecting the height of my impassioned ideas . . .].

81. Ibid., 91.

82. Olivier de Magny, *Les Gayetez*, ed. Alistair R. MacKay (Geneva: Droz, 1966), 3.

83. Mathieu-Castellani, "Les Marques du féminin," 196. See also Mathieu-Castellani, *La quenouille et la lyre* (Paris: J. Corti, 1998), 176.

84. I have changed the transcription "fecondes" to "secondes."

85. Baker, *Subject of Desire*, 152.

86. Pontus de Tyard, *Solitaire second, ou Prose de la musique*, ed. Cathy Yandell (Geneva: Droz, 1980). See also Frances Yates, *The French Academies of the Sixteenth Century* (London: The Warburg Institute, 1947); and Robert Aulotte, ed. *Musique et humanisme à la Renaissance* (Paris: Presses de l'Ecole Normale Supérieure, 1993).

87. François Rouget, "Olivier de Magny, amant libertaire et poète de l'inconstance," *Revue des Amis de Ronsard* 11 (June 1998): 105–6.

88. Magny, *Les Gayetez*, 70.

89. Line Catherine Pouchard, "Louise Labé in Dialogue with Her Lute: Silence Constructs a Poetic Subject," *History of European Ideas* 20 (1995): 714–22.

90. "Isotopy" has been defined by A. J. Greimas as "a complex of manifold semantic categories making possible the uniform reading" of a text. Greimas, *Du sens* (Paris: Seuil, 1979), 88; cited by Umberto Eco, *Interpretation and Overinterpretation*, ed. Stefan Collini (Cambridge: Cambridge University Press, 1992), 62.

91. For further analysis of these "signes d'amante," see Baker, *Subject of Desire*, 146–47; Gillian Jondorf, "Petrarchan Variations in Pernette Du Guillet and Louise Labé," *Modern Language Review* 71 (1976): 766–78; and Sharlene May Poliner, "'Signes d'amante' and the Dispossessed Lover: Louise Labé's Poetics of Inheritance," *Bibliothèque d'humanisme et Renaissance* 46 (1984): 323–42.

92. For further readings of this preface, see Baker, *Subject of Desire*, 11–40; and Rigolot, "La préface à la Renaissance," 121–35. Paula Sommers analyzes the extent to which the speaker assumes her own body in the prefatory letter in "Louise Labé: The Body in the Text," in *Renaissance Women Writers,* ed. Larsen and Winn, 88–90.

93. Frances M. Biscoglio, "*Unspun* Heroes: Iconography of the Spinning Woman in the Middle Ages," *Journal of Medieval and Renaissance Studies* 25 (1995): 164. On the gendering of tasks, see also Merry Wiesner-Hanks, who shows that in Reformation ideology, when women performed an activity such as sewing clothes, it was defined as domestic work, whereas when men performed the same activity, also in their own homes, it was considered production, "'A learned task and given to men alone': The Gendering of Tasks in Early Modern German Cities," *Journal of Medieval and Renaissance Studies* 25 (1995): 95.

94. See Juliana Schiesari, *The Gendering of Melancholia: Feminism, Psychoanalysis, and the Symbolics of Loss in Renaissance Literature* (Ithaca: Cornell University Press, 1992), 55–56; Jordan, *Renaissance Feminism*, 100–105; Ferguson, Quilligan, and Vickers, eds., *Rewriting the Renaissance,* xv–xxxi.

95. Biscoglio, "*Unspun* Heroes," 165.

96. "C'est pourquoi ceux-là font fort bien, qui ne voulant pas faire apprendre un métier

à leurs filles, à cause de leurs grandes richesses ou de la dignité de leur rang et de leur fortune, leur apprennent l'art de travailler en tapisserie, ou de filer de la soïe, ou de joüer de quelque instrument, afin qu'elles aïent dequoi éviter l'oisiveté" (Erasmus, *Le mariage chrétien*, 106–7). [This is why they who do not wish their daughters to learn a trade, because of their great riches or the dignity of their status and fortune, do quite well to teach them the art of tapestry or spinning silk or playing some instrument, so that [the daughters] will have something to do to keep idleness at bay].

97. Vives, *Institution de la femme chrétienne*, 242.

98. Compare verses 36–39 of Theocritus's "The Distaff," a possible model for Ronsard's poem, where the spindle serves the male poet's purposes in a different way:

> Theugenis shall have the name
> of the best bespindled wife,
> to remind her all her life
> of her poetry-loving friend.

The Poems of Theocritus, trans. Anna Rist (Chapel Hill: University of North Carolina Press, 1978), 201.

99. Hélisenne de Crenne, *Œuvres* (1560; reprint, Geneva: Slatkine, 1977), O4v. For an analysis of Catherine's poem, see below, chapter 5, pp. 180–82.

100. *Petrarch's Lyric Poems*, ed. Durling, 37.

101. Tyard, *Les Erreurs amoureuses*, 96.

102. Labé writes the first sonnet of her collection in Italian, and the influence of Petrarch on her work is unmistakable.

103. For analyses of these poems, see Nicolas Ruwet, "Un sonnet de Louise Labé," *Langage, musique, poésie* (Paris: Seuil, 1972), 176–99; Jones, *Currency of Eros*, 164–65; Françoise Charpentier's preface to Louise Labé's *Œuvres poétiques* (Paris: Gallimard, 1983), 29–30; Labé, *Œuvres complètes*, ed. Rigolot, 22–23.

104. While a negative construction begins Labé's Italian sonnet ("Non havria Ulysse o qualunqu'altro mai," in *Œuvres complètes*, ed. Rigolot, 121), it does not technically constitute a retraction.

105. Jones, *Currency of Eros*, 171.

106. A Klein bottle is a three-dimensional version of the two-dimensional Möbius strip. A Möbius strip can be pictured by taking a band of paper as if to make it into a ring, but turning over one of them when the two ends are attached. It then becomes impossible to determine which side of the planar figure is the inside and which is the outside. Just as a Möbius strip is a two-dimensional figure functioning in three dimensions, so the Klein bottle is a three-dimensional figure functioning in four.

CHAPTER 4. ANNE DE MARQUETS AND NICOLE ESTIENNE

1. See Maïté Albistur and Daniel Armogathe, *Histoire du féminisme français* (Paris: des femmes, 1977), 94–111; and Madeleine Lazard, *Images littéraires de la femme à la Renaissance* (Paris: Presses Universitaires de France, 1985), 115–73. Lazard treats other possibilities as well: prostitutes, pimps *(entremetteuses),* and witches, 174–230. See also Natalie Zemon Davis, *Society and Culture in Early Modern France* (Stanford, Calif.: Stanford University Press, 1975), 69ff.

2. Jordan, *Renaissance Feminism*, 56–57.

3. As Ann Rosalind Jones points out, the wife's obedience to her husband fit into the conception of the household as a microcosm of the hierarchy that structured the public world (*Currency of Eros*, 14).

4. Mary Hilarine Seiler, *Anne de Marquets, poétesse religieuse du XVIe siècle* (Washington, D.C.: Catholic University of America Press, 1931; reprint, New York: AMS Press, 1969); Enea Balmas, "Anne de Marquets, Claude d'Espence et la fortuna del Flaminio in Francia," in *Saggi e studi sul Rinascimento francese* (Padova: Liviana, 1982), 135–62; Hannah S. Fournier, "La voix textuelle des 'Sonnets spirituels' d'Anne de Marquets," *Etudes Littéraires* 20, no. 2 (Autumn 1987): 77–92; Kirk D. Read, "In Search of Literary Community: Liminal Strategies in Women's Writings of Sixteenth-Century France" (diss., Princeton University, 1990); Gary Ferguson, "Biblical Exegesis and Social and Theological Commentary in the *Sonnets spirituels* of Anne de Marquets," *Œuvres et Critiques: Revue Internationale d'Etude de la Reception Critique d'Etude des Œuvres Litteraires* 20, no. 2 (1995): 111–22; Anne de Marquets, *Sonets spirituels*, ed. Gary Ferguson (Geneva: Droz, 1997).

5. However, two fine studies of Marguerite de Navarre's religious poetry have appeared in the past fifteen years: Robert D. Cottrell, *The Grammar of Silence* (Washington, D.C.: Catholic University of America Press, 1986); and Paula Sommers, *Celestial Ladders: Readings in Marguerite de Navarre's Poetry of Spiritual Ascent* (Geneva: Droz, 1989).

6. Hilarion de Coste, *Les Eloges et les vies des reynes des princesses, et des dames illustres en pieté, en courage & en Doctrine, qui ont fleury de nostre temps, & du temps de nos Peres* (Paris: Gabriel Cramoisy, 1647), vol. 1, Addition fol. PPppp r.

7. The *Memoires concernant le prieuré de Poissy*, Paris, BN, ms. ff. 5009 (1719) of Poissy begins with "les princesses qui ont eté Religieuses," 1v. Aside from lists of nuns living in the convent, the *Memoires* contains records of nuns who died between 1522 and 1613. More careful records seem to have been kept of their deaths than of their entry into the convent. Most of the deaths and wakes were rather uneventful, including that of Anne de Marquets in 1588. But a few years earlier an unusual death is described: "Le dimanche 14 Mars 1585 deceda noble Religiuse Soeur Marguerite . . . agée de 22 ans à sept heures du matin. On a commencé le service de Requiem quapres midy par les vigilles pour le doutte quelle fut bien morte" (20v) [Sunday 14 March 1585 the noble Sister Marguerite died . . . twenty-two years of age, at seven o'clock in the morning. The Requiem service did not begin until the afternoon with the vigil because we weren't certain that she was really dead]. On the royal nature of Poissy, see also Seiler, *Anne de Marquets,* 11. For a very useful synopsis of the convent's history and situation in the sixteenth century, see Gary Ferguson's introduction to the *Sonets spirituels,* 13–17. Compare also S. Moreau-Rendu, *Le Prieuré royal de Saint-Louis de Poissy* (Colmar: Alsatia, 1968).

8. Jacques Le Goff, *Time, Work, and Culture in the Middle Ages*, trans. Arthur Goldhammer (Chicago: University of Chicago Press, 1980), 35.

9. Rabelais, *Gargantua*, ed. Defaux, 443.

10. On daily life in the monastery of Poissy, see Seiler, *Anne de Marquets,* 10–20.

11. In 1400, Christine de Pizan had described the monastery in elegiac verses that are reproduced in Edmond Bories, *Histoire de la Ville de Poissy* (1925; reprint, Marseille: Lafitte, 1977), 53–69.

12. *Sonets, prières et devises en forme de pasquins pour l'assemblée de messieurs les prélats et docteurs* (Paris: Guillaume Morel, 1562), a6r; also in Ronsard's *Œuvres complètes*, L. XIV, 200; P.II, 1115. Further references to the *Sonets, prières* are to the Morel edition.

13. References to the *Sonets spirituels* will be first to the original edition, *Sonets spirituels de feüe très vertueuse et très-docte dame Sr Anne de Marquets, religieuse à Poissi, sur les dimanches et principales solennitez de l'année* (Paris: Claude Morel, 1605), followed by the page numbering in Gary Ferguson's recent edition (Geneva: Droz, 1997).

14. Léon Feugère, *Les Femmes poètes au 16ᵉ siècle* (1860; reprint, Geneva: Slatkine, 1969), 63.

15. "Car ayant quitté ses parents & ses biens, & pour prendre le voile et l'habit de l'ordre de saint Dominique . . . , elle y mena une vie digne du Ciel, & s'adonna entierement . . ." (Coste, *Les Eloges et les vies,* vol. I, Addition, fol. PPppp r–v) [For having left her parents and possessions to take the veil and habit of the order of Saint Dominic . . . , she lived a life worthy of heaven, and gave herself entirely to it].

16. Anne de Marquets, trans., *Les Divines poésies,* by Marco Antonio Flaminio (Paris: Nicolas Chesneau, 1568), e4v, a translation of Flaminio's *De rebus divinis carmina*. References to *Les Divines poésies* are to this edition. It should also be noted, however, that Anne de Marquets was encouraged to write by a doctor of theology, Claude d'Espence (Ferguson in Marquets, *Sonets spirituels,* ed. Ferguson, 23–25).

17. Caroline Walker Bynum, "'And Woman His Humanity': Female Imagery in the Religious Writing of the Later Middle Ages," in *Gender and Religion,* ed. Caroline Walker Bynum, Stevan Harrell, and Paula Richman (Boston: Beacon Press, 1986), 258. See also Gary Ferguson, who argues that by their writings and the "female space" of the convent, women were included in the religious discourse of medieval and Renaissance Europe. Ferguson, "Biblical Exegesis," 112, 119 n. 4.

18. Agrippa, *De la Noblesse,* D6v.

19. Antoine Favre's *Entretiens spirituels* appeared in 1602 and Anne de Marquets's *Sonets spirituels* were published posthumously in 1605. Gary Ferguson notes that while the sonnets cycles of Jacques de Billy, Gabrielle de Coignard, and Anne de Marquets were roughly contemporaneous, Marquet's is the most highly developed (*Sonets spirituels*, ed. Ferguson, 33).

20. Seiler, *Anne de Marquets,* 79–80.

21. Hannah Fournier signals the importance of the female textual voice in Anne de Marquets's work, evidenced both by the topoi addressed (fecundity and maternity, familial intimacy, God's feminine qualities, the paradox of the great within the small) and by her insistence on female biblical characters (Mary, Judith, the queen of Sheba, Jahel, Miriam), 77–92. Mary B. McKinley shows that in Marguerite de Navarre's *Heptameron*, the almost silent narrative voice appropriates authority by portraying powerful women characters. "Telling Secrets: Sacramental Confession and Narrative Authority," in *Critical Tales: New Studies of the Heptameron and Early Modern Culture,* ed. John D. Lyons and Mary B. McKinley (Philadelphia: University of Pennsylvania Press, 1993), 146–71.

22. See, for example, Davis, *Society and Culture,* 68ff.

23. Ibid., 93–94.

24. Antoine Favre, *Entretiens spirituels* (Paris: Pierre Chevalier, 1602), 118.

25. Ibid., 137.

26. Marquets, trans., *Les Divines poésies,* 26.

27. Vives, *Institution de la femme chrétienne,* 28.

28. On this attribution, see Seiler, *Anne de Marquets,* 105 and Marquets, *Sonets spirituels,* ed. Ferguson, 88 n. 1.

29. Several critics have explored the humility topos among other rhetorical strategies in prefaces of early modern women writers. See chapter 1, p. 223 n. 50, above. In the *Sonets*

spirituels, Anne de Marquets praises Christian humility in various forms; see, for example, Sonets 36, 49, 76, 80, and 223.

30. See Sonet 413 in the Assumption poems of *Sonets spirituels:* "Je suis, disoit la Vierge, ainsi haut exaltée, / Que le Cedre au Liban, qu'en Sion le Cypres . . ." (308; 331) [I am as exalted as the cedar in Lebanon, the cypress in Zion . . .]. This is a paraphrase of Ecclus. 24:13 ("There I grew like a cedar of Lebanon, like a cypress on the slopes of Hermon . . .").

31. Jean-Hippolyte Mariéjol recounts that "Catherine se flattait de réussir là où Charles-Quint avec toute sa puissance avait échoué. . . . La Reine espérait que théologiens protestants et catholiques, mis en présence, débattraient leurs différends et, comme en un congrès de diplomates, les régleraient par des concessions réciproques" [Catherine flattered herself in thinking she could succeed where Charles V and his power had failed. . . . The Queen hoped that Protestant and Catholic theologians, in the presence of one another, would debate their differences and, as in a diplomatic meeting, would resolve them by reciprocal concessions]. *Catherine de Médicis* (Paris: Hachette, 1920), 101. Jean Héritier further describes the unfolding of the colloquium: "Elle [Catherine de Médicis] ne prévoyait pas . . . que les docteurs protestants, faisant appel à l'arbitrage royal, ne rencontreraient point, devant eux, des adversaires, mais des juges consentant à écouter les hérétiques, non pour arriver à une entente, tout au contraire, pour les confondre et les condamner" [Catherine de Médicis did not foresee . . . that the Protestant scholars, appealing to royal arbitration, would not be faced with adversaries, but with judges consenting to receive heretics, not to come to an agreement, but to disconcert and condemn them]. *Catherine de Médicis* (Paris: Fayard, 1959), 156.

32. The two speeches took place on 9 September 1561 and 16 September 1561. For an interesting account of these speeches, see also Condé, *Mémoires de Condé ou Recueil pour servir à l'Histoire de France* (London: Claude du Bosse, J. Nillor, 1740), 2:688–718. A detailed synopsis of the colloquium can be found in Lucien Romier, *Catholiques et huguenots à la cour de Charles IX* (Paris: Perrin, 1924), 173–87.

33. *Mémoires de Condé,* 2:726–27.

34. Seiler, *Anne de Marquets,* 89.

35. Read, "In Search of Literary Community," 294.

36. In his introduction, Favre mentions in connection with the holy rosary the "victoires gaignees sur les infideles par la pieté" (*Entretiens spirituels,* A2r) [victories won over infidels by piety]. This presumably refers to the Feast of the Rosary, which was a day of thanksgiving declared by Pope Pius V to celebrate the Christian victory over the Turks between the gulfs of Corinth and Patras on 7 October 1571. The battle took place at the same time as the process of the Orders of the Rosary in Rome, whence the name originates. See Baudot and Chaussin, *Vies des saints et des bienheureux* (Paris: Letouzey, 1952), 208–12.

37. Caroline Walker Bynum, *Fragmentation and Redemption* (New York: Urzone, 1991), 183–95.

38. Cave, *Devotional Poetry in France,* 187–88.

39. Sonnet 3 in Favre, *Entretiens spirituels,* 144.

40. This sense was fairly common in sixteenth-century usage. See Huguet, *Dictionnaire,* s.v. "espace." Georges Matoré argues more broadly that time becomes spatialized in the sixteenth century, which removes time's mysteries from the terrestrial world ("Le temps au seizième siecle," 4). In this section I do not intend to claim that Anne de Marquets is the only poet who brings a spatial dimension to time, but rather to illustrate her particular strategies for doing so and to draw parallels between these and other concretizations in her texts.

41. On the question of the active exemplum, Jean-Philippe Beaulieu and Diane

Desrosiers-Bonin treat the concept of "exemplarité expérientielle" in "Allégorie et épistolarité: Les jetées de l'érudition féminine chez Hélisenne de Crenne," a paper presented at the Sixteenth Century Studies conference, 25 October 1996. See also Diane Desrosiers-Bonin, "Les lieux de l'immortalité héroïque," *Nouvelle Revue du Seizième Siècle* 12, no. 1 (1994): 21–32.

42. Ferguson points out, for example, that the repeated *hodie* ("today") of the liturgy serves to abolish the temporal distance between the believer and the historical religious events (*Sonets spirituels*, ed. Ferguson, 37–38).

43. Petrarch, *Seniles*, bk. 15, letter 3, translated by Ricardo Quinones in *The Renaissance Discovery of Time*, 121–22.

44. Aristotle, *Generation of Animals*, trans. Peck, 4.1.765b1. On the subject of Aristotle's biology and Renaissance readings of it, see Jordan, *Renaissance Feminism*, 29–34; Ian Maclean, *The Renaissance Notion of Woman* (Cambridge: Cambridge University Press, 1980), 31ff.; and Maryanne Cline Horowitz, "Aristotle and Woman," *Journal of the History of Biology* 9, no. 2 (1979): 183–213. For another record of the theory that without men, women would produce unformed fleshy substances, see Plutarch (*Les Œuvres meslees de Plutarque*, translated into French by Jacques Amyot in 1572), cited by Guillerm et al., eds., *Le Miroir des femmes*, 1:39.

45. Petrarch, *Letters on Family Matters*, bk. 23, letter 19, 301–2. See also Greene, *The Light in Troy: Imitation and Discovery in Renaissance Poetry* (New Haven: Yale University Press, 1982), 95.

46. This work differs from her unpublished *Stanzes du mariage* (n.d., 1570s), an antithetical response to Philippe Desportes's *Les stances contre le mariage*. For an analysis of this "exercice de virtuosité," see Evelyne Berriot-Salvadore, "Evocation et représentation du mariage dans la poésie féminine," *Le Mariage au temps de la Renaissance*, ed. M. T. Jones-Davies (Paris: Klincksieck, 1993), 211–27.

47. Hélisenne de Crenne, *Œuvres*, K5v.

48. Heather Dubrow, *A Happier Eden: The Politics of Marriage in the Stuart Epithalamium* (Ithaca: Cornell University Press, 1990), 12.

49. Vives, *Institution de la femme chrétienne*, 4:1.

50. Ibid., 214.

51. Pierre Lesnauderie, *Le Louange de mariage* (Paris: F. Regrault, 1523), fol. 1v.

52. Pierre Charron, *De la sagesse* (1601) (Geneva: Slatkine, 1968), III, 62–63.

53. François de Billon, *Le Fort inexpugnable de l'honneur du sexe feminin* (Paris: Ian d'Allyer, 1555), A1v.

54. See Marie Cerati, *Marguerite de Navarre* (Paris: Sorbier, 1981), 12; and Nancy Lyman Roelker, *Queen of Navarre: Jeanne d'Albret* (Cambridge: Harvard University Press, 1968), 46–47.

55. Diefendorf, *Paris City Councillors*, 181.

56. See Evelyne Berriot-Salvadore, *Les femmes dans la société française de la Renaissance* (Geneva: Droz, 1990), 29.

57. See Diefendorf, *Paris City Councillors*, 181–84.

58. See Zinguer, *Misères et grandeurs*, 49.

59. On wife beating, see *Les Evangiles des quenouilles*, which suggests that when a husband beats his wife, he should obtain his wife's pardon before asking the Virgin Mary's grace. *Les Evangiles des quenouilles*, ed. Madeleine Jeay (Montreal: Presses de l'Université de Montréal, 1985), 83. See also Davis, *Society and Culture*, 313 n. 37.

60. Davis recounts Vallée's and Goberde's stories in *Fiction in the Archives*, 77–79, 93–94.

61. Berriot-Salvadore, *Les femmes,* 210.

62. On this and other details concerning Charles Estienne, see Roman d'Amat, *Dictionnaire de biographie française* (Paris: Letouzey et Ané, 1975).

63. L.-G. Michaud, *Biographie universelle* (Paris: Michaud, 1843–65), s.v. "Charles Estienne."

64. Jacques Grévin, *L'Olimpe* (Paris: Robert Estienne, 1560), 40.

65. Jacques Lavaud, "Quelques poésies oubliées de N. Estienne," *Revue du seizième siècle* 18 (1931): 341ff.

66. See Lucien Pinvert, *Jacques Grévin* (Paris: Fontemoing, 1899), 37–38.

67. *Poètes du XVIe siècle,* ed. Schmidt, 738.

68. Another historical detail would provide further fodder for the psychoanalytic cannon: Nicole's only child, Marie Liébaut, married an "auditeur aux comptes" [an examiner of accounts in the royal treasury]! (Lavaud, "Quelques poésies," 344).

69. Ibid.

70. Ibid., 343.

71. Michaud, *Biographie universelle,* s.v. "Jean Liébaut."

72. Philippe Renouard, *Imprimeurs parisiens depuis l'introduction de l'imprimerie à Paris (1470) jusqu'à la fin du seizième siècle* (Paris: A. Claudin, 1898), 265.

73. Lavaud, "Quelques poésies," 344.

74. The portrait to which Lavaud refers is by François Clouet and can be found at the Bibliothèque Nationale (Estampes Na 22 rés boîte 15 n° 7). It is reproduced in several places, including Henri Bouchot, *Les Clouet et Corneille de Lyon* (Paris, 1892), 26–28, and Pinvert, *Jacques Grévin,* 375.

75. "Reponce par Madame Liebaut," Manuscript, Bibliothèque Nationale, Fonds Dupuy, 360v; Zinguer, *Misères et grandeurs,* 41.

76. MS Dupuy 360v–361r; Zinguer, *Misères et grandeurs,* 42–43.

77. MS Dupuy 361r.

78. Vives, *Institution de la femme chrétienne,* 341.

79. *Poètes du Seizième Siècle,* ed. Albert-Marie Schmidt, Bibliothèque de la Pléiade (Paris: Gallimard, 1953), 737.

80. Zinguer, *Misères et grandeurs,* 21.

81. Madame Liébaut, *Les Misères de la femme mariée, où se peuvent voir les peines et tourmens qu'elle reçoit durant sa vie* (Paris: Pierre Mesnier, n.d. [ca. 1587]), a4r; Zinguer, *Misères et grandeurs,* 32. All subsequent textual references will be to these two editions.

82. See Pinvert, *Jacques Grévin,* 252, 253, 255, 256, 258, 258, 264, 279, 293, 295.

83. Ibid., 277.

84. Zinguer, *Misères et grandeurs,* 23.

85. On the term "semantic isotopy," see above, chapter 3, pp. 119 and 239 n. 90.

86. Baker, *Subject of Desire,* 22.

87. The placement of commas may well have been the printer's decision. The effect of listing by including substantives without conjunctions, however, remains the poet's own.

88. See, for example, the parallels she establishes between marriage and taking religious vows. *Les Misères,* b1r; 34. Also, her suggestions for improving the institution imply her faith in the possibility of a good marriage.

89. Several tales of Marguerite de Navarre's *Heptameron* of course involve domestic violence, but they are recounted by the *devisants* rather than the women themselves.

90. François d'Amboise, *Dialogues et devis des damoiselles pour les rendre vertueuses et bienheureuses en la vraye et parfaicte amitié* (Paris: V. Norment, 1581), 190r–v.

91. Claude Mermet, *Le temps passé: Contenant le bon droit des femmes* (Lyons: B. Bouquet, 1585), 81.

92. By "interpreter," I mean to encompass the function of interpreting, translating, or inscribing the "je," a problem elegantly exposed in Charles d'Orléans's rondeau "Le truchement de ma pensée." See *Charles d'Orléans*, ed. Jacques Charpier (Paris: Seghers, 1958), 195. On the problem of authorial consciousness in fifteenth-century poetry, see Leonard W. Johnson, *Poets as Players: Theme and Variation in Late Medieval French Poetry* (Stanford, Calif.: Stanford University Press, 1990), 109ff. On the problematic notion of women's individuality as a liberating force, see Gayatri Spivak, "Three Women's Texts and a Critique of Imperialism," in *Feminisms,* ed. Warhol and Herndl, 800–812.

93. Jean-Louis Flandrin, *Les amours paysannes: XVI–XIX Siècles* (Paris: Gallimard, 1993), 31.

94. In her response to Philippe Desportes's misogynistic *Stances du mariage*, Nicole Estienne had already written a series of poems in defense of the promises of marriage: ". . . Heureuse et saincte loy, source de vos plaisirs, / . . . Des corps et des esprits heureuse liaison . . . " [Happy and holy law, source of your pleasures, / The fortunate joining of bodies and spirits . . .]. "Stanzes du mariage par Madame Liebault, femme de medecin," MS 500 des Cinq Cents de Colbert, fol. 87r.

95. Both Anne de Marquets's explicit responses to her Protestant detractor in favor of the prelates at Poissy and her admonition of the princess Marguerite can be seen as political action in the largest sense of the term.

CHAPTER 5. *LE TEMPS RETROUVÉ:* CATHERINE DES ROCHES

1. Catherine's symbiotic relationship with her mother Madeleine doubtless constitutes another reason for her refusal to marry. In her writings, however, Catherine presents a sustained argument only for the pursuit of letters, as this chapter demonstrates.

2. On women's social status in sixteenth-century France, see Jones, *Currency of Eros,* 11–15; Berriot-Salvadore, *Les femmes,* esp. 11–238; Jordan, *Renaissance Feminism,* 16ff.; Davis and Farge, *Histoire des femmes en occident,* vol. 3; Joan Kelly, "Did Women Have a Renaissance?" in *Becoming Visible,* ed. Renate Bridenthal and Claudia Koonz (Boston: Houghton Mifflin, 1977), 137–64. Kelly's pioneering work concentrates on Italy, but many of the questions she addresses apply to France as well (19–49); it is followed by an excellent bibliography of early work in the social history of Renaissance women (49–50). For an original theoretical treatment of the social control of women in a developing Renaissance state, see Peter Stallybrass, "Patriarchal Territories: The Body Enclosed," in *Rewriting the Renaissance,* ed. Ferguson, Quilligan, and Vickers, 123–42.

3. For more complete details on this and other biographical questions, see Madeleine des Roches et Catherine des Roches, *Les Œuvres,* ed. Anne R. Larsen (Geneva: Droz, 1993), 16–47 (further textual references to *Les Œuvres* will be to this edition); George Diller, *Les Dames des Roches: Etude sur la vie littéraire à Poitiers dans la deuxième moitié du XVIe siècle* (Paris: Droz, 1936), 1–86; Gabriel-A. Pérouse, *Nouvelles Françaises du XVIe siècle: Images de la vie du temps* (Geneva: Droz, 1977), 218–26; Michaud, *Biographie universelle,* s.v. "Les Dames des Roches."

4. The Dames des Roches were able to maintain their acclaimed salon, for example, entertaining both local and distant luminaries. See Diller, *Les Dames des Roches,* 61–74;

and des Roches, *Les Œuvres*, ed. Larsen, 26–29. Jones shows, however, that both Catherine and Madeleine were eager to accept payment for their work (*Currency of Eros*, 52–53).

5. Barbara Diefendorf notes the more independent and active role assumed by French (notably Parisian) widows as distinguished from the more passive role of Florentine widows in the sixteenth century. "Family Culture, Renaissance Culture," 677.

6. The debts range from 40 écus to to 949 livres 15 solz. For a summary of the law suits and investments, see Diller, *Les Dames des Roches,* 8–10, 18 and 168–75.

7. To appreciate the rarity of adopting the name of the mother's land, see Jean-Louis Flandrin, *Families in Former Times: Kinship, Household and Sexuality in Early Modern France*, trans. Richard Southern (Cambridge: Cambridge University Press, 1979), 11ff. On the denomination "des Roches," see des Roches, *Les Œuvres*, ed. Larsen, 17.

8. On Catherine's education by her mother, see Coste, *Les Eloges et les vies*, 2:235–36; Diller, *Les Dames des Roches,* 7–8; and des Roches, *Les Œuvres*, ed. Larsen, 22–23.

9. See Diller, *Les Dames des Roches,* 188–91; and des Roches, *Les Œuvres,* ed. Larsen, 418–19.

10. Timothy Hampton, *Writing from History* (Ithaca: Cornell University Press, 1990), 29. Compare also Larry Scanlon, who defines the exemplum as "a narrative enactment of a cultural authority." *Narrative, Authority and Power* (Cambridge: Cambridge University Press, 1994), 34.

11. On the notion of "opening up," "unpacking" or "unfolding," see Hampton, *Writing from History,* 25ff.

12. Ibid., 19.

13. Terence Cave, "The Mimesis of Reading in the Renaissance," in *Mimesis from Mirror to Method, Augustine to Descartes* (Hanover, N.H.: University Press of New England, 1982), 155.

14. Hampton, *Writing from History,* x–xi.

15. Ibid., 298.

16. Madeleine and Catherine des Roches, *Les secondes œuvres* (Poitiers: Nicolas Courtoys, 1583), 37r. Later references in the text to *Les secondes œuvres* are to this edition.

17. This figure includes two Greek editions, ten Latin editions, and four French translations.

18. Berriot-Salvadore, *Les femmes,* 16.

19. For a convincing analysis of the social significance of Catherine's adaptation of this biblical passage, see Anne R. Larsen, "Legitimizing the Daughter's Writing: Catherine des Roches's proverbial good Wife," *Sixteenth Century Journal* 21 (1990): 563–74.

20. Des Roches, *Les Œuvres*, ed. Larsen, 330.

21. Bèze, "Les Vertus," 1:21–22.

22. Anne Larsen usefully notes that this passage "challenges exegetical views on woman's visibility by transgressing the limits considered normative for women in bourgeois family theory." Larsen, "Legitimizing the Daughter's Writing," 570. For a subtle treatment of female speech as a type of counterdiscourse (among other functions), see Heather Dubrow, *Echoes of Desire* (Ithaca: Cornell University Press, 1995), 40–45; 90–92.

23. Théodore de Bèze's "femme fidèle" is not depicted as drawing pleasure from her work, but because of her good household management she avoids unpleasant tasks, "rien qui luy desplaise" ("Les Vertus," 21) [nothing that displeases her].

24. Diller notes that the form of this text is reminiscent of medieval dialogues (*Les Dames des Roches,* 117). For specific examples of other works that treat the harmony among body parts (or the lack thereof), see Larsen's introduction to des Roches, *Les Œuvres*, ed.

Larsen, 218 n. 40; Cathy Yandell, "*Corps* and *Corpus:* Montaigne's 'Sur des vers de Virgile'" (1986), reprinted in *Language and Meaning*, vol. 4 of *Montaigne: A Collection of Essays*, ed. Dikka Berven (New York: Garland, 1995), 201–11; Richard Peterson, "Critical Calculations: Measure and Symmetry in Literature," *PMLA* 91 (1976): 367–75.

25. For an analysis of iconographic and symbolic aspects of the distaff, see above, chapter 3, pp. 120–22.

26. Anne Larsen, "The French Humanist Scholars: Les Dames des Roches," in *Women Writers of the Renaissance and Reformation*, ed. Wilson, 239; Colette Winn, "Mère/fille/femme/muse: Maternité et créativité dans les œuvres des Dames des Roches," *Travaux de Littérature* 4 (1991): 55–68.

27. Tilde Sankovitch, *French Women Writers and the Book: Myths of Access and Desire* (Syracuse, N.Y.: Syracuse University Press, 1988), 53.

28. Ann Rosalind Jones, "Surprising Fame: Renaissance Gender Ideology and Women's Lyric," in *The Poetics of Gender,* ed. Nancy K. Miller (New York: Columbia University Press, 1985), 85

29. Jones, *Currency of Eros,* 61. See also Constance Jordan, who sees the spindle as "a sign promising the realization of a poetic vision of heroic dimensions." *Renaissance Feminism,* 183.

30. I am indebted to Robert Cottrell in his *Grammar of Silence* for this term, which I use in a somewhat broader context and explain more fully below.

31. Typical of early modern women's prefatory strategies, Catherine claims that she does not aspire to poetic immortality: "[C]e n'est pas que j'espere me tracer avec la plume une vie plus durable que celle que je tien [*sic*] de Lachesis . . ."(*Les Œuvres*, ed. Larsen, 184) [{I}t's not that I hope to trace with my pen a longer lasting life than the one Lachesis gave me . . .]. In "A mes escrits, " Catherine postulates that her work will be incapable of conquering oblivion or time (*Les Œuvres*, ed. Larsen, 293). In both cases, the very mention of her poetry's longevity acknowledges the enduring potential of writing and confirms her aspirations. On the (false) modesty of women's prefaces, see Colette Winn, "La femme écrivain au XVIe siècle: Ecriture et transgression," *Poétique* 21 (1990): 435–52; Kirk Read and François Rigolot, "Discours liminaire et identité littéraire: Remarques sur la préface féminine au XVIe siècle," *Versants* 15 (1989): 75–98; Larsen, "Un honneste passetemps."

32. "Tu dis que femmes sont de rudes et obnubilez espritz. parquoy tu conclus, qu'autre occupation ne doibvent avoir que le filer. . . . J'ay certaine evidence par cela, que si en ta faculté estoit, tu prohiberois le benefice literaire au sexe femenin, l'improperant de n'estre capable des bonnes lettres" [You say that women are ignorant and murky spirits. From this you conclude that women should have no other occupation than spinning. . . . I have reason to believe that if it were in your power, you would prohibit the female sex from the privilege of writing, reproaching women for being incapable of learning]. Hélisenne de Crenne, Epistre Invective 4, in *Œuvres*, O4v. Compare Marie de Gournay: "[I]l ne suffit pas à quelques gens de leur preferer le sexe masculin, s'ils ne les confinoient encores d'un arrest irrefragable et necessaire à la quenoüille, ouy mesme à la quenouille seule" [{I}t isn't enough for some people to prefer the male sex over the female; they also issue an inviolable and mandatory sentence to the distaff, yes to the distaff alone]. *Egalité des hommes et des femmes* (1622), in *La fille d'alliance de Montaigne*, ed. Mario Schiff (1910; reprint, Geneva: Slatkine, 1978), 61.

33. Regarding the des Roches' excellent reputation, in a letter to Monsieur Pithou, Estienne Pasquier describes the daily schedule of the Dames des Roches: "Brief, je vous pleuvis sa maison pour une vraye escole d'honneur. Le matin, vous trouverez la mere et la

fille, aprés avoir donné l'ordre à leur mesnage, se mettre sur les livres, puis tantost, faire un sage vers, tantost une epistre bien dictée. Les aprés-disnées et souppées, la porte est ouverte à tout honneste homme. Là l'on traite divers discours, ores de Philosophie, ores d'histoire, ou du temps, ou bien quelques propos gaillards. Et nul n'y entre qui n'en sorte, ou plus sçavant, ou mieux edifié" (bk. 6, letter 8 in Pasquier, *Œuvres complètes*, 2:165–66). [In short, I assure you that her house is true school of honor. In the morning, you will see mother and daughter, after having put the house in order, occupied with their books and then writing some intelligent verse or clever letter. In the afternoons and evenings, the door is open to any gentleman. There they discuss philosophy, history, time/the season or sometimes more lively topics. And no one enters there who does not emerge either wiser or more cultivated].

34. Erasmus, *Le mariage chrétien*, 106–7.

35. Catherine des Roches, Response 11, in *Les Missives de Mesdames de Roches de Poitiers, mère et fille, avec le Ravissement de Proserpine* (Paris: Abel L'Angelier, 1586), 73r.

36. E.g., keeping her husband company (*Œuvres*, 328), fleeing idleness (329), watching over husband, children and servants (329), and providing nourishment (330).

37. In fact, if Pierre de L'Estoile's journal can be taken at face value, Henri's cross-dressing was a common occurrence. September 1576: "Le roi cependant courait la bague, vêtu en amazone, et faisait tous les jours festins nouveaux" [Meanwhile, the king played "lance the ring" dressed as an Amazon, and every day engaged in new festivities]. February 1577: "Cependant le roi faisait tournois, joutes et ballets et force mascarades où il se trouvait ordinairement habillé en femme, ouvrait son pourpoint et découvrait sa gorge, y portant un collier de perles . . ." [Meanwhile, the king had tournaments, jousts, dances, and masked balls where he was normally dressed as a woman, opened his tunic and revealed his neck, where he was wearing a string of pearls . . .]. Cited by Jacqueline Boucher, *La cour de Henri III* (Rennes: Ouest-France, 1986), 25.

38. Boucher, *Société et mentalité autour de Henri III*, 4 vols. (Paris: Champion, 1981), 3:1, 3:111.

39. Christine de Pizan recounts the story of "Marthésie" in sec. I.16.1 of *La Cité des Dames*, ed. Eric Hicks and Thérèse Moreau (Paris: Stock, 1986), 71–72.

40. Tilde Sankovich reads this poem as a writing woman's manifesto: "Through the Book, women may be freed from their destructive imprisonment in an impoverished and limited occupation, and find access to life, honor, and poetic immortality." *French Women Writers and the Book*, 65.

41. The name Pasithée is probably from the Greek *pasis,* possession and *theos,* God. See Roy-Chevrier, *Mémoires de la société d'histoire et d'archéologie de Chalon-sur-Saône*, 2 série, 12 (1924): 173, cited by John A. McClelland, in Tyard, *Erreurs amoureuses,* ed. McClelland (Geneva: Droz, 1967), 82 n. 143. Frances Yates proposes that for Tyard, Pasithée represents a condensed symbol for Apollo and the Muses (*French Academies*, 61, 99, 133). The name "Pasithée" enjoyed a vogue in sixteenth-century literary circles: Tyard had chosen it for his prima donna ("Dame") in the *Erreurs amoureuses*, ed. McClelland, 21, 82–83, 284, and for the charming interlocutor of both the *Solitaire premier* and the *Solitaire second*. "Pasithée" was also a widely accepted pseudonym for the Maréchale de Retz (consult, for example, the poems addressed to "Pasitée" in the Maréchale de Retz's album, 36r–55v). See also Pontus de Tyard, *Solitaire second*, ed. Yandell, 16–18.

42. Catherine's character Charite is more frequently identified with the poet, but I believe that Pasithée, too, serves as Catherine's mouthpiece. Since Pasithée addresses much

more explicitly the importance of study, I have chosen to concentrate on her as an exemplum for the humanist woman, though many of the same arguments apply equally to Charite.

43. In the copy of the *Secondes œuvres* at the Bibliothèque de l'Arsenal, an anonymous commentator reveals his disapproval of a father's refusal to let his daughter read good books, with the following exception: "sinon un pauvre homme qui auroyt besoing du travail manuel de sa fille pour la nourriture de sa famille, au moins en jours ouvrables" (47v) [except a poor man who needed the manual labor of his daughter to feed his family, at least on business days].

44. Compare Beroalde de Verville, *Les aventures de Floride* (1594): "On dit que si les femmes savaient elles voudraient commander. O proposition indigne d'être pensée de tout brave courage! Heé, y a-t-il rien qui apporte plus d'humilité que la science?" [They say that if women knew, they would want to lead. Oh, what an indignant proposal to be thought by any brave heart! Is there anything that brings more humility than knowledge?]. Beroalde de Verville, *Les aventures de Floride*, in *Misères et grandeurs de la femme au XVIe siècle*, ed. Zinguer, 82.

45. Both this estate law and the possibility of revoking it are mentioned in the J. Calvini (W. Kahl), *Lexicon Juridicum* (Geneva: Chouët, 1752), 932.

46. For an engaging analysis of this dialogue, see Ann Rosalind Jones, "The Muse of Indirection: Feminist Ventriloquism in the Dialogues of Catherine des Roches," in *The Dialogue in Early Modern France: Art and Argument,* ed. Colette Winn (Washington, D.C.: Catholic University of America Press, 1993), 201–14.

47. Catherine's mother, Madeleine, in a letter to her daughter had similarly elaborated the inestimable power of letters, evoking the Aristotelian terms of matter and form:

> La lettre peut changer le vitieux,
> La lettre accroist le cueur du vertueux,
> La lettre est l'art qui prenant la matiere
> Luy peut donner sa forme plus entiere.
>
> (*Les Œuvres*, 82)

[Letters can change the vice-ridden / Letters augment the courage of the virtuous / Letters are the art that can give form to matter.]

48. I have replaced the fautive question mark in the original text by a period.

49. I am thinking particularly of conflicts between work and family; between teaching and writing; between engaging in a measurably useful activity (such as working with the homeless) and a less measurably useful one (such as academic endeavors), and so forth.

50. On Mary and Martha and the "mixed life," see Cottrell, *Grammar of Silence*, 4–5, 9–10, 311.

51. Thomas More's dedicatory letter to Peter Giles, in *Utopia* (1516), trans. Ralph Robynson (1551) (Oxford: Clarendon Press, 1895), 4.

52. Montaigne, *Essais,* I,39; 1:271.

53. As Colette Winn notes, "le choix délibéré d'une vie sans engagements a donc ici la valeur d'une contestation, d'une résistance à la Loi" [The deliberate choice of a life without personal commitments thus takes on the value of a contestation, a resistance to the Law]. "Mère/fille/femme/muse: Maternité et créativité dans les œuvres des Dames des Roches," *Travaux de Littérature* 4 (1991): 62.

54. Montaigne, *Essais,* III,3; 2:248–50.

55. Pasquier, *Œuvres complètes,* bk. 6, letter 8, 2:165–66.

56. In her odes, Madeleine des Roches laments the injustice of men's laws for women and the particularly difficult position of women who write:

> Je voudroy bien m'arester sur le livre,
> Et au papier mes peines souspirer;
> Mais quelque soing m'en vient tousjours tirer,
> Disant qu'il faut ma profession suivre.
>
> (*Œuvres,* 89)

[I would like to dwell on books / And sigh out my afflictions on paper; / But some care always draws me away, / Saying that I must follow my profession.]

57. Hampton, *Writing from History,* 29.

58. As illustrated in the expression "Fille trop en rue, tost perdue" [Girl in the street too much, soon lost]. See above, chapter 3, p. 88.

59. On the publication of her *Missives,* Catherine writes in a letter to her editor that he should choose the name that will sell best: "Nommez-le donc ainsi que bon vous semblera, du tiltre de Missives, ou de Lettres, ou d'Epistres: pource que la curiosité des hommes en rendra peut-estre la despesche plus prompte" [Call it whatever seems right to you—Missives, Letters or Epistles—because maybe people's curiosity will speed up the book's distribution.]. Des Roches, *Les Missives,* Letter 70, 40v.

60. Christine de Pizan, *La Cité des Dames,* 37–38. It should be noted that Christine de Pizan's rhetorical rejection of the female body in this passage powerfully expresses the alienation a woman might experience in a highly misogynous culture. On Christine's ultimate status as an influential spokeswoman, see Charity Cannon Willard, "Christine de Pizan: From Poet to Political Commentator," in *Politics, Gender and Genre: The Political Thought of Christine de Pizan,* ed. Margaret Brabant (Boulder and San Francisco: Westview Press, 1992), 17–32.

61. On the related subject of the eroticization of the female voice by male poets, see Heather Dubrow, *Echoes of Desire: English Petrarchism and Its Counterdiscourses* (Ithaca: Cornell University Press, 1995), 87–89.

62. Jones, "Surprising Fame," 84.

63. Evelyne Berriot-Salvadore, "Les héritières de Louise Labé," in *Louise Labé, les voix du lyrisme,* ed. Guy Demerson (Saint-Etienne: Institut Claude Longeon; Paris: Editions du CNRS, 1990), 94, 104.

64. Kazimierz Kupisz analyzes these borrowings in "Dans le sillage de Louise Labé (Louise Labé et Catherine des Roches)," in *Il Rinascimento a Lione,* ed. Antonio Possenti and Giulia Mastrangelo (Rome: dell'Ateneo, 1988), 531–47.

65. Clark L. Keating, *Studies on the Literary Salon in France, 1550–1615* (Cambridge: Harvard University Press, 1941), 68.

66. Pasquier, *Œuvres complètes,* 2:992.

67. Ibid., 2:993.

68. Jean-Michel Pelous, *Amour précieux amour galant (1654–1675): Essai sur la représentation de l'amour dans la littérature et la société mondaines* (Paris: Klincksieck, 1980), 18–22.

69. Crenne, *Œuvres,* N6r.

70. The husband details the nefarious effects of women's beauty in ibid., N5v ff.

71. Ibid., Epitre invective 3, N8v.

72. On Catherine's relationship with her mother, see Scévole de Sainte-Marthe, who notes the unbelievable unity of sentiments ("incredibilis consensus") between mother and daughter, cited by Diller, *Les Dames des Roches,* 51. See also Larsen, "Legitimizing the Daughter's Writing," 559–62; and Winn, "Mère/fille/femme/muse." Diller hesitatingly qualifies Catherine's filial love as abnormal (*Les Dames des Roches,* 52), and Pérouse signals what he calls a "troublante identification" between the daughter and the mother (*Nouvelles Françaises du XVIe siècle: Images de la vie du temps* [Geneva: Droz, 1977], 219 n. 133). In the *Secondes œuvres,* Catherine herself warns against overly zealous parents:

> Ne sortez point de vous en la faveur d'autruy,
> C'est se precipiter et destruire son estre:
> L'homme trop desireux de celuy qu'il fait naistre,
> Souvent se meurt en soy, afin de vivre en luy.
>
> (16r)

[Do not leave yourself in favor of another, / Rushing in and destroying your being: / He who is too involved in his offspring / Often dies in himself to live in the other].

73. Jones, *Currency of Eros,* 76; des Roches, *Les Œuvres,* ed. Larsen, 51.

74. On the widespread admiration of both Madeleine and Catherine des Roches, see La Croix du Maine, who describes the Dames des Roches as "les deux perles de tout le Poitou . . . [qui ne] cessent de travailler pour se rendre immortelles" (La Croix du Maine and Du Verdier, *Bibliothèques françoises* [1584], ed. Rigoley de Juvigny [Paris: Saillant et Nyon, 1772], 2:71) [The two pearls of Poitou, who never stop working to make themselves immortal]. Compare Feugère, *Femmes poetes au XVI siècle,* 39ff. Public approval did not necessarily extend to Catherine's refusal to marry, however, as we saw above in Pasquier's letter to Monsieur Pithou. Pasquier, in *Le Monophile,* cites other reasons for women to remain chaste before marriage: the husband will remember past favors and wonder if the wife is now sharing them with someone else (*Œuvres complètes,* 2:716) or else the wife will be abandoned like Medea and Oenone (2:717). Pasquier the poet, on the other hand, when faced with a resisting, chaste woman, seems not to be hampered by the same bother some tenets:

> Je feray d'elle encor' si grand' poursuite,
> Que me rangeant tout à sa volonté,
> Et flechissant d'un long traict sa fierté,
> On la verra sous mon pouvoir reduite.
>
> (*Œuvres complètes*, 2:843)

[I will pursue her so valiantly, / Doing everything she wants / And shooting down her pride with a long arrow, / That she will be reduced under my power.]

75. Margaret L. King, "Book-Lined Cells: Women and Humanism in the Early Italian Renaissance," in *Beyond Their Sex: Learned Women of the European Past,* ed. Patricia H. Labalme (New York: New York University Press), 78. See also Jones, who demonstrates the subversiveness of Catherine's apparently conformist strategy in "la femme forte descritte par Salomon," wherein the poet appears to endorse both the marital theory of the Old

Testament and the men of her social class as she praises the active force of the housewife ("Surprising Fame," 84–85, 92).

76. Epicurus, in a letter to Menoeceus, expresses a similar sentiment. *The Epicurus Reader: Selected Writings and Testimonia*, trans. and ed. Brad Inswood and L. P. Gerson (Indianapolis: Hackett, 1994), 28.

77. E.g., "Hymne de la mort" (L.VIII,161; P.II,601); "Epitaphe de François Rabelais" (L.VI,20; P.II,986), "Elegie [à Robert de la Haye]" (L.X, 315; P.II,366); "Si le grain de forment ne se pourrist en terre" [Epitaphe de Charles IX] (L.XVII, 383; P.II,903).

78. In "L'Hynne de l'Esté" (L.XII,35; P.II,554), for example, Ronsard depicts Time as an impotent old man, "aussi froid qu'un rocher, / Descharné, deshallé, sans puissance ny force, / N'ayant plus rien de vif sinon un peu d'escorce" [as cold as a rock, fleshless and exhausted, without power or force, with nothing alive save the skin].

79. Michaud, *Biographie universelle*, s.v. "DESROCHES (Madeleine-Neveu, dame)." Hilarion de Coste also describes Catherine as "avantagée singulierement du Ciel des beautez du corps" (*Les Eloge et les vies*, 2:235) [singularly blessed by Heaven in physical beauty].

80. For readings of Catherine's contribution to this collection, see Cathy Yandell, "Of Lice and Women," 123–35, which argues that although it may first appear that Catherine has simply joined in the literary game of paradoxical encomia to the flea, her poem, by subverting Petrarchan and other commonplace rhetorical practices and by representing a feminized mythology, ultimately undermines the collection as a whole. See also Jones, *Currency of Eros*, 58–59; and idem, "Contentious Readings: Urban Humanism and Gender Difference in *La Puce de Madame Des-Roches* (1582)," *Renaissance Quarterly* 8 (1995): 109–27.

81. E.g., "no one steps into the same river twice." For similar thoughts expressed by Pythagoras and Epimarchus, see Quinones, *Renaissance Discovery of Time,* 209.

82. This humanist "Pasithée" is the young interlocutor in Tyard's *Solitaire premier* and *Solitaire second*. See above, p. 249 n. 41.

83. For a discussion of the term *vertu* in the sixteenth century, see above, chapter 3, pp. 85–90.

84. Roughly one hundred years later in Mexico, Sor Juana, in her "Escoge antes el morir" and "Proscura desmientir los elogios," employs many of these same arguments against the poetic flatterers who praise transitory beauty. See Elizabeth Howe, "The Feminine Mistake: Nature, Illusion, and Cosmetics in the *Siglo de Oro*," *Hispania* 68, no. 3 (1985): 443–51.

85. Pasquier, *Lettres familières,* ed. D. Thickett (Geneva: Droz, 1974), bk. 2, letter 4; idem, *Œuvres complètes,* 2:34.

86. Des Roches, *Les Missives,* letter 44, 32v.

EPILOGUE: THE BRIDGES OF CHRONOS

1. Greene, *Light in Troy*, 118–20.

2. Stephen W. Hawking, *A Brief History of Time* (New York: Bantam, 1988); *Stephen Hawking's A Brief History of Time: A Reader's Companion,* ed. Stephen Hawking and Gene Stone (New York: Bantam, 1992); Jeremy Rifkin, *Time Wars* (New York: Henry Holt, 1987).

3. "Time saving" in this context is of course a relative term. For every nanosecond saved in editing, for example, another is lost in tending an ailing printer; for every electronic mail message quickly sent, three others are written that would not otherwise have been, ad infinitum.

4. Agrippa, *De la Noblesse,* 68v.

Bibliography of Works Cited

Primary Sources

(followed by call numbers from the Bibliothèque Nationale de France or the Bibliothèque de l'Arsenal (Ars.) where applicable).

Agrippa, Henricus Cornelius (Henri Corneille). *De la Noblesse et Preexcellence du sexe foeminin.* Paris: Denys Janot, n.d. [1529]. Rés. p. R. 858.

Alberti, Leone Battista. *Opere Volgari.* Edited by D. A. Bonucci. 2 vols. Florence: Galileiana, 1844.

Album de la Maréchale de Retz. Bibliothèque Nationale, MS fr. 25455.

Amboise, François d'. *Dialogues et devis des damoiselles pour les rendre vertueuses et bienheureuses en la vraye et parfaicte amitié.* Paris: V. Norment, 1581. Rés Z.2449.

Aristotle. *Physics.* Translated by Edward Hussey. Oxford: Clarendon, 1983.

Artus, Thomas. *Qu'il est bienséant que les filles soient sçavantes* (1600). In *Misères et grandeur de la femme au XVIe siècle,* edited by Ilana Zinguer. Geneva: Slatkine, 1982.

Augustine. *Confessions.* Translated by Henry Chadwick. Oxford: Oxford University Press, 1992.

Ausonius, Decimus Magnus. *Ausonius.* Translated by Hugh G. Evelyn White. 2 vols. London: William Heinemann, 1919.

Barbaro, François (Francesco). *Deux livres de l'estat du mariage.* Translated by Claude Joly. Paris: Guillaume de Luyne, 1567.

Beaujeu, Anne de (Anne de France). *Les enseignements d'Anne de France à sa fille Suzanne de Bourbon.* Lyons: Le Price, n.d. [1521]. Rés. D. 80004.

Bembo, Pietro. *Les Azolains* (1545). Translated by Jan Martin. In *Le Miroir des femmes,* edited by J. P. Guillerm, L. Guillerm, L. Hordoir, and M.F. Piejus, 1:135–42. Lille: Presses Universitaires de Lille, 1983.

———. *Rime.* Venice: G.A. de Nicolini da Sabio, 1535.

Benedicti, Jean. *Somme des Pechez.* Paris, 1601. D 6502.

Bèze, Théodore de. "Les Vertus de la femme fidele et bonne mesnagere" (1556). In *Le Miroir des femmes,* edited by J. P. Guillerm, L. Guillerm, L. Hordoir, and M. F. Piejus, 1:21–22. Lille: Presses Universitaires de Lille, 1983.

Billon, François de. *Le Fort inexpugnable de l'honneur du sexe feminin*. Paris: Ian d'Allyer, 1555. 4 Z.1326 and Rés.Z.872.

Blasons anatomiques du corps féminin. In *Blasons, Poésies anciennes des XVe et XVIe siècles*, edited by D. H. Méon. Paris: Guillemot et Nicolle, 1809.

Bouchet, Jean. *Les Triumphes de la noble et amoureuse dame, et l'art de honnestement aymer*. Paris: Galliot du Pré, 1535. In-fol. Vélins 585.

———. *Panégyric du Chevalier sans reproche*. Poitiers: Jacques Bouchet, 1527. Rés. Ln[27]. 11678 and 11678a; microfilm m. 8172.

Brantôme [Pierre de Bourdeille]. *Oeuvres complètes*. Edited by Ludovic Lalanne. 10 vols. Paris: Jules Renouard, 1864–82.

———. *Recueil des Dames, poésies et tombeaux*. Edited by Etienne Vaucheret. Paris: Gallimard, 1991. 16 Z.15297 380.

Budé, Guillaume. *De l'institution du Prince*. Paris: J. Foucher, 1547.

Callimachus. *Hymns. Epigrams*. Translated by A. W. Ari. Loeb Classical Library. Cambridge: Harvard University Press, 1969.

Calvini, J. [W. Kahl]. *Lexicon Juridicum*. Geneva: Chouët, 1752.

Castiglione, Baldessar. *Le Courtisan [Il Libro del Cortegiano]*. Translated by Jacques Colin. Lyons: François Juste, 1538. Rés. R. 2049.

Champier, Symphorien. *La Nef des dames vertueuses*. Lyons: J. Arnollet, 1503. Rés. Vélins 1972.

Charron, Pierre. *De la sagesse* (1601). 3 vols. Geneva: Slatkine, 1968.

Cholières, Le seigneur de (Nicholas de Cholières). *Les Neuf Matinées*. Paris: J. Richer, 1585. Rés. Y2 8460 and Y2 2030. Ars. 8 B.L. 18912 et 13.

Christine de Pizan. *La Cité des Dames*. Edited by Eric Hicks and Thérèse Moreau. Paris: Stock, 1986.

Colletet, Guillaume. *Vies des poètes françois*. Bibliothèque Nationale, MS Nouvelles Acquisitions Françaises 3073.

Condé, Louis Ier de Bourbon, prince de. *Mémoires de Condé ou Recueil pour servir à l'Histoire de France. Contenant ce qui s'est passé de plus memorable dans ce Royaume sous les Regnes de François II et de Charles IX*. 2 vols. London: Claude du Bosse, J. Nillor, 1740. La22.3

Coste, Hilarion de. *Les Eloges et les vies des reynes des princesses, et des dames illustres en pieté, en courage & en Doctrine, qui ont fleury de nostre temps, & du temps de nos Peres*. Vol. 1, Addition. Paris: Gabriel Cramoisy, 1647.

Cotgrave, Randle. *Dictionarie of the French and English Tongues*. 1611. Reprint, Columbia: University of South Carolina Press, 1950.

Crenne, Hélisenne de. *Œuvres*. 1560. Geneva: Slatkine, 1977.

Des Périers, Bonaventure. *Œuvres*. Edited by Louis Lacour. 2 vols. Paris: P. Jannet, 1856.

———. *Recueil des œuvres de feu Bonaventure Des Périers*. Lyons: J. de Tournes, 1544. Rés. Ye. 1445; microfilm m.2082(1).

des Roches, Catherine. In *La Puce de Madame des Roches. Qui est un recueil de divers poemes Grecs, Latins et François, composez par plusieurs doctes personnages aux Grands Jours tenus à Poitiers l'an M. D. LXXIX*. Paris: Abel l'Angelier, 1582.

des Roches, Madeleine, and Catherine des Roches. *Les Missives de Mesdames de Roches* de Poitiers, mère et fille, avec le Ravissement de Proserpine. Paris: Abel L'Angelier, 1586. Rés. Ye. 527; microfilm m. 1607.

———. Les Oeuvres. 1579. Edited by Anne R. Larsen. Geneva: Droz, 1993.

———. Les secondes œuvres de Mes-dames des Roches de Poictiers, Mere et fille. Poitiers: Nicolas Courtoys, 1583. Rés. p. Ye. 410. Ars. 4 B.L. 2912.

Du Bellay, Joachim. Les Antiquitez de Rome and "Songe." In Poètes du Seizième Siècle, edited by Albert-Marie Schmidt, 418–37. Bibliothèque de la Pléiade. Paris: Gallimard, 1953.

———. L'Olive. Edited by E. Caldarini. Geneva: Droz, 1974.

Du Guillet, Pernette. Rymes. 1545. Edited by Victor Graham. Geneva: Droz, 1968.

———. Poésies, Précédé d'une notice extraite des Vies des poètes français par G. Colletet. Lyons: L. Perrin, 1830. Rés. Ye. 3922. Reprint, Geneva: Slatkine, 1970.

Du Pont, Gratien. La beaulté que femme doibt avoir: Les controverses des sexes masculin et femenin. Toulouse: J. Colomies, 1534. Rés Ye. 48.

Ebreo, Leone. De l'Amour. Translated by Pontus de Tyard. Lyons: Jean de Tournes, 1541. Z.16907–16908 and microfilm m. 3433.

Epicurus. The Epicurus Reader. Selected Writings and Testimonia. Translated and edited by Brad Inswood and L. P. Gerson. Indianapolis, Ind.: Hackett, 1994.

Erasmus. Colloquies. Translated by Craig R. Thompson. Chicago: University of Chicago Press, 1965.

———. Le mariage chrétien. Paris: François Babuty, 1714. D.25502 and microfiche D. 14012. A translation into French by Cl. Bosc of Institutio matrimonii christiani (1526).

Estienne, Charles. Paradoxes. Paris: Charles Estienne, 1553. Microfiche m. 23984.

Estienne, Nicole. [Madame Liébaut/Liébault]. Les Misères de la femme mariée, où se peuvent voir les peines et tourmens qu'elle reçoit durant sa vie. Paris: Pierre Mesnier, n.d. [ca. 1587]. Rés. Ye. 2043; microfilm m. 1597.

———. "Reponce par Madame Liebaut." Bibliothèque Nationale, MS Fonds Dupuy. 360v–361r.

———. Stanzes du mariage par Madame Liebault, femme de medecin. MS 500 des Cinq-Cents de Colbert, fol. 87r–90r.

Les Evangiles des quenouilles. Edited by Madeleine Jeay. Montreal: Presses de l'Université de Montréal, 1985.

Favre, Antoine. Entretiens spirituels. Paris: Pierre Chevalier, 1602. Ars. 8 B.L. 10779.

Ferrand, Jacques. Traité de l'essence et guérison de l'amour, ou De la mélancholie érotique. Toulouse: J. and R. Colombiez, 1610.

Firenzuola, Agnolo. Dialogo della bellezza del donne. Fiorenza: Bernardo di Giunta, 1548.

François Premier. Œuvres Poétiques. Edited by J. E. Kane. Geneva: Slatkine, 1984.

Gournay, Marie de. Egalité des hommes et des femmes. 1622. In La fille d'alliance de Montaigne, edited by Mario Schiff, 61–77. 1910. Reprint, Geneva: Slatkine, 1978.

The Greek Anthology (Anthologia Palatina). Translated by Alan Marshfield. Edited by Peter Jay. Oxford: Oxford University Press, 1973.

Grévin, Jacques. L'Olimpe. Paris: Robert Estienne, 1560.

L'Hermite, Jehan. Le passetemps. 1890–1896. Edited by Charles Ruelens et al. Geneva: Slatkine, 1971.

Horace. *The Odes and Epodes.* Translated by C. E. Bennett. Loeb Classical Library. Cambridge: Harvard University Press, 1968.

Labé, Louise. *Œuvres complètes.* 1555. Edited by François Rigolot. Paris: Flammarion, 1986.

Lemaire de Belges, Jean. *La Concorde des deux langages.* Edited by Jean Frappier. Paris: Droz, 1947.

Le Caron, Louis. *Dialogues.* Edited by Joan A. Buhlmann and Donald Gilman. Geneva: Droz, 1986.

Le Roux de Lincy. *Le livre des proverbes français et leur emploi dans la littérature du Moyen Age et de la Renaissance.* 1859. Geneva: Slatkine, 1968.

Lesnauderie, Pierre. *La Louange de mariage.* Paris: F. Regnault, 1523.

Magny, Olivier de. *Les Amours.* Paris: Estienne Groulleau, 1553. Rés. Ye. 1667.

———. *Les Gayetez.* Edited by Alistair R. MacKay. Geneva: Droz, 1966.

Marguerite de Navarre. *L'Heptameron.* Edited by Simone de Reyff. Paris: Flammarion, 1982.

———. *Lettres de Marguerite d'Angoulême.* Paris: Jules Renouard, 1841.

Marot, Clément. *Œuvres poétiques.* Edited by Gérard Defaux. 2 vols. Paris: Bordas, 1993.

Marquets, Anne de. *Sonets, prières et devises en forme de pasquins pour l'assemblée de messieurs les prélats et docteurs.* Paris: Guillaume Morel, 1562. Rés. Ye. 4359. Microfilm m. 1608. Ars. 8 B.L. 11614 Rés.

———. *Sonets spirituels de feüe très vertueuse et très-docte dame Sr Anne de Marquets, religieuse à Poissi, sur les dimanches et principales solennitez de l'année.* Paris: Claude Morel, 1605. Rés. Ye. 2058 & Ars. 8 B.L.11619.

———. *Sonets spirituels.* Edited by Gary Ferguson. Geneva: Droz, 1997.

Marquets, Anne de, trans. *Les Divines poésies,* by Marco Antonio Flaminio. Paris: Nicolas Chesneau, 1568. Rés. B 4479, Rés. Ye. 2695. Microfilm Dm. 1744; Ars. 8 B.L. 5321.

Medici, Lorenzo de'. *Poesie volgari.* Venice: Aldo, 1554.

Memoires concernant le prieuré de Poissy, receuillis [sic] sur les archives de la maison, par Madame Susanne de Hennequin, etc. Bibliothèque Nationale, MS ff. 5009 (1719).

Mermet, Claude. *Le temps passé de Claude Mermet de Sainct Rambert en Savoye. Contenant le bon droict des femmes.* Lyons: B. Bouquet, 1585. Rés. Ye. 1641.

Meurier, Gabriel. *Thresor de sentences dorees, proverbes et dicts communs selon l'ordre alphabeticque. Avec le Bouquet de philosophie morale, reduit par demandes et reponses.* Lyons: Jean d'Ogerolles, 1577. Ars. 8 B.L.33.177.

Montaigne, Michel de. *The Complete Essays of Montaigne.* Translated by Donald M. Frame. Stanford, Calif.: Stanford University Press, 1965.

———. *Essais.* Edited by Maurice Rat. Paris: Garnier, 1962.

———. *Montaigne's Essays and Selected Writings.* Translated by Donald M. Frame. New York: St. Martin's Press, 1963.

More, Thomas. *Utopia.* Translated by Ralph Robynson. 1551. Reprint, Oxford: Clarendon, 1895.

Motte-Messemé, Seigneur de la [François Le Poulcre]. *Le Passe-temps.* Paris: Jean Leblanc, 1595. Rés. Y2. 2039.

Muret, Marc-Antoine de. *Commentaire au premier livre des Amours de Ronsard. Les Oeuvres de Pierre de Ronsard*. 1622. Edited by Jacques Chomarat, Marie-Madeleine Fragonard, and Gisèle Mathieu-Castellani. Geneva: Droz, 1985.

Ovid. *Ars Amatoria*. Edited by A. S. Hollis. Book 1. Oxford: Clarendon, 1977.

Paré, Ambroise. *Les Œuvres*. Paris: G. Buon, 1585. Fol. Td72.1.

Pasquier, Estienne. *Œuvres complètes*. 2 vols. Geneva: Slatkine, 1971.

———. *Lettres familières*. Edited by D. Thickett. Geneva: Droz, 1974.

Petrarca, Francesco. *Familiarium rerum libri*. Edited by V. Rossi et al. Florence: Sansoni, 1933–42.

———. *Letters from Petrarch*. Edited by Morris Bishop. Bloomington: Indiana University Press, 1966.

———. *Letters on Family Matters: Rerum Familiarium Libri, IX–XVI*. Translated by Aldo S. Bernardo. Baltimore: Johns Hopkins University Press, 1982.

———. *Petrarch's Lyric Poems*. Edited and translated by Robert M. Durling. Cambridge: Harvard University Press, 1976.

Piccolomini, Alessandro. *Instruction pour les jeunes dames en forme de dialogue, par laquelle les dames apprendront comme elles doivent se bien gouverner en amour*. 1597. Edited by Concetta Menna Scognamiglio. Fasano: Schena; Paris: Nizet, 1992.

———. *La Raffaella: Dialogue de la gentille éducation des femmes*. Edited and translated by Alcide Bonneau. Paris: Liseux, 1884. Rés. p. Y2. 154.

Plato. *Symposium*. Translated by Benjamin Jowett. Revised by Hayden Pelliccia. New York. Modern Library, 1996.

Poètes du seizième siècle. Edited by Albert-Marie Schmidt. Paris: Gallimard, 1953.

Poitiers, Diane de. *Lettres inédites*. 1866. Edited by Georges Guiffrey. Geneva: Slatkine, 1970.

Poliziano, Agnolo, and Lorenzo de' Medici. *Canzone*. Florence: Giunti, 1568. Rés. p. Yd. 67.

Rabelais, François. *Gargantua*. Edited by Gérard Defaux. Paris: Librairie Générale Française, 1994.

———. *Pantagruel*, Edited by Gérard Defaux. Paris: Librairie Générale Française, 1994.

———. *Le Tiers livre*. Edited by Pierre Michel. Paris. Livre de Poche, 1966.

Ronsard, Pierre de. *Les Amours*. Paris: M. de la Porte, 1552.

———. *Les amours . . . nouvellement augmentées par lui, et commentées par M. A. de Muret*. Paris: chez la veuve M. de la Porte, 1553. Res. Ye. 1905; Microfilm m. 2072.

———. *Œuvres complètes*. Edited by Paul Laumonier. 25 vols. Paris: Société des Textes Français Modernes, 1914–75.

———. *Œuvres complètes*. Edited by Jean Céard, Daniel Ménager, and Michel Simonin. 2 vols. Paris: Gallimard, 1993–94.

Scève, Maurice. *The "Délie" of Maurice Scève*. Edited by I. D. McFarlane. Cambridge: Cambridge University Press, 1966.

Tahureau, Jacques. *Les Dialogues non moins profitables que facétieux*. 1565. Edited by Max Gauna. Geneva: Droz, 1981.

Taillemont, Claude de. *Discours des Champs faez à l'honneur et exaltation de l'Amour, et des Dames*. Paris: Galiot du Pré, 1571.

Theocritus. *The Poems of Theocritus*. Translated by Anna Rist. Chapel Hill: University of North Carolina Press, 1978.

Tyard, Pontus de. *Discours du Temps, de l'an et de ses parties*. In *Discours philosophiques*. Paris: Abel l'Angelier, 1587.

———. *Les Erreurs amoureuses*. Edited by John McClelland. Geneva: Droz, 1967.

———. *Solitaire premier*. Edited by Sylvio Baridon. Geneva: Droz, 1950.

———. *Solitaire second*. Edited by Cathy Yandell. Geneva: Droz, 1980.

Verville, Beroalde de. *Les aventures de Floride* (1594). In *Misères et grandeurs de la femme au XVIe siècle*, edited by Ilana Zinguer. Geneva: Slatkine, 1982.

Vives, Juan Luis. *Institution de la femme chrétienne*. Translated by Pierre de Changy. Lyons: S. Sabon, n.d. [ca. 1541–49].

CRITICAL AND THEORETICAL WORKS

Albistur, Maïté, and Daniel Armogathe. *Histoire du féminisme français*. Paris: des femmes, 1977.

Amat, Roman d'. *Dictionnaire de biographie française*. Paris: Letouzey et Ané, 1975.

Ardouin, Paul. *Maurice Scève, Pernette du Guillet, Louise Labé: L'amour à Lyon au temps de la Renaissance*. Paris: Nizet, 1981.

Aulotte, Robert, ed. *Musique et humanisme à la Renaissance*. Paris: Presses de l'Ecole Normale Supérieure, 1993.

Baker, Deborah Lesko. *Narcissus and the Lover: Mythic Recovery and Reinvention in Scève's Délie*. Saratoga, Calif.: Anma Libri, 1986.

Bailbé, Jacques. "Le thème de la vieille femme dans la poésie satirique du 16e siècle et début du 17e siècle." *Bibliothèque d'Humanisme et Renaissance* 26 (1964): 98–119.

Baudot and Chaussin. *Vies des saints et des bienheureux*. Paris: Letouzey, 1952.

Beaulieu, Jean-Philippe, and Diane Desrosiers-Bonin. "Allégorie et épistolarité: Les jetées de l'érudition féminine chez Hélisenne de Crenne." Paper presented at Sixteenth Century Studies conference, St. Louis, 25 October 1996.

Béguin, Sylvie, Oreste Binenbaum, André Chastel, W. McAllister Johnson, Sylvia Pressouyre, and Henri Zerner. *La Galerie François Ier au Chateau de Fontainebleau*. Paris: Flammarion, 1972.

Bellenger, Yvonne. *Le jour dans la poésie française*. Tübingen: Gunter Narr Verlag, 1979.

———. "Le vocabulaire de la journée et des moments dans la poésie du XVIe siècle." *Revue Belge de Philologie et d'Histoire* 55 (1977): 760–84.

Berriot-Salvadore, Evelyne. *Les femmes dans la société française de la Renaissance*. Geneva: Droz, 1990.

Bonney, Richard. *The European Dynastic States: 1494–1660*. Oxford: Oxford University Press, 1991.

Bories, Edmond. *Histoire de la Ville de Poissy*. 1925. Reprint, Marseille: Lafitte, 1977.

Boucher, Jacqueline. *La cour de Henri III*. Rennes: Ouest-France, 1986.

———. *Société et mentalité autour de Henri III*. Paris: Champion, 1981.

Braudel, Fernand. *The Limits of the Possible*. Vol. 1 of *Structures of Everyday Life*, translated by Siân Reynolds. New York: Harper and Row, 1981.

Bynum, Caroline Walker. "'And Woman His Humanity': Female Imagery in the Religious Writing of the Later Middle Ages." In *Gender and Religion*, edited by Caroline Walker Bynum, Stevan Harrell, and Paula Richman, 257–88. Boston: Beacon Press, 1986.

———. *Fragmentation and Redemption* (New York: Urzone, 1991).

Cave, Terence. *Devotional Poetry in France, 1570–1613*. Cambridge: Cambridge University Press, 1969.

———. "The Mimesis of Reading in the Renaissance." In *Mimesis from Mirror to Method, Augustine to Descartes*, 149–65. Hanover, N.H.: University Press of New England, 1982.

Cerati, Marie. *Marguerite de Navarre*. Paris: Sorbier, 1981.

Chamard, Henri. *Histoire de la Pléiade*. 2 vols. Paris: Didier, 1939–40.

Chojnacki, Stanley. "Comment: Blurring Genders." *Renaissance Quarterly* 4, nos. 3–4 (1987): 743–51.

Colie, Rosalie. *Paradoxica Epidemica*. Princeton: Princeton University Press, 1966.

Conley, Tom. *The Graphic Unconscious in Early Modern French Writing*. Cambridge: Cambridge University Press, 1992.

Cottrell, Robert D. *The Grammar of Silence: A Reading of Marguerite de Navarre's Poetry*. Washington, D.C.: Catholic University of America Press, 1986.

Cropper, Elizabeth. "The Beauty of Women: Problems in the Rhetoric of Renaissance Portraiture." In *Rewriting the Renaissance: The Discourses of Sexual Difference in Early Modern Europe*, edited by Margaret W. Ferguson, Maureen Quilligan, and Nancy Vickers, 175–90. Chicago: University of Chicago Press, 1986.

Curtius, Ernst. *La littérature européenne*. Translated by Jean Bréjoux. Paris: Presses Universitaires de France, 1986.

Davis, Natalie Zemon. *Fiction in the Archives: Pardon Tales and their Tellers in Sixteenth-Century France*. Stanford, Calif.: Stanford University Press, 1987.

———. *Society and Culture in Early Modern France*. Stanford, Calif.: Stanford University Press, 1975.

Davis, Natalie Zemon, and Arlette Farge, eds. Vol. 3 of *Histoire des femmes en occident, XVIe–XVIIIe siècles*, edited by Georges Duby and Michelle Perrot. Paris: Plon, 1991.

Defaux, Gérard. *Marot, Rabelais, Montaigne: L'Ecriture comme présence*. Paris: Champion, 1987.

de Man, Paul. "The Rhetoric of Temporality." In *Interpretation: Theory and Practice*, edited by Charles S. Singleton, 173–209. Baltimore: Johns Hopkins University Press, 1969.

Desrosiers-Bonin, Diane. "Les lieux de l'immortalité héroïque." *Nouvelle Revue du Seizième Siècle* 12, no. 1 (1994): 21–32.

Diefendorf, Barbara B. "Family Culture, Renaissance Culture." *Renaissance Quarterly* 4, no. 3–4 (1987): 661–81.

———. *Paris City Councillors in the Sixteenth Century: The Politics of Patrimony*. Princeton: Princeton University Press, 1983.

Dubrow, Heather. *Echoes of Desire: English Petrarchism and Its Counterdiscourses*. Ithaca: Cornell University Press, 1995.

———. *A Happier Eden: The Politics of Marriage in the Stuart Epithalamium*. Ithaca: Cornell University Press, 1990.

———. "Navel-Battles: Interpreting Renaissance Gynecological Manuals." *American Notes and Queries* 5 (1992): 67–71.

Eco, Umberto. *Interpretation and Overinterpretation*. Edited by Stefan Collini. Cambridge: Cambridge University Press, 1992.

Febvre, Lucien. *Le problème de l'incroyance au XVIᵉ siècle*. Paris: Michel, 1962.

Ferguson, Margaret W., Maureen Quilligan, and Nancy Vickers, eds. *Rewriting the Renaissance: The Discourse of Sexual Difference in Early Modern Europe*. Chicago: University of Chicago Press, 1986.

Feugère, Léon. *Les Femmes poètes au 16ᵉ siècle*. 1860. Geneva: Slatkine, 1969.

Flandrin, Jean-Louis. *Les amours paysannes: XVI–XIX Siècles*. Paris: Gallimard, 1993.

———. *Families in Former Times: Kinship, Household and Sexuality in Early Modern France*. Translated by Richard Southern. Cambridge: Cambridge University Press, 1979.

Foucault, Michel. *Les mots et les choses*. Paris: Gallimard, 1966.

Glasser, Richard. *Time in French Life and Thought*. Translated by C. G. Pearson. Manchester: Manchester University Press, 1972.

Greenblatt, Stephen. *Renaissance Self-Fashioning*. Chicago: University of Chicago Press, 1980.

Greene, Thomas M. *The Light in Troy: Imitation and Discovery in Renaissance Poetry*. New Haven: Yale University Press, 1982.

Hampton, Timothy. *Writing from History*. Ithaca: Cornell University Press, 1990.

Héritier, Jean. *Catherine de Médicis*. Paris: Fayard, 1959.

Horowitz, Maryanne Cline. "Aristotle and Woman." *Journal of the History of Biology* 9, no. 2 (1979): 183–213.

Howe, Elizabeth Teresa. "The Feminine Mistake: Nature, Illusion, and Cosmetics in the *Siglo de Oro*." *Hispania* 68, no. 3 (1985): 443–51.

Huguet, Edmond. *Dictionnaire de la langue française du seizième siècle*. Paris: Champion, 1925.

Hutton, James. *The Greek Anthology in France and in the Latin Writers of the Netherlands to the Year 1800*. Ithaca: Cornell University Press, 1946.

Jakobson, Roman. *Language in Literature*. Edited by Krystyna Pomorska and Stephen Rudy. Cambridge: Harvard University Press, 1987.

Jehlen, Myra. "The Paradox of Feminist Criticism." In *Feminisms*, edited by Robyn R. Warhol and Diane Price Herndl. New Brunswick, N.J.: Rutgers University Press, 1991.

Johnson, Leonard W. *Poets as Players: Theme and Variation in Late Medieval French Poetry*. Stanford, Calif.: Stanford University Press, 1990.

Jondorf, Gillian. "Petrarchan Variations in Pernette Du Guillet and Louise Labé." *Modern Language Review* 71 (1976): 766–78.

Jones, Ann Rosalind. "Assimilation with a Difference." *Yale French Studies* 62 (1981): 135–53.

———. *The Currency of Eros: Women's Love Lyric in Europe, 1540–1620*. Bloomington: Indiana University Press, 1990.

———. "Surprising Fame: Renaissance Gender Ideology and Women's Lyric." In *The Poetics of Gender*, edited by Nancy K. Miller, 74–95. New York: Columbia University Press, 1985.

Jong, Edy de. "Pearls of Virtue and Pearls of Vice." *Simiolus* 8 (1975–76): 73–85.

Jordan, Constance. *Renaissance Feminism: Literary Texts and Political Models.* Ithaca: Cornell University Press, 1990.

Joukovsky, Françoise. *Le feu et le fleuve: Héraclite et la Renaissance française.* Geneva: Droz, 1991.

———. *Montaigne et le problème du temps.* Paris: Nizet, 1972.

Joukovsky, Françoise and Pierre Joukovsky. *A Travers la Galerie François Ier.* Paris: Champion, 1992.

Kelly, Joan. "Did Women Have a Renaissance?" In *Becoming Visible,* edited by Renate Bridenthal and Claudia Koonz, 137–64. Boston: Houghton Mifflin, 1977.

Kelso, Ruth. *Doctrine for the Lady of the Renaissance.* Urbana: University of Illinois Press, 1978.

Kermode, Frank. "Changing Epochs." In *What's Happened to the Humanities?,* edited by Alvin Kernan, 162–78. Princeton: Princeton University Press, 1997.

King, Margaret L. "Book-Lined Cells: Women and Humanism in the Early Italian Renaissance." In *Beyond Their Sex: Learned Women of the European Past,* edited by Patricia H. Labalme, 66–90. New York: New York University Press.

———. *Women of the Renaissance.* Chicago: University of Chicago Press, 1991.

Kristeva, Julia. "Women's Time." Translated by Alice Jardine and Harry Blake. *Signs* 7 (1981): 13–35.

Kritzman, Lawrence D. *The Rhetoric of Sexuality and the Literature of the French Renaissance.* Cambridge: Cambridge University Press, 1991.

Kushner, Eva. "Le rôle de la temporalité dans la pensée de Pontus de Tyard." In *Le temps et la durée dans la littérature du Moyen Age et à la Renaissance.* Paris: Nizet, 1986.

Laplanche, Jean, and J.-B. Pontalis. *Vocabulaire de la psychanalyse.* Paris: Presses Universitaires de France, 1976.

Laqueur, Thomas. *Making Sex: Body and Gender from the Greeks to Freud.* Cambridge: Harvard University Press, 1990.

Larsen, Anne R. "'Un honneste passetems': Strategies of Legitimation in French Renaissance Women's Prefaces." *L'Esprit Créateur* 30 (1990): 11–22.

Lazard, Madeleine. "La France en Arcadie: La pastorale politique du XVIe siècle." In *Vérité et illusion dans le théâtre au temps de la Renaissance,* edited by M. T. Jones-Davies, 27–39. Paris: Touzot, 1983.

———. *Images littéraires de la femme à la Renaissance.* Paris: Presses Universitaires de France, 1985.

———. "Protestations et revendications féminines dans la littérature française du XVIe siècle." *Revue d'histoire littéraire de la France* 6 (1991): 859–77.

Le Goff, Jacques. *Time, Work, and Culture in the Middle Ages.* Translated by Arthur Goldhammer. Chicago: University of Chicago Press, 1980.

Le Roy Ladurie, Emmanuel. "Family Structures and Inheritance Customs in Sixteenth-Century France." In *Family and Inheritance,* edited by Jack Goody, Joan Thirsk, and E. P. Thompson. Cambridge: Cambridge University Press, 1976), 37–70.

Levinas, Emmanuel. *Le temps et l'autre.* Paris: Presses Universitaires de France, 1983.

Levine, Laura. *Men in Women's Clothing: Anti-theatricality and effeminization, 1579-1642.* Cambridge: Cambridge University Press, 1994.

L'Hoest, Benoît. *L'Amour enfermé: Sentiment et sexualité à la Renaissance.* Paris: Olivier Orban, 1990.

Lock, Richard. *Aspects of Time in Medieval Literature.* New York: Garland, 1985.

Losse, Deborah N. "Women Addressing Women: The Differentiated Text." In *French Women Writers: French Texts/American Contexts,* edited by Anne R. Larsen and Colette H. Winn, 23–37. Detroit: Wayne State University Press, 1994.

MacLean, Ian. *The Renaissance Notion of Woman.* Cambridge: Cambridge University Press, 1980.

Mariéjol, Jean-Hippolyte. *Catherine de Médicis.* Paris: Hachette, 1920.

Mathieu-Castellani, Gisèle. *La poésie amoureuse de l'âge baroque.* Paris: Librairie Générale Française, 1991.

———. *La quenouille et la lyre.* Paris: J. Corti, 1998.

Matoré, Georges. "Le temps au seizième siecle." *L'Information Grammaticale* 32 (1987): 3–8.

———. *Le vocabulaire et la société du XVIᵉ siècle.* Paris: Presses Universitaires de France, 1989.

McKinley, Mary B. "Telling Secrets: Sacramental Confession and Narrative Authority in the *Heptameron.*" In *Critical Tales: New Studies of the "Heptaméron" and Early Modern Culture,* edited by John D. Lyons and Mary B. McKinley, 147–71. Philadelphia: University of Pennsylvania Press, 1993.

Merleau-Ponty, M. *Le visible et l'invisible.* Paris: Gallimard, 1964.

Michaud, L.-G. *Biographie universelle.* 45 vols. Paris: Michaud, 1843–65.

Le Miroir des femmes. Edited by J. P. Guillerm, L. Guillerm, L. Hordoir, and M. F. Piejus. Lille: Presses Universitaires de Lille, 1983.

Muchembled, Robert. *Popular Culture and Elite Culture in France, 1400–1750.* Translated by Lydia Cochrane. Baton Rouge: Louisiana State University Press, 1985.

Mulvey, Laura. *Visual and Other Pleasures.* Bloomington: Indiana University Press, 1989.

Ostriker, Alicia. "Body Language: Imagery of the Body in Women's Poetry." In *The State of Language,* edited by Leonard Michaels and Christopher Rickes, 247–63. Berkeley: University of California Press, 1980.

Pelous, Jean-Michel. *Amour précieux amour galant (1654–1675): Essai sur la représentation de l'amour dans la littérature et la société mondaines.* Paris: Klincksieck, 1980.

Peterson, Richard. "Critical Calculations: Measure and Symmetry in Literature." *PMLA* 91 (1976): 367–75.

Picard, Michel. *Lire le temps.* Paris: Minuit, 1989.

Pinvert, Lucien. *Jacques Grévin, 1538–1570: Etude biographique et littéraire.* Paris: Thorin, 1899.

Poirion, Daniel. "Le temps perdu et retrouvé . . . au seizième siècle." *Revue des sciences humaines* 183 (1981): 71–84.

Poulet, Georges. *Mesure de l'instant.* Vol. 2 of *Etudes sur le temps humain.* Paris: Presses Pocket, 1990.

Putnam, Michael C. J. *Artifices of Eternity: Horace's Fourth Book of Odes.* Ithaca: Cornell University Press, 1986.

Quinones, Ricardo J. *The Renaissance Discovery of Time.* Cambridge: Harvard University Press, 1972.

Read, Kirk D., and François Rigolot. "Discours liminaire et identité littéraire. Remarques sur la préface féminine au XVIe siècle." *Versants* 15 (1989): 75–98.

Renouard, Philippe. *Imprimeurs parisiens depuis l'introduction de l'imprimerie à Paris (1470) jusqu'à la fin du seizième siècle.* Paris: A. Claudin, 1898.

Ricoeur, Paul. *Le temps raconté.* Paris: Seuil, 1985.

Rifkin, Jeremy. *Time Wars.* New York: Henry Holt, 1987.

Rigolot, François. "La préface à la Renaissance: Un discours sexué?" *Cahiers de l'association des études françaises* 42 (1990): 121–36.

Roelker, Nancy Lyman. *Queen of Navarre: Jeanne d'Albret.* Cambridge: Harvard University Press, 1968.

Romier, Lucien. *Catholiques et huguenots à la cours de Charles IX.* Paris: Perrin, 1924. Microfiche Lb. 33–564.

Rouget, François. "Olivier de Magny, amant libertaire et poète de l'inconstance." *Revue des Amis de Ronsard* 11 (June 1998): 99–115.

Saunders, Alison. *The Sixteenth Century Blason Poétique.* Bern: Peter Lang, 1981.

Scanlon, Larry. *Narrative, Authority and Power.* Cambridge: Cambridge University Press, 1994.

Schiesari, Juliana. *The Gendering of Melancholia: Feminism, Psychoanalysis, and the Symbolics of Loss in Renaissance Literature.* Ithaca: Cornell University Press, 1992.

Scott, Joan W. "Gender: A Useful Category of Historical Analysis." *American Historical Review* 91 (1986): 1053–75.

Sommers, Paula. *Celestial Ladders: Readings in Marguerite de Navarre's Poetry of Spiritual Ascent.* Geneva: Droz, 1989.

Saulnier, Verdun-L. *Maurice Scève.* 2 vols. Paris: Klincksieck, 1948.

Spivak, Gayatri Chakravorty. "Three Women's Texts and a Critique of Imperialism." In *Feminisms,* edited by Robyn R. Warhol and Diane Price Herndl, 798–814. New Brunswick, N.J.: Rutgers University Press, 1991.

Stalleybrass, Peter. "Patriarchal Territories: The Body Enclosed." In *Rewriting the Renaissance: The Discourses of Sexual Difference in Early Modern Europe,* edited by Margaret W. Ferguson, Maureen Quilligan, and Nancy J. Vickers, 123–42. Chicago: University of Chicago Press, 1986.

Telle, E.-V. *L'œuvre de Marguerite d'Angoulême, reine de Navarre, et la querelle des femmes.* 1937. Paris: Slatkine, 1969.

Tomarken, Annette H. *The Smile of Truth: The French Satirical Eulogy and Its Antecedents.* Princeton: Princeton University Press, 1990.

Vickers, Nancy. "Diana Described: Scattered Woman and Scattered Rhyme." *Critical Inquiry* 8 (1976): 265–79.

Weber, Henri. *La Création poétique au XVIe siècle en France.* Paris: Nizet, 1955.

Weisner-Hanks, Merry "'A learned task and given to men alone': The Gendering of Tasks in Early Modern German Cities." *The Journal of Medieval and Renaissance Studies* 25 (1995): 89–106.

Winn, Colette H. "La femme écrivain au XVIe siècle: Ecriture et transgression." *Poétique* 21 (1990): 435–52.

Woodward, Kathleen."The Mirror Stage of Old Age." In *Memory and Desire: Aging-Literature-Psychoanalysis*, edited by Kathleen Woodward and Murray Schwartz. Bloomington: Indiana University Press, 1986.

Yandell, Cathy. *"A la recherche du corps perdu:* A capstone of the Renaissance *Blasons anatomiques." Romance Notes* 26 (1986): 135–42.

———. "Carpe Diem, Poetic Immortality and the Gendered Ideology of Time." In *Renaissance Women Writers: French Texts/American Contexts,* edited by Anne R. Larsen and Colette H. Winn. Detroit: Wayne State University Press, 1994.

———. "*Corps* and *Corpus:* Montaigne's 'Sur des vers de Virgile.'" In *Language and Meaning*, vol. 4 of *Montaigne: A Collection of Essays*, edited by Dikka Berven, 201–11. New York: Garland, 1995.

———. "The Dialogic Delusion: Jacques Tahureau's *Dialogues* and the Rhetoric of Closure." In *The Dialogue in Early Modern France, 1547–1630: Art and Argumentation*, edited by Colette H. Winn, 158–89 Washington, D.C.: The Catholic University Press of America, 1993.

Yates, Frances. *The French Academies of the Sixteenth Century.* London: The Warburg Institute, 1947.

Individual Authors

RONSARD

Ahmed, Ehsan. "'Quel genre de querelle?' Pierre de Ronsard and Janne." *Romance Notes* 38 (1998): 255–61.

Armstrong, Elizabeth. *Ronsard and the Age of Gold.* Cambridge: Cambridge University Press, 1968.

Bellenger, Yvonne. "Temps mythique et mythes du temps dans les *Hymnes* de Ronsard (*Hymnes* de 1555–56 et de 1563)." In *Le Temps et la durée dans la littérature au Moyen Age et à la Renaissance*, edited by Yvonne Bellenger. Paris: Nizet, 1986.

Bellenger, Yvonne, et al., eds. *Ronsard en son IVe centenaire: Ronsard hier et aujourd'hui.* Genève: Droz, 1988.

Berg, Elizabeth. "Iconoclastic Moments: Reading the *Sonnets for Hélène*, Writing the Portuguese Letters." In *The Poetics of Gender*, edited by Nancy K. Miller, 208–21. New York: Columbia University Press, 1986.

Binet, Claude. *Discours de la vie de Pierre de Ronsard* (1586). In *Les Amours,* edited by Jean de Bonnot. Paris: Jean de Bonnot, 1980.

Blum, Claude. "Peinture de la souffrance et représentation du moi dans la poésie amoureuse de Ronsard." In *Sur des vers de Ronsard, 1585–1985: Actes du colloque international,* edited by Marcel Tetel, 29–36. Paris: Aux Amateurs de Livres, 1990.

Clements, Robert J. *Critical Theory and Practice of the Pléiade.* Cambridge: Harvard University Press, 1942.

Creore, Alvin Emerson. *A Word-Index to the Poetic Works of Ronsard.* 2 vols. Leeds: W. S. Maney, 1972.

Desan, Philippe. "The Tribulations of a Young Poet: Ronsard from 1547 to 1552." In *Renaissance Rereadings,* edited by Maryanne Horowitz, Anne Cruz, and Wendy Furman, 184–202. Urbana and Chicago: University of Illinois Press, 1988.

Duval, Edwin. M. "Ronsard's Conflation of Classical Texts." *Classical and Modern Literature* 1, no. 4 (Summer 1981): 255–66.

Fenoaltea, Doranne. *Du palais au jardin: l'architecture des "Odes" de Ronsard.* Geneva: Droz, 1990.

Joukovsky, Françoise. "Temps et éternité dans les *Hymnes.*" In *Autour des 'Hymnes' de Ronsard,* edited by Madeleine Lazard, 53–82. Paris: Champion, 1984.

Kritzman, Lawrence. "Le corps de la fiction et la fiction du corps chez Ronsard." In *Sur des vers de Ronsard, 1585–1985: Actes du colloque international,* edited by Marcel Tetel, 71–83. Paris: Aux Amateurs de Livres, 1990.

Langer, Ullrich. *Invention, Death and Self-Definition in the Poetry of Pierre de Ronsard.* Saratoga, Calif.: Anma Libri, 1986.

Laumonier, Paul. *Ronsard, poète lyrique: étude historique et littéraire.* 1923. Reprint, Geneva: Slatkine, 1972.

Longnon, Henri. *Pierre de Ronsard, essai de biographie.* 1912. Reprint, Geneva: Slatkine, 1975.

Mathieu-Castellani, Gisèle. "La main dextre et l'autre, ou la rhétorique détournée." In *Sur des vers de Ronsard, 1585–1985: Actes du colloque international,* edited by Marcel Tetel, 85–92. Paris: Aux Amateurs de Livres, 1990.

McFarlane, I. D. "Aspects of Ronsard's Poetic Vision." In *Ronsard the Poet,* edited by Terence Cave, 13–78. London: Methuen, 1973.

Ménager, Daniel. "L'amour au féminin." In *Sur des vers de Ronsard, 1585–1985: Actes du colloque international,* edited by Marcel Tetel, 105–16. Paris: Aux Amateurs de Livres, 1990.

Moss, Ann. "Ronsard et son Narcisse." In *Poétique et narration: Mélanges offerts à Guy Demerson,* 215–33. Paris: Champion, 1993.

Perry, Kathleen. *Another Reality: Metamorphosis and the Imagination in the Poetry of Pierre de Ronsard.* New York: Peter Lang, 1990.

Quainton, Malcolm D. *Ronsard's Ordered Chaos:* Visions of Flux and Stability in the Poetry of Pierre de Ronsard. Manchester: Manchester University Press, 1980.

Rigolot, François. "Rhétorique de la métamorphose chez Ronsard." In *Textes et Intertextes: Etudes sur le seizième siècle pour Alfred Glauser,* edited by Floyd Gray and Marcel Tetel, 147–59. Paris: Nizet, 1979.

Silver, Isidore. *Ronsard's Philosophic Thought.* Vol. 3 of *The Intellectual Revolution of Ronsard.* Geneva: Droz, 1992.

Simonin, Michel. "Hélène avant Surgères: pour une lecture humaniste des *Sonnets pour Hélène.*" In *Sur des vers de Ronsard, 1585–1985: Actes du colloque international,* edited by Marcel Tetel, 127–43. Paris: Aux Amateurs de Livres, 1990.

Stone, Donald, Jr. *Ronsard's Sonnet Cycles: A Study in Tone and Vision.* New Haven: Yale University Press, 1966.

Tetel, Marcel, ed. *Sur des vers de Ronsard, 1585–1985: Actes du colloque international.* Paris: Aux Amateurs de Livres, 1990.

PERNETTE DU GUILLET

Boney, Jan. "Ardeur de veoir: Reading Knowledge in Pernette Du Guillet's *Rymes.*" *Esprit Créateur* 30, no. 4 (1990): 54–58.

Charpentier, Françoise. "Projet poétique, travail poétique dans les *Rymes* de Pernette Du Guillet: Autour de trois quatrains." In *Poétique et narration: Mélanges offerts à Guy Demerson,* edited by Marotin François and Jacques-Philippe Saint-Gérand, 143–56. Paris: Champion, 1993.

Cottrell, Robert D. "Pernette du Guillet and the Logic of Aggressivity." In *Writing the Renaissance,* edited by Raymond La Charité, 93–113. Lexington, Ky.: French Forum, 1992.

———. "Pernette du Guillet's *Rymes:* An Adventure in Ideal Love." *Bibliothèque d'Humanisme et Renaissance* 31 (1969): 553–71.

DellaNeva, JoAnn. "Mutare/Mutatus: Pernette Du Guillet's Actaeon Myth and the Silencing of the Poetic Voice." In *Women in French Literature,* edited by Michel Guggenheim, 47–55. Saratoga, Calif.: Anma Libri, 1988.

Donaldson-Evans, Lance K. "The Taming of the Muse: The Female Poetic Voice in Pernette Du Guillet's *Rymes.*" In *Pre-Pléiade Poetry,* edited by Jerry C. Nash, 84–96. Lexington, Ky.: French Forum, 1985.

Jones, Ann Rosalind. "Pernette du Guillet: The Lyonnais Neoplatonist." In *Women Writers of the Renaissance and Reformation,* edited by Katharina Wilson, 219–31. Athens: University of Georgia Press, 1987.

Mathieu-Castellani, Gisèle. "La parole chétive: Les *Rymes* de Pernette du Guillet." *Littérature* 73 (1989): 47–60.

Miller, Joyce. "In the Margins of Amatory Discourse: The 'Responces' of Pernette Du Guillet." *Sixteenth Century Journal* 24, no. 2 (1993): 351–68.

Perry, T. Anthony. "Pernette Du Guillet's Poetry of Love and Desire." *Bibliothèque d'Humanisme et Renaissance* 35 (1973): 259–71.

Read, Kirk D. "Poolside Transformations: Diana and Actaeon Revisited by French Renaissance Women Lyricists." In *Renaissance Women Writers: French Texts/American Contexts,* edited by Anne R. Larsen and Colette H. Winn, 38–54. Detroit: Wayne State University Press, 1994.

Rothstein, Marian. "Pernette du Guillet." In *French Women Writers: A Bio-Biographical Source Book,* edited by Eva Martin Sartori and Dorothy Wynne Zimmerman, 143–52. New York: Greenwood Press, 1991.

Saulnier, V.-L. "Etude sur Pernette du Guillet et ses *Rymes.*" *Bibliothèque d'Humanisme et Renaissance* 4 (1944): 7–110.

Winn, Colette H. "Le chant de la nouvelle née: Les *Rymes* de Pernette du Guillet." *Poétique* 20 (1989): 207–17.

———. "Le procès du même et de l'autre: Pernette du Guillet et le mythe ovidien de Diane et Actéon." In *Les représentations de l'Autre du Moyen Age au XVIIe siècle,* edited by Evelyne Berriot-Salvadore, 263–71. Saint-Etienne: Publications de l'Université de Saint-Etienne, 1995.

LOUISE LABÉ

Baker, Deborah Lesko. "Louise Labé's Conditional Imperatives: Subversion and Transcendence of the Petrarchan Tradition." *Sixteenth Century Journal* 21, no. 4 (1990): 523–41.

———. *The Subject of Desire: Petrarchan Poetics and the Female Voice in Louise Labé.* West Lafayette, Ind.: Purdue University Press, 1996.

Berriot-Salvadore, Evelyne. "Les héritières de Louise Labé." In *Louise Labé, la voix du lyrisme,* edited by Guy Demerson, 93–105. Saint-Etienne: Institut Claude Longeon; Paris: Editions du CNRS, 1990.

Charpentier, Françoise. "L'ordre et triomphe du corps." In *Œuvres poétiques*, by Louise Labé, edited by Françoise Charpentier, 12–16. Paris: Gallimard, 1983.

———. "Les Voix du désir: Le *Debat de Folie et d'Amour* de Louise Labé." In *Le Signe et le Texte: Etudes sur l'écriture au XVIe siècle en France,* edited by Lawrence D. Kritzman, 27–38. Lexington, Ky.: French Forum, 1990.

Conley, Tom. "Engendering Letters: Louise Labé Polygraph." In *Renaissance Women Writers: French Texts/American Contexts,* edited by Anne R. Larsen and Colette H. Winn, 160–71. Detroit: Wayne State University Press, 1994.

Mathieu-Castellani, Gisèle. "Les marques du féminin dans la parole amoureuse de Louise Labé." In *Louise Labé: Les voix du lyrisme,* edited by Guy Demerson, 189–205. Saint-Etienne: Institut Claude Longeon. Paris: CNRS, 1990.

Nash, Jerry C. "Louise Labé and Learned Levity." *Romance Notes* 21 (1980): 1–7.

Poliner, Sharlene May. "'Signes d'amante' and the Dispossessed Lover: Louise Labé's Poetics of Inheritance." *Bibliothèque d'humanisme et Renaissance* 46 (1984): 323–42.

Pouchard, Line Catherine. "Louise Labé in Dialogue with Her Lute: Silence Constructs a Poetic Subject." *History of European Ideas* 20 (1995): 714–22.

Read, Kirk D. "Louise Labé in Search of Time Past: Prefatory Strategies and Rhetorical Transformations." *Critical Matrix: Princeton Working Papers in Women's Studies* 5 (1990): 63–88.

Rigolot, François. "Louise Labé et les 'Dames Lionnoises': Les ambiguïtés de la censure." In *Le signe et le texte: Etudes sur l'écriture au XVIe siècle en France,* edited by Lawrence D. Kritzman, 13–25. Lexington, Ky.: French Forum Publishers, 1990.

Ruwet, Nicolas. "Un sonnet de Louise Labé." In *Langage, musique, poésie,* 176–99. Paris: Seuil, 1972.

Sommers, Paula. "Louise Labé: The Body in the Text." In *Renaissance Women Writers: French Texts/American Contexts*, edited by Anne R. Larsen and Colette H. Winn, 85–98. Detroit: Wayne State University Press, 1994.

ANNE DE MARQUETS

Balmas, Enea. "Anne de Marquets, Claude d'Espence et la fortuna del Flaminio in Francia." In *Saggi e studi sul Rinascimento francese,* 135–62. Padova: Liviana, 1982.

Cave, Terence. *Devotional Poetry in France, 1570–1613.* Cambridge: Cambridge University Press, 1969.

Ferguson, Gary. "Biblical Exegesis and Social and Theological Commentary in the *Sonets spirituels* of Anne de Marquets." *Œuvres et Critiques: Revue Internationale d'Etude de la Reception Critique d'Etude des Œuvres Litteraires* 20, no. 2 (1995): 111–22.

Feugère, Léon. *Les Femmes poètes au 16ᵉ siècle.* Paris: Didier, 1860. Geneva: Slatkine, 1969.

Fournier, Hannah S. "La voix textuelle des 'Sonnets spirituels' de Anne de Marquets." *Etudes Littéraires* 20, no. 2 (Autumn 1987): 77–92.

Lazard, Madeleine. *Images littéraires de la femme à la Renaissance.* Paris: Presses Universitaires de France, 1985.

Read, Kirk D. "In Search of Literary Community: Liminal Strategies in Women's Writings of Sixteenth-Century France." Dissertation, Princeton University, 1990.

Seiler, Mary Hilarine. *Anne de Marquets, poétesse religieuse du XVIᵉ siècle.* Washington, D.C.: Catholic University of America Press, 1931. 8 Ln. 27 63934. Reprint, New York: AMS Press, 1969.

NICOLE ESTIENNE (MADAME LIÉBAUT)

Berriot-Salvadore, Evelyne. "Evocation et représentation du mariage dans la poésie féminine." In *Le Mariage au temps de la Renaissance,* edited by M. T. Jones-Davies, 211–27. Paris: Klincksieck, 1993.

———. "Les femmes dans les cercles intellectuels de la Renaissance: De la fille prodige à la précieuse." In *Mélanges Pitti-Ferrandi: Etudes corses, études littéraires,* 210–37. Paris: Le Cerf, 1989.

Lavaud, Jacques. "Quelques poésies oubliées de N. Estienne." *Revue du seizième siècle.* 18 (1931): 341–51.

Zinguer, Ilana. *Misères et grandeur de la femme au XVIᵉ siècle.* Geneva: Slatkine, 1982.

CATHERINE DES ROCHES

Berriot-Salvadore, Evelyne. *Les femmes dans la société française de la Renaissance.* Geneva: Droz, 1990.

———. "Les femmes dans les cercles intellectuels de la Renaissance: De la fille prodige à la précieuse." In *Mélanges Pitti-Ferrandi: Etudes corses, études littéraires,* 210–37. Paris: Le Cerf, 1989.

Jones, Ann Rosalind. "Contentious Readings: Urban Humanism and Gender Difference in *La Puce de Madame Des-Roches* (1582)." *Renaissance Quarterly* 8 (1995): 109–27.

Diller, George. *Les Dames des Roches: Etude sur la vie littéraire à Poitiers dans la deuxième moitié du XVIᵉ siècle.* Paris: Droz, 1936.

Keating, L. Clark. *Studies on the Literary Salon in France, 1550–1615.* Cambridge: Harvard University Press, 1941.

Kupisz, Kazimierz. "Dans le sillage de Louise Labé (Louise Labé et Catherine des Roches)." In *Il Rinascimento a Lione,* edited by Antonio Possenti and Giulia Mastrangelo, 2:529–47. Rome: dell'Ateneo, 1988.

Larsen, Anne R. "Catherine des Roches (1542–1587): Humanism and the Learned Woman."

Journal of the Rocky Mountain Medieval and Renaissance Association 8 (1987): 97–117.

———. "The French Humanist Scholars: Les Dames des Roches." In *Women Writers of the Renaissance and Reformation,* edited by Katharina Wilson, 232–59. Athens: University of Georgia Press, 1987.

———. "Legitimizing the Daughter's Writing: Catherine des Roches's Proverbial Good Wife." *The Sixteenth Century Journal* 21 (1990): 559–74.

Pérouse, Gabriel-A. *Nouvelles Françaises du XVIe siècle: Images de la vie du temps,* 218–26. Geneva: Droz, 1977.

Sankovitch, Tilde. "Catherine des Roches's *Le Ravissement de Proserpine:* A Humanist/Feminist Translation." In *Renaissance Women Writers: French Texts/American Contexts*, edited by Anne R. Larsen and Colette H. Winn, 55–66. Detroit: Wayne State University Press, 1994.

———. *French Women Writers and the Book: Myths of Access and Desire.* Syracuse, N.Y.: Syracuse University Press, 1988.

Winn, Colette. "Mère/fille/femme/muse: Maternité et créativité dans les œuvres des Dames des Roches." *Travaux de Littérature* 4 (1991): 53–68.

Yandell, Cathy. "Of Lice and Women: 'La Puce de Madame des Roches.'" *Journal of Medieval and Renaissance Studies* 20 (1990): 123–35.

Index

Note: Italicized page numbers indicate illustrations.

Académie de Poésie et de Musique, 118
Agathias, 226–27n. 31
aging: beauty lost in, 43–46, 67–72; death as more auspicious than, 61–62, 72–73; fear of, 15–16, 42–47, 49, 60, 72–74, 76–79, 82; female body as representative of, 40–46, 60–61, 69–72, 82, 203–5, 213; gender blurred in, 45–46, 73–74; life cycle and, 34–39, 203–7, 210; physical suffering linked to, 65; replaced by memory of youth, 76–77; Ronsard on, 43, 48, 49, 60, 68–74, 76–82, 205, 208, 215, 221n. 56; subversion of, 17; as threat, 206, 209–10. See also *carpe diem* (pluck the day)
Agrippa, Henricus Cornelius, 89, 128, 132, 216
Ahmed, Ehsan, 228n. 56
Alberti, Leone Battista, 28
Alexander the Great, 44
Allen, Woody, 215–16
Amazons, as exemplars, 183–88, 192–93
Amboise, François d', 168–69
Amours (Ronsard): *carpe diem* motif in, 72–73, 226n. 28; *exegi monumentum* in, 50–65; poetic immortality claimed in, 50–51; poet's identities in, 82–84; Ronsard and Cassandre in, 51, *52,* 54, 83, 225n. 10, 225n. 13; transcendence subverted in, 49

Angoulême, count of, 156
Anne de France, 88
Ardouin, Paul, 232–33n. 35
Argensola, Lupercio Leonardo de, 66
Ariosto, 184
Aristotle: on matter and "motive principle," 154, 232n. 26; on time, 27, 82; on woman, 14, 37–38, 88. Works: *Physics,* 27, 82; *Politics,* 88
Armstrong, Elizabeth, 223n. 5
Artus, Thomas, 89–90
Asclepiades, 226–27n. 31, 227n. 34
Aubert, Guillaume, 81
Augustine, 27, 219n. 18
authority: of texts, 176–77; time and, 71–72; of woman poet, 139–40, 143–44

Bade, Josse, 66, 218n. 8
Baïf, Jean-Antoine de, 157–58
Baker, Deborah Lesko: on Labé, 236n. 91; on memory, 116; on signs of enslavement, 166; on women's prefaces, 220n. 50
Balmas, Enea, 238n. 4
Barbaro, Francesco, 38
Beaulieu, Jean-Philippe, 240–41n. 41
beauty: created by male writing, 54; death's link to, 40–41; lost in aging, 43–46, 67–72; moral goodness linked to, 194–95, 206–7; negative consequences of, 200–203; obsession with,

268

72, 206, 213, 215; pleasure from, 195–96; rejection of ideal, 45; rhetorical aging and, 80–81; subversion of, 190, 196, 206–10; writing as substitute for, 159–60; youth as component of, 45–46, 72–73, 213
Bel, Philippe le, 129
Bellay, Joachim du. *See* Du Bellay, Joachim
Bellenger, Yvonne, 97, 226 n. 28, 228 n. 50, 233 n. 37
Bembo, Pietro, 14–15, 50
Berg, Elizabeth, 226 n. 28
Berriot-Salvadore, Evelyne, 157, 178, 197, 234–35 n. 68
Berthoff, Warner, 230 n. 4
Bèze, Théodore de, 87, 94, 139, 178
Bible: contemplation vs. good works in (Mary and Martha), 192; Crucifixion story, 147–49; feminization of (Proverbs), 178–80, 182–83; life cycle in (Ecclesiastes), 204–5; on marriage (Paul), 168; serving others/serving Christ (Matthew and Luke), 147
Billon, François de, 14, 156
Billy, Jacques de, 239 n. 19
Binet, Claude, 48
bird-catcher, symbolism of, 165
Biscoglio, Frances, 121
Blasons anatomiques du corps féminin (text), 72
Bloch, Oscar, 86
Blum, Claude, 229 n. 65
body: eroticism and, 194–203; flower linked to, 67–75; future linked to, 50–51, 65; mind vs., 191; temporality and, 203–11, 213; time and functions of, 30; time measured through, 15, 23, 40–41, 49; woman as, 193–94. *See also* aging; beauty; female body; human life
Boney, Jan, 230 n. 5
Bonney, Richard, 34
Boucher, Jacqueline, 183
Bouchet, Jean: on time, 90, 127, 211; on virtue, 87, 88. Works: *Panégyric du Chevalier sans reproche*, 87, 88, *Les Triumphes de la noble et amoureuse dame et l'art de honnestement aymer*, 73
Bourges, Clémence de, 112, 113, 235 n. 76
Brantôme [Pierre de Bourdeille], 41, 45, 153, 225 n. 13
Braudel, Fernand, 34, 42, 221 n. 53
Budé, Guillaume, 87, 231 n. 10
Buhlman, Joan, 226 n. 22
Bynum, Carolyn Walker, 132, 147

Cabassoles, Philippe de, 28
Caesar, Julius, 44
Callimachus, 58, 59, 225 n. 16
carpe diem (pluck the day): des Roches's use of, 17, 205–11, 213; doubled activities and, 30; gendered use of, 11–12, 47, 213; Horace's use of, 65–66, 77–79; human agency in, 29; origins of, 65–66; Ovid's use of, 67; popular use of, 23–25; rhetorical strategies and, 79–81; Ronsard's use of, 15–16, 47, 49, 50, 67–82, 84, 226 n. 28; Rufinus's use of, 67–69; youth linked to, 77–82. *See also* aging; death
Castiglione, Baldassare, 88, 230 n. 4
Catherine de Médicis, 59, 139, 240 n. 31
Catherine de Navarre, 159
Catholic Church: in colloquium debate, 139–40, 240 n. 31, 240 n. 32; Crucifixion and, 147–49; defense of, 138; Huguenots vs., 132–33; sonnets celebrating rituals of, 145–47. *See also* confession; Jesus (biblical); Mary (biblical)
Cave, Terence, 26, 147, 176–77
Céard, Jean, 229 n. 59
celibacy, as guardian, 202–3
Chamard, Henri, 224 n. 9, 225 n. 13
Champier, Symphorien: on time, 30, 90, 127; on virtue, 87–88
Charles V (Holy Roman Emperor and king of Spain), 42
Charles VIII (king of France), 88
Charles IX (king of France), 25
Charpentier, Françoise, 86, 99, 106
Charron, Pierre, 155
Chassignet, Jean-Baptiste, 129

chastity: celibacy as militant, 202–3; emphasis on, 231n. 10; erotic body and, 196; Ronsard vs. des Roches on, 184–86; virtue's link to, 86–87, 90, 95. *See also* virginity; virtue/*vertu*
children: of body vs. soul, 224n. 8; timing conception of, 30
Chojnacki, Stanley, 12–13
Cholières, Nicholas de, 31–32, 38–39
Christine de Pizan: as exemplar, 177; on female body, 194, 248n. 60; on Marthésie, 246n. 39; at Poissy, 129, 238n. 11. Works: *La Cité des Dames,* 194
Cicero, 219n. 18
civility, sexual difference and, 13
Clements, Robert J., 224n. 7
Clèves, duc de, 156
clocks: construction of, 24; regulation by, 129–30; as tyrants, 30–31
Clouet, François (artist), 242n. 74
Coignard, Gabrielle de, 239n. 19
Cointerel, P., 130
Colletet, Guillaume, 158
concordia discors (discordant concourse), 12
conduct manuals: on education, 89; female body in, 13; on marriage, 155; on virtue, 87–89
confession: Labé's treatment of, 123, 124–25; for wife beating, 241n. 59
Conley, Tom, 225n. 19, 226n. 28
contentment, use of term, 102–11, 207
convent: as choice for women, 128, 130–31, 168, 173–74; time as seen from, 16, 128–29; time's regulation in, 130. *See also* Marquets, Anne de; Poissy, La Royale Maison de (Le Prieuré de Saint-Louis de Poissy, convent)
corporality, gendered use of, 60
Coste, Hilarion de, 131, 239n. 15, 250 n. 79
Costelay, Guillaume, 118
costume: as disguise, 183, 246n. 37; gender altered by, 222–23n. 95
Cotgrave, Randle, 86, 95, 121
Cottrell, Robert D.: on Marguerite de Navarre, 238n. 5; on "mixed life,"

245n. 30; on Pernette, 97, 234n. 68, 235n. 70
court celebrations, Amazon disguises at, 183, 246n. 37
Cousin, Jean, 51, *52*
Crenne, Hélisenne de: on beauty, 201; on distaff, 122, 182, 245n. 32; on domestic violence, 168; on marriage, 39, 154–55; writing and, 34
Creore, Alvin Emerson, 49, 72
Crucifixion, depiction of suffering in, 147–49
Curtius, Ernst, 224n. 7
Cyrus, 44

dance, as pastime, 33
Dasypodius, Conrad, 24
Davis, Natalie Zemon, 34, 132, 157
day ("jour"), use of term, 96–102, 111
death: beauty's link to, 40–41; as commonality, 67–69; as escape, 65; preferred to aging, 61–62, 72–73; records of, 238n. 7; as threat, 67–69; of woman poet, 91–92. See also *carpe diem* (pluck the day); immortality
Délie (Scève): Pernette's verse compared to, 100–101, 103–6, 107–9; repentance in, 123; time's linearity in, 213
Dellaneva, Joann, 234n. 68, 235n. 70
Denisot, Nicolas, 51, *52,* 224n. 9
Desan, Philippe, 223n. 2
Des Périers, Bonaventure, 23, 33–34
Desportes, Philippe, 63, 241n. 46, 243 n. 94
des Roches, Catherine: admiration of, 249n. 74; *carpe diem* motif and, 17, 205–11, 213; on chastity, 184–86, 202–3; on distaff, 122; entertaining by, 182, 198, 243–44n. 4; on erotic body, 194–203; exemplars of, 176, 177–93; (false) modesty of, 245n. 31; influences on, 197, 205, 206; marriage rejected by, 192–93; name of, 175–76, 244n. 7; publication and, 243–44n. 4, 248n. 59; schedule of, 245–46n. 33; social environment of, 13, 175–76, 212; temporal ideology of, 11–12, 203–11, 213, 215; on woman as body,

193–94, 203–11; on writing, 34, 175. Works: "A ma quenoille," 122, 180–83, 198; "Chanson des amazones," 183, 185–86; *Dialogue d'Amour de Beauté et de Physis,* 200–201; *Dialogue de la main, du pié et de la bouche,* 180; *Dialogue de Placide et Severe,* 177–78, 188–90; *Dialogue de Sincero et de Charite,* 198–200; *Dialogue de Vieillesse et Jeunesse,* 203–5; *Dialogue d'Iris et Pasithée,* 190–92, 195–96, 208–11; "La femme forte descritte par Salomon," 178–80, 196; *Missives,* 248n. 59; "Pour une mascarade d'amazones," 183–84; *Sonnets de Sincero à Charite,* 202–3; *Tobie,* 201–2. See also *Œuvres* (des Roches); *Secondes Œuvres* (des Roches)

des Roches, Madeleine (Madeleine Neveu): admiration of, 249n. 74; Catherine's relations with, 249n. 72, entertaining by, 182, 198, 243–44n. 4; on men's laws and women writers, 248n. 56; role of, 175–76; schedule of, 245–46n. 33; on writing, 247n. 47

Desrosiers-Bonin, Diane, 240–41n. 41
Diefendorf, Barbara, 38, 156, 244n. 5
Diller, George, 244–45n. 24, 249n. 72
Diotima, 224n. 8
distaff: Amazons and, 186; pen vs., 181–83, 192, 244n. 22, 245n. 32, 246n. 40; symbolism of, 120–22, 237n. 98
Divines poésies, Les (Marquets): humility in, 142–44; materiality in, 150–51; publication of, 131, 145
domesticity: erotic body and, 196; exemplars in, 177–83, 192–93; rejection of, 178, 180–81; resistance to, 121; as women's sphere, 212
domestic violence, 157, 168–69, 241n. 59
Donaldson-Evans, Lance, 103, 234n. 68, 235n. 70
Donne, John, 66
Dorat, Jean, 130
double: addressee as "body double," 60; Pernette's use of, 96–97; Ronsard's use of, 229n. 60

Du Bartas (Guillaume de Salluste), 11
Du Bellay, Joachim: on past and present, 61, 223n. 5; on time and decay, 25–26, 29. Works: *Les Antiquités de Rome,* 25, 61; *L'Olive,* 26, 114; "Songe," 26
Dubrow, Heather, 155, 241n. 48, 248n. 61
Du Guillet, Pernette: birth of, 232n. 30; contentment used by, 102–7, 110–11, 207; death of, 47, 91; editor of, 34; epitaphs for, 107–9; influences on, 212; "jour" and "journée" used by, 96–102, 111; present privileged by, 90–111; sense of becoming, 97–102; temporal ideology of, 11–12, 16, 126–27, 213, 215; on virtue and time, 16, 85, 93–96, 230n. 5, 232n. 32. See also *Rymes* (Du Guillet)
du Pont, Gratien, 39, 41
Duval, Edwin, 226–27n. 31
Du Verdier, Antoine, 161

Eboissard, François, 175
Ebreo, Leone, 102–11, 234n. 58
Eco, Umberto, 119, 164
education. See women's education
Empedocles, 16
Epicurus, 25, 218n. 8, 250n. 76
Epimarchus, 250n. 81
equality: establishment of, 111–12; in marriage, 172–73; in virtue, 96, 99
Erasmus: on education, 89; on female body, 14, on idleness, 231n. 10; on marriage age, 36; on women's occupations, 121, 128, 182, 236–37n. 96; on women's time, 210–11. Works: "A Girl with No Interest in Marriage," 128; *Praise of Folly,* 14
Espence, Claude d', 239n. 16
Estienne, Charles, 86–87, 157–58. Works: *Agriculture et maison rustique,* 158; *Paradoxes,* 86–87
Estienne, Nicole Liébaut: on alternatives, 169–74, 243n. 94; appearance of, 159–60; background of, 155–59, 242n. 68, challenge by, 153, 154–55, 161–62, 168–69, 173, 174, 212; on convent vs. marriage, 242n. 88; language and, 169–71; marriage critique by, 16–17,

Estienne, Nicole Liébaut *(continued):* 39, 153, 154–55, 157, 161, 166; present privileged by, 162–63, 173–74; signature anagram of, 159–60; temporal ideology of, 11–12, 15–17, 129, 162–63, 173–74. See also *Misères de la femme mariée, Les* (Estienne)

Evangiles des quenouilles, Les (collection), 120–21

exegi monumentum (I have raised a monument): gendered use of, 11–12, 51, 213; Magny's use of, 115; overview of, 224n. 7; popular use of, 23–24; Ronsard's use of, 48–65, 84. See also future; immortality

exemplars, women as: Amazons as, 183–88, 192–93; body and, 193–94; definition of, 176–77, 244n. 10; housewives as, 177–83, 192–93; humanist women as, 176–77, 187–93

Farge, Arlette, 34

Favre, Antoine: on Feast of the Rosary, 240n. 36; Marquets compared to, 145–46, 148, 239n. 19; on Virgin's veneration, 133

Febvre, Lucien, 24

female body: aging represented by, 40–46, 60–61, 69–72, 82, 203–5, 213; ambivalence toward, 193–94; eroticicism and, 194–203; flower as, 67–75; as impetus for poet, 58–63, 65; as literary site for measuring time, 23, 40; male poet's body evoked by, 60–62; materiality of, 150–51; religious connection via, 146–50; sexual difference of, 13–15; sublimation of physical, 197–98; temporality and, 203–11, 213. See also beauty

feminization, of religious texts, 131–32, 134–35, 146–47, 178–80, 182–83

Ferguson, Gary, 238n. 7, 239n. 16, 239 n. 17, 241n. 42

Ferguson, Margaret, 227n. 39

Ferrand, Jacques, 13–14

Feugère, Léon, 130

Flaminio: on disembodied soul, 150–51; illness poem of, 151–53; Marquets's translations of, 131, 134–35, 142–43

Flandrin, Jean-Louis, 171–72, 244n. 7

Fleur de Poésie Françoyse, 234n. 58

flower, symbolism of, 67–75, 208–9. See also lily; rose

Fortia, Sister Maria de, 144–45

Fournier, Hannah, 238n. 4, 239n. 21

Fradonnet, André, 175

François I (king of France): pardons by, 157; Ronsard's link to, 56–57; on time's length, 29; treatise dedicated to, 87

François II (dauphin), 59

Françon, Marcel, 45

free will, interest in, 87

fugit irreparabile tempus (irrecoverable time flees), 25, 29

future: epitaphs dominated by, 107–9; human body linked to, 50–51, 65; Pernette's exclusion of, 109–11; as Ronsard's focus, 84; women poets on, 91, 162–63, 213, 215. See also immortality

Galen, 13–14, 36

gambling, as pastime, 33

Gandhi, Mahatma, 182

Garcilaso de la Vega, 66

gender: blurring of, 45–46, 73–74; *carpe diem* motif and, 11–12, 47, 213; costume for altering, 222–23n. 95; definition of virtue by, 86–88, 230–31n. 9; *exegi monumentum* motif and, 11–12, 51, 213; immortalization differences by, 55–60; occupations and, 236n. 93; in Ronsard's work, 83–84; sexual dysfunction and, 41; temporal ideology and, 11–17, 23–24, 46–47, 126–27, 212–16, 234n. 59; use of term, 13. See also beauty; men; women

gestation: appropriate length for, 219n. 29; of Gargantua, 29–30

Gilman, Donald, 226n. 22

Glasser, Richard, 23, 226n. 28

glory, Labé's use of, 127

Goberde, Bonne, 157

God, changing concepts of, 218–19n. 16
Góngora, Luis de, 66
Good Samaritan parable, 147
Gournay, Marie de, 182, 245n. 32
Graham, Victor, 234n. 58
Greenblatt, Stephen, 229–30n. 68
Greene, Thomas, 69, 215
Greimas, A. J., 236n. 90
Grévin, Jacques, 23, 158, 161, 163–64
Groton, Anne, 225n. 16, 227n. 32
Guersens, Caye-Jules de, 205

Hampton, Timothy, 176–77, 193
Hawking, Stephen, 215
Henri II (king of France): death of, 25; lover of, 45; Ronsard's odes for, 55–57, 59, 60
Henri III (king of France), 25, 183, 246 n. 37
Henri IV (king of France), 25
Heraclitus, 25, 206
Héritier, Jean, 240n. 31
Herrick, Robert, 66
"heureux," use of term, 103–4
Hopkins, Gerald Manley, 106
Horace: on aged former lover, 228–29 n. 57; *carpe diem* motif of, 65–66, 77–79; influence by, 15, 50, 58, 62, 224 n. 7; rhetorical strategies of, 79–81. Works: "Ad Ligurinum," 77–81; "Aequam memento rebus in arduis," 81; *Carmina,* 66; "Ode to Lyce," 228–29n. 57; *Opera,* 66
housewives, as exemplars, 177–83, 192–93
Huguenots vs. Catholics, 132–33
Huguet, Edmond, 86, 97, 103
humanism: exemplars in, 176–77, 187–93; on marriage, 154, 156; on temporality, 13, 25–29; virtue in, 230–31n. 9; on women's education, 89–90
human life: as cyclical, 34–39, 203–7, 210; in humanism's concept of time, 13, 25–29; pastimes for, 32–34; schedules and, 29–34; tensions in, 192–93. *See also* aging; body
humility, symbolism of, 138–43, 239–40 n. 29

hunting, as pastime, 33
Husserl, Edmund, 227n. 35
Hutton, James, 227n. 34

iconography: of pearls, 51, 54, 225n. 11; Time's image in, 25, 203
idleness: avoidance of, 88, 111; men's vs. women's, 15, 87–88, 231n. 10; negative consequences of, 211; spinning as safeguard against, 121–22
immortality: absent in Pernette's *Rymes,* 109–11; ambivalence about, 62–65; contemporary attitudes toward, 215–16; gendered attitudes toward, 55–60; as reversal of aging, 61–62; Ronsard's claim of, 50–51, 57, 60–62, 118, 213; Scève's obsession with, 107–9, 110, 127; of song, 55; study of poetic, 224n. 7; virtue linked to, 93, 107–9. *See also* exegi monumentum (I have raised a monument); future
isotopy: definition of, 236n. 90; in Estienne and Grévin, 164; of production, 119

Jakobson, Roman, 106
Jannequin, Clément, 118
Jehlen, Myra, 12
Jesus (biblical): Mary compared to, 133–35; nourishment for, 146–47; suffering with, 147–49
Johnson, Leonard, 227n. 36, 243n. 92
Jondorf, Gillian, 236n. 91
Jones, Ann Rosalind: on erotic body, 196; on "journée," 233n. 37; on Labé, 126; on marriage, 238n. 3; on pen and distaff, 181; on Scève vs. Pernette, 105; on subversiveness, 249–50n. 75; on virtue, 85
Jones-Davies, M. T., 223n. 5
Jongh, Edy de, 225n. 11
Jordan, Constance, 128, 236n. 94, 245 n. 29
Joukovsky, Françoise: definition of time, 212; on Epicurus, 218n. 8, on Montaigne, 219n. 20; on time and eternity, 223n. 4, 226n. 24

"jour" and "journée," use of terms, 96–102, 111
Juana (sister), 250n. 84
Julianus, 70–71
Justinian, 37

Kelly, Joan, 243n. 2
Kermode, Frank, 217n. 1
King, Margaret, 203
Klein bottle, 127, 237n. 106
Kristeva, Julia, 47, 234n. 59
Kritzman, Lawrence, 83, 234n. 68, 235 n. 71
Kupisz, Kazimierz, 248n. 64
Kushner, Eva, 235n. 74

Labé, Louise: on aging, 45, 222n. 93; influences on, 212, 237n. 102; lute playing by, 117–19; marriage of, 38; present privileged by, 112, 114, 115–19, 126; temporal ideology of, 16, 120–27, 213, 215; on virtue and time, 85, 90, 111–14; on women's roles, 13, 17; on writing, 34, 111–12, 120, 126, 175, 197, 213, 235n. 73. Works: *Euvres,* 111–12; "Tant que mes yeux pourront larmes espandre," 116–17
La Bruyère, Jean de, 177
La Croix du Maine, François Grudé de, 158, 249n. 74
La Fontaine, Jean de, 177
La Motte-Messemé. *See* Motte-Messemé
Lando, Ortensio, 157
languages, time spent learning, 92
Laplanche, Jean, 228n. 51
Laqueur, Thomas, 13
Larsen, Anne: on des Roches, 184; on distaff, 181; on transgression, 244n. 22; on women's prefaces, 220–21n. 50
Lascaris, J., *Greek Anthology,* 66–67, 70
Laumonier, Paul: on *carpe diem* motif, 66, 226n. 28; on Denisot, 224n. 9; on Horace, 79; on Ronsard, 226n. 28, 228n. 43
Lavaud, Jacques, 158, 159, 160–61
law: on marriageable age, 37; women's study of, 189; women writers and, 248n. 56

Lazard, Madeleine, 223n. 5, 237n. 1
Le Caron, Louis, 62
Le Goff, Jacques, 129–30
Lemaire de Belges, Jean, 42–43
Leonardo da Vinci, 58
Le Roux de Lincy, 72, 88
Lesnauderie, Pierre, 111, 155
L'Estoile, Pierre de, 246n. 37
Le Villain, Claude, 168
Levinas, Emmanuel, 84, 85
Levine, Laura, 46
L'Heptameron (Marguerite de Navarre): age in, 35, 222n. 70; on chastity, 86; domestic violence in, 242n. 89; genesis of, 32–33; on marriage, 222 n. 70, 222n. 76; strategies in, 239n. 21
L'Hermite, Jehan, 21
l'Hospital, Michel de, 139–40
Liébaut, Jean, 158–59, 161
Liébaut, Madame de. *See* Estienne, Nicole Liébaut
Liébaut, Marie, 242n. 68
life expectancy, 34–35
lily, symbolism of, 228n. 46
Littré, Emile, 32
Lorraine, Charles de Guise (Cardinal de), 139–40
Losse, Deborah, 220–21n. 50
love: aged body in, 228–29n. 57; beating linked to, 169; des Roches's female body and, 197–200; enslavement by, 164–66; negative consequences of, 200–203; passing of, 208–9; as withering, 81–82
Lucretius, 218n. 8
lute, symbolism of, 117–19
lyre, symbolism of, 118

Machiavelli, Niccolò, 88
Magny, Olivier de: Cassandra and, 225 n. 11; *exegi monumentum* motif and, 23, 114–15; Labé compared to, 112; poetic immortality claimed by, 118; retraction used by, 125–26; Ronsard and, 223n. 2; temporal ideology of, 115, 126–27, 213. Works: *Les Amours,* 225n. 11; *Gayetez,* 112, 114, 115, 118
Mallarmé, Stéphane, 49

Index   275

Mandrou, Robert, 33
manuscript culture, Marquets's poems in, 139–40, 145–46
Marguerite de France: Grévin and, 158; Ronsard's odes for, 57–59, 60
Marguerite de Navarre: aging of, 35; on chastity, 86; on marriage, 222n. 76; marriage age and, 222n. 70; pastimes of, 33–34; studies of, 238n. 5, 239 n. 21. See also *L'Heptameron* (Marguerite de Navarre)
Marie de Clermont, 129
Marie de France, 129
Mariéjol, Jean-Hippolyte, 240n. 31
Marillac, Monsieur de, 211
Marot, Clément, 23, 40–41, 96
Marquets, Anne de: as authoritative voice, 139–40, 143–44; background of, 13, 129–30; death of, 144, 238n. 7; decision to become nun, 130–31; hierarchical displacements by, 16, 131–32, 174; humility and, 138–44; illness poem of, 151–53; key motifs of, 239n. 21; on Mary, 132, 133–38, 146–50, 153; present privileged by, 146, 151–53, 174; response to Protestant challenge, 138, 140–42, 243n. 95; as subversive, 173–74; temporal ideology of, 16, 17, 129, 149–53, 212, 213; writing as process for, 145–47, 153. See also *Divines poésies, Les* (Marquets); *Sonets, prieres et devises* (Marquets); *Sonets spirituels* (Marquets)
marriage: age for, 36–39, 72, 156–57, 166–67; challenge to, 153, 154–55, 161–62, 168–69, 173, 174, 212; as choice for women, 128, 173–74, 242 n. 88; intellectual bias against, 153–54; negative consequences of, 201–2; rejection of, 192–93; suggestions for ameliorating, 169–73, 243n. 94; time as seen from, 16–17, 128–29, 162–63, 166–67; wife beating in, 157, 168–69, 241n. 59; women's subjugation/enslavement in, 16–17, 156–57, 163–68, 238n. 3
Marsili, Father Luigi, 28

Marullus, *Epigrammata et Hymni,* 67
Marvell, Andrew, 66
Mary (biblical): humility and, 138–39; Marquets linked to, 135–38, 150, 153; as model, 149–50; role of, 131–33; suffering of, 148–49; time consecrated via, 149–50; veneration of, 132–34, 146–47
Masten, Jeffrey, 109
materiality: of female body, 150–51; as symbol of aging and death, 61–62
Mathieu-Castellani, Gisèle, 115, 223n. 1, 234n. 68, 235n. 72
Matoré, Georges, 240n. 40
Maumont, Jean, 157–58
McClelland, John, 114, 246n. 41
McFarlane, I. D., 105, 226n. 21, 233n. 42
McKinley, Mary B., 239n. 21
medical treatises: on bodily functions and time, 30; on life cycle, 35–36
Medici, Lorenzo de', 67
Meleager, 228n. 46
Memoires concernant le prieuré de Poissy (records), 238n. 7
memory: writing's link to, 16, 116; of youth, 76–77
men: fear of aging of, 42–46; marriage age for, 37–39, 156–57, 166–67; pastimes for, 33; spinning by, 182, 186; time regulated by, 31–32; virtue of, 85–88, 201. *See also* men poets
Ménager, Daniel, 83, 229n. 59
men poets: on circularity, 213; female aging emphasized by, 40–46; female body as impetus for, 58–63, 65; poetic immortality claimed by, 154; temporal context of, 15–17; time and gender linked for, 12; time as freedom for, 17; writing as pastime for, 34. *See also specific poets*
Mercury, time's passage and, 21, 22, 23
Mermet, Claude, 169
Mesnier, Pierre, 159
metamorphoses, in Ronsard's sonnets, 83–84, 229n. 61
Meurier, Gabriel, 35
Michaud, L.-G., 157–58, 159, 205
Miller, Joyce, 222n. 89, 233–34n. 55

miroir de la vie et de la mort, Le (engraving), 213, *214*
mirror: aging and, 78; Mary as, 149–50. *See also* reciprocity
Misères de la femme mariée, Les (Estienne): on age gap in marriage, 39, 157, 166; as challenge, 153, 154–55, 168–69, 173, 174; circularity in, 170, 173, 174; commentary on, 159–62; context of, 155–59; language in, 169–71; on married woman, 16–17; suggestions in, 169–73; temporal backdrop of, 163; on women's suffering, 163–68, 170–71
misogyny, privatization linked to, 121
Möbius strip, 237n. 106
Monsigot, 131
Montaigne, Michel de: on aging and self, 77–78; on beauty, 43–44; on *passetemps,* 32–33, 220n. 43; Ronsard as precursor for, 84; on tensions of time, 192–93; on time as subjective, 29; on youth, 222n. 84. Works: "Of Physiognomy," 43–44
Montchrestien, Antoine de, 136
moral treatises: on age gap in marriage, 38–39; on aging and beauty, 44–45; on bodily functions and time, 30
More, Thomas, 192
motherhood: physicality inspired by, 59; separation and, 201–2. *See also* Mary (biblical)
Motte-Messemé, Le Seigneur de la, 33
Moulin, Antoine du, 90, 91–93
Muchembled, Robert, 221n. 52
Mulvey, Laura, 225n. 17
music: accomplishments in, 117–19; as pastime, 33, 191; time spent learning, 92, 111
myrtle, symbolism of, 62, 226n. 21

Nahom-Grappe, Véronique, 40
Neoplatonism, on meaning of time, 25
Nietzsche, Friedrich, 16, 107

occupations, gendering of, 236n. 93. *See also* women's work
Œuvres (des Roches): Amazon in, 183–88, 192–93; body and temporality in, 203–5, 211; female body in, 194–203; housewife in, 177–83, 192–93. *See also Secondes Œuvres* (des Roches)
Orleans, Charles d', 243n. 92
Ostriker, Alicia, 233n. 36
Other: aging projected onto, 77–78; poet as, 74; self-fashioning and, 229–30 n. 68; self vs., 77; temporality and, 82–84, 85
Ovid, 67, 186, 219n. 18

paintings, on passage of time, 21, *22, 23*
Paré, Ambroise, 30, 36–38
Pasquier, Estienne: *carpe diem* poems for des Roches by, 23, 205; on des Roches, 192–93, 245–46n. 33, 249 n. 74; on marriage age, 36–37; mock rivalry with des Roches, 197–98; on time, 211. Works: *La Puce de Madame des Roches,* 205
passetemps: activities in, 33–34; meanings of, 32–33; spinning as, 120–21; women's link to, 32, 34, 92–93
past: repentance for, 123–25; retraction of, 125–26, 237n. 104; symbols of, 61; writing as recuperation of, 114–19
pastimes. See *passetemps*
patriarchy: role of, 12–13; women's education and, 190
pearls, iconography of, 51, 54, 225n. 11
Pellejay, Claude, 205
Pelous, Jean-Michel, 198
Pernette. *See* Du Guillet, Pernette
Pérouse, Gabriel-A., 249n. 72
Perry, Anthony, 234n. 68
Perry, Kathleen, 229n. 61
Petit, Jean, 218n. 8
Petit Jehan de Saintré (Antoine de La Sale), 31
Petrarch: on aging, 49, 223n. 3; on marriage, 153–54, 173; as model, 59, 226–27n. 31, 237n. 102; on repentance, 123, 124; retraction used by, 125; Ronsard on, 75–76; secular subjectivization of time and, 27–28; on time, 11, 30. Works: "I'mi vivea," 226–27n. 31; *Rime sparse,* 123

Philip II (king of Spain), 42
philosophy, on meaning of time, 25–28.
    See also humanism; *specific philosophers*
Piccolomini, Alessandro, 44–45
Pindar, 55, 58, 59
Plato, 44
Pléiade poets: *carpe diem* motif of, 66; on circularity, 213; fear of aging of, 43; influence by, 129, 179; on love, 200; on music, 118; on time and decay, 25. *See also specific poets*
Plotinus, 27
Plutarch, 176, 189
poetry: determining intention of, 119; music's link to, 118; translations of, 17–18, 131, 134–35, 142–43; Tyard on progress of, 114–16. *See also* men poets; women poets; writing; *specific poets*
Poirion, Daniel, 218–19n. 16
Poissy, La Royale Maison de (Le Prieuré de Saint-Louis de Poissy, convent): Colloquium at, 139–40, 240n. 31, 240n. 32; deaths at, 238n. 7; status of, 129; time's regulation at, 130
Poitiers, Diane de, 45, 220n. 48
Poitiers, siege of, 175
Poliziano, Agnolo, 67
Pontalis, J.-B., 228n. 51
Poulet, Georges, 108, 218–19n. 16
Précieuses, suitors and, 197–200
present: past explained in, 124; privileging of, 90–111, 112, 114–19, 126, 146, 151–53, 174. *See also* women's time
production, centrality of, 119
projection, definition of, 228n. 51
Propertius, 67
Protestants: in colloquium debate, 139–40, 240n. 31, 240n. 32; as Marquets's detractors, 137–38, 140–41
psychology, in meaning of time, 27
publication/printing: permission for, 131; poets' protests of, 112–13, 140–41; posthumous, 91, 129, 144–45, 239 n. 19; status of, 157, 215; urgency of, 54–55

public sphere, women's writing and, 120
Pythagoras, 35–36, 250n. 81

Quainton, Malcolm D., 82, 227n. 33
"quenouille," use of term, 120–21
Quevedo y Villegas, Francisco de, 66
Quinones, Ricardo, 23, 32, 226n. 28

Rabelais, François: authoritative tone of, 143; on human activity duration, 29–31; on time and decay, 25. Works: *Gargantua*, 29–31, 130, 215; *Pantagruel*, 29–30; *Tiers Livre*, 25
Read, Kirk D.: on Labé, 220–21n. 50; on Marquets, 145; on Pernette, 234–35 n. 68, 235n. 71
readers: Estienne's appeal to, 162; Labé's appeal to, 125–26; Marquets's appeal to, 146–49; women as, 113–14, 186–87. *See also* exemplars, women as
reciprocity, Pernette's use of, 106, 107
religious texts: Crucifixion in, 147–49; feminization of, 131–32, 134–35, 146–47, 178–80, 182–83; illness poem in, 151–53; paradox in, 139. *See also* Bible; Catholic Church; Jesus (biblical); Mary (biblical); Protestants
religious wars, 25, 26
Renouard, Philippe, 159
repentance, Labé's treatment of, 123–25
repetition: Estienne's use of, 163–64, 166–68, 170–71, 173; Pernette's use of, 106–7; role of in poetry, 106
Retz, Catherine de Clermont, maréchale de, 112, 113–14, 246n. 41
Rhetoriqueurs, wordplay of, 106
Ricchieri, L., 218n. 1
Rifkin, Jeremy, 215
Rigolot, François: on gendered prefaces, 220–21n. 50; on Ronsard, 227n. 35; on *vertu*, 85–86
Rilke, Rainer Maria, 235n. 76
Robert, Paul, 86
Roman de Renart (book), 185
Ronsard, Pierre de: on aging, 43, 48, 49, 60, 68–74, 76–82, 205, 208, 215, 221n. 56; ambivalence about immortality of, 62–65; amorous mythology

Ronsard, Pierre de *(continued):* of, 223 n. 2; body as central axis for, 54–55; *carpe diem* motif used by, 15–16, 47, 49, 50, 67–82, 84; Cassandre and, 51, *52,* 54, 81–82, 225n. 10, 225n. 13; on chastity, 184–85; on children, 224n. 8; death of, 229n. 64; *exegi monumentum* used by, 23, 48–65, 84; female body as impetus for, 58–63, 65; immortalization by, 55–57; on Marquets, 130; poetic immortality claimed by, 50–51, 57, 60–62, 118, 213; rhetorical strategies of, 79–84; sexuality and, 74–76; temporal ideology of, 11, 15, 49, 213, 250n. 78; on time and change, 26–27, 29, 71–72; use of name, 223 n. 1; on women's occupations, 121–22, 182; youth glorified by, 72–79. Works: "A Charles de Pisseleu," 26–27; "A Janne impitoyable," 77–81; "A la royne Catherine de Medicis," 59; "A Madame Marguerite," 57–59; "Comme une belle fleur assise entre les fleurs," 81; *Continuation des Amours,* 75–76; "Dame au gros cœur, pourquoy t'espargnes-tu?" 227n. 34; "Dedans des Prés je vis une Dryade," 72–74; *Derniers vers,* 49, 63–65, 82; "Elegie à Marie," 62–63; "En vain pour vous ce bouquet je compose," 228 n. 46; *La Franciade,* 49; "Ha, Seigneur Dieu," 83; "Ha! Belacueil, que ta douce parolle," 83; "Hymne de France," 118; "L'Hynne de l'Esté," 250n. 78; "J'ay ce matin amassé de ma main," 69–70; "Je voudroy bien richement jaunissant," 83; "Je vous envoye un bouquet que ma main," 67–69, 74; "Mignogne, levés-vous, vous estes paresseuse," 83; "Mignonne, allons voir," 227n. 35; "Nimphe aus beaus yeus," 81–82; "Ode au Roy Henri II," 55–57; *Odes,* 55–57, 59; "Pren este rose aimable comme toy," 228 n. 46; "Quand je suis vingt ou trente mois," 72; "Quand vous serez bien vieille," 60–62, 76, 207; "Quelle nouvelle fleur apparoist à noz yeux?", 130; "La royne sa femme," 59; *Second livre des meslanges,* 121–22; "Sonnet à Sinope," 77; *Sonnets pour Hélène,* 75, 82, 122, 213, 229n. 60; *Stances,* 64–65; "Le trophée de la chasteté," 184; "Le trophée de l'amour," 184; "Verson ces roses en ce vin," 81. See also *Amours* (Ronsard)

rose, symbolism of, 71–72, 74–75, 81, 205–6, 227n. 35, 227n. 46, 228n. 46
Rosso Fiorentino, 21, *22,* 23, 47
Rothstein, Marian, 233n. 55
Rouget, François, 118
Royale Maison de Poissy, La. *See* Poissy, La Royale Maison de (Le Prieuré de Saint-Louis de Poissy, convent)
Rufinus: *carpe diem* motif of, 67–69; influence by, 15, 226–27n. 31. Works: "To Rhodoklea," 67–69
Ruwet, Nicolas, 237n. 103
Rymes (Du Guillet): contentment used in, 102–7, 110–11; denigration of, 92–93, 110–11; gender in, 103; immortality absent in, 109–11; "jour" and "journée" used in, 96–102, 111; publication of, 91; repetition in, 106–7; on virtue, 93–96

Sainte-Marthe, Scévole de, 249n. 72
Saint Gelais, Mellin de, 23
Sales, François de, 33
Sankovitch, Tilde, 181, 246n. 40
Saulnier, Verdun: on Pernette, 90, 105, 234n. 67; role of, 232n. 29; on virtue, 230n. 5
Saunders, Alison, 227n. 39
Savoie, Louise de, 156
Scaliger, J. C., 157–58
Scanlon, Larry, 244n. 10
Scève, Maurice: *carpe diem* motif of, 23; on immortality, 107–9, 110, 127; as "le Jour," 96–100; Pernette compared to, 16, 100–101, 103–6, 107–8; on repentance, 123, 124; temporal ideology of, 11, 107–8, 126–27, 213; on time, 90–91; virtue and, 85, 93–94, 230n. 5. See also *Délie* (Scève)

Index

schedules: convent, 130; des Roches's, 245–46n. 33; obsession with, 29–34
Schiesara, Juliana, 236n. 94
Schmidt, Albert-Marie, 161
scientific treatises, on bodily functions and time, 30
Scott, Joan, 13
Secondes Œuvres (des Roches): body and temporality in, 206–10; *carpe diem* in, 17, 205–11; female body in, 195–96; humanist woman in, 176–77, 187–93; marginalia on copy of, 247n. 43
Secundus, Johannes, 67
Seiler, Sister Mary Hilarine, 129, 130, 132, 145
self: aging and, 77–78; fashioning of, 229–30n. 68; Other vs., 77
Seneca, 189, 206, 219n. 18
sexual dysfunction, gender difference in, 41
sexual intercourse, timing of, 30, 31
sexuality: difference and, 13–15; rhetorical strategies and, 79
Shakespeare, William, 66
Silver, Isidore, 63–65, 228n. 49
Simonin, Michel, 229n. 59, 229n. 60
social class: education and, 89; life expectancy and, 34; marriage age and, 37, 156; temporal ideology and, 46; virtue and, 87–88, 230n. 4; women's work and, 236–37n. 96
Socrates, 44, 224n. 8
Sommers, Paula, 236n. 92, 238n. 5
Sonets, prières et devises (Marquets): publication of, 145; as response to Protestant challenge, 138, 140–42, 243n. 95; Ronsard's poem in, 130
Sonets spirituels (Marquets): Assumption poems in, 240n. 30; Crucifixion in, 147–49; on decision to become nun, 130–31; humility in, 138–40; Mary in, 132, 133–38, 146–50; publication of, 129, 144–45, 239n. 19
spinning. *See* distaff
Sponde, Jean de, 129
Stallybrass, Peter, 243n. 2
Stobaeus, J., 66
Stoicism, on meaning of time, 25
Stone, Donald, 225n. 19, 226n. 28
Strasbourg, clock in, 24
subversion: of aging, 17; approach to, 173–74; of beauty, 190, 196, 206–10; in Des Roches, 249–50n. 75, 250 n. 80; of transcendence, 49
sun, symbolism of, 163

Tahureau, Jacques, 33
Taillemont, Claude, 230–31n. 9
temporal ideology: body and, 203–11, 213; concretization in, 149–51; context of, 15–17; definition of, 13; gendered differences in, 11–17, 23–24, 46–47, 126–27, 212–16, 234n. 59; humanism on, 13, 25–29; Other and, 82–84, 85; social class and, 46; virtue and, 85, 90, 93–96, 111–14, 210–11, 230n. 5, 232n. 32. *See also* future; past; present; time
Tetel, Marcel, 227n. 35
theater, effeminization in, 46
Theocritus, 237n. 98
time: approach to, 11–13; authority and, 71–72; as circular, 13, 25–39, 170, 173, 174, 192–93, 203–7, 210, 213; contemporary attitudes toward, 215–16; as enemy, 23–25, 81–82, 206, 209–10; flight of, 25, 29; as human phenomenon, 27–29; as linear, 97–100, 106, 107–11, 114–19, 126–27, 213; measured through body, 15, 23, 40–41, 49; Other in, 82–84, 85; paintings on, 21, 22, 23; Pernette's relationship to, 91–92; preciousness of, 21, 28–29; reclaimed, 192–93; scarcity of, 111–12; secular subjectivization of, 27–29; as seen from marriage, 16–17, 128–29, 162–63, 166–67; spatialization of, 149–53, 240n. 40; symbols for, 25, 203–5, 250n. 78; "true," 27; use of term, 13; women associated with worldly, 156. *See also* aging; death; future; immortality; past; present; temporal ideology; women's time
Tournes, Jean de, 90, 93, 112
twinship *(la gémellité)*, 229n. 60

Tyard, Pontus de: aging of, 35; Labé compared to, 112–14; on music, 118; names used by, 246n. 41, 250n. 82; on repentance, 123, 124; temporal ideology of, 114–15, 126–27, 209, 213; on time and uncertainty, 25–26. Works: *Discours du Temps,* 25–26; *Erreurs amoureuses,* 112–14, 123, 213; *Solitaire second, ou Prose de la musique,* 118, 250n. 82

ubi sunt (where are), Ronsard's use of, 49–50
Ursprung, Andrea, 225n. 16

Valasque, virtue of, 86
Vallée, Marguerite, 157
vanitas vanitatum (vanity of vanities), meaning of, 25, 26
Verville, Beroalde de, 89, 247n. 44
vice, definition of, 125
Vickers, Nancy, 227n. 39
Viret, Pierre, 24
Virgil, 25, 73, 226n. 21
virginity, symbolism of, 135–37. *See also* chastity
virtù: definition of, 230n. 4; fear of loss of, 42–46; virtue stemming from, 86
virtue: social class and, 87–88, 230n. 4
virtue/*vertu:* acquisition of, 88, 92–93; as beauty, 160; chastity's link to, 86–87, 90, 95; as defense, 232n. 32; definition of, 85–90, 94–95, 231n. 10; education linked to, 17, 87–90, 209–10; equality in, 96, 99; humanism on, 230–31n. 9; immortality through, 93, 107–9; importance of Christian, 144; maintenance of, 88–90, 94–95; Scève and, 85, 93–94, 230n. 5; temporality of, 85, 90, 93–96, 111–14, 210–11, 230n. 5, 232n. 32; writing linked to, 17, 93, 111–14, 120
Vives, Juan Luis: on age, 72; on idleness, 111, 121, 126; on marriage, 155; on older women, 42; on sexual difference, 14; on time, 90; on virginity, 135–36; on virtue, 87, 94; on women's education, 89; on women's time, 210–11. Works: *De institutio foeminae christianae,* 14, 87; *Institution de la femme chrétienne,* 72, 155
Voltaire, 79

Wartburg, Walther von, 86
Weber, Henri, 72, 226n. 28, 228n. 46
Wiesner-Hanks, Merry, 236n. 93
wind, symbolism of, 71–72
Winn, Colette: on distaff, 181; on Pernette, 102, 234–35n. 68; on transgression and resistance, 220–21n. 50, 247n. 53
women: aging of, 35, 40–42, 221n. 56; as bodies, 193–94; choices of, 128, 237 n. 1, 242n. 88; community of, 187, 195; corporality linked to, 60; courting of, 198–200; denigration of, 158–59; excluded from politics, 14–15; as literary subjects, 213; marriage age for, 36–39, 72, 156–57; pastimes for, 33–34; as readers, 113–14, 186–87; role reversal for, 169–70; sexual difference of, 13–15; subordination of, 13–17, 120–22, 153–54, 156–57, 163–68, 238n. 3; virtue of, 16, 85–90, 93, 94–95, 111–14; as widows, 244n. 5. *See also* convent; exemplars, women as; female body; marriage; women's education; women's time; women's work
women poets: on aging, 45; Amazons linked to, 183–84, 192–93; surveillance of, 131; temporal context of, 15–17, 46–47; temporality reformulated by, 23–24; writing as pastime for, 34. *See also specific poets*
women's education: freedom linked to, 190; humanism and, 176–77, 187–93; social class and, 89–90; virtue and, 17, 87–90, 209–10; wisdom acquired through, 209–11
women's time: alleged misuse of, 87–88; as circular, 13, 25–39, 170, 173, 174, 192–93, 203–7, 210, 213; for distaff and pen, 181–83; as fleeting, 92; gendered expectations of, 15; as housewife, 178–79, 192–93; intelligent use of, 176, 191–92; life

expectancy and, 34–35; past in present, 126; reclaimed by women, 192–93; regulation of, 15; as resource, 211, 212; virtue and writing in, 111–14; for women poets, 12, 212–16. *See also* distaff; *passetemps*

women's work: choices in, 128; daily tasks of, 34, 120–22, 155–56, 166–68, 170, 221n. 51; guidance in, 189–90; pleasure in, 179–80, 244n. 23; Ronsard on, 121–22, 182; social class and, 236–37n. 96; valorization of, 177–80. *See also* distaff

Woodward, Kathleen, 228n. 53

writing: beauty created by male, 54; domesticity rejected through, 175, 178, 180–81, 197; encouragement of women's, 111–14, 116, 120, 126, 175; immortality of, 50–51; memory's link to, 16, 116; past and present linked in, 114–19; as pastime, 34, 235n. 73; payment for women's, 243–44n. 4; pleasures of, 115–16; power of, 247 n. 47; as process, 145–46, 153; as substitute for beauty, 159–60; time as reason for, 212–13; virtue linked to, 17, 93, 111–14, 120; women as anathema to, 154. *See also* poetry; readers

Xenophon, women's education and, 177–78, 189

Yates, Frances, 246n. 41

youth: authenticity linked to, 78; beauty and, 45–46, 72–73, 213; *carpe diem* linked to, 77–82; as female, 21, *22,* 23; glorification of, 42–43, 72–79, 82; pleasures of, 64–65; sexuality and, 74–76

Zenobie, virtue of, 86

Zinguer, Ilana, 161–62